Humanitarian Invasion
Global Development in Cold War Afghanistan

Humanitarian Invasion is the first book of its kind: a ground-level inside account of what development and humanitarianism meant for Afghanistan, a country touched by international aid like no other. Relying on Soviet, Western, and NGO archives, interviews with Soviet advisers and NGO workers, and Afghan sources, Timothy Nunan forges a vivid account of the impact of development on a country on the front lines of the Cold War.

Nunan argues that Afghanistan functioned as a laboratory for the future of the Third World nation-state. If, in the 1960s, Soviets, Americans, and Germans sought to make a territorial national economy for Afghanistan, then later, under Soviet military occupation, Soviet nation-builders, French and Swedish humanitarians, and Pakistani-supported guerrillas fought a transnational civil war over Afghan statehood. Covering the entire period from the Cold War to Taliban rule, *Humanitarian Invasion* signals the beginning of a new stage in the writing of international history.

Timothy Nunan is an Academy Scholar at the Harvard Academy for International and Area Studies. Previously, he was an Alexander von Humboldt Postdoctoral Research Fellow at the Zentralasien-Seminar of the Humboldt-Universität zu Berlin.

Global and International History

Series Editors

Erez Manela, *Harvard University*
John McNeill, *Georgetown University*
Aviel Roshwald, *Georgetown University*

The Global and International History series seeks to highlight and explore the convergences between the new International History and the new World History. Its editors are interested in approaches that mix traditional units of analysis such as civilizations, nations, and states with other concepts such as transnationalism, diasporas, and international institutions.

Titles in the Series
Timothy Nunan, *Humanitarian Invasion: Global Development in Cold War Afghanistan*
Stephen J. Macekura, *Of Limits and Growth: International Environmentalism and the Rise of "Sustainable Development" in the Twentieth Century*
Michael Goebel, *Anti-Imperial Metropolis: Interwar Paris and the Seeds of Third World Nationalism*

Humanitarian Invasion

Global Development in Cold War Afghanistan

TIMOTHY NUNAN

Harvard University

CAMBRIDGE
UNIVERSITY PRESS

CAMBRIDGE
UNIVERSITY PRESS

32 Avenue of the Americas, New York, NY 10013-2473, USA

Cambridge University Press is part of the University of Cambridge.

It furthers the University's mission by disseminating knowledge in the pursuit of education, learning, and research at the highest international levels of excellence.

www.cambridge.org
Information on this title: www.cambridge.org/9781107112070

© Timothy Nunan 2016

First published 2016

Printed in the United Kingdom by Clays, St Ives plc.

A catalog record for this publication is available from the British Library.

ISBN 978-1-107-11207-0 Hardback

For my parents

Contents

Acknowledgments

Books in development flourish only with advising, economic aid, and a certain number of humanitarian interventions. This book began as a D.Phil. dissertation at the University of Oxford under the supervision of Catriona Kelly and Alexander Morrison, but that I was able to learn anything from them I owe to earlier teachers like Michael Gordin, Anthony Grafton, Will Howarth, Michael Jennings, Anson Rabinbach, and Froma Zeitlin. It is, however, thanks to even earlier teachers like George Ramos and Mark Wiedenmann that I found my way to the humanities at all.

Several colleagues improved the dissertation when it was still in its infancy. Thanks to Stephen Kotkin, for inspiring my interest in Soviet history in the first place and stoking it with comments and criticism; to James Pickett, for helping me think through Chapter 5 at a very early stage; to Robert Crews, for testing ideas; to David Engerman, Thomas Barfield, and David Ekbladh, for humoring me during an early visit to Boston; to Artemy Kalinovsky, for breaking ground in the field and sharing his experiences with me; and to Lori Maguire, for taking an interest in this project from the very start and opening her home to me one damp evening in Paris.

Thanks to Rodric Braithwaite for discussing the Soviet Union, Afghanistan, and careers with an uncertain graduate student; to Ryan Irwin, Jason Parker, and Robert Rakove, for tolerating a slightly less uncertain graduate student on strolls through Serbian castles; to Navid Hamid and Matthew McCartney, for introducing me to Pakistan; and to Azam and Theresa Chaudry, for being indefatigable hosts in Lahore. Thanks to Inomjon Mamadiliev for furnishing interview contacts in Khujand and sharing his insights into Central Asian history. Thanks to Andreas Eckert, Marc Frey, Mario del Pero, and Sara Lorenzini for inviting me to Trento; to Mark Mazower for conversations in Paris; and to Stephen Batalden and Mark von Hagen, for the same in Arizona. Timothy D. Snyder may not know it, but his lecture at a memorial event for Tony Judt at

King's College, Cambridge, and subsequent lectures on global history informed my thoughts about how to write regional history in a global context. Similarly, my dissertation examiners, Odd Arne Westad and David Priestland, challenged me to turn a dissertation focused on the Soviet Union into a work that could speak beyond the confines of Russian and Eurasian history.

At Harvard, conversations with Erez Manela, Terry Martin, Kelly O'Neill, Roger Owen, Serhii Plokhii, and Brad Simpson helped me think about the kind of international history I wanted to write. Friendships at the Harvard Academy for International and Area Studies with Naor Ben-Yehoyada, Jeffrey Kahn, and Caroline Schuster fed me with reading lists of anthropology, while Nazanin Shahrokni was a patient conversational partner in Persian. Laurence Winnie, the Executive Officer of the Harvard Academy, kept up morale on cold winter mornings. Kathleen Hoover, the Program Coordinator for the Academy, made it all work behind the scenes. During that year, a conference organized by the Havighurst Center of Miami University connected me with Edward Holland, who provided a probing critique of Chapter 6. M. Jamil Hanifi reached out early on to provide guidance as I tried to recreate the world he had grown up in. Erez Manela and Aviel Roshwald offered constructive criticism as I prepared the manuscript for submission, while two anonymous reviewers provided comments and criticism that helped me rethink the manuscript in its final stages. Elise Alexander saved the manuscript from many infelicities and errors.

The research for this book relied on the support of several institutions. The Rhodes Trust generously funded my studies at Oxford, while grants from the International Research and Exchanges Board made possible two separate long research trips to Russia, Tajikistan, and Uzbekistan. Grants from Mr. MJB Palmer and Dr. David Frederick facilitated early research trips to Germany. Corpus Christi College funded a research trip to Kyrgyzstan, while a Scatcherd European Scholarship supported a visit to Moscow that proved essential for gathering key material I had missed during earlier stays. The Harvard Academy for International and Area Studies supported a year of rewriting the dissertation into a book manuscript and organized an author's conference to discuss the book manuscript when it was still in gestation. Thanks go, then, not only to the attendees of that gathering – Thomas Barfield, David Engerman, Shah Mahmoud Hanifi, Charles S. Maier, and Stephen Kotkin – but also to Timothy Colton for chairing the conference and to Benjamin Siegel for serving as our *munshi*. Last, but not least, the Harvard Academy and the American Institute for Afghanistan Studies sponsored a final research trip to the archives of the Swedish Committee for Afghanistan and Doctors Without Borders.

During that and other archival trips, I relied on the expertise and judgment of several archivists who made my research possible. Among others, I would like to thank three in particular. Professor Shaista Wahab was exceptionally helpful with navigating the Arthur Paul Collection at the University of Nebraska-Omaha and Galina Tokareva, the chief archivist of the Komsomol archive of the

Russian State Archive for Socio-Political History, made me aware of Komsomol's Afghanistan operations in the first place. Klas Bjürstrom, of the Swedish Committee for Afghanistan (SCA), became involved in this project relatively late, but I am deeply thankful to him for not only scouting out the Swedish National Archives for me in advance of my visit, but also for introducing me to Södermalm, multiple interview contacts, and, most importantly, *fika*, during my stay in Stockholm.

Yet if books owe their germs to foundations, libraries, and archives, it is friendships that coax them to sprout and finally blossom. Andreas Knab and Ryan Berg provided succor during our year together in Oxford, while friendships with Eirik Bjorge, Lucas Brown, Kyle Haddad-Fonda, Vincent Hofer, Harvey Lederman, Zachary Miller, Scott Moore, Geoffrey Shaw, Luke Swiderski, Ardevan Yaghoubi, and Anton Zykov sustained me. In Moscow, Octavie Bellavance, Alex Hazanov, Tom Hooker, and Alessandro Iandolo were appreciated comrades. Elsewhere, Jonathan Fluger, Kayvon Tehranian, and William Wachter were probing critics but, more importantly, friends. I have accrued unrepayable debts to Sean Griffin and John Raimo for asking them to read sections of the manuscript several times. And thanks to M.S. for holding my hand through the meadows along the Elbe and beyond.

Several families opened their homes to me during my research. In Moscow, the Bystrov family hosted me for a month, while the Kruteev family treated me to a tour of Elektrostal' and an elaborate feast at their home. The Zhanyberdaev family provided shelter during a frigid Bishkek winter; the Barno family, the same during a sweltering Dushanbe summer. Zamira Yusufjonova helped out in Khujand, while Lia Ilsar stepped admirably into the role of host mother during later trips to the Russian capital. The family to which I owe the most, however, is my own. From providing me with the opportunity to study history with inspiring teachers to holding their breath as I depart on research trips, they have supported me throughout this entire journey. The world that they have given me, the world that we share, has not always been an easy one to bear, as they have born the cross of a child with autism. But it is ours – a world that all the members of our family enrich, enliven, and continually create. This book is dedicated to them.

Note on Language and Transliteration

This book adheres to the standards of the American Library Association and the Library of Congress for transliteration from foreign languages into English. In the case of well-known personalities whose names are in widespread use in English, however, I use the more common spelling. Hence, the KGB Director and General Secretary of the USSR goes as Yuri Andropov, while the Soviet Orientalist goes as Iurii Gankovskii. Unless otherwise noted in the footnotes, all translations are the author's own.

Chapter Five of this book appeared in modified form, "Under a Red Veil: Staging Afghan Emancipation in Moscow," *The Soviet and Post-Soviet Review* 38:1 (2011): 30–62. That material is used with permission from (c) Koninklijke Brill NV, Leiden, 2011.

Introduction

It was an afternoon like any other at the airport in Tashkent, one of the largest cities in the Soviet Union and the capital of the Uzbek Soviet Socialist Republic. The morning return flights on Aeroflot Il'iushin IL-18s to Bukhara and Samarkand had long left, and at one of the gates there idled a FinnAir DC-8, refueling on a stopover from Bangkok to Helsinki. A connection from Novosibirsk, in the Russian Soviet Federative Socialist Republic, descended onto the bromegrass-lined runway; its passengers disembarked from the plane. Inside the terminal, servers dished out Uzbek *plov* at the cafeteria, but even that couldn't shake the stale monotony of a Soviet airport: the same tired buffets that could be found everywhere from Riga to Vladivistok and the same metallic coffee found, if less commonly, from Kiev to Kazan.[1] At once expansive and insular, the Soviet Union could feel more like a world than a country. And yet if one looked closely, even at airports like Tashkent's, hints of a world beyond beckoned.

Among the passengers on the Novosibirsk flight was Viktor Samoĭlenko, a journalist who had won accolades for his reporting from the Democratic Republic of Afghanistan, the world's youngest socialist state and the Soviet Union's neighbor to the south. Samoĭlenko was no stranger to the airport layovers, the endless trips across Soviet Eurasia. Yet here in Tashkent Samoĭlenko recognized something new. "They say," he wrote, "that the Tashkent Airport, in spite of its resemblance to every other Soviet airport, leaves a stronger, longer-lasting impression on you than others. Here, like nowhere else," Samoĭlenko noticed the peculiarities of his fellow Soviet citizens. "I met with young Heroes of the Soviet Union. And it was clear to everyone: they had won the Gold Star 'there' in fulfillment of their international duty."[2] Samoĭlenko found his

[1] Author Interview, Iuriĭ Sal'nikov, Volgograd, Russian Federation, November 4, 2012.
[2] Viktor Samoĭlenko, *Kak otkryvaesh' stranu: Afganistan glazami ochevidstev* (Novosibirsk: Knizhnoe Izdatel'stvo, 1986), 11.

gate, which was still disgorging passengers: "people who had spent some time 'there' – Soviet specialists returning from their trips, as well as children whose parents had died at the hands of the enemy." The boarding call for his flight rang out. It was time to return "there" – to Afghanistan.

Samoïlenko was not alone. Waiting in line, he spoke with a Belarusian Party worker who shared his life story. The Soviet state had evacuated him from Nazi killing squads to Tashkent, the Belarusian explained, where an Uzbek family, the Alimjanovs, raised him. For much of his childhood, he had assumed that his biological parents had perished, and he soon took on the last name of his Uzbek parents. But his biological mother had survived. After fifteen years of searching, she found him in Uzbekistan. The Komsomol worker considered reclaiming his original Belarusian surname, yet he retained the Uzbek surname in honor of "those to whom I had an unpaid debt."[3] Alimjanov, wrote Samoïlenko, embodied the virtues his own generation had drawn from the past, such as when Soviet families took in refugees from the Spanish Civil War: "the Soviet person as a patriot and internationalist."

Samoïlenko, Alimjanov, and a piebald procession of "geologists, construction workers, and agronomists" boarded the plane in groups by profession. A gregarious and numerate engineer seated next to Samoïlenko explained what awaited them in Afghanistan. "Now imagine," he said. "We're flying to a country that only recently was the 127th country in the world by level of education, 119th by level of health care, and 108th by national income per head – not only that, but the average life expectancy for an Afghan man is only forty years."[4] As the plane took off and headed south, the journalist Samoïlenko awaited a familiar ritual. Whenever he had flown abroad before on Aeroflot flights, there came "a moment when they announce that the foreign heavens have begun."[5] He and the other passengers looked out their windows: they were approaching the Amu-Darya River, the southern border of the USSR. The light for the PA system turned on. Samoïlenko perked his ears. The PA system rang out: "Afghanistan!"

The plane had entered the airspace of a country at the heart of Central Asia, bordered to its north by the Soviet Union, to its west by Iran, and to its east and south by Pakistan. As the plane flew over the country's northern marches, inhabited by Turkic- and Persian-speakers, the Hindu Kush loomed. Until Soviet engineers built a tunnel piercing the mountains in 1964, the range had divided not only the watershed of the Amu-Darya River from that of the Indus, but also Afghanistan itself. The Il'iushin crested a low point and descended toward Kabul, the capital, located in the densely populated east of the country. Eastward still lay the Safed Koh range, straddling the border between Afghanistan and Pakistan and intersected by the Kabul River, a tributary of the Indus. Further south, along an American-built ring road, lay the

---

[3] Ibid., 12.
[4] Ibid., 14.
[5] Ibid., 15.

FIGURE 1. Cold War Central Asia, c.1947–91 with countries, regions, and Soviet SSRs noted. The colonial-era Durand Line, marked on the map as a dotted line, formed the *de facto* border between Afghanistan and Pakistan, but Kabul never recognized the line as a legitimate international boundary.
Source: Author Map.

orchards and plantations of the Helmand watershed, dominated by the country's second-largest city, Qandahar. Together, these eastern and southern borderlands constituted the homelands of the Pashtun people, speakers of Pashto, an Indo-Iranian language. Informed guesses placed them at seven or eight million people, making them a plurality of Afghanistan's population. More Pashtuns, however, lived outside of Afghanistan than in it, most in neighboring Pakistan. Apart from the Pashtuns, a mix of Tajiks, Uzbeks, Hazara, Qizilbash, and other ethnicities populated Afghanistan. Little wonder, then, that some saw Afghanistan as "an anthropologist's dream."[6]

---

[6] Louis Dupree, Untitled Book Manuscript, 45. Louis Dupree Papers, Box 5, Peabody Natural History Museum Special Collections, Harvard University.

Afghanistan had been a monarchy since 1747 and independent from the British since 1919. Since 1929, the same lineage of Mohammadzai Durrani Pashtuns, a subtribe from southern Afghanistan, had ruled the country. The new Shah (King) was assassinated after only three years on the throne, but his son, Mohammad Zahir Shah (no relation to the Shah of Iran), reigned for thirty-nine years, during which time both his regents, Prime Ministers, and he himself remained content to keep society at arm's length. Modernization remained limited. The state asked little of the people; the people, little of the state. It seemed shrewd, for against the regional background of imperial collapse, revolution, world wars, and Partition, Afghanistan experienced fifty years of peace. And rather than throwing itself in with Washington or Moscow, cautious Kabul lured foreign experts to oversee development projects and reform the state. And even when Zahir Shah's cousin and former Prime Minister, Mohammad Daoud Khan, overthrew the monarchy in the summer of 1973, Afghanistan remained an island of relative stability in a tumultuous Cold War world.

That soon changed. On the evening of April 27, 1978, a group of Afghan Communists, the People's Democratic Party of Afghanistan (PDPA), overthrew and murdered Daoud and declared Afghanistan a Democratic Republic, making it one of the world's two Muslim-majority communist states (South Yemen was the first) and one of several socialist countries in the Third World. But in contrast to their monarchical predecessors, PDPA élites, many of them Ghilzai Pashtuns from eastern Afghanistan, imposed radical and violent change on the countryside. Civil war threatened a country that lay directly on the southern border of the USSR, and Afghan Communists exacerbated the crisis by murdering one another. The Soviet Union, which had played no role in inciting the so-called April Revolution, intervened militarily, first on December 24, 1979, with commandos to assassinate and replace PDPA leadership and, shortly thereafter, with tens of thousands of soldiers to occupy the country. The intervention led to disaster: of the perhaps fifteen million souls inhabiting Afghanistan in 1979, one third would become refugees outside the country, while another third would end up wounded or internally displaced. Over a million Afghans would be killed. Parallel to this carnage, however, thousands of Soviet nation-builders – the men and women on Samoïlenko's flight – and tens of thousands of Afghan Communists would seek to turn Afghanistan into a test site for the construction of socialism at the scale of the nation-state.

But these nation-builders had enemies. Hundreds of thousands of rebels operating from the other side of the Durand Line, the colonial-era boundary dividing Afghanistan from Pakistan, conducted attacks against the Afghan communist state and Soviet occupying forces. Supported by the Pakistani intelligence services and billions of dollars in American military aid, these Afghan warriors – *mujāhidin* – formed a formidable enemy in what was to become one of the defining conflicts of the Cold War. Yet also operating among the *mujāhidin* were NGOs, led by European humanitarians who believed that the future was neither socialism, nor the nation-state, but rather the overcoming of both through transnational morality. Emanating from a disenchanted European Left, this project of humanitarian postterritoriality collided with "real existing socialism" in a space on the planet where colonial cartography allowed them to overlap. No mere Cold War theater between the Soviet Union and its enemies, Afghanistan had become a battleground for debates about the relationship of the global Left to the Third World nation-state. Once among empires, once within borders, Afghanistan had become a battleground between two very different visions of Third World sovereignty – Soviet-style territorial authoritarianism on the one hand, and poststate humanitarianism on the other. The battle between these two projects, both enmeshed in a trans-regional civil war, would reveal Afghanistan's role not as "the graveyard of empires," but rather as the graveyard of the Third World nation-state.

How this happened is the story of men like Samoïlenko and his colleagues on board that flight to Kabul. It is the story of the American and West German state-makers who preceded them and of the European humanitarians who opposed them. It is the story of the Afghans who became interlocutors to all of the above. It is the story of the struggle between a territorial order of states and a transnational order of human beings – a story at once entangled in the Cold War while also in some ways above it. It is, in short, the story of this book. Before telling that story, however, it bears situating it in its historiographical context and dwelling on how to write the history of a country whose present very much begins with the interaction of global projects described and analyzed in what follows.

In Search of Modern Afghanistan

"Compared to its neighboring countries," writes historian Nile Green, "Afghanistan remains something of a blank spot on the historiographical map. Falling between Middle Eastern, South Asian, and Central Asian fields of expertise, it is in many respects the last great unclaimed territory of historical studies, not so much competed over as ignored by scholars."[7] Institutes for the study of "East Asia," the "Middle East," or "South Asia" abound, but there exist few centers for the study of Central Asia, much less Afghanistan itself. "Despite a rich burst of scholarship in the 1960s," continues Green, "and the efforts of a small but distinguished cadre of scholars since then, Afghan history has neither truly developed as a historical field in its own right nor [has it] been successfully absorbed into the study of any of its adjacent regions."

How did this happen? The continuities between Persia, Afghanistan, and the southern realms of Russian Turkestan were obvious to Russian and British imperialists, not to mention people who actually lived in the region. During the 1950s and 1960s, however, old imperial boundaries conspired with

---

[7] Nile Green, "Introduction," Roundtable on "The Future of Afghan History," *International Journal of Middle East Studies* 45 (2013), 127.

Cold War optics to render the study of Afghanistan homeless. The Iron Curtain bracketed not just "Eastern Europe" from "Western Europe," but also Soviet Eurasia from the rest of the Turko-Persianate world, both politically and epistemologically.[8] If Soviet academic institutions distinguished between "Middle Asia" (the Uzbek, Tajik, Turkmen, and Kyrgyz SSRs) and the "Middle East" (Turkey, Iran, Afghanistan, and Pakistan), American "Soviet Studies" grouped the entire Soviet Union together, fragmenting possible approaches to Eurasian history. Worse, academic centers typically located Iran in an Arab-dominated "Middle East" and Pakistan in "South Asia." Younger scholars trained in these paradigms. An elder generation of Orientologists retired just as learned critiques of English and French attitudes toward the Arab World discredited Orientology writ large. Much of what was no longer taught was forgotten.

How, then, to overcome the schematic categories that the Cold War imposed? Clearly, we need to do more than simply knit together a patchwork quilt of nationalist histories. The problems with this approach are especially visible in the case of Afghanistan, where, explains Afghan-American historian Shah Mahmoud Hanifi, there is a perpetual confusion about what was meant by the term "Afghan," particularly in relation to the terms "Pathan" or "Pashtun."[9] More fundamentally, Afghan national history is rendered murkier by the shifts in the meanings of the word "Afghanistan" itself between 1747 and 1893. Further, these confusions were often distilled by colonial authors like Mountstuart Elphinstone to cement a view of Afghanistan as an unchanging unit of geographic analysis, run from Kabul under Pashtun state domination, and yet also somehow threatened by Pashtun tribes.[10] Rather than merely placing this colonially-inflected Afghan national story alongside its Iranian, Pakistani, or (post-)Soviet counterparts, we need to pursue a transregional analysis, understanding how such nationalist narratives were themselves the product of sustained, and often violent, material, military, and epistemological intercourse with empire.[11]

Doing so demands grappling with the Cold War historiographical traditions that continue to govern the production of expert knowledge. American scholarship on Afghanistan, writes Hanifi, remained "fully nested within Cold War politics and U.S. intelligence gathering."[12] Donald Wilber, an OSS veteran who completed a PhD in Persian architectural history before directing the 1953

---

[8] Timothy D. Snyder, Remarks at Memorial Event to Tony Judt, March 23, 2012, King's College, Cambridge, United Kingdom.

[9] Shah Mahmoud Hanifi, "Quandaries of the Afghan Nation," in *Under the Drones: Modern Lives in the Afghanistan-Pakistan Borderlands*, eds. Robert Crews and Shahzad Bashir (Cambridge, MA: Harvard University Press, 2012), 86.

[10] Ibid., 87–8.

[11] Christine Noelle-Karimi, "Maps and Spaces," Roundtable on "The Future of Afghan History," *International Journal of Middle East Studies* 45 (2013), 142. One promising work in this direction (although appearing after this book went into print) is Robert Crews, *Afghan Modern: The History of a Global Nation* (Cambridge, MA: Harvard University Press, 2015).

[12] Hanifi, 96.

Anglo-American coup against Iranian Prime Minister Mohammad Mossadegh, wrote the first serious area studies-inflected work on Afghanistan in 1962.[13] Yet it was Louis Dupree, a veteran and trained archaeologist, who dominated American studies of Afghanistan during the Cold War.[14] Living in Kabul from 1959 to 1978 and based in Peshawar from 1978 to 1983, Dupree embodied the disinterested American capable of interpreting "inward looking" or "xenophobic" peoples to outsiders.[15] The "enthusiasm" and "passion" of these scholars, however, masks the weak institutionalization of the study of Afghanistan and an absence of sustained critical engagement with concepts like "Afghan" and "Afghanistan."

It would be wrong to conclude from Hanifi's reflection, however, that Americans dominated the literature on Afghanistan in the twentieth century. Instead, it was *Soviet* scholars who pursued the richest lines of inquiry. And yet, our appreciation for the Soviet scholarly legacy remains weak. Why? One reason is the rise of tendentious approaches to Russian history enabled by Cold War xenophobia. As Anatol Lieven explains, scholars like Richard Pipes stressed "deep continuities running through and even largely determining the course of Russian history from the Middle Ages through the Tsarist empire and to the Soviet Union to the post-Soviet present."[16] Others downplayed Russian internal despotism and to play up a Russian external expansionism, seeing "Russians and Russian culture as deeply, perennially and primordially imperialist, aggressive and expansionist." Excellent work by Jerry Hough, Francis Fukuyama, and Andrezj Korbonski aside, the Cold War view of Russia as fundamentally paranoid discouraged serious engagement with the Soviet Union's own production of area studies knowledge, much less the intersection of ideas and policy.

Writing on Soviet-Afghan relations presents its own special challenges. Anglophone writings often reach back upon an older British tradition of writing about Afghanistan as a "graveyard of empires," as if the context of imperial war had not changed since the 1880s, or if the near-total extermination of the Afghan people by three percent of total Soviet Armed Forces constituted a noble victory.[17] But these Anglophone views have also informed Afghan

[13] Donald Wilber, *Afghanistan: Its People, Its Society, Its Culture* (New Haven: HRAF Press, 1962).

[14] Dupree's magnum opus was *Afghanistan* (Princeton: Princeton University Press, 1973).

[15] According to Shah Mahmoud Hanifi, when his father (a graduate of élite secondary institutions in Afghanistan and then studying in the United States) met Louis Dupree for the first time in the mid-1950s, the first question that Dupree asked him was whether the Afghan Ministry of Defense had its own intelligence agency – an odd opening from a man whose primary training was in archaeology. The Soviet Union, it bears recalling, would have only just begun training the Afghan Army when Dupree asked his question. Personal Communication, Shah Mahmoud Hanifi, April 4, 2014.

[16] Anatol Lieven, *Chechnya: Tombstone of Russian Power* (New Haven: Yale University Press, 1998), 5.

[17] The phrase "graveyard of empires" is usually attributed to twentieth-century Afghan intellectual Mahmud Tarzi.

historical framings. Afghan-American historian Mohammad Hassan Kakar describes Russians as "latecomers to the fold of civilization" and members of a politically backwards civilization.[18] Kakar contends that "godless Communists" sought to "ruthlessly suppress" Afghans just as "the Russians" had done to "Muslim Bukhara." Former Council of Ministers Chairman Muhammad Hassan Sharq also connects the Soviet invasion to a demonic logic of Russian expansion.[19] Ironically, a view of Afghans as fanatical Muslims that was "diligently cultivated and craftily deployed by the British in India" has been recycled by former Afghan Communists in order to stress their native authority.[20] Outlawed for much of the twentieth century, Afghan historiography remains captive to the categories of colonial and Cold War knowledge originally designed to dominate it.

This scholarly inheritance presents problems and opportunities for the historian who wishes to write on Afghanistan's twentieth century, particularly the years between 1929 and 1978. Traditionally, writes Nile Green, those brackets – the collapse of the Amanullah regime and the overthrow of the Musahibans – have enthralled scholars to the exclusion of unpacking the decades in between. Yet this mode of processing history "is a classic model of nationalist analysis: Afghans built the nation, non-Afghans destroyed it. What we lose sight of is both the multiplicity of voices drowned in the clarion call of the nation and the larger sequence of transnational dynamics through the entire twentieth century."[21] As a result, any "processual glue" that would link together the apparently national moment of the early twentieth century with the global moment of the 1970s is lost, leaving historians "with a narrow set of agents and analyses." If *space* constitutes the first dimension in which one must relocate Afghanistan, then the alleged globality or nonglobality of its history at different points in the twentieth century is the second.

In Search of Global History

But what would it mean to write a global history of Afghanistan, or indeed of any country? "How," as one scholar asks, "should the history of global flows and connections be conceptualized when it encompasses potentially nothing less than 'the world,' since all-inclusiveness is obviously not an option?"[22] Any answer to this question must disentangle a global scale from that of diplomatic

[18] M. Hassan Kakar, *Afghanistan: The Soviet Invasion and the Afghan Response, 1979–1982* (Berkeley: University of California Press, 1995), 125–6.

[19] Muhammad Hassan Sharq, *The Bare-Foot in Coarse Clothes* (Peshawar: Area Study Centre of University of Peshawar, 2000).

[20] Hanifi, 95.

[21] Nile Green, "Locating Afghan History," Roundtable on "The Future of Afghan History," *International Journal of Middle East Studies* 45 (2013), 132.

[22] Vanessa Ogle, "Whose Time Is It? The Pluralization of Time and the Global Condition, 1870s-1940s," *American Historical Review* 188(5) (December 2013), 1377.

exchange, or, in the case of the twentieth century, the Cold War. Traditionally, historians took for granted that scrupulous study of the diplomatic record could reveal "the secret stratagems of monarchs and statesmen" and uncover "the pattern of the past which explained the present."[23] By the early 1980s, however, diplomatic history was embattled.[24] "The history of international relations," wrote one scholar, "cannot, alas, be counted among the pioneering fields of the discipline during the 1970s."[25]

Fortunately, both new sources and methodological innovations enabled scholars to respond to these charges. An imperial turn in many national historiographies, including that of the United States, prompted historians to investigate exchange beyond just the political or diplomatic plane. Exploiting the archives of businesses, NGOs, and universities and making use of postcolonial theory, historians of international relations have made theirs a field that now studies not just war but also cotton, community development, or suburbs as legitimate research subjects.[26] Two and a half decades after the opening of Eastern Bloc, Chinese, Yugoslav, and other national archives, scholars have turned Cold War history into a thriving discipline with journals, institutes, and debates of its own.[27]

Sometimes, however, an insistence that "the most fundamental issue is the question of war and peace" can lead to an over-emphasis on writing history from the point of view of a National Security Adviser – or a Politburo member.[28] Obviously, exchanges between Foreign Ministries, or between

[23] Roger Bullen, "What Is Diplomatic History?" in *What Is History Today?*, ed. Juliet Gardiner (London: Macmillan Education, 1988), 135.

[24] Charles S. Maier, "Marking Time: Contemporary Historical Writing in the United States," in *The Past Before Us: Contemporary Historical Writing in the United States* (Ithaca: Cornell University Press, 1980), 355–387; Alexander de Conde, "What's Wrong With American Diplomatic History?" *Newsletter of the Society of Historians of American Foreign Relations* 1 (May 1970); David S. Patterson, "What's Wrong (And Right) with American Diplomatic History? A Diagnosis and a Prescription," SHAFR *Newsletter* 9 (September 1978), 1–14.

[25] Maier, "Marking Time," 355. For a reflection by Maier on the state of the field decades later, see "Return to Rome: Half a Century of American Historiography in Light of the 1955 Congress for International Historical Studies," in *La storiografia tra passato e futuro (Il X Congreso Internazionale di Scienze Storiche (Roma 1955) cinquant'anni dopo* (Rome: 2008), 189–211).

[26] Sven Beckert, *Empire of Cotton: A Global History* (New York: Knopf, 2014); Daniel Immerwahr, *Thinking Small: The United States and the Lure of Community Development* (Cambridge, MA: Harvard University Press, 2015); Andrew Friedman, *Covert Capital: Landscapes of Denial and the Making of U.S. Empire in the Suburbs of Northern Virginia* (Berkeley: University of California Press, 2013).

[27] Consider, for example, the works in the University of North Carolina Press's New Cold War History Series, or the work of that Series' editor, Odd Arne Westad's *The Global Cold War: Third World Interventions and the Making of Our Times* (Cambridge: Cambridge University Press, 2005).

[28] Mark Trachtenberg, "What's the Problem? A Research Agenda for Diplomatic History," H-Diplo State of the Field Essay, October 10, 2014; Mario del Pero, "Tra lunghe paci i guerre fredde. La storiografia di John Lewis Gaddis" (2005); Tony Judt, "A Story Still to Be Told," *New York Review of Books*, March 23, 2006.

Presidents and General Secretaries, were fundamental, since "policymakers could effect the most fundamental changes in how people lived and worked." But so, too, could the real or perceived threat of overpopulation, smallpox, or global warming.[29] The most compelling works reject divisions between structural change and diplomatic exchange, exploring how "the changing forms of the transnational itself" interact with the story culled from state archives.[30] They stress how the bipolar conflict was necessarily embedded in a developing global condition with roots dating to the 1870s, but which changed dramatically in the 1970s.[31] While global history itself now constitutes a field of its own, the global turn has itself irreversibly affected every national historiographic field, not least that of Russia and the Soviet Union.[32]

Humanitarian Invasion builds upon this conversation by placing the history of development in Afghanistan in the context of global transformations in the concept of sovereignty. More specifically, this book argues that Afghanistan's tumultuous Cold War experience is best understood through the lens of global debates about the rights and responsibilities associated with postcolonial sovereignty. Far from an obscure location fundamentally distant from global processes, Afghanistan and its twentieth-century journey from British protectorate to international protectorate – by way of independence and Soviet

---

[29] Matthew Connelly, *A Diplomatic Revolution: Algeria's Fight for Independence and the Origins of the Post-Cold War Era* (Oxford: Oxford University Press, 2002), x; Nick Cullather, *The Hungry World: America's Cold War Battle Against Poverty in Asia* (Cambridge, MA: Harvard University Press, 2010); Matthew Connelly, *Fatal Misconception: The Struggle to Control World Population* (Cambridge, MA: Harvard University Press, 2008); Erez Manela, "A Pox on Your Narrative: Writing Disease Control into Cold War History," *Diplomatic History* 34(2) (April 2010), 299–323.

[30] Sven Beckert, "Das Reich der Baumwolle: Eine globale Geschichte," in *Das Kaiserreich transnational: Deutschland in der Welt 1870–1914*, eds. Sebastian Conrad and Jürgen Osterhammel (Göttingen: Vandenhoeck & Ruprecht, 2004), 301; C.A. Bayly, *The Birth of the Modern World, 1780–1914* (Malden: Blackwell, 2004); Jürgen Osterhammel, *Die Verwandlung der Welt. Eine Geschichte des 19. Jahrhunderts* (Munich: C.H. Beck, 2009); Stefan Link, "Transnational Fordism: Ford Motor Company, Nazi Germany, and the Soviet Union in the Interwar Years" (PhD Dissertation, Harvard University, 2012); Heidi Tworek, "Magic Connections: German News Agencies and Global News Networks, 1905–45," (PhD Dissertation, Harvard University, 2012); Vanessa Ogle, *The Global Transformation of Time, 1879–1950* (Cambridge, MA: Harvard University Press, 2015); Mira Siegelberg, *Statelessness: An International History, 1921–1961* (Cambridge, MA: Harvard University Press, forthcoming).

[31] Michael Geyer and Charles Bright, "World History in a Global Age," *The American Historical Review* 100(4) (October 1995), 1034–60; Charles Maier, "Consigning the Twentieth Century to History: Alternative Narratives for the Modern Era," *American Historical Review* 105(3), 807–31; Geyer and Bright, "Where in the World is America? The History of the United States in the Global Age," in *Rethinking American History in a Global Age*, ed. Thomas Bender (Berkeley: University of California Press, 2002), 63–100.

[32] See (although focused more explicitly on Soviet-Third World exchanges than any global condition) David Engerman, "The Second World's Third World," *Kritika* 12(1) (Winter 2011), 183–211; for one example from the field of American history, see *Rethinking American History in a Global Age*, ed. Thomas Bender (Berkeley: University of California Press, 2002).

occupation – would remain inexplicable without reference to shifts in global norms about the promises and pitfalls of post-imperial statehood. For while other postcolonial countries underwent similar journeys in the global order, not only was Afghanistan's search for a place in the world longer than almost any other postcolonial state, its engagement with Soviet socialism, European humanitarianism, and transnational Islam was more diverse and intimate than perhaps that of any other country. It is because of the diversity of Afghanistan's encounters with such different visions of postcolonial statehood and international order that the history of this seemingly obscure place actually reveals a very big story.

A Look Ahead

Afghanistan assumed this role as a mirror of global order because of its tortured place in the history of territorial statehood itself. The Durrani Empire, which occupied much of the territories comprising present-day Afghanistan and Pakistan in the early nineteenth century, epitomized the style of rule best suited for arid, sparsely-populated Central Asia: "control the best bits...and leave at arm's length territories deemed unprofitable to rule or of little strategic value."[33] Lacking "the geographer's impulse" of fixing subjects in space, Durrani leaders never mapped their own borders or conducted censuses.[34] But from 1871 to 1896, surrounding empires delineated the borders of Persia, Russian Turkestan, the Emirate of Bukhara, the Qing Empire, and British Empire with Afghanistan. Most fatefully, however, in 1893, British colonial officials raised cash subsidies to Kabul by half in exchange for the Anglo-Afghan demarcation of a boundary line, the Durand Line.[35] Drawn a year later, the 1,640-mile long Durand Line served as the functional border between British India and the Emirate of Afghanistan. While the British retained control over Afghanistan's foreign affairs, they committed not to intervene west of the Line, creating, in effect, a space of Afghan sovereignty.

Afghanistan had thus entered a territorial state system, but without ever developing the personnel or expertise required to "do" territoriality. Further, once locked into the territorial process, there was no way out. Following the Third Anglo-Afghan War, Afghanistan became a sovereign postcolonial state before it was fashionable. But when the Partition of British India in 1947 carved Pakistan out of the Raj, Afghanistan became only further locked into a territorial jigsaw. It was, however, a jigsaw secured by the colonial Durand Line, even if Kabul never recognized the Line as a border. Soon, the indeterminacy

---

[33] Thomas Barfield, *Afghanistan: A Cultural and Political History* (Princeton: Princeton University Press, 2010), 68.

[34] Charles S. Maier, *Leviathan 2.0: Inventing Modern Statehood* (Cambridge, MA: The Belknap Press of Harvard University Press, 2012), 166.

[35] Shah Mahmoud Hanifi, "Mapping Afghanistan" (Unpublished Paper), 3.

of the Durand Line became at once an opportunity and a specter. Regarding the border as a marker of closed territorial space meant dooming Afghanistan to become a "failed state." Reframing it as an irredentist whisper waiting to explode through the map, however, offered Kabul with a means to pressure Pakistan. As military trainers, economists, and draftsmen built territorial states and national economies on both sides of the Line, the indeterminacy of the colonial cartographic archive loomed large.

And yet it was clashes after the "development decade" of the 1960s that would interact most fatefully with Afghanistan's ambiguous territoriality. Crucial here was the role of the Soviet Union, whose emergence as a defender of territoriality few would have predicted. For much of Soviet history, official ideology held that the USSR would become a utopian Communist society.[36] Eventually, the state was supposed to wither away. But in the 1970s, as actors had to cope with the new ubiquity of the nation-state and postcolonial territorial sovereignty, the official line shifted.[37] Soviet and Eastern Bloc leaders insisted that they had built "developed socialism" or "real existing socialism," the most utopian project actually *achievable* given the circumstances of capitalist encirclement. "Nonutopian" Soviet socialism was the only realistic vision of the future as a political proposition.[38] Imperialist aggression forced socialists to abandon world revolution in favor of revolution at the scale of the nation-state, relying on norms of territorial sovereignty to transform the societies within.

This reinvention of socialism inspired the reinvention of Western humanitarianism as a challenge to socialism and the Third World nation-state – a crucial turn without which the upsurge in European humanitarian interest in Afghanistan, formerly one of the most obscure countries in the world, would remain inexplicable. The turn is particularly striking in the case of France and Sweden, the two countries that would form the two largest transnational humanitarian operations to challenge Soviet socialism in Afghanistan. In France, the group that became *Médecins sans Frontières* (MSF) was led by ex-Communists old enough to be disillusioned once by the Prague Spring and then again by the international refugee crisis of the Vietnamese "boat people." Motivated less by universal human rights than "the right to life of the Vietnamese," MSF soon embraced an antitotalitarian stance that viewed authoritarian borders as meaningless where precarious lives were at stake.[39] In Sweden, intellectuals sublimated early Maoist opposition to Soviet imperialism to organize

---

[36] In his October 31, 1961, speech at the 22nd CPSU Party Congress, Nikita Khrushchëv declared that "the current generation of Soviet people will live under Communism," while the CPSU program at the conference confirmed that by 1980 "in the USSR a Communist society will have been fundamentally constructed."

[37] Ryan M. Irwin, "Decolonization and the Cold War," in *The Routledge Handbook of the Cold War*, eds. Artemy Kalinovsky and Craig Daigle (London: Routledge, 2014), 91–104.

[38] Timothy D. Snyder, Public Lecture, "Not Even Past: History, Russia, Ukraine and Europe," June 4, 2014, available online at: www.youtube.com/watch?v=mgIqL_mxKI8.

[39] Rony Brauman, *Mémoires* (Paris, Juillard, 1983) quoted in Anne Vallaeys, *Médecins sans Frontières: La biographie* (Paris: Fayard, 2004), 290.

the largest humanitarian campaign inside of occupied Afghanistan. The cult of the guerrilla gave way to the religion of humanity. As one activist reflected, "there [had been] many of us who not only regarded the Vietnam War as a justified defensive struggle but saw the Vietnamese as another kind of human being, more noble than us. But the whole point was that they were basically like us."[40] Just as the Soviets emphasized the nation-state as the proper scale for political confrontation, European Leftists tacked in a different direction. Socialism in one country had ceded ground to morality in one planet.

Hence, when the Soviet Union invaded Afghanistan on December 24, 1979, and drove millions of Afghan refugees into Pakistan, it furnished a justification for Western humanitarians to intervene. But the way in which humanitarian NGOs did so augured an important shift in the form and politics of the Left. Against Soviet state-builders, NGOs emerged "not as challengers pressing up against the state *from below* but as *horizontal* contemporaries of the organs of the state," exploiting the cartographic indeterminacy of the Durand Line to challenge socialism at the scale of the nation-state with morality at the scale of the human.[41] Sovereign individualism, not subaltern internationalism, was their watchword. If Soviet advisers saw Afghans as political beings ready to be molded in the shape of a movement for justice, humanitarians justified their intervention into Afghan state space in the language of suffering. They worked not to erase inequality, but to restore society to its pre-disaster condition. Compared to the 100,000 Soviet troops and thousands of Soviet advisers stationed on Afghan territory, the dozen or so people in Peshawar field offices seemed trifling. But their work was embedded inside the transnational armies of several hundred thousand *mujāhidin*, themselves armed with modern weapons and with both command and knowledge of the vast majority of Afghanistan that lay beyond the Soviet-controlled roads and cities. Even before the USSR withdrew from Afghanistan in 1989, an unlikely alliance of ex-Leftists and Islamists was ministering to perhaps the majority of Afghans inside what was still, technically, a sovereign state.

Both the Soviet and the humanitarian invasion of Afghanistan ended with deeply ambiguous consequences. In the region itself, Pakistan fused the *mujāhidin* rebels and refugee bodies generated by the Soviet invasion with the transnational anti-statism of humanitarian groups to degrade and destroy the Democratic Republic of Afghanistan. For decades, Pashtun irredentism, often coming from the Left, had threatened Pakistan's territorial integrity. When attempts to seal the Durand Line forever as a border between the two states faltered, however, Pakistan exploited the two dominant tendencies in the late twentieth century global Left – Soviet territoriality and humanitarian postterritoriality – to transform the territory at the semantic core of Afghan

---

[40] Staffan Forssell, "För Afghanistan!" in *Tio år av solidaritet* (Special 1991 Issue of *Afghanistan-Nytt*), 6. Personal Archive of Anders Forsberg, Uppsala, Sweden.

[41] James Ferguson and Akhil Gupta, "Spatializing States: Towards an Ethnography of Neoliberal Governmentality," *American Ethnologist* 29(4) (November 2002), 994.

irredentism into a novel space of not just bio- but also geopolitical experimentation.

On a global scale, moreover, the hopes and ambitions that the USSR and humanitarians invested into the Third World nation-state waned. While MSF and SCA challenged Soviet socialism in the arena of the Third World itself, by the mid 1980s, both European socialists and Soviet Communists diverted their political energies from the Third World to Europe. When Moscow not only withdrew from Afghanistan but also authorized the insertion of the United Nations into the theater, the decline of the Third World nation-state's sovereign privileges was complete. Ransacked by Pakistani-sponsored *mujāhidin* and kept alive by NGOs, Afghanistan had become a model of the "nongovernmentality" about to define much of the former Third World.[42]

Methodology

This book draws on archival sources, manuscripts, and interviews from several different countries. In addition to material from Soviet archives in Russia, Tajikistan, and Kyrgyzstan, this book relies on dozens of semi-structured interviews with former Soviet advisers. In the United States, the journals of Arthur Paul and Robert Nathan, held at the University of Nebraska-Omaha and Cornell University, respectively, offered insight into the worlds of two American consultants in Afghanistan. In Germany, materials from the archives of the West German Federal Ministry for Economic Cooperation at the Federal Archives in Koblenz and the Political Archive of the Foreign Office provided detail on West German economic assistance to Afghanistan. The archives of Human Rights Watch at Columbia University and the Javier Pérez de Cuéllar papers at Yale University clarified points of contact between the Soviet Union, the United Nations, and American NGOs. Likewise, in Sweden and France, the archives of the Swedish Committee for Afghanistan and MSF provided a view beyond Anglophone human rights organizations and into the two groups with the largest presence in Soviet-occupied Afghanistan. In the United Kingdom, materials from the National Archives as well as the papers of Vasiliĭ Mitrokhin held crucial trade statistics and information about Soviet academia's connection to the intelligence services. For interviews, I have anonymized the name of informants who wished to not be mentioned specifically.

Security conditions and the politics of memory in Afghanistan make sustained in-country research challenging. During the Afghan Civil War, *mujāhidin* looted the National Archives and sold documents at bazaars in Peshawar.[43] Provincial archives, meanwhile, were either nonexistent before 1979 or

---

[42] Gregory Mann, *From Empires to NGOs in the West African Sahel: The Road to Nongovernmentality* (Cambridge: Cambridge University Press, 2015).

[43] Habibo Brechna, *Die Geschichte Afghanistans. Historische Ereignisse, Erzählungen und Erinnerungen* (Zürich: Hochschulverlag AG, 2012), 446.

destroyed during the civil war. The remaining holdings of the National Archives in Kabul, while rich, are not cataloged, and the extent of holdings on the Communist era remains unclear. More importantly, Afghans remain disenfranchised from their own history. Many of the leading figures in Afghanistan's political life today are former members of the PDPA whose past has not always been critically examined. Tellingly, when the Afghan Human Rights Commission completed an independent 800-page study on mass killing in Afghanistan in December 2011, its publication was suppressed because it threatened to name many current members of Karzai Administration.[44]

Thus, this book is not a social or political history *of* Afghanistan, nor is it a history of the Soviet invasion and occupation *per se*; it is a history of international development and humanitarianism *in* Afghanistan. Readers looking for a Cold War story *per se* will search in vain, too, for while my story took place within the Cold War and was impossible without it, the reinventions of Afghan sovereignty documented here go beyond the dynamic of great power conflict. If what might seem like obvious narrative turning points – most obviously, the Soviet decision-making process to invade Afghanistan – appear deemphasized here, it is not because they were unimportant. Many excellent books have been written on those turning points, but *Humanitarian Invasion* aspires to something else.[45] What follows here is a story of how territorial state power, and the archive of knowledge that came with it, interacted with a part of the world never formally incorporated into empire. It is a story of how ideas and ambitions for "Afghanistan" qua nation-state conspired to make and break Afghanistan as a real place.

Throughout, therefore, an important methodological issue – what one might dub the interlocutor problem – cannot be forgotten. During the Cold War, even the best-informed experts could imagine an Afghan economy and state out of only a few conversations, or a walk around the right couple of blocks of Kabul. Frequently, "development" meant less building a state or economy than injecting meaning into fragments of both. Seen in isolation, however, and preferably with the interlocution of native informants, experts could read into a factory, a canal, a gas pipeline, a spreadsheet, or sawmill a functioning but in reality barely existent Afghan state. American smallpox vaccinators could be ordered "to do 100 percent coverage, from the moment of birth to the moment of death" when the Ministry of Health literally did not have a piece of paper.[46] Soviet petroleum

[44] Rod Nordland, "Top Afghans Tied to '90s Carnage," *New York Times*, July 22, 2012.

[45] Aleksandr Liakhovskiĭ, *Tragediia i doblest' Afgana* (Moscow: GPI Iskona, 1995); Barnett R. Rubin, *The Fragmentation of Afghanistan: State Formation and Collapse in the International System* (New Haven: Yale University Press, 1995); Pierre Allan and Dieter Kläy, *Zwischen Bürokratie und Ideologie. Entscheidungsprozesse in Moskaus Afghanistankonflikt* (Bern: Paul Haupt Verlag, 1999); Rodric Braithwaite, *Afgantsy: The Russians in Afghanistan, 1979–89* (London: Profile Books, 2011); Artemy Kalinovsky, *A Long Goodbye: The Soviet Withdrawal from Afghanistan* (Cambridge, MA: Harvard University Press, 2011).

[46] Linda Kuhn Berryhill and Deezie Stebbins Flower, Interview, *Once in Afghanistan* (2008).

engineers could take pride in the construction of oil derricks and steel pipelines while the majority of the country burned dung for warmth. The Afghan state of the late 1970s was an adventitious thing: microscopic state size, microscopic state capacity, and yet nonetheless a success by the measure of getting foreigners to pay its bills, indeed, to imagine it into existence.

Structure

This book consists of seven chapters. Chapter 1 explores the intellectual history of the study of Afghanistan and the Third World in the Soviet Union, showing how in spite of sustained investment into an area studies infrastructure, Soviet élites and experts were intellectually unprepared for Afghan Communists' coup d'état in Kabul in April 1978. Chapter 2, the longest in this book, explores the history of development in Afghanistan from the 1930s to the late 1960s. While the first half of the Chapter consists of a traditional chronological narrative of Afghanistan's journey from independence to becoming a Cold War developmental hothouse, the latter half of the chapter uses four case studies using different resources and developmental actors to understand statebuilding at its high point: American and Soviet financial and trade advisers in Kabul; American hydrologists in southern Afghanistan; Soviet petroleum engineers in northern Afghanistan; and, lastly, West German foresters in eastern Afghanistan. This second half of the chapter could have perhaps formed a chapter unto itself, but such a division might have risked narratively separating Afghanistan's Cold War dilemmas from the interwar context with which they were intimately connected. Chapter 3 moves into the 1970s, with an emphasis on regional geopolitics, the reinvention of Soviet socialism, and European humanitarianism. Chapter 4 follows Soviet youth advisers into occupied Afghanistan, showing how Soviet territoriality faltered along a colonial borderscape. Chapter 5 explores how Soviet activists and their Afghan interlocutors approached "the woman question"; Chapter 6, the transformation of northern Afghanistan into a Soviet and humanitarian co-constituted landscape. Chapter 7 returns to Afghanistan's southern and eastern borders to show how an alliance of *mujāhidin* fighters and humanitarian NGOs usurped power from not only the Kabuli state but also the UN, raising painful questions about statebuilding and humanitarianism in the process.

Readers will notice a shift in narrative scale throughout *Humanitarian Invasion*. More than just a narrative choice, however, this shift reflects the changing intellectual stakes during the periods whose histories we write. The first half of this book is about projects that were literally embedded in the planet itself: carbon extracted from the ground by drills and pumps, water collected from the mountains in canals, cedar trees sliced in sawmills. People could invest their hopes for the postcolonial nation-state into these objects in the earth. It is a story of a moment when people more often sought freedom *in*, rather than *from*, the nation-state.[47]

But as the abuses of sovereignty became more apparent, as postcolonial national self-determination lost its teleological vigor, statehood measured in steel tonnage and kilowatt-hours enchanted less. The postutopian visions of the 1970s fantasized less about the materiality of development. Rather than planting things in the *surface* of the planet, one needed to challenge its *structure*, that is, the global concept of sovereignty. Whereas the first half of this book is richly grounded in the materiality of development, in the second half, the bulldozers recede into the background; Western humanitarian and Soviet organizations concerned with children's welfare, with women, creep into the foreground. It is this shift, I suspect, from the territoriality of the nation-state to the postterritorial morality of our present moment that accounts for the narrative reframing ahead.

Here, then, you will find a history of sovereignty in Afghanistan seen through foreign eyes. Mine is a story of youth advisers; of women's activists who sought to "rescue" Afghan women from barbarism; of agronomists who wanted to make cedar forests bloom; of economists and statisticians who wanted to make the state as legible as a spreadsheet; of experts like those who boarded Viktor Samoïlenko's flight from Tashkent to Kabul.

Flying over the Amu-Darya, Viktor Samoïlenko recorded his thoughts. "What threw itself into our eyes?" he wrote. "Well-groomed land with fields and woodlands, lakes and canals, roads and villages leading up to the Amu-Darya, as though they were stumbling toward an insurmountable barrier. The banks of river ended, yielding their place to the uniform gray background upon which could be seen the bright brown hills with vague outlines of scalloped dunes reminding one of light ripples on water. Occasionally something resembling a settlement became visible – flat, gray like the land around it, and hence unexpected in the landscape. A few aquatic plants floated in the spindly ponds down below, but once soon they disappeared from view, and there was nothing below to stop or even hold one's gaze."[48] The numerate engineer seated next to Samoïlenko cleared his throat. "You and I have been thrown a couple of years back in time – perhaps 150 years into the past," he said. "It's time to land."

Even if one arrived armed with the developing powers that economics, social science, or seven decades of socialism furnished, transforming Afghanistan promised to be no easy task. But for over four decades, two generations of Soviets, Americans, Germans, Afghans, Pakistanis, and others would try. I traveled widely to read these people's diaries. I read the reports they wrote to their

[47] Jeremi Suri, *Power and Protest: Global Revolution and the Rise of Detente* (Cambridge, MA: Harvard University Press, 2003), 259.

[48] Samoïlenko, 12.

supervisors. I tracked them down and listened as they shared the history of the ideas that were supposed to reinvent Afghan statehood.

The dreams these advisers brought to Afghanistan would spawn nightmares. The Soviet occupation and the Afghan Civil War, by destroying so much and killing so many, obscured the historical processes that made the invasion and war possible in the first place. Not only that, because the Soviet Union and its vision of the planet collapsed so suddenly, it became possible to overlook how it influenced the conceptual vocabulary of development, sovereignty, and humanitarianism for decades to come. But is precisely for those reasons that this past – this sediment material and mnemonic – demands unearthing. *Humanitarian Invasion* presents itself as one possible beginning to a conversation inviting foreigners and Afghans to come to terms with the human and material debts associated with Afghanistan's Cold War encounters.

How to Write the History of Afghanistan

The historical process of development, to say nothing of the construction of a new socialist society, isn't a stroll down the Nevskiĭ Prospect of Petrograd, nor is the road there as straight and as flat.[1]

When the airborne Samoĭlenko described the landscape below him as a "uniform gray background" with nothing to arrest his gaze, he was only repeating one of many clichés about Afghanistan.[2] For some, the country beggared comprehension: it was "from another planet," "where time had stopped," Biblical, medieval.[3] But as Samoĭlenko's projection of timelessness onto the monochrome marshes below him demonstrated, Afghanistan's landscape was in fact "a palimpsest which bores the inattentive but seduces the curious."[4] Here, sediments of history lay stacked upon one another like the sheaves of the Persian, Pashto, and Turkic manuscripts Orientologists jealously poached. The possibilities for how to write the history of Afghanistan seemed endless. As modernizing Afghan regimes created native intelligentsias ready and willing to interact with foreign delegations, moreover, the possibilities for a shared Orientological and historiographical world made by words seemed electric. Throughout the twentieth century, Soviet scholars of Afghanistan would turn their gaze, excitedly, toward the lands that had bored Samoĭlenko.

[1] Dmitriĭ Fyodorovich Solovëv, "Vospominaniie o Vladimire Il'iche Lenine chlena Kommunisticheskoĭ Partii Sovetskogo Soiuza s 1919 goda, Solovëva Dmitriia Fëdorovicha–3.9.1968, Kiev," Tsentral'nyĭ Gosudarstvennyĭ Arkhiv Politicheskoĭ Dokumentatsii Respubliki Kirgizii, f. 391, op. 424, l. 66.

[2] Viktor Samoĭlenko, Kak otkryvaesh' stranu: Afganistan glazami ochevidstev (Novosibirsk: Knizhnoe Izdatel'stvo, 1986), 11.

[3] Vladimir Basov and Genrikh Poliakov, Afganistan: Trudnye sud'by revoliutsii (Moscow: Znaniie, 1988), 3.

[4] Anthony Grafton, "Hello to Berlin," New York Review of Books, August 14, 1997, available online at: www.nybooks.com/articles/archives/1997/aug/14/hello-to-berlin/

Mentions of Orientology might prompt readers to reach for *Orientalism*, the influential 1978 volume by Edward Said that argued that Orientology was a "cultural apparatus" that "elided the Orient's difference with weakness."[5] "In a nutshell," summarizes one scholar, "Said's *Orientalism* argues that the scholarly apparatus whereby the West studies the East is a means to oppress it."[6] And yet Soviet Orientology presents a problem for the Saidian framework. Said barely mentioned Russian or Soviet Oriental Studies in his work, even though the Soviet Union ruled tens of millions of Muslims. Soviet Orientology explicitly framed itself in opposition to Western imperialism; a quarter century before Said, Soviet encyclopedias explained how "from the very beginning bourgeois Orientology diametrically opposed the civilizations of the so-called 'West' with those of the 'East'," which reflected "the colonialist–racist worldview of the European and American bourgeoisie."[7] None of this diminishes Said's destruction of British and French attitudes toward the Arab World, but it does speak for the need to take Soviet Orientology on its own terms, not to "Occidentalize" scholars who saw Orientology as a weapon against, not for the colonial domination of non-Europeans.

Indeed, what made Soviet scholars most different from the Saidian caricature of Orientology was their position in a revolutionary state. When Soviet Orientologists noted that their methodology was "the Marxist–Leninist doctrine on the state," they were not just making a scholarly decision. The Soviet Union was a Marxist–Leninist state that claimed to know the "scientific" laws of historical development – indeed, not just to know, but to embody. Yet as former parts of the Ottoman Empire, protectorates like Afghanistan, and, later, European colonies gained their independence, the relevance of Marxism–Leninism to those countries' history and future demanded elucidation. When Bolsheviks dreamed of Communist revolution, they had projected it upon "the land of long chimneys" – industrialized Europe.[8] But revolution had to travel a different path: through the steppes of Central Asia, the rice paddies of China, or the Gangetic plains of India. The more that scholars bent orthodox Marxism–Leninism to analyze extra-Soviet reality, the more questionable the Soviet Union's claim to offer universally applicable advice on the road from serfdom to socialism became. Understanding, much less guiding, development in the Third World would turn out to be a task rather more complicated than an amble down Nevskiĭ Prospect.

The Soviet Union's engagement with Afghanistan forms an essential part of this story. Even prior to the Soviet invasion, understanding Afghanistan

5 Edward Said, *Orientalism* (New York: Vintage Books, 1978), 204.
6 David Schmmelpennick van der Oye, *Russian Orientalism: Asia in the Russian Mind from Peter the Great to the Emigration* (New Haven: Yale University Press, 2010), 6.
7 *Bol'shaia sovetskaia entsiklopediia*, 2nd Edition (1951), Entry for "Vostokovedenie" (Orientology).
8 Thomas Ashton, quoted in Sven Beckert, *Empire of Cotton: A Global History* (New York: Knopf, 2014), 80.

mattered for several reasons. Firstly, Afghanistan bordered the Soviet Union. After Afghanistan declared its independence from the British Empire on August 19, 1919, the Soviet Union was the first country in the world to recognize Kabul, transforming Afghanistan from irredentum to actor in an anticolonial international system. Secondly, many of the people inhabiting Afghanistan were, in some sense, the same as those inhabiting the Soviet Union, speakers of Turkic and Persian languages later ethnographized as Uzbeks and Tajiks. Indeed, such people had sought refuge in Afghanistan following Stalinist repressions. Hence, when Soviet scholars approached the country, they faced a bevy of questions about how to write the history, and imagine the future, of Afghanistan. What did it mean that anticolonial Afghanistan was a monarchy? Could countries with no working class have revolutions? Which nationality or ethnicity was supposed to take power in a "tribal" society? And, crucially, how were native Communist Parties to arise in such conditions?

This opening chapter is an intellectual history of Soviet scholarship on Afghanistan and Soviet engagement with the Third World more broadly, showing how the Soviet Union sought to find answers to these questions. Moscow studied Afghanistan more effectively than did the United States or any European competitor, and yet numerous seemingly trivial problems conspired in a way that made it difficult to understand a revolution from the Left in 1978. Tajik Persianate biases accrued in Soviet higher education, reinforcing an image of Pashtun barbarism that intersected with the Kabuli Persianate marketing of "Pashtunistan." All the while, the overthrow of a progressive Afghan monarchical regime in 1929 haunted Soviet scholars. If Afghanistan had failed to launch revolution in Asia in the 1920s, could not the coup d'état of April 1978 offer a second chance to do so?

A History Lesson for the Future

Soviet development thought had its origins in early Marxist–Leninist debates. Marxism offered a guide to historical development: societies marched through five discrete "formations." Communal societies transitioned into slaveholding ones, then feudalism, then capitalism, and, finally, after a transitional phase of socialism, communism. For Bolsheviks looking onto Europe, history's amble seemed clear. A mere year after the October Revolution, Germany descended into revolution, with a workers' republic being declared in Munich and Spartacist uprisings in Berlin. Even after interventions by right-wing thugs put down these attempts at revolution, a socialist republic was declared in Hungary in 1919. With the Red Army charging through Poland, a general European revolution still seemed possible. But as Soviet offensives stalled, the Hungarian Republic was invaded by Romania, and a fragile republican government consolidated itself in Berlin. The Revolution turned out to be stillborn.

Moscow needed new options. Revolutionaries like Trotsky insisted that "the road to India could turn out to be shorter and more passable for us at the given moment than the road to Hungary," and that "the path to Paris and London goes through the cities of Afghanistan, the Punjab, and Bengal."[9] As the Soviet Union's southern neighbor, Afghanistan, won its independence from the British Empire, Bolshevik armies captured Baku, and as the revolution stalled in Europe, Trotsky's argument had obvious appeal.

There was only one theoretical problem. The orthodox Marxist explanation for historical development was intended to apply only to advanced industrial European societies. Marx had stressed that Asian societies did *not* follow this five-stage (*piatichlennaia*) path. There, Marx explained, an "Asian mode of production" dominated, since "land in Asian peasant society was owned by the state or the peasant commune rather than by landlords."[10] This Asian mode of production had not led to English- or German-style capitalism, which meant that there were precious few proletarians. Of course, these contradictions were also present in former Russian colonies like Turkestan or Soviet clients, like Mongolia. But the crucial difference between these and Iran or China was that Soviet ideas did not hold hegemony in the latter. Soviet republics like Uzbekistan or Transcaucasia could become test sites in a way unthinkable one inch south of the southern border of the USSR.[11] All the same, the USSR derived its legitimacy from being the vanguard of an international revolutionary movement and had to promote progressive forces abroad – even if they were, as was the case in Kabul, monarchs.

Hence, not long after Afghanistan declared independence in 1919, a ragtag team of Soviet diplomats, intellectuals, and spies took leave of the fort in Kushka, Transcaspia, to travel via Herat, Qandahar, and Ghazni, to Kabul, where they sought to realign Afghanistan toward Moscow. All RSFSR (later Soviet) plenipotentiaries to interwar Kabul worked closely with the Comintern to incite rebellion in the British Empire's Pashtun frontier.[12] But intrigue and diplomacy demanded brainpower, too. Young scholar–diplomats like Igor' Reĭsner served as translators and advisers in the RSFSR Embassy; after their service, they returned to Moscow to transform an already-rich tradition of Tsarist scholarship on Afghanistan into *Soviet* Afghan Studies.[13]

[9] Leon Trotsky, Letter, August 5, 1919, RGASPI f. 325, op. 1, d. 47, l. 1–2, referenced in "Protokol ob"edinennogo zasedaniia Politbiuro i Orgbiuro TsK RKP(b), 2 avgusta 1919," in *Politbiuro TsK RKP(b)–VKP(b) i Komintern. 1919–1943. Dokumenty* (Moscow, 2004), 31.

[10] V.N. Nikoforov, *Sovetskie istoriki o problemakh Kitaia* (Moscow: Nauka, 1970), 204.

[11] Terry Martin, *The Affirmative Action Empire: Nations and Nationalism in the Soviet Union, 1923–1939* (Ithaca: Cornell University Press, 2001); Francine Hirsch, *Empire of Nations: Ethnographic Knowledge and the Making of the Soviet Union* (Ithaca: Cornell University Press, 2005).

[12] Iuriĭ Tikhonov, *Afganskaia voĭna Stalina: bitva za tsentral'niuiu Aziiu* (Moscow: Eksmo, 2008), 48.

[13] For more on the prehistory of Soviet Afghan studies, see R.T. Akhramovich, "Taqiqāt dar bāreh-yi tārikh-i Afghānistān dar Atahād-i Shuruvi," in *Afghānshanāsi-yi shuruvi dar 'arseh-yi chehel sāl*, ed. R.T. Akhramovich (Moscow, 1959), 9–14.

During the exhilarating decade after Afghan independence, Soviet scholars rediscovered, reinterpreted, and reimagined the country to their south whose sovereignty Soviet recognition had reified. Scholars like Aleksandr Semënov translated descriptions of northern Afghanistan into Russian and made academic publics aware of Afghan court historians like Faiẓ Mohammad Kātib.[14] Others, like I.F. Ludshveĭt and V.N. Durdenevskiĭ, translated Afghanistan's 1923 Constitution into Russian.[15] At a time when the British were massacring innocents in the Punjab and Reza Shah was crushing opposition in Persia, Afghanistan represented a ray of anti-imperialist hope.

Russian intellectuals in Kabul chronicled the electric atmosphere there – and, inadvertently, the interlocutor problem that would plague so many subsequent visitors. Larisa Reĭsner, Igor Reĭsner's sister, and the wife of the lead Soviet diplomat, took a trip one day to the *māshin khāneh*, the Kabul State Arsenal built by British engineers for 'Abd al-Rahmān Khan in the 1890s.[16] The "machine house" had been built as "the material and geographic point of origin for the subsidy-fueled violence that 'Abd al-Rahmān projected out from Kabul upon peoples and territories coercively bound into Afghanistan."[17] Reĭsner, however, found in this peripheral expression of British global capitalism hope for a workers' movement. The *māshin khāneh*, Reĭsner wrote, constituted the only point of life in an otherwise oppressively still, timeless, and dusty Oriental landscape. There, presses, stamps, and levers chiseled peasant arms into workers' biceps, just as twelve-hour workdays emaciated laborers' bellies and fattened those of their overseers. Witness to the explosive contradictions of industrial capitalism, Reĭsner read into the exploited workers "the solitary, indeed almost mystical, premonition of revolution."[18] Fellow Embassy member Lev Nikulin was similarly optimistic about the prospects for a revolution from the frontier. "Not without reason," he mockingly wrote in 1923, "did Lord Curzon claim that every family in England would give away its youngest son in the event that British power in India were threatened by any danger. *Every* family?"[19]

---

[14] Burhān al-Din Khān Kushkeki, *Kattagan i Badakhshan: dannye po geografii strany, estestvenno-istoricheskim usloviiam, naseleniiu, ekonomike i putiam soobshchenia*, trans. P.P. Vvedenskiĭ, E.V. Levkovskiĭ, B.I. Dolgopolov, ed. A.A. Semënov (Tashkent: Obshestvo dlia izucheniia Tadzhikistana i iranskikh narodnosteĭ za ego predelami, 1926); Semënov's study on Katib was published in *Soobshcheniia turkestanskogo otdela russkogo geograficheskogo obshchestva* 16 (Tashkent, 1923), 121–74.

[15] V.N. Durdenevskiĭ, *Konstitutsii Vostoka* (Leningrad: Gosudarstvennoe izdatel'stvo, 1926), 27–80.

[16] Shah Mahmoud Hanifi, "Mapping Afghanistan: Colonial, National, and Post-Colonial Cartographies," 3; Shah Mahmoud Hanifi, *Connecting Histories in Afghanistan: Market Relations and State Formation on a Colonial Frontier* (Stanford: Stanford University Press, 2011), Chapter 4.

[17] Hanifi, "Mapping Afghanistan," 3.

[18] Larisa Reĭsner, *Afganistan* (Moscow: Gosudarstvennoe Izdatel'stvo, 1925), 35.

[19] Lev Nikulin, *Chetyrnadtsat' mesiatsev v Afganistane* (Izdatel'stvo Krasnaia Nov', Moscow, 1923), 57.

Yet events soon cast the Revolution's trajectory into doubt. Amanullah Khan's regime was overthrown in 1929, leading Soviet scholars and diplomats to reflect on what had gone wrong. Some saw the coup as the result of Pashtun exploitation of the non-Pashtun north and British intrigues among conservative, reactionary Pashtun tribes.[20] Others worried that revolutionary optimism had blinded scholars to objective conditions in the country. "In the course of studies of documents relating to the collapse of the Young Afghan government," wrote one scholar years later, "there was a difference of opinion among Soviet Afghanologists with respect to some issues. Some scholars exaggerated the development of class movements in Afghanistan; others did not take into account the level of social and economic progress in this country that was only at the first stages of capitalism. Moreover, the reactionary role of the national bourgeoisie, then in its process of formation and working to preserve the territorial integrity of the country, was not sufficiently taken into consideration."[21]

A new generation of scholars would learn its lessons. Prerevolutionary scholars like Ivan Yagorskiĭ and Vasiliĭ Bartol'd had long passed away, making the interwar period the crucible for the first generation of Soviet specialists: Reĭsner taught at the Foreign Ministry from 1935; and Martiros Aslanov, who learned Pashto while serving in the Embassy (1930–38), later taught the language at the Moscow Institute of Oriental Studies (MIV).[22] Students of Aslanov's, like Konstantin Lebedev, continued in this tradition; Lebedev taught Pashto at MIV until 1985. Thanks to men like these, the building blocks were laid for Soviet–Afghan worlds made by words in which linguists and historians could thrive. In the meantime, moreover, the Soviet transformation of Central Asia was setting an example for the rest of the region. Even after the 1929 Afghan collapse, one Soviet scholar could mention, almost in passing, that "it is well known that Afghanistan [finds] itself on the path away from India and toward Soviet Central Asia."[23]

But even as the study of Afghanistan professionalized itself, intuitions were hardening before they had been questioned. Amanullah's ouster seemed to offer lessons: seek alliance with the Pashtun Left and oppressed northerners; beware Anglo-Indian schemes from the east and south. But these intuitions also jived with the ideology of "Pashtunophobia" vended to foreigners by the new Musahiban élite inhabiting Kabul.[24] (The term *musahibān*, Persian for "companions" or "consorts," was not a family name, but rather referred to the

---

[20] "Tezizy vostochnogo sekretariata IKKI 'K polozheniiu v Afganistane,'" December 12, 1931, RGASPI f. 495, op. 154, d. 417–a.

[21] R.T. Akhramovich, "Taqiqāt dar bāreh-yi tārikh-i Āfghānistān dar Ātahād-i Shuruvi," 19.

[22] Moscow State Institute for International Relations, "Pushtu," available online at: www.mgimo.ru/study/languages/list/document6594.pdf.

[23] P. Alekseenkov, *Agrarnyĭ vopros v afganskom Turkestane* (Moscow: Mezhdunarodnyĭ agrarnyĭ institut, 1933), 5.

[24] M. Jamil Hanifi, "Vending Distorted Afghanistan Through Patriotic 'Anthropology'" (Review of Thomas Barfield, *Afghanistan*), *Critique of Anthropology* 31(3), 264.

family's history as advisers to the court of Amanullah Khan.)[25] While Nadir Shah and the Ministers who governed as regents for his son marketed themselves as "Pashtun" to foreigners based on "the numerical majority and historical prestige of Pashtun tribes" in Afghanistan, they *also* pushed a parallel story about 1929 that portrayed Pashtuns, especially eastern Pashtuns, as the "chronic disrupters and opponents of the state."[26] Soviet academia's insistence on "ontological nationalities" and on the "objective" existence of nations hindered critical engagement with these claims. Rather than deconstructing "Afghanistan" as a concept, Soviet scholars conflated the categories of Afghan and Pashtun, of the Afghan state and an "Afghan nation." It all complicated writing the history of Afghanistan, much less reading its future.

Making things more difficult still, however, was the deep freeze that Stalin's drive for collectivization and industrialization imposed on the Soviet historical imagination. If scholars earlier drew a differentiated developmental timeline between the industrialized world and Asia, now they asserted the Soviet Union's primacy as the world's leading socialist state, one whose model could be applied to Asian countries. In 1931, Egyptologist Vasiliĭ Struve proposed that the five-stage model did apply to Asia; and in a 1938 article, Stalin argued that Asia had already passed through feudalism.[27] There was no point in waiting for societies like Afghanistan or China to progress through a phase they had long left behind. Academic debates on the timing of feudalism in the past excepted, the universalist *piatichlennaia* model became orthodoxy.[28] Yet it remained unclear how workerless monarchies were supposed to become workers' republics.

The contingencies of war rendered this question academic for a moment, but the unexpected collapse of colonial empires forced Moscow to return to it. In territories not under the sway of the Red Army, it became clear, influence would depend on hard-won relationships with nationalist élites. The USSR learned how to operate within the postwar internationalist order without fully being part of it. Committed to revolution but also a status quo power, it joined the United Nations and contributed to specialized agencies like the United Nations Children's Fund (UNICEF), the United Nations Development Programme (UNDP), and the Food and Agricultural Organization (FAO). Moreover, by the mid 1950s, Moscow had signed foreign aid deals of $100 million each with Afghanistan, Ethiopia, Indonesia, Argentina, and Cuba parallel to its partnerships with Mao and North Korea's Kim Il-Sung.[29]

New countries and new policies demanded new expertise. In 1950, the Oriental Institute of the Academy of Sciences of the Soviet Union (IV AN SSSR) was

---

[25] My thanks to Haschmat Hosseini for clarifying this point.

[26] Ibid., 264.

[27] Stalin, "O dialekticheskom i istoricheskom materializme," *Pravda*, September 12, 1938.

[28] Jerry Hough notes that "almost every issue of the major historical journal, *Voprosy istorii*, carried at least one article on this subject from November 1949 through February 1951." See *The Struggle for the Third World: Soviet Debates and American Options* (Washington: Brookings Institution, 1986), 44.

[29] Louis Dupree, *Afghanistan* (Princeton: Princeton University Press, 1973), 517.

uprooted and moved from Leningrad to Moscow.[30] In 1954, the Moscow State Institute for International Relations (MGIMO), the professional school for the Soviet Ministry of Foreign Affairs, absorbed the older Moscow Oriental Institute (MIV). In 1956, the Institute for the World Economic and International Relations (IMEMO), the reincarnation of an earlier institute of international politics, was also established in the capital. And in 1958, an Institute of Foreign Trade was transplanted from Leningrad to MGIMO.

But putting new signs on buildings was one thing; encouraging new scholarly traditions was another. Old experts had to don new hats. In 1961, for example, when one scholar joined the Africa section of the International Department of the Central Committee of the Communist Party of the Soviet Union (CPSU), its director was a scholar of Greece and Albania who knew no African languages, much less English, French, or Portuguese.[31] MGIMO did not offer a track for Africa specialists until 1960; when one student graduated in 1956 for his first of several assignments in Addis Ababa, a former Italian colony, the only available course was in the history of the British Empire.[32]

Soviet scholarship on Afghanistan constituted an oasis in this institutional desert. Igor' Reĭsner, who had written books on Afghan and Indian history, became the Chair of IV AN SSSR's newly formed Indian Section in 1957. Pupils of the interwar moment were coming of age too – pupils like Nikolaĭ Dvoriankov – a scholar of the Pashto language and Pashto literature who would play a crucial role in Soviet–Afghan relations in years to come. Born to a working-class family in Moscow in 1923, Dvoriankov began to study Pashto at the Military Institute for Translators in Moscow in 1940.[33] During the war, the Institute was transferred to Tashkent, where Dvoriankov continued his studies. After the war, Dvorianko taught Pashto at MIV alongside Lebedev. Yet Dvoriankov was more than just a linguist. He translated Mayakovsky and Pushkin into Pashto and later authored primers on both Afghanistan and the Pashto language; soon, in 1957, he became MIV's Deputy Director.[34] After only four years, in 1961, he became the Head of MIV's Indian, Iranian, and Semitic Languages Section, a position he held for decades.[35]

[30] Author Interview, Anna Matveeva, London, United Kingdom, April 18, 2012.

[31] Karen Brutents, *Tridtsat' let na staroĭ ploshchadi* (Moscow: Mezhdunarodnye Otnosheniia, 1998), 197–8.

[32] Sergeĭ Sinitsyn, *Missiia v Efiopii: Efiopiia, Afrikanskiĭ Rog i politika SSSR glazami sovetskogo diplomata 1956–1982 gg.* (Moscow: Izdatel'skiĭ dom "XXI vek–soglasie," 2001), 10.

[33] Author Correspondence, Viktor Korgun, November 28, 2013; Vladimir Plastun and Vladimir Andrianov, *Nadzhibulla: Afganistan v tiskakh geopolitiki* (Moscow: Russkiĭ biograficheskiĭ institut/Agenstvo "sokrat," 1998), 28.

[34] Vladimir Snegirëv and Valeriĭ Samunin, *Virus "A": Kak my zaboleli vtorzheniiem v Afganistane* (Moscow: Rossiĭskaia Gazeta, 2011), 211 (Page 267 of English translation), 267; N.A. Dvoriankov, *Iazyk pushtu* (Moscow: Izdatel'stvo vostochnoĭ literatury, 1960).

[35] Michael Roshchin, "Evgeniĭ M. Primakov: Arabist and KGB Middleman, Director and Statesman," in *The Heritage of Soviet Oriental Studies*, eds. Michael Kemper and Stephan Conermann (Routledge: Abdingon, 2011), 107.

Charismatic, brilliant, and a gifted linguist, Dvoriankov dazzled Kabul polite society by giving lectures at Kabul University, emceeing poetry readings, and delivering interviews in Pashto, switching on demand between dialects.[36] Soviet–Afghan worlds, once shattered, were recrudescent. During one of his visits during the 1960s, Dvoriankov befriended a certain Nur Mohammad Taraki, then a struggling author who wrote "sentimental stories on the difficulties of life among the poor in Afghanistan."[37] The pair traveled the country together, coming to share the belief that only radical revolution could transform Afghanistan's "feudal" society. United by their love for the Pashto language and a belief in the power of literature to document the social question, the professor and his pupil would soon shape Soviet and Afghan history.[38] Better-connected with the regime every year as his Moscow students marched through institutions of state and Party, Dvoriankov made Taraki known to élites through trips sponsored by the Soviet Writers' Union and the Soviet–Afghan Friendship Society.[39]

But Dvoriankov's enthusiasm obscured key epistemological issues. In the *Sektor Afganistan* at IV AN SSSR, Aleksandr Davydov and Naum Gurevich (both Reĭsner students) modified their mentor's *piatichlennaia* view of Afghan economic history. Conducting painstaking research into Tsarist trade archives in Tashkent, Gurevich argued that Afghanistan was *permanently* stuck in feudalism; Davydov, researching Afghanistan's bazaar economy, argued that the country was inching toward capitalism.[40] Yet either conclusion bore political consequences. If Afghanistan were only on the verge of transition from feudalism to capitalism, radical redistribution could unleash mayhem. And if it were permanently feudal, then auspicious revolutionary conditions could be millennia away.

In addition to these disagreements over Afghanistan's economic history, a linguistic and intellectual gulf crystallized among Orientologists. Scholars like Aslanov and Lebedev had built an institutional presence for Pashto at MIV/MGIMO, but these were schools for diplomats, not future scholars. Reĭsner worked primarily as a scholar of a Persianate cosmopolis defined by the Persian language, Islam, and high culture. Path dependencies had crowded out sustained nonphilological research on Pashtun, Baluch, or Punjabi culture. Reĭsner and Aslanov had trained on the job at the Soviet Embassy in Kabul, but there were no such Embassies in British India, and the British had not even let *American* social scientists into the Raj.[41]

---

[36] Plastun and Andrianov, 28.

[37] Snegirëv and Samunin, *Virus "A,"* 211.

[38] Author Correspondence, Vladimir Plastun, November 28, 2013.

[39] Snegirëv and Samunin, 211.

[40] Author Interview, Viktor Korgun, Moscow, Russian Federation, October 15, 2012. For Reĭsner, see *Razvitie feodalizma i obrazovanie gosudarstva u afgantsev* (Moscow: Izdatel'stvo Akademii Nauk SSSR, 1954). For a critical review of Reĭsner's work, see A.Z. Arabadzhan's review in *Sovetskoe vostokovedenie* 6 (1956), 146.

[41] Daniel Immerwahr, *Thinking Small: The United States and the Lure of Community Development* (Cambridge, MA: Harvard University Press, 2015), 53.

Further, the "discovery" of Soviet Tajikistan further institutionalized sustained disattention to Pashto. When ethnographers carved the Tajik ASSR out of the Uzbek SSR in 1924 before declaring it a full-fledged SSR in 1929, scholars like Aleksandr Semënov devoted themselves to inventing *Tajik* traditions for the new Soviet republic. As Soviet Tajik intellectuals like Bobojon Ghafurov, the Director of IV AN SSSR from 1956 to 1977, assumed power, the study of Tajikistan took off. Other, older IV AN SSSR-trained Tajik scholars like Muhammad Osimi (the President of the Tajik Academy of Sciences), teamed up with Russian colleagues to build a Republican Oriental Institute in Dushanbe, a research center to which Tajik students could return after training in Moscow.[42] The Persianate Musahiban regime patronized Pashto philology and history, but Soviet Orientology lacked for a true center for the study of Pashtuns.

This sustained focus on a Persianate, as opposed to Pashtun, space may seem trivial, but it created blind spots with regard to the politics of Pashtun self-determination. After 1947, when Partition in the Indian Subcontinent turned millions of "Pathans" into Pakistanis, Kabul began agitating for the formation of "Pashtunistan," a proposed Pashtun nation-state to be carved out of the Pakistani frontier. Scrutinized closely, Kabul's position was designed more for foreign consumption than as foreign policy. The overwhelming majority of materials produced about "Pashtunistan" (itself a Persian toponym) were in Persian, not Pashto, and most people who lived in the putative territories of the place were unaware that they were in "Pashtunistan."

The point, however, is less that of Kabuli hypocrisy than how Kabul's performance of Pashtun identity politics would muddle foreigners' interpretations of the region. In spite of Afghanistan's premature decolonization and its bewildering ethnic makeup, the Musahibans, especially after 1947, positioned themselves as leaders of a Pashtun-dominated Afghan state demanding the self-determination of…another Pashtun nation-state. Itself an artifact of a brief interwar moment of decolonization, Afghanistan and its leaders had embraced the trope of Pashtun state domination to legitimate themselves to foreign and domestic audiences. They did so, however, while also embracing a postwar vision of decolonization that saw freedom not in religious but in national self-determination – that is, in the nation-state. Without the philological and in-country background to discredit Afghan state claims of Pashtun authenticity on their own terms, foreign scholars had either to accept Kabul's claims or argue, as some did, that Pakistan did in fact provide an alternative, if not superior, vehicle for national aspirations than the interwar postcolony (Afghanistan) or its identitarian postwar cousin ("Pashtunistan").

Moscow had scholars capable of deconstructing this jabberwocky, but the weak institutionalization of the study of Afghanistan hindered serious research.

---

[42] R. Mamadshoev, "Vklad Iu. V. Gankovskogo v razvitie vostokovedeniia v Tadzhikistane," Presented Paper, April 6, 2011, Oriental Institute of the Russian Academy of Sciences.

Scholars with good Pashto, like Davydov, worked in terms of "the Afghan peasantry," not nationalities.[43] Lebedev taught Pashto at MGIMO, but IV AN SSSR provided instruction in only Persian and Hindustani. Particularly for Tajik nationalists like Ghafurov, sustained study of Pashtun civilization challenged the legitimacy of the Persian language and a Persianate state as features of modernity.[44] Those who cobbled together Pashto instruction at MGIMO, among them a young diplomat, Vladimir Basov, remained marginal. And when Pashto was finally offered at IV AN SSSR in the early 1980s, patterns of language study became gendered. Well-connected students in an overwhelmingly male student body, desirous of work in glamorous (compared to Moscow) Baghdad or Damascus, studied Arabic; students who came from less élite backgrounds were left with Korean (a one-way ticket to Pyongyang) or Pashto.[45]

And yet the very presence of more women in the scene underscores how academic reforms had unleashed new ways to plot a socialist life. Soviet academic transformed the lives of people like Vadim Romodin, a former merchant marine sailor from Bishkek who defended a *kandidat nauk* dissertation on Yusufzai tribes (defended in 1952) and later coauthored the first general Marxist history of Afghanistan with archaeologist V.M. Masson.[46] Marianna Arunova, a fixture in the intellectual scene, turned her *doktor nauk* dissertation into a study of the early Afsharid state, paralleling the work of her colleague Iuriĭ Gankovskiĭ (of whom more in a moment).[47] Rectors like Ghafurov promoted the careers of Soviet Tajiks like Saulatshah Merganov, who studied Pashto in Dushanbe before serving as an interpreter in the Soviet Embassy in Kabul in 1968–9, during which time he met Dvoriankov. Following his service in the Embassy, he moved to IV AN SSSR to complete a dissertation and serve as Dvoriankov's interlocutor with the Kabuli Left.[48] Slowly, haltingly, messily, Soviet academia was creating a world made by words between Russians, Tajiks, and Pashtuns, between Moscow and Kabul, between Pushkin and Taraki, out of the ashes of Amanullah's experiment and into the revolutionary future.

---

[43] A.D. Davydov, *Razvitie kapitalisticheskikh otnosheniĭ v zemledelii Afganistana* (Moscow: Izdatel'stvo vostochnoĭ literatury, 1962); A.D. Davydov, *O sel'skoĭ obshchine i eë khoziastvennoj znachenii v Afganistane (rajony s preiumshchestvenno tadzhikskim naseleniem) – voprosy ekonomiki Afganistana* (Moscow: 1963); *Agrarnyĭ stroĭ Afganistana: osnovnye etapy razvitiia* (Moscow: Nauka, 1967); *Afganskaia derevniia. Sel'skaia obshchina I rassloeniie krest'ianstva* (Moscow: Nauka, 1969).

[44] James M. Caron, "Cultural Histories of Pashtun Nationalism, Public Participation and Social Inequality in Monarchic Afghanistan, 1905–1960" (PhD Dissertation: University of Pennsylvania, 2009), 20.

[45] Author Interview, Anna Matveeva, London, United Kingdom, April 18, 2012.

[46] V.M. Masson and V.A. Romodin, *Istoriia Afganistana* (Moscow: Nauka, 1965).

[47] Marianna Arunova, *Gosudarstvo Nadir-Shakha Afshara: ocherki obshchestvennyk otnosheniĭ v Irane 30–40 godov XVIII veka* (Moscow: Izdatel'stvo vostochnoĭ literatury, 1958). The book was later translated into Persian and published in Iran on the eve of the Islamic Revolution as *Dawlat-i Nādir Shāh* (Tehran: Shabgir, 1977).

[48] Author Correspondence, Viktor Korgun, November 28, 2013.

But the mirage of "Pashtunistan" created new tensions. For elder scholars like Reĭsner or Rostislav Ul'ianovskiĭ (chair of the CPSU International Department's Developing Countries Section), disputes between Karachi and Kabul posed a quandary: should the Soviet Union support the self-determination of postcolonial states or peoples? If decolonization was what mattered, then one could view Pakistan as a progressive front in the struggle against British imperialism. But if the postcolonial nation-state was the higher goal, the imposition of Urdu on Pakistani Pashtuns or Balochis seemed unjust. Ul'ianovskiĭ, however, remained unimpressed by such logic. Moscow lavished aid on India and Afghanistan, but it never heaped scorn on Pakistan, and in 1961, the first Soviet–Pakistani aid deal was inked. Practically, however, such a stance meant that "up until 1978, in Soviet institutions of higher education, including those for the secret services, the number of students studying the little-used language of Urdu, which does not belong to one of the fundamental nationalities of Pakistan, exceeded the number of those studying Pashto, which was spoken by tens of millions of Pashtuns in the region."[49]

This statement, from Soviet Afghanistan hand Vasiliĭ Kravtsov, was an exaggeration, such as it glossed over the complexities of postcolonial diglossia. But it neatly captured a revolutionary point of view vended by Kabul and embraced by many well-meaning scholars of nations without states. If one took postwar national self-determination seriously and applied it consistently, *and* held the Third World nation-state to be the privileged vehicle of anticolonialism, then artifacts like Turkey with its Kurds, Pakistan with its Pashtuns, and any number of other states full of the stateless needed to be shattered. For a self-proclaimed revolutionary state not to support such aspirations, not to treat their languages and cultures as coequal with Turkish or Urdu, was nothing less than hypocrisy.

To observers like this, Kravtsov events within the area studies community were about to take on a conspiratorial bent. In 1958, the sixty-year-old Reĭsner died following a research trip to Tajikistan, allowing Reĭsner's forty-year-old student Iuriĭ Gankovskiĭ to take over his chair.[50] Gankovskiĭ cemented his reputation with a monograph on the history of the Durrani Empire, the basis for a brilliant career that blended academia with consulting work for the KGB.[51] Yet Gankovskiĭ also became the chair of the Pakistani-funded Soviet "Friends of Pakistan" Association. On the surface, the Society was devoted to benign

---

[49] V.B. Kravtsov, Introduction to V.V. Basov, *Natsional'noe i plemennoe v Afganistane: k ponimaniiu nevoennykh istokov afganskogo krizisa*, ed. V.B. Kravtsov (Moscow: NIF FSKN Rossii, 2011), 10.

[50] Author Interview, Vasiliĭ Kravtsov, Moscow, Russian Federation, November 15, 2012.

[51] Iuriĭ Gankovskiĭ, *Imperiia Durrani: ocherki administrativnoĭ i voennoĭ sistemy* (Moscow: Izdatel'stvo vostochnoĭ literatury, 1958); on Gankovskiĭ's work with the KGB's Second Directorate, see "Appendix 2 – KGB Officers and Agents of Soviet Nationality," MITN 1/6/7, 651e. Vasiliĭ Mitrokhin Papers, Churchill Archives Centre, Churchill College, Cambridge University, Cambridge, United Kingdom.

cultural exchanges. Working with his Pakistani counterpart, the poet Faiẓ Ahmad Faiẓ, Gankovskiĭ burnished Pakistan's image in a country saturated with Indian cultural diplomacy. Thanks to Gankovskiĭ, Faiẓ won the Lenin Peace Prize in 1962 and saw most of his oeuvre translated into Russian. But Kravtsov suspected that the organization was a cover.[52] "If you ask me as a KGB man," said Kravtsov, "factually, [the Friends of Pakistan Society] was [Pakistan's] secret service."[53]

Gankovskiĭ's ties with Pakistan formed one part of a complicated life. Like his father (and like Ul'ianovskiĭ), Gankovskiĭ had been imprisoned in the GULaG from 1947 to 1955, yet he remained an orthodox Marxist–Leninist.[54] Discussing the circumstances of his arrest remained taboo, but from what one student could piece together, when Gankovskiĭ was a Red Army officer, he had prevented the execution of a soldier accused of a political crime. Doing so saved the man's life, but it also earned Gankovskiĭ an eight-year sentence to the Kazakh steppe.[55] "Gankovskiĭ had a double personality," recalled his friend Hafeez Malik.[56] "This prolonged confinement in the Soviet jail did not embitter Yuri toward the Soviet system. In fact he became an ardent supporter of the Soviet policies, but he was always very cautious in what he said and did."[57] To Gankovskiĭ, Malik recalled, "austere and spartan life was natural and 'socialist.' In the long Russian winter he dressed himself in one miserable suit and its lighter version in the summer. On one occasion I presented him a few nice shirts with a friendly hint: 'Yuri, please wear them in good health.' He gave them away."

But Gankovskiĭ's biography ought not to distract from his impressive scholarly output. In his magisterial history of the Durrani Empire, Gankovskiĭ sketched out a financial and administrative history that hinted toward conclusions just as political as those in Davydov's economic history. As Gankovskiĭ explained, the Sadozai Emperor taxed the core, poor Pashtun territories of the Empire lightly in comparison to the empire's wealthy periphery. Wealthy outlying provinces like Sindh, Punjab, and Kashmir supplied a majority of the Empire's tax income. Indeed, during the First Anglo-Afghan War, the would-be Afghan king-in-exile Shah Shuja explained to the British that funds for Afghanistan's armies had derived primarily "from the revenues of the dependent countries of Punjab, Sindh, Cashmere and Moultan and part of

---

[52] V.B. Kravtsov, Introduction to Basov, *Natsional'noe i plemennoe*, 9.

[53] Author Interview, Vasiliĭ Kravtsov, Moscow, Russian Federation, November 15, 2012.

[54] Author Interview, Viktor Korgun, Moscow, Russian Federation, October 15, 2012; Hafeez Malik, "The Soviet Union, Russia: Yuri and I. A Memoir," *Journal of South Asian and Middle Eastern Studies* XXXV 3 (Spring 2012), 59.

[55] Author Interview, Viktor Korgun, Moscow, Russian Federation, October 15, 2012.

[56] Author Interview, Hafeez Malik, conducted via telephone from Cambridge, MA, September 4, 2013.

[57] Malik, 59.

FIGURE 2. Soviet Orientalist Iuriĭ Gankovskiĭ. "Soviet orientalist, Professor, Doctor of
Historical Sciences Yuri Gankovsky, the head of the Near and Middle East department
of the Institute of Oriental Studies, USSR Academy of Sciences."
Source: Photographed by Boris Babanov, 1979. Courtesy of RIA Novosti.

Khoorasan" – until, that is, a nascent Sikh Empire conquered them from
Kabul.[58]

But the wealthy lowland regions and Kashmir then assembled into the Sikh
Empire now belonged to Pakistan. Partition had transformed the historic financial core of an Afghan state into Pakistani territory. It was no mystery that a

---

[58] Shah Shuja to Lord Auckland (January 15, 1840), Series No. 75–7, Foreign, Secret Consultations, National Archives of India, cited in William Dalrymple, *Return of a King: The Battle for
Afghanistan, 1839–42* (New York: Alfred A. Knopf, 2013), 231.

postimperial Afghan state, stripped of its wealthy lowland possessions, perpetually lacked for cash. History showed that Afghan empire could *only* be built through domination of the Punjab and Kashmir. In a later book, Gankovskiĭ tackled the history of nationalist movements in Pakistan, as if to historically contextualize, and potentially delegitimize, the Leftist Pashtun nationalist forces that threatened to tear Pakistan apart with centrifugal violence.[59] Rather than endorsing romantic left-wing Pashtun nationalism, however, Gankovskiĭ showed how conservative Pashtun élites and *māliks* (wealthy landlords) had conspired with the Pakistan Army and Punjabi-dominated Muslim League élites to stymie the realization of a "Pashtunistan" dominated by progressive forces, which they viewed as a threat to their privileges. Pashtun élites had used the military and police apparatus of the Pakistani state to dominate the peasantry and working class.[60] Sympathize as one might with Pashtun Leftists, in short, one could not accept Kabuli propaganda about the One Unit scheme and Pakistani "Pathans" at face value. Intelligent Marxists had to diagnose the very real class interests that held Pakistan together, not to assume the existence of a bourgeois Punjabi dictatorship on the brink of collapse.

According to Kravtsov, however, Gankovskiĭ's scholarship on and lobbying for Pakistan became blurred.[61] Because of the Muslim League's shallow ties with foreign governments, independent Karachi opportunistically sought allies beyond just Washington. Pakistani diplomats were willing and able to pay bribes to representatives of the Ministry of Foreign Affairs and the KGB. Gankovskiĭ would travel to Pakistan to give two lectures, but would receive honoraria for ten talks. Nor was Gankovskiĭ always a generous mentor. Pashto specialists more sympathetic to Pashtun self-determination like Vladimir Basov found their work criticized by Gankovskiĭ; while Basov quickly rose through the ranks in the Ministry of Foreign Affairs, prestigious organs like IV AN SSSR's *Special Bulletin* rejected his scholarship.

Working with Ul'ianovskiĭ in the International Department, Gankovskiĭ offered his Pakistani patrons a softer Soviet line on South Asian policy. Moscow's close ties with New Delhi limited any overtly pro-Pakistani line; India was "objectively" a Soviet ally, and experts like Genrikh Poliakov and Oleg Zharov monopolized Afghanistan-specific policy. Still, in 1971, claimed Kravtsov, Ul'ianovskiĭ called Delhi to plead with Indira Gandhi not to invade the Punjab. Nor is this claim inconsistent with other accounts. In April 1971, D.P. Dhar, a trusted adviser of Gandhi and the Indian Ambassador to the Soviet Union, wrote to Foreign Secretary T.N. Kaul to suggest that Kabul "help the oppressed East Bengalis materially by reviving their vocal interest in the

---

[59] Iu. V. Gankovskiĭ, *Natsional'nyĭ vopros i natsional'nye dvizheniia v Pakistane* (Moscow: Nauka, 1967), 183–4.
[60] Ibid., 184.
[61] Author Interview, Vasiliĭ Kravtsov, Moscow, Russian Federation, May 27, 2013.

Pakhtoon movement."[62] In a secret meeting with Indian diplomats in London in June 1971, India's Foreign Minister Swaran Singh openly contemplated exploiting Pashtun nationalism to fragment West Pakistan.[63] Nor were the Indians only imagining Kabul's interest in revisionist politics. Gankovskiĭ leaked to Hafeez Malik the fact that Moscow had discouraged Zahir Shah from acceding to his generals' requests to take Peshawar in 1971.[64]

The Ul'ianovskiĭ–Gankovskiĭ axis seemed in the ascendancy for much of the Cold War.[65] Nor were their achievements inconsiderable. After years of USSR–Pakistan tension since the U-2 incident, Moscow remained neutral during the 1965 Indo-Pakistani War and welcomed Ayub Khan to Moscow in April 1965. Party leaders finally had their chance to show off the relevance of Central Asia, but not within circumstances of their own choosing. If Tajikistan had once stood "at the gates of Hindustan," forty-one years later, Tashkent hosted peace talks resolving the Indo-Pakistani War, settling the conflict within the framework of the UN with the USSR as a guarantor.[66] After years of talks, in 1968, Soviet Premier Alekseĭ Kosygin visited Rawalpindi to sign an arms deal. The Bangladesh Liberation War strained relations, as did the August 1971 signing of an Indo-Soviet Treaty of Friendship and Cooperation, but even during that conflict "Gandhi could not quite extract a Soviet endorsement for a war" against Pakistan. Andreĭ Gromyko, visiting Washington at the same time, assured Nixon that "it was Soviet policy to do everything possible to prevent a confrontation."[67]

And yet had not Moscow's acceptance of the internationalist order emasculated its revolutionary visions? In a heartless colonial world, the Soviet Union and Kingdom of Afghanistan had needed one another to exist: Moscow had been the first government to recognize Afghanistan's right to exist as an international actor; Afghanistan, the first to recognize the Soviet Union. When diplomats like Vladimir Basov traveled to Kabul, they would have seen testaments to fifty years of Soviet–Afghan friendship: the buildings, the Russian-speaking students, the Army officers. They would have seen the major cultural production devoted to Soviet–Afghan friendship, the 1971 film *Mission to Kabul* (shot on site in Afghanistan and India with thousands of extras), glamorizing

---

[62] Letter, D.P. Dhar to T.N. Kaul (April 4, 1971), Subject File 165, P.N. Haksar Papers, Nehru Memorial Museum and Library (NMML).

[63] Swaran Singh Briefing in London (June 1971), Subject File 19, T.N. Kaul Papers, NMML.

[64] Malik, 64–5.

[65] According to Viktor Korgun, in April 1978, Gankovskiĭ was solicited by the CPSU CC for his views – unsurprisingly so, given Gankovskiĭ's work with the Second Directorate of the KGB. S.N. Kamenev, "Konferentsiia, posviashchennaia 90–letiiu so dnia rozhdeniia Iu. V. Gankovskogo," *Vostok. Afroaziatskie obshchestva, istoriia i sovremennost'*, 5 (2011), 169–73.

[66] Joseph Stalin, March 25, 1925; RGASPI, f. 17, op. 56, d. 722 l. 127; *The Awakened East: A Report by Soviet Journalists on the Visit of N.S. Khrushchov to India, Burma, Indonesia and Afghanistan* (Moscow: Foreign Languages Publishing House, 1960), 23–4.

[67] "Memorandum for the President's File," in *FRUS*, Vol. XI (South Asia Crisis) (Washington: United States Government Office, 2005), 425.

the diplomats who had wrested Afghanistan into a noncolonial international order.[68]

Yet victory in the Great Patriotic War and the explosion in the number of nation-states that looked up to Moscow had shifted Moscow's reliance on Kabul in the international arena. *Mission to Kabul* presented 1921 as the end of national liberation, not the beginning of a struggle aborted in 1929. Soviet diplomats watched as an authoritarian monarchy brutalized intellectuals who advocated democratization and constitutional rule.[69] When one intellectual, Mohammad Ghulam Gubar, wrote a progressive history of Afghanistan from ancient times to Amanullah, Zahir Shah had almost all of the copies seized.[70] When doctors diagnosed Gubar with hepatitis, the Daoud regime rejected his application to travel to the Soviet Union for medical treatment. He emigrated instead to West Germany, but died there in the spring of 1978. Détente had brought peace, but at the cost of justice. Could aging Soviet leadership manage if crisis intruded?

Accelerating Justice, Decelerating Time

Cracks in the Soviet outreach toward the Third World were visible not long after it began. An increasingly belligerent People's Republic of China (PRC), led by Mao Zedong and Zhou Enlai, offered a vibrant alternative to Soviet socialism.[71] The Maoist challenge led postcolonial countries to disparage the Soviet Union as a content *status quo* power that had made peace with white imperialists rather than to stoke antiimperialist Revolution. In those countries where the Left was out of power, Leftists squabbled over whether Moscow or Beijing represented "authentic" antiimperialist socialism.[72] Over the winter of 1963–4, Zhou traveled to ten African countries, Burma, and Pakistan, offering aid. Beijing soon built a major railway project in Tanzania to connect copper-rich Zambia with the Indian Ocean port of Dar es Salaam. China, in short, forced the Soviet Union to choose between two trajectories: "either continue the path of peaceful coexistence and hope to win the battle with capitalism through economic competition both within the Soviet Union itself and through the example of its protégés in the developing world or reinforce its rear against the Chinese challenge, risking relations with the West in order to promote a more militant brand of revolution."[73]

---

[68] *Missiia v Kabul* (1971), directed by Leonid Kvinkhidze.

[69] "Mir Gulam Mukhammad Gubar. Ocherk zhizni i deiatel'nosti," in Mir Gulam Muhammad Gubar, *Afganistan na puti istorii* (Moscow: Nauka, 1987).

[70] Ibid., 14.

[71] *Brothers in Arms: The Rise and Fall of the Sino-Soviet Alliance*, ed. Odd Arne Westad (Stanford: Stanford University Press, 1998); and Lorenz M. Lüthi, *The Sino-Soviet Split: Cold War in the Communist World* (Princeton: Princeton University Press, 2008); Austin Jersild, *The Sino Soviet Alliance: An International History* (Chapel Hill: University of North Carolina Press, 2014).

[72] Jeremy Friedman, "Reviving Revolution: The Sino-Soviet Split, the 'Third World,' and the Fate of the Left" (PhD Dissertation, Princeton University, May 2011).

[73] Friedman, "Reviving Revolution," 143; RGANI f. 5. o. 30 d.481, ll. 1–7, cited in Friedman, 175.

Nor was Beijing the only problem. Many of the projects Moscow had sponsored in the Third World failed to yield political dividends. Consider what occurred in Guinea, the earliest site of major Soviet engagement in Sub-Saharan Africa.[74] Shortly after Guinea rejected membership in a French Community in favor of full independence on October 2, 1958, its leader, Sekou Touré, signed agreements with the Soviet Union and Czechoslovakia to secure commodities and heavy weaponry.[75] It seemed like a promising start: Touré had studied Marxism–Leninism with French Communists under colonial rule and was famous as "the founding father of Guinean trade unions."[76]

But irreconcilable differences soon reared their head. Touré remained enthralled with the elimination of social differences and the promotion of agricultural output, not Soviet dreams of proletarian class consciousness and industrialization.[77] Touré, Soviet diplomats complained, stole aid to build prestige projects.[78] Soviet advisers, the Guineans complained, built useless projects: the American Ambassador to the country at the time noted that a "Soviet tomato cannery up in Mamou was constructed without regard to the absence of tomatoes or water in the area."[79] Touré distanced himself from Moscow, and in the wake of a teachers' strike, he expelled the Soviet ambassador from the country, crying conspiracy.[80] Chinese delegations soon replaced their Soviet predecessors, impressing Guineans with their policy of not exceeding the local standard of living.[81] "National democrats" like Touré, once supposed to deliver socialism through economics, were now suspect as nationalists susceptible to Maoist appeals.

It was time to refurbish old concepts. The old Stalinist five-stage consensus had classified societies based on their mode of production, but sophisticated Marxists knew that reality was more complex. Scholars recognized that different modes of production could exist simultaneously at times of transition.

[74] The very first Soviet overtures to Sub-Saharan Africa actually occurred in Liberia, where a Soviet delegation was invited to Monrovia from December 31, 1955 to January 12, 1956. Another delegation visited in January 1960. However, other than the establishment of diplomatic relations, little came out of these visits, and Soviet–Liberian ties remained ephemeral. See Sergeï Mazov, *A Distant Front in the Cold War: The USSR in West Africa and the Congo, 1956–1964* (Washington: Woodrow Wilson Center Press, 2010), 32–43.

[75] Mazov, 68.

[76] Ibid., 58.

[77] Friedman, 108.

[78] *Rossiia i Afrika. Dokumenty i materialy, XVIII v.–1960 g.*, Vol. II: 1918–1960 gg., eds. Apollon Davidson and Sergeï Mazov (Moscow: IVI RAN, 1999), 22–5, 208–11; Alessandro Iandolo, "The Rise and Fall of the 'Soviet Model of Development' in West Africa, 1957–64," *Cold War History* 12(4) (2012), 699.

[79] William Attwood, *The Reds and the Blacks: A Personal Adventure – Two Tours on Duty in Revolutionary Africa as Kennedy's Ambassador to Guinea and Johnson's to Kenya* (New York: Harper & Row, 1967), 68–9.

[80] Mazov, 187–8.

[81] Friedman, 120.

Economic eschatology meant that pre-socialist societies carried in them the seeds not only of their own destruction, but also of the next historical stage's mode of production.[82] Quoting Lenin, theorists dubbed these subordinate modes of production and the social structures they produced *uklady* (structures). The term derived from a 1918 Lenin essay in which he described Soviet Russia as a "multistructural" (*mnogoukladnyĭ*) society that featured nomadic, private capitalist, and state capitalist economies existing side by side. But in the mid 1950s, scholars like Ul'ianovskiĭ reused the concept to justify aid to "national democracies" like Guinea and monarchies like Afghanistan.[83] National bourgeois parties might exist alongside admittedly small working classes, but all as part of a gradual process of scientifically proven development toward socialism. The arc of the economic universe was long, so to speak, but it bent toward socialism – especially if the Soviet Union provided the factory workers.

But African adventures, not to mention the spree of right-wing coups from Brasilia to Bamako that swept the world in the late 1960s, prompted theorists to think more seriously about how socialists could realistically seize power. Party élites exhorted scholars to devote more time to policy-relevant research on the threat that armies, coups, and ethnic divisions posed to left-wing governments.[84] In a series of shifts that began with the concept of "revolutionary democracy" and culminated with the declaration of the concept of "countries of socialist orientation" at the 1971 CPSU Party Congress, Soviet theoreticians came "full-circle to the Leninist position that political and ideological control, in the form of a centralized party structure, could compensate for economic concessions while economics alone was not enough to assure the success of revolution."[85] Practically, this meant close cooperation with governments like Ba'athist Iraq or Daoud's Afghanistan, where "bourgeois" regimes included Communists in government and remained dependent on Soviet military aid.

Yet the new approach had its own pitfalls. Consider the case of Somalia. As in Guinea, where Soviet trade had surged from nothing to dominating Conakry's

[82] Hough, 55.

[83] V.A. Maslennikov, "Diskussia ob ekonomicheskom razvitii kolonial'nykh I zavisimykh stran v epokhu imperializma," *Sovetskoe vostokovedenie*, 4 (1955), 139; R.A. Ul'ianovskiĭ, "Agrarnye reformy v stranakh Blizhnego i Srednego Vostoka, Indii, i iugo-vostochnoĭ Azii," *Narody Azii i Afriki*, 1 (1961), 13.

[84] "Armiia i osvoboditel'noe dvizheniie," *Aziia i Afrika segoniia* (September 1966), 2–4; V. Iordanskiĭ, "O kharaktere voennykh diktatur v tropicheskoĭ Afrike," *Narody Azii i Afriki* 4 (1967), 22–37; G. Mirskiĭ, "Politicheskaia rol' armii v stranakh Azii i Afriki," *Narody Azii i Afriki* 6 (1968), 3–14; Iu. Symbatiian, "Armiia v politicheskoĭ sisteme natsional'noĭ demokratii," *Narody Azii i Afriki* 4 (1969), 34–8.

[85] V. Iordanskiĭ, "Tropicheskaia Afrika: o prirode mezhetnicheskikh konfliktov," *Mirovaia Ekonomika i Mezhdunarodnye Otnosheniia* 1 (1967), 47–56; I. Pronichev, "Nekapitalisticheskiĭ put' razvitiia i ego mesto v istoricheskom protsesse," *Mirovaia Ekonomika i Mezhdunarodnye Otnosheniia* 12 (1966), 6.

trade balance, Moscow sought political and military influence in Mogadishu after a 1969 coup. Yet given its lack of competitive export industries, Moscow struggled to build up "objective" influence in the Horn. As one Africa hand noted, Moscow's renewed Leninist position of obtaining political influence without economic penetration meant that "unlike the former colonialists – the Italians – [we] did not have any 'ingrown interests' in Somalia."[86] Once political relations went pear-shaped – when Somalia invaded neighboring Ethiopia (itself a Soviet ally) – a familiar pattern repeated itself: Soviets out, Chinese (and Americans) in.

The exception to the rule, however, was Afghanistan, where the Soviet Union accounted for more than a third of Afghanistan's total trade, thrice that of any other competitor. Even there, however, as Davydov had argued, *capitalist* relations were barely forming.[87] Davydov suggested that the solution was land reform along the lines of the White Revolution in Iran: break up feudal estates, even if they ended up in the hands of commercial farming groups as well as peasants. But this contention ran against the new orthodoxy. If Davydov was right, then all of the work that Dvoriankov had put into Taraki was premature. Afghanistan was "objectively" evolving, but at a glacial pace and toward the emergence of a national market and capitalism. Imposing the crash land redistribution that Afghan Communists championed was likely to delegitimize the Left, not bolster it.

Then again, why listen to the academics at all? The shift away from economics to politics had proven them of marginal utility.[88] Applied area studies of the kind that IV AN SSSR patronized declined in prestige, for if *the* core independent variable affecting societies' paths to development (and socialism) was the state and, more specifically, control of the state by Soviet-aligned Communist Parties, then there was no reason to waste time with Pashtun tribes, Uzbek verbs, or Tajik kinship patterns. The central area studies truth had been that place – language, religion, economics, history – determined politics; the central Leninist truth, that politics could save a place from its own peculiarities. Nor did the fickleness of Soviet alliance formation according to the new paradigm help. One day, it was Somalia that was the ally and Ethiopia the enemy; the next day it was the reverse. Egypt was an ally one day, an American stooge the next.

Policy intellectuals bemoaned this turn as an ersatz strategy. The "Czechoslovak epic of 1968," reflected Karen Brutents, "served as a kind of rehearsal for future events. The apparent achievement of goals, the flabby reaction of

---

[86] Sinitsyn, 274.

[87] Davydov, *Sotsial'no-ekonomicheskaia struktura derevni Afganistana: osobennosti evoliutsii* (Moscow: Nauka, 1976); Anna R. Patterson, "Scholars, Advisers, and State-Builders: Soviet Afghan Studies in Light of Present-Day Afghan Development," in *The Heritage of Soviet Oriental Studies*, eds. Michael Kemper and Stephan Conermann (Abdingdon: Routledge, 2012), 156.

[88] "Moĭ marksizm–eto ne marksizm sovetskikh uchebnikov...," (Interview with Nodari Simoniia), *Mezhdunarodnye protsessy: zhurnal teorii mezhdunarodnykh otnosheniĭ i mirovoĭ politiki* 7, available online at: www.intertrends.ru/seventh/009.htm.

a West which had factually accepted a philosophy of treating these interventions as 'traffic accidents'[...] strengthened Moscow's belief in the omnipotence of military methods and impunity. In this sense, the road to Angola and Ethiopia, as well as to Kabul, led through Prague."[89] With its European territorial claims secure, the USSR flung itself into the Horn. "A policy of using 'whatever opportunities turned up' dominated. We were thrown more into the global conflict than into the formation of our own stable base in Africa. More than that, no economic or even serious military–strategic motives were guiding us."[90] Given, however, that "the USSR seemed to be at the apogee of its influence toward those countries more ideologically disposed toward it in Africa and Asia," strategic retrenchment would have been seen as a sign of weakness – especially, noted one Ethiopia expert, "insofar as subjective factors played such an unjustifiable large role."[91]

This was a charitable way of saying that the gerontocracy was growing incompetent. Brutents cited an April 27, 1978, meeting to illustrate his point. There, Mikhaïl Suslov and Dmitriï Ustinov lavished praise on Brezhnev on his "success" in recent negotiations over arms reduction with American Secretary of State Cyrus Vance, avoiding any substantive discussion of the financial and diplomatic costs that came with maintaining tens of thousands of nuclear warheads.[92] What would happen if a more immediate crisis presented itself – as it did that evening, as Afghan communists stormed the Presidential Palace in Kabul and overthrew the dynasty that had ruled Afghanistan for half a century?

Durrani Commonwealth?

The decades-long dream of a genuine Leftist coup d'état in the Third World had come to fruition, but what did it mean? Eastern Bloc officials flew to Moscow to listen to the Orientologists. "The current revolution," argued Ul'ianovskiï to a visiting East German delegation on May 12, "is overwhelmingly marked by the participation of the masses. This is a rare event in the 'Third World.'"[93] Yet the Pashtun ghosts that by now constituted accepted wisdom haunted Ul'ianovskiï. "The question of the tribes in the south of Afghanistan is a politically serious problem. The Pathans and the Pashtuns, as the *ur*-population of Afghanistan have always played a counterrevolutionary role. They've always come in groups of 10,000–100,000 men from the mountains, invaded the cities, and carried out acts of violence. It was always through them that monarchical power was

---

[89] Brutents, 238.
[90] Ibid., 215.
[91] Sinitsyn, *Missiia v Efiopii*, 277.
[92] Brutents, 305.
[93] "Information zur gegenwärtigen Lage in Afghanistan–Gespräch des Genossen Friedel Trappen mit Genossen R.A. Uljanowski im ZK der KPDSU am 12.5.1978," May 16, 1978, Bundesarchiv SAPMO, DY-30/13673, 12.

restored in Afghanistan."[94] Uli'ianovskiĭ had fallen prey to the "colonially constructed intellectual battleship" of Afghanistan as both dominated and undermined by Pashtuns. Relying on colonial stereotypes of Pashtuns as chronic state disruptors, Ul'ianovskiĭ was not alone in missing how the mix of Soviet-sponsored Leftism, Kabul-sponsored Pashtun chauvinism, and visions of the nation-state as the vehicle for nationalist aspirations had created a monstrosity.

Orientologists arrived in Kabul to diagnose the post-revolutionary situation. Gankovskiĭ had a full schedule, shuttling between lectures at the Kabul Embassy, the Lubyanka (the KGB's Headquarters in Central Moscow), and the Central Committee of the CPSU.[95] Gankovskiĭ's student Viktor Korgun was seconded as a consultant to the Afghan Ministry of Higher Education in the summer of 1978, and soon he, too, was aboard the familiar Moscow–Kabul flight. "Afghanistan was my bread and butter," joked Korgun. After Korgun turned in his passport to the Soviet Embassy for safekeeping, a Soviet diplomat drove Korgun to the hotel. They wound through the streets of the capital and inadvertently ran into a giant PDPA-organized youth parade. Dozens of Afghan children streamed by the car, shouting slogans in support of Nur Muhammad Taraki, now General Secretary of the Afghan Communist Party. When Korgun tried to get out of the car to greet the children, however, he was yanked back in: Kabul, the minder told him was a spy den. Peeved, the puckish Korgun escaped his Soviet minders to travel the countryside, where, as late as September 1978, he recalled, he could travel without any fear for his security. But doubts plagued him. What did Afghan peasants have in common with the PDPA intelligentsia?

Such thoughts were far from the mind of Dvoriankov. For a committed revolutionary Marxist who had guided Taraki to the precipice of the Afghan state, traveling to Kabul felt like a homecoming. Afghan Army officers and a former pupil of Dvoriankov – married to a Russian woman and now the head of the Afghan Academy of Sciences – met the philologist at the airport and drove him to the Hotel Kabul.[96] There, however, Valeriĭ Starostin, a young KGB officer, intercepted Dvoriankov. Starostin grilled the scholar on the state of the revolution. But Taraki's louts interrupted the conversation: they had to shuttle Dvoriankov to a private dinner with the General Secretary. Over dinner, however, Dvoriankov found Taraki out of touch with reality. He had, it appeared, delegated governing to his thuggish deputy Hafizullāh Amin – precisely the kind of development that would have interested KGB officers interested in managing Afghanistan's turn to socialism.[97]

---

[94] Ibid., 14.
[95] S.N. Kamenev, "Konferentsiia, posviashchennaia 90 – letiiu so dnia rozhdeniia Iu. V. Gankovskogo," 169–73; Author Interview, Viktor Korgun, Moscow, Russian Federation, October 15, 2012.
[96] Snegirëv and Samumin, *Virus "A,"* 106.
[97] Ibid., 213–14.

Undeterred, Starostin continued to search for the professor. The next day, he returned to Hotel Kabul, where he plucked Dvoriankov out of a symposium with Afghan intellectuals. When the KGB officer criticized the PDPA's executions of political opponents, however, Dvoriankov snapped back, explaining that the revolution demanded violence.[98] Later, after returning home to Moscow, Dvoriankov savaged Starostin and Ambassador Puzanov as pusillanimous revolutionaries. He demanded to work full-time as an informal adviser to the ruling Khalq wing of the PDPA and cautioned against working with moderates if the Revolution was to survive.[99] Dvoriankov was being petulant, but he had merely internalized the key dogma of the ideological shift of the 1970s: politics, not economics, was fundamental.

Vladimir Basov, working in the Soviet Embassy at the time, shared Starostin's suspicion of Afghan Communists. "It was an unpleasant surprise for us, for many of the major workers in the Party and state," he reflected. "There was much that was unexpected, a race forward."[100] Even skeptics like Soviet Ambassador Puzanov refused to distance themselves from the PDPA. Basov unintentionally grasped the key point. For Persianate rulers like Musahibans incapable of "doing Pashto," much less speaking Pashto, "Pashtunistan" had always been a shell game, a way of reinterpreting the Durand Line in a way to make Afghanistan geopolitically relevant.[101] It constituted a foreign policy, but only as long as the dog never caught the bus.

The problem now, however, was that parvenus like Taraki and their foreign interlocutors like Dvoriankov had understood Pashtunistan as an ends rather than a means. Such Khalqists, explained Basov, "turned out to be mere adventurists, if not something worse … people who imagined themselves as the head of all Pashtuns, of a Great Pashtunistan that would include Afghan and Pakistani Pashtuns, striving to smash together the interests of the United States and the Soviet Union, of Pakistan and Iran like wood chips to ignite a bonfire over which they could cook their little omelet (*nebol'shuiu iachnitsu*), so to speak, and claim their political ambitions. That was more or less their calculation."[102] By dreaming of Afghanistan as a Pashtun nation-state, the PDPA leaders and Dvoriankov had transformed the postcolonial optic of Pashtunistan into actual policy.

Horrified, Gankovskiĭ sought to make his own intervention. The academic had been busy through the spring of 1979 assessing the KGB's work in Kabul, but after he had lambasted its spy work, his reputation with Party élites plummeted, and he was reassigned to the more mundane task of editing the

---

[98] Ibid., 215–16.

[99] Ibid., 225.

[100] Vladimir Basov, Interview with Russian television (2004), available online at: www.youtube.com/watch?v=ab6bpIsUg_g&list=WLph1vvPu535MLrryLnpjA_xxiifFGlBog.

[101] M.J. Hanifi, "Vending Distorted Afghanistan," 264.

[102] Vladimir Basov, Interview with Russian television.

Russian-language *Encyclopedia of Pakistan.*[103] At the same time, however, Gankovskiĭ published his own historical contextualization of the crisis in an article, "Several International Aspects of the Pashtun Problem," in a policy journal distributed internally to Party and academic élites by IV AN SSSR.[104] British incursions into Afghanistan, explained Gankovskiĭ, resulted in the 1893 Anglo-Afghan Agreement, which compelled Afghanistan to recognize the "suzerainty of the British powers in the territory of the independent Pashtun tribes." Afghanistan, moreover, recognized the legitimacy of the Durand Line with the Treaty of Rawalpindi in 1921.[105] But after the formation of Pakistan, Afghan élites reneged on the agreement: Pakistan was not a formal successor state to the British Raj, Kabul argued, so all earlier Anglo-Afghan treaties were void.[106]

Here, however, Gankovskiĭ elided "Pashtunistan" as an actual foreign policy with "Pashtunistan" as a diplomatic marketing strategy. "If we are to talk about the actual goals of Afghan policy from 1947 to 1977," wrote the scholar, "as opposed to their diplomatic camouflage, then one has to recognize that Afghan ruling élites didn't want the formation of an independent Pashtunistan, and that in their minds, the meaning of the realization of the slogan 'Freedom for Pashtuns!' was the annexation of a part of the territory of Pakistan to Afghanistan." Since, however, Kabul recognized that it could not achieve this goal alone, it had enlisted "the most ambitious direct support of third party great powers interested in the extermination of Pakistan. In other words, the realization of the Afghan plans would mean an enormous war in South Asia."[107]

Such schemes, however, were not only based on a false diagnosis of Pakistani society but also eroded Moscow's strategic position. Prior to the April Revolution, Gankovskiĭ reckoned, India's desire to become the "undeniable hegemon in the vast region of South Asia and the northern part of the Indian Ocean" had been checked by the existence of Pakistan. New Delhi strove to dismember Pakistan into an independent Punjab, Sindh, and "Urdustan," but it could not muster the resources to do so.[108] Now, however, with a friendly regime in Kabul, Indian strategists could forge a regional architecture that shielded "Hindu-Brahmin imperialism" from Soviet, American, or Chinese meddling.[109] Here, then, was the long-term challenge of "the Pashtun problem." Even if one

---

[103] Author Correspondence, Viktor Korgun, November 28, 2013; *Entsiklopediia Pakistana*, ed. Iu. V. Gankovskiĭ (Moscow: Fundamenta Press, 1998).

[104] Gankovskiĭ, "Nekotorye mezhdunarodnye aspekty pushtunskoĭ problemy," *Vostok i sovremennost'* 1 (1979), 111–24.

[105] Ibid., 116.

[106] Ibid., 117.

[107] Ibid., 119.

[108] Ibid., 123.

[109] Ibid., 124. Gankovskiĭ echoed this view in his private discussions over the years with Malik, where he noted "for better or worse, India was determined to establish a policy of hegemony over all the states of South Asia, including Pakistan. This was, in India's eyes, a logical historical development."

considered India an ally, a South Asia with Pakistan was more predictable than one without it.[110]

Gankovskiĭ saw a way out of the labyrinth. He reminded readers that the government of Afghanistan had conceded that Pashtuns would "live in the territory of two sovereign states" in an 1838 agreement between Shah Shuja, Ranjit Singh, and Lord Auckland. As the spiritual, if not legal, successor state to Ranjit Singh's Sikh Empire, Islamabad "noted that in both countries the Pashtun nation would play an important role in state and social life." It agreed "not to reserve for itself the right to speak in the name of all Pashtuns, and did not recognize that right on the part of Afghanistan." In contrast to the PDPA's hegemonic designs, Pakistani leaders had "declared that their country not only has no objections to the possibility of the formation of the closest ties 'between two brotherly Muslim states,' but that they also even agree to 'the reconstruction of the empire of Ahmad Shah Durrani' (insofar as this does not contradict Pakistani interests). The route to such a 'reconstruction' could be a confederation or federation of the two countries, by means of which the Pashtun problem would automatically be solved, since then all Pashtuns would turn up living within the borders of a united state formation." The only way out of the nightmare created by the fusion of Pashtun self-determination with the imaginary of the nation-state, in short, was Pakistani hegemony.

Gankovskiĭ remained guarded on the question of the Soviet Union's role in the region, but this ended up mattering little. The decision to invade would be made without academic input. As Viktor Korgun recalled, in the summer of 1979, the CPSU's International Department requested Afghanistan experts at IV AN SSSR to outline possible outcomes to an intervention in Afghanistan.[111] The group offered four possible positive eventualities and sixteen negative ones, but the International Department never responded. Later that autumn, Dvoriankov, by then ailing with heart problems and stress, submitted a letter of protest to the Central Committee cautioning against a military intervention. This, too, received no response. After four decades of investment into expertise, Moscow willfully ignored the knowledge on hand at IV AN SSSR, a fifteen-minute walk from the Central Committee buildings around Staraia Square. Perhaps the one figure at IV AN SSSR with enough personal prestige to halt an intervention, Bobojon Ghafurov, had died in 1977.[112]

A morbid air of confusion descended upon IV AN SSSR. One student recalled faculty meetings "where it became clear that no one really knew what was going on."[113] "In all," said Southeast Asia specialist Nodari Simoniia, "I think among our academicians and specialists not more than five or six persons

[110] Christopher Andrew and Vasiliĭ Mitrokhin, *The World Was Going Our Way: The KGB and the Battle for the Third World* (New York: Basic Books, 2005), 321.
[111] Author Interview, Viktor Korgun, Moscow, Russian Federation, October 15, 2012.
[112] Author Interview, Mamadsho Davlatov, Khujand, Tajikistan, September 6, 2012.
[113] Author Interview, Anna Matveeva, London, United Kingdom, April 18, 2012.

understood what had really happened at the time." The turn toward "countries of socialist orientation" had borne rotten fruit. Élites erred in thinking that "whenever a particular leader anywhere said anything positive about our country, then we classified him as our friend and perhaps even called him 'progressive.'" In doing so, they created the impression "that there is a 'world revolution' going on and today two or three additional countries have joined the socialist camp. Hence why Afghanistan looked like a socialist revolution, not a coup. "Everyone," said Simoniia, "had the idea that in three days everything will be solved. Some people thought it will be not three days, but rather three months. Then, one year. And then, as two or three years passed and more of the dead returned to their families, everyone understood that something difficult was happening in Afghanistan."[114]

Dvoriankov bore the stress poorly. Only fifteen years ago, the vigorous professor had kicked his students out of their shared hotel rooms during conference travel to invite one of his (numerous) lovers in Alma-Ata or Tashkent over for a tryst. Now he looked like an old man. Dvoriankov died of a heart attack on December 17, 1979.[115] His passing marked a loss at a crucial time. Dvoriankov, recalled Korgun, commanded respect from Afghans and Pakistanis alike; his was one of the few Moscow funerals that both the Pakistani and Afghan Ambassadors, who despised one another, attended. As pallbearers lowered Dvoriankov's casket into the ground, his forehead covered with the scarlet lipstick of a former lover who had kissed him goodbye, it marked a farewell to not only a friend but also a half-century of Soviet–Afghan friendship.[116] Moscow was in serious trouble.

Conclusion

By 1979, the Soviet social sciences had traversed an exhilarating journey. The Soviet state's position in the world had been embattled from the start, but the five-stage model of history provided teleological certainty. But the project of explaining the Russian revolutionary experience in a Marxist–Leninist paradigm soon became something else, namely a project of interpreting and managing postcolonial revolution.

That project had changed lives. To a degree often uncommon in Western academia, female intellectuals imbibed in the prestige of "international work." The sons of workers, like Dvoriankov, found opportunities at the pinnacle of academia in ways too often uncommon in the West. The sons of peasants, like Kravtsov, discovered a way out of the marshes and cow pastures of southern Belarus. Every day, recalled Kravtsov of his childhood, he carried with him a

---

[114] Lawrence Lifschultz, Interview with Nodari Simoniia, *Economic and Political Weekly*, 23–30 December 1989, Arthur Paul Collection, University of Nebraska-Omaha.

[115] Author Correspondence, Viktor Korgun, November 28, 2013; Plastun and Andrianov, 28.

[116] Author Interview, Viktor Korgun, Moscow, Russian Federation, October 15, 2012.

satchel of books as he gathered cows from the pasture, reading when he had a spare moment. "If it was hot outside, if it was raining, no one cared," he said, thinking back to his rustic childhood.[117] To go from "deepest, darkest Belarus" to Afghanistan marked an incredible journey.

And yet the lessons that Moscow had drawn from its Third World engagements doomed the dream of Orientology in an antiimperialist key. The Orientological institutes that established themselves in Moscow in the mid 1950s may have positioned themselves as more practical, more attuned to geopolitics, than the cobwebbed academicians left behind in Leningrad. But Third World losses underscored the lesson that only disciplined Marxist–Leninists, brutal armies, and ideological hegemony could secure revolution.[118] And following the invasion of Afghanistan in December 1979, opposition to the war was professionally impossible. Scholars became implicated in the production of a Soviet archive of colonial knowledge, a black page in a history of Orientology that otherwise boasted a rich tradition of agitating against imperialism.

Having interpreted Afghanistan's history, Soviet experts were now embarking upon a journey to change its future. But they were entering a country touched not only by epistemologies, but also by bulldozers, cranes, and roadgraders. During the mid twentieth century, Afghan élites, recognizing their financial constraints, exploited the Cold War to finance their own visions of renewal. Since Pakistan had affixed to the former financial core of Afghan empire, a much-reduced twentieth century Afghanistan required a fusion of foreign expertise, hardware, and cash to fulfill even its élites' modest expectations. Kabul had to become relevant, somehow, to the outside world, if it was to finance modernization. Yet Kabuli élites' exploitation of Pashtun nationalism as a device to do so would prove dangerous. As this chapter has hinted at, the myth of "Pashtunistan" as an "insufficiently imagined" nation-state would hybridize with foreign influences in unpredictable ways.[119] Infrastructure and imagination – the physical and mental work needed to turn a proposition into a country – had touched down at the foot of the Hindu Kush. Afghanistan's developmental moment had begun.

---

[117] Author Interview, Vasiliĭ Kravtsov, Moscow, Russian Federation, October 23, 2012.

[118] Vera Tolz, *Russia's Own Orient: The Politics of Identity and Oriental Studies in the Late Imperial and Early Soviet Periods* (Oxford: University of Oxford Press, 2011), 74. Alessandro Iandolo, "The Rise and Fall of the 'Soviet Model of Development' in West Africa, 1957–64," 683–704; Friedman, "Reviving Revolution," 235–6.

[119] Salman Rushdie, *Shame* (New York: Knopf, 1983), 91–2.

2

Afghanistan's Developmental Moment?

Studies designed to enlist social science in the diagnosis and treatment of social maladies did not provide an appropriate forum in which to express reservations about social science. Such studies had to observe rigorous standards of measurement, to lay out the evidence in the form of charts and tables, to remind the reader at every opportunity that the problem was fearfully complex (though by no means insoluble), and thus to justify the claim that experts alone knew how to solve it.[1]

Area studies and development theory were about ideas, but they also were about places – places like Afghanistan, which the Cold War transformed into a hothouse of modernization, a crucible where development economics traditions from both sides of the Iron Curtain competed side by side. The Soviet-built bread factory used American-supplied grain to bake bread for West German-trained police officers; female American Peace Corps volunteers used freeze-dried Soviet smallpox vaccine to inoculate Afghan women.[2] As foreign-built road networks halved travel times between cities and foreign cartographers drew the first reliable maps of Afghanistan in history, the parameters of Afghan time and space shifted – even if, as foreigners often remarked, the country seemed stuck in the fourteenth century (which, of course, it was, at least according to the Islamic lunar calendar). Then again, to dream a state and impose it on Afghanistan – did not that quest extend as far into the future as Afghanistan lived in the past? Shrouded by myth and nostalgia, Afghanistan's developmental moment demands reconstruction.

---

[1] Christopher Lasch, *The True and Only Heaven: Progress and Its Critics* (New York: W.W. Norton, 1991), 447.

[2] C. Edward Wardle, Interview with Charlene McGrath, March 26, 1995, 5; Louie B. Nunn, Center for Oral History, University of Kentucky.

Whether Soviet, American, or German, foreigners in Afghanistan operated on contemporary assumptions about territoriality: namely, the idea that modern national life was defined by a central capital issuing orders over bordered political space.[3] In an age of restricted capital flows, ample development aid, and Chinese and Indian peasants locked out of the global labor market, territorial nation-states furnished postcolonial leaders with an ideal platform. The concept of interdependence was still years in coming; it was the realist age of "politics among nations." The development mono-economics of the day, however, had little to say about how states formed, or about the great diversity among states.

This made for a blinkered view of Afghanistan's recent history, in which borders' double existence as lines both spectral and pregnant played a prominent role. Afghanistan had historically thrived as a connecting space between Persia, Turkestan, and the Punjab. But independence and Partition unintentionally forged a territorial Afghan state. Even as Afghan élites never accepted their territoriality as legitimate, they had to work within it. But after 1947, the formation of Pakistan turned an iron cage into a house of sand; old models of statehood no longer worked. Crisis drove Afghans to the superpowers to conceptualize and finance a state of borders.

But Kabul knew that it could not count on magnanimity alone to realize its ambitions. If three decades of engagement with the outside world offered a lesson, it was that Afghans' stories mattered. Tempting as it may be to assign inherent geopolitical magnetism to Afghanistan, the real question is what global narratives prompted foreigners to lavish attention and money on the country at all. Outsiders had to be convinced that obscure, remote Afghanistan mattered. Without one empire already engaged in the region, it was difficult to foster competition. Kabul needed a postcolonial marketing strategy that would render the country relevant to Soviets, Americans, and others.

The answer was "Pashtunistan" – Afghanistan's demand for a Pashtun nation-state to be carved out of western Pakistan. The specifics were deliberately vague: one U.S. Ambassador to Pakistan understood it only as "a very vague concept concerning the Pushtan [sic] tribes, which involved a part of what is now Pakistan."[4] Indeed, the idea was full of contradictions. Why were élites whose preferred court language was Persian so intent on defending Pashtun self-determination? Why were Afghans, who got their decolonization before practically anyone, so obsessed with someone else's nation-state? Maybe, however, ambiguity was the point. Generating contradictory but mutually

---

[3] Odd Arne Westad, Remarks, "A True Alternative? The Nonaligned Movement in the Cold War," conference held in Belgade, Serbia, May 24–6, 2012.

[4] Niel M. Johnson, Interview with Henry Byroade, September 19 and September 21, 1988; Harry S. Truman, Library and Museum, available online at: www.trumanlibrary.org/oralhist/byroade .htm.

constitutive myths about Afghanistan as a "failed state" and a Pashtun state, "Pashtunistan" became for Kabul an optical foreign policy that promised to lure both Soviets and Americans. And yet misreadings of such propaganda could bring serious consequences. Pakistani élites took "Pashtunistan" seriously. In Islamabad, Kabul's strategy seemed like an attempt to finagle foreign expertise, hardware, and cash to build tumors along the border, showing Pakistani "Pathans" the plight of their situation. Indeed, the territorial nationalism that justified "Pashtunistan" contradicted the two-nation theory that justified Pakistan's existence. Nor were the generals in Rawalpindi the only unintended consumers of Kabul's exported Pashtun nationalism. Increasingly, a generation of Afghan Communists understood "Pashtunistan" as an actual foreign policy. Pakistan, they insisted, was a failure of Jinnah and Iqbal's dreaming minds; "Pashtunistan," the real geography about to shatter the palimpsest imposed.[5] Time was of the essence, however, for every day, the known world of Pakistan hardened and covered up what needed recovering.

Westerners turned out not to care about, much less understand, Kabul's vending of "Pashtunistan" and Pashtun state domination. Whether they arrived from Moscow, Washington, or Bonn, experts fit the square peg of Afghanistan into the round hole of development. Natural resources, too, resources like water, oil, and wood demanded transformation. Advisers toured Afghanistan's borderlands to transform the land itself into the basis for a national economy and territorial political space. But experts imported not just infrastructure but also institutions scrupulous finance ministries, quarellous legislatures, perspicacious tax collectors, and praetorian officer and border guard corps. Development promised a manageable postcolonial world, whether one defined by economic growth that neutralized Communist temptation or the formation of an industrial proletariat that could globalize the work begun in Russia. When foreigners arrived, then, Afghanistan was a walking contradiction: it had never wanted to conform to "politics among nations," yet had hired on expertise to help it conform to precisely that international geometry so easily processed by dueling Cold War projects.

The dreams of foreign experts, Kabul, and the Afghan Left were about to clash with the nightmare of Rawalpindi. Obscure locations would play host to the intersection of economic and nationalist dreams. Afghans and foreigners would together build islands of development, but without ever really building a state. They would translate Kabul's ambitions for glacial change into the language of the national economy, of postcolonial socialism, of "Pashtunistan." Yet development flagged; none of these dreams proved viable. Ecological, financial, and ideological crises transmogrified the former canvas for the dreaming Pashtun mind into an arena for regional and global conflicts far removed from

5 Rushdie, Shame, 91–2.

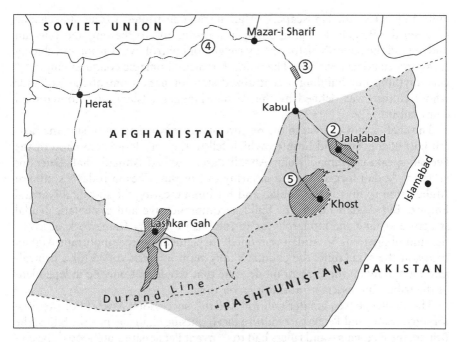

FIGURE 3. Cold War development and "Pashtunistan." During Afghanistan's developmental moment, conceptions of Pashtun nationalism as an inherent feature of the Afghan state structure, visions of the nation-state as the only possible postcolonial future, and American, Soviet, and West German aid would collide fatefully. Shaded areas represent regions with a majority Pashtun population; diagonally hashed and numbered areas represent project sites discussed in this chapter: (1) Helmand Valley, (2) Jalalabad Irrigation Project, (3) Salang Tunnel, (4) Soviet hydrocarbon infrastructure, and (5) Paktia Project.
Source: Author Map.

the provincial settings of the development decade. As development economics gained in maturity what it had lost in excitement, Afghan Communists seized power, ready to fuse ecstatic nationalism and ghoulish violence to master the challenge that dismal politics and mono-economics more dismal still failed to address.

From Independence to Dependence

So dominant have territorial states been since decolonization that it can be difficult to imagine the planet in any other way than the polygons and lines of political maps. Yet the arid regions bound by the Iranian Plateau in the west, the Central Asian steppe in the north, and the Indus River in the east demand alternative paradigms. Here, "rulers did not seek to impose their authority uniformly across the landscape."[6] Afghanistan constituted a zone of exchange between the Punjab, Kashmir, Sindh, Khorasan, and Turkestan, and one can understand the region's history as a struggle for control over surplus-producing areas and customs revenues. The point, for such "nomadic conquest empires," was anything but building a centralized state or nation out of the badlands whose culture was defined by the Persian language, Islam, and nonnational court cultures.[7]

The challenge was great in the resource-poor territories comprising the eastern half of the Afsharid Empire, which fell to the very loose command of the Persian-speaking Ahmad Khān Abdāli (later dubbed Ahmad Shah Durrani) in 1747. Abdāli forged a standing army out of the tribes in today's southern Afghanistan to invade the Punjab and Kashmir, creating the so-called Durrani Empire. But Abdāli failed "to build a comprehensive and systematic feudal structure around the monarchy or to establish a lasting framework of loyalties and obligations."[8] Abdāli remained "dependent on the important Afghan tribes; at the same time, the country's long-term interests called for a centralized monarchy on the Persian model, one that would not only be independent of the tribes, but assert its authority over them."

The challenge was greater still for Abdāli's successors. A world of preterritoriality, trade, and Persianate culture faced outside challengers – the Sikhs, the British, the Russians – and rulers had to reinvent Persianate statehood or be colonized. The territories to the east of the Durand Line were colonized, but incorporation into the British Empire as Sikhs and "Pathans" brought their dwellers into far more global networks of commercial resources and capital than those available to people in the impoverished Emirate of Afghanistan. By the late nineteenth century, Anglo-Indian concerns in Shikarpur dominated many of the markets in Afghanistan.[9] By the early twentieth century, German merchants had entered the *karakul* wool trade, too, exporting *karakul* to Leipzig, whence it went on to a second life in fashionable garments sold from Paris to New York. But corporations based in Sindh still remained dominant, and indeed financed the First Anglo-Afghan War (1839–42) in a harebrained scheme to restore business empires penetrating into Turkestan. Nonetheless, the point was clear: the nomadic empires that had formerly terrorized Persianate Asia were

---

[6] Thomas Barfield, *Afghanistan: A Cultural and Political History* (Princeton: Princeton University Press, 2010), 10–11.

[7] Hanifi, "Quandaries of the Afghan Nation," 88.

[8] Vartan Gregorian, *The Emergence of Modern Afghanistan: Politics of Reform and Modernization, 1880–1946* (Stanford: Stanford University Press, 1969), 49.

[9] N.M. Gurevich, *Afganistan: Nekotorye osobennosti sotsial'no-ekonomicheskogo razvitiia, 1919–1977* (Moscow: Nauka, 1983), 21; Stephen Dale, *Indian Merchants and Eurasian Trade, 1600–1750* (Cambridge: Cambridge University Press, 1994); Claude Markovits, *Merchants, Traders, Entrepreneurs: Indian Business in the Colonial Era* (Basingstoke: Palgrave Macmillan, 2008).

no match for European empire and the network effects they provided to the subjects imbricated in them. The Third Anglo-Afghan War (1919), which resulted in Afghan independence at the cost of the withdrawal of British subsidies, placed a dilemma at the feet of Kabul's rulers. Rather than relying on handouts from the British, Afghan élites had either to enact reforms that could grant them a foothold in a world of imperial trade, or resign themselves to becoming a British possession in all but name. Into this conjuncture stepped a new Emir, Amanullah. The new ruler may be best remembered for his "Westernizing" reforms: a new penal code, funding for foreign education that exceeded military spending, and the compulsory wearing of Western clothing in Kabul. British military intelligence in Kabul reported of how "the first victim of the new rule was the ex-Emir of Bukhara, who was asked by a policeman to remove his silk turban and was then fined a shilling for not wearing a Hamburg hat."[10]

But such colorful anecdotes mask Amanullah's more substantial accomplishments. Amanullah halted official discrimination against Indian merchants and invited non-Muslim Indians into the Afghan civil service (British soldiers had just slaughtered protesters in Amritsar).[11] Soon crowding Kabul were 19,000 former British subjects with knowledge of the global networks beyond the Durand Line.[12] Other outside events helped, too. The Russian Civil War had blocked Afghan goods' northward outlet on the Trans-Caspian Railway, but it also generated such a backlog of goods in Bukhara that Afghanistan's *southward* transit trade boomed. Ties between northern Afghan and Bukharan trading houses grew. While London shuttered Afghan merchants operating in Sindh or the Punjab, Moscow encouraged Afghan traders to open representations in Soviet cities.[13] And when Soviet Turkestan stabilized, demand for goods expanded the fortunes of Afghan merchants.

Still more meaningful were new fiscal, trade, and monetary policies. Amanullah authorized the founding of *sherkats*, corporations granted a trade monopoly for certain goods with majority Afghan ownership.[14] But Amanullah was a mercantilist, not a xenophobe. Visiting Leipzig on his 1928 grand tour, he announced that he wished to see more direct German–Afghan trade without going through Anglo-Indian intermediaries.[15] Afghan trade offices in Europe opened. And yet the distance between ambition and accomplishment remained

---

[10] Gubar, *Afganistan na puti istorii*, 135; Letter from Sir F. Humphrey to Lord Cushendun, November 26, 1928, NA PRO AIR 5/736, in *Afghanistan Strategic Intelligence: British Records, 1919–1970*, ed. A.L.P. Burnett (Cambridge: Archive Editions Limited, 2002), Vol. 1, 907.

[11] N.M. Gurevich, *Vneshniaia torgovlia Afganistana* (Moscow: Izdatel'stvo vostochnoĭ literatury, 1959), 158.

[12] Hanifi, "Mapping Afghanistan," 5.

[13] Gurevich, *Vneshniaia torgovlia Afganistana*, 165–6.

[14] Ibid.; *Amān-i Afghān*, June 18, 1928. See also *Biulleten' pressy Srednego Vostoka* 4–5 (1928), 142–3.

[15] *Biulleten' pressy Srednego Vostoka* 2 (1928), 125.

great. When Amanullah's court tallied customs duties in the late 1920s, data showed that Anglo-Indian houses still dominated the *karakul* trade.[16] One Soviet commercial journal lamented that neither Afghan nor Soviet merchants could compete with Peshawari firms.[17] "All of the financial operations [in Herat]," reported a Soviet newspaper in 1929, "are carried out by the money changers, most of whom are Hindus who finance the enterprises, make investments, and engage in usury."[18] One Afghan merchant estimated that foreign merchants still controlled some sixty percent of the total foreign trade.[19] Ironically, moreover, Amanullah's opposition to foreign investment discouraged the development of resources like the gas fields of the north.[20]

Merchants inhabiting the poorer territories between Persia and the Punjab seemingly had little to do but to accommodate their designs to the mediocrity of their circumstances, doomed due to the inability of the Afghan state to pursue mercantilist policies in promotion of a "national interest." Indeed, the state itself was imploding. Having invested land and customs taxes into education, not the army, and having alienated many by deploying German- and Soviet-piloted airplanes to exterminate rebels from the air, Amanullah was forced to abdicate when a Tajik highwayman and his followers stormed the capital in the winter of 1928–9.

When Nadir Shah and the Musahiban brothers recaptured Kabul in the summer of 1929, they sought outside expertise to manage their fiscal house. Nadir turned to a thirty-seven-year-old Afghan banker, 'Abd al-Majid Zabuli, the son of a Herati businessman who had been educated in Tashkent and commanded a business empire between the Soviet Union, Afghanistan, Iran, and Germany.[21] Married to a Russian woman and fluent in Persian, Russian, and German, Zabuli was just the type the Musahibans needed. Telegrams arrived at his Berlin office from the Afghan Embassy – invitations from Nadir Shah to come to Afghanistan.[22] Zabuli declined, but in 1932, Nadir Shah's brother, the Ambassador to Germany, called Zabuli to demand that he come to the Embassy. The banker arrived there, where he was told that he was being taken to Kabul. Soon, Zabuli was booked aboard a train across the Soviet Union to the Afghan border.

Along the way, Zabuli recalled, "the Ambassador drew a description of the unorganized economic condition of Afghanistan for me." The government had only eight thousand *afghānis* on hand, and so it needed someone who "had

---

[16] Ibid., 169–71.
[17] *Torgovlia Rossii s Vostokom* 5–7 (1925), 4.
[18] *Bol'shevik* 3 (1929), 59.
[19] Gurevich, *Vneshniaia torgovlia Afganistana*, 171.
[20] Gregorian, *The Emergence of Modern Afghanistan: Politics of Reform and Modernization, 1880–1946*, 272.
[21] Ludwig W. Adamec, *Afghanistan's Foreign Affairs to the Mid-twentieth Century: Relations with the USSR, Germany, and Britain* (Tucson: University of Arizona Press, 1974), 242.
[22] 'Abd al-Majid Zabuli, *Yāddāshthā-yi 'Abd al-Majid Zābali* (Peshawar, 2001), 7.

been entered into the science of economics and who could build the economy of the country on a normative basis, which is required of the developments of today's world." His Majesty, the Ambassador continued, "has chosen you for this important task." After a stop in the western Afghan city of Herat to win support from merchants, the pair continued to Kabul, where Nadir Shah explained how he wanted to free Afghanistan from dependence on foreign money changers.[23] By exporting *karakul* through European and American representations and concentrating capital in a national bank, Zabuli was to "improve the work of the nation and unite the rural and mountainous regions around the cities and centers." Fortunately, while Zabuli was in Herat, he had secured commitments of five million *afghāni*s to found a private import–export bank; in Kabul, he secured two million more from Nadir Shah.[24]

Yet the Afghan state remained brittle. "The State Treasury was empty," Zabuli wrote, "and all of its contents had disappeared. The reserves of arms had been looted and all of the offices and ministries had become the objects of plunder. Until August 1933, the state could not pay for the livelihood of the army."[25] Foreign trade remained a wreck. "Exports and trade had completely fallen into the hands of foreign Jews and Hindustanis, and they also had a monopoly on foreign exchange." It was little wonder, then, that Zabuli counted no fewer than seventeen attempts to overthrow the government between his arrival and the Second World War alone.[26]

This lack of what we would call "state capacity" expressed itself in more subtle ways. The Amanullah regime had produced hardly any maps of itself for public consumption. This changed under Nadir Shah, as annual state almanacs produced (in Persian and French) maps of the country, maps of Asia, and "itineraries of European politicians in Mediterranean-centered Europe."[27] But the state-produced maps of the country itself were refreshingly candid, noting that they were "prepared in great haste, [have] errors, and should not be trusted for determining border/frontier lines with neighbors."[28] Afghanistan remained far from the territorial state regimes of the late nineteenth century, which obsessed over "counting every point [that] had a quantity of human energy resources linked to it."[29] Then again, why did this matter? No mere Persian-speaking imposters, the Musahibans mastered a precarious political ecology of Kabul and countryside, ceding not only "resources but also the right

---

[23] *Iṣlāh*, June 28, 1947.
[24] Zābali, 8; N.M. Gurevich, *Ocherk istorii torgovogo kapitala v Afganistane* (Moscow: Nauka, 1967), 43; *Sālnāmeh-yi Kabul* 1319, 409; I.A. Shah, *Trade with Afghanistan* (Kabul, 1946), 67; *Iṣlāh*, June 28, 1947.
[25] Zābali, 8.
[26] Ibid., 9.
[27] Hanifi, "Mapping Afghanistan," 10.
[28] *Sālnāmeh-yi majaleh-yi Kābal* (1933).
[29] Maier, *Leviathan 2.0: Inventing Modern Statehood*, 168.

of domestic conquest and overlordship to select Pashtun lineages, and forging personal ties of monarchic influence over them."[30]

Zabuli was aware that he had to work within these limitations, but pressed upon the merchants of Herat, Qandahar, Kabul, and other centers of trade to form *sherkats* – corporations with import–export monopolies on valuable goods. The import–export bank that Zabuli and the Royal Government had chartered, Afghan National Bank (ANB), then invested its capital into these corporations. Attempts to lure Soviet investment into the oil and gas fields of northern Afghanistan proved abortive, but an agricultural and industrial revolution made up for it.[31] In 1937, ANB invested in the Spinzar and Pamba Cotton Companies, which deployed Soviet cottonseed and Pashtun settler labor to penetrate the countryside.[32] In one year, national cotton production doubled.[33] In 1938, ANB established a sugar factory in Baghlan and encouraged the cultivation of sugar beet in the province. Swampy lands in Baghlan Province were drained, soon resettled by six hundred Pashtun households.[34] Sugar beet production quadrupled from 1940 to 1945.[35] Slowly, Indian merchants wilted in influence.[36]

Zabuli had performed impressively. But to the Musahibans, the German-aligned, Russophile Zabuli represented a threat to their personal autocracy. Nadir Shah had literally been delivered to Afghanistan from Paris via Peshawar by the British, whence he and his brothers were installed with the help of British-organized Waziri militias.[37] Not only had they outsourced much to Pashtun grandees, "they had firsthand information about British military might" and feared that rapprochement with Berlin or Moscow could undo the regional and international alliances they had cultivated.[38]

Zabuli became the Minister of the National Economy in 1936 and authored Afghanistan's first Five-Year Plan three years later; but his base of power at court was shrinking.[39] Audits into ANB revealed that Zabuli's associates had

[30] James M. Caron, "Cultural Histories of Pashtun Nationalism, Public Participation, and Social Inequality in Monarchic Afghanistan, 1905–1960," 106.

[31] Zābali, 34–7.

[32] Ali Banuazizi, and Myron Weiner, *The State, Religion, and Ethnic Politics: Afghanistan, Iran and Pakistan* (Syracuse: Syracuse University Press, 1986), 54; Ubaïd Vafobekovich Okimbekov, "Problemy ekonomicheskogo i sotsial'nogo razvitiia Severo–Vostoka Afganistana," (*Kandidat nauk* Dissertation, Institut Vostokovedeniia Rossiĭskoĭ Akademii Nauk, 2003), 149.

[33] Gurevich, *Voprosy ekonomiki Afganistana* (Moscow: Izdatel'stvo Akademii Nauk SSSR, 1963), 224.

[34] Sh. Zaripov, *Proizvoditel'nye sily sel'skogo khoziaĭstva sovremennogo Afganistana* (1972), 111.

[35] Okimbekov, 130.

[36] Ibid., 49.

[37] M. Jamil Hanifi, "Vending Distorted Afghanistan Through Patriotic 'Anthropology,'" *Critique of Anthropology* 31 (September 2011), 262.

[38] Faridullah Bezhan, "The Second World War and Political Dynamics in Afghanistan," *Middle Eastern Studies* 50(2) (2014), 176.

[39] Mir Hekmatullah Sadat, "The Life of a 102 year-old Afghan Entrepreneur: an Economic Perspective," available online at: www.afghanmagazine.com/jan99/articles/zabuli.html.

been laundering foreign cash out of the country. Court élites then lobbied for a genuine state bank, which took the Pashto name *Da Afghānistān Bānk* (Bank of Afghanistan/BA).[40] The decision was partly cosmetic, since Zabuli's ANB staff were the only people in Kabul who knew anything about finance and soon staffed BA's offices. But when BA gained a monopoly over foreign exchange, the tides seemed to be shifting.

The Second World War offered both factions a chance to do the other in. Zabuli seemed to have relinquished his ambitions when he withdrew to a Swiss chalet, while the Musahibans turned to the British for military and intelligence aid. With the pro-Amanullah Nazis and Soviets on the march, the Musahibans feared that Berlin and Moscow might collaborate to return Amanullah to Kabul. Panicked about the possibility of a spring 1940 Soviet offensive into northern Afghanistan, "where the inhabitants are poorly armed, relatively unwarlike, and not comparable as fighting material to the tribes of Eastern Afghanistan," London ramped up aid to the Afghan Air Force.[41] The summer 1941 Nazi invasion of the USSR dampened these particular fears, but anxieties over German intrigue ran high, as Zabuli traveled to Berlin to hint that Kabul would look favorably on a postwar South Asian settlement extending the Afghan–Indian border to the Indus River.[42] German diplomats in Kabul gloated that "Hitler would be in London by the middle of August and [offer] Afghanistan the restoration of the Durrani Empire."[43] Call it irresponsible diplomacy, but with German trade and investment increasing, such intrigue kept the economy afloat.[44] Zabuli, however, picked the wrong side. An Anglo-Soviet invasion of neighboring Iran in September 1941 made enthusiasm for a German breakthrough more tepid, and dreams of Afghan empire on the shores of the Indus died on the battlefields of Stalingrad.[45]

More importantly, however, the Raj was crumbling. Pashtuns with long-standing ties to their Afghan cousins populated the Northwest Frontier Province (NWFP), the Frontier Regions, and the Tribal Agencies of British India. But when Clement Atlee announced on February 20, 1947, that London intended "to transfer full power to Indian hands," he had little to say about

[40] Maxwell J. Fry, *The Afghan Economy: Money, Finance, and the Critical Constraints to Economic Development* (Leiden, E.J. Brill, 1974), 86; *Sālnāmeh-yi Kābul* 1319, 409.

[41] "Strategic Problems" (Afghanistan/July 1939), NA WO 33/2377, in *Afghanistan Strategic Intelligence*, Vol. 3, 56.

[42] Sadat, "The Life of a 102 Year-Old Afghan Entrepreneur: An Economic Perspective"; Gregorian, *The Emergence of Modern Afghanistan: Politics of Reform and Modernization, 1880–1946*, 387.

[43] William Kerr Fraser-Tytler, "The Expulsion of Axis Nationals from Afghanistan," in *The Middle East in the War*, ed. George Kirk and Arnold Toynbee (London: Oxford University Press, 1953), 153.

[44] After 1939, free passage for Afghan traders to the USSR was closed. Louis Dupree, Field Diary (Second Afghan Expedition, American Museum of Natural History, August 1950 to February 1951), December 3, 1950, 206; Louis Dupree Papers, Peabody Natural History Museum Special Collections, Harvard University.

[45] Gregorian, 388.

Pashtun self-determination. Kabuli newspapers demanded that "the Pashtuns living in the regions lying between the Durand Line and the Indus River be given the opportunity of freely expressing their view."[46] London announced a referendum to be held between July 7 and 16, 1947, in the NWFP; tribal assemblies would vote in the Tribal Agencies and the Frontier Regions. But voters were only given the choice of whether to join India or Pakistan, not to found "Pashtunistan." Boycotts limited turnout to around fifty percent, but the results were decisive: ninety-nine percent for Pakistan, one percent for India.[47] Most countries recognized Pakistan (Iran was the first); Moscow extended diplomatic recognition to Karachi in May 1948.

But Kabul rejected the vote. "Until such time as the Afghans living between the Durand Line and the Indus River obtain the right to vote freely," declared Afghan papers, "we shall recognize no referendum as legal."[48] In June 1949, the Afghan National Assembly unanimously endorsed a policy of ensuring "all Afghans on the other side of the Durand Line independence and prosperity, and to grant them the right to decide their destiny themselves."[49] Newspapers also supported local governments in the Tribal Agencies and Frontier Regions as a step "toward the establishment of a single government and an independent Pashtun state."[50] Outraged, Pakistan announced an embargo on Afghanistan. A Soviet–Afghan barter deal eased its impact, but Karachi had made itself clear.

Worse, international opinion remained unkind. When Indian journalist Shiva Rao published an article critical of Pakistan's treatment of Pashtuns in the American magazine *The Nation*, Pakistani Embassy officials swiftly criticized it and received apologies from editors.[51] Yet when a Secretary at the Afghan Embassy in Washington criticized *The Nation*'s depiction of "the independent area between the former British India and Afghanistan," editors dismissed the "Pathanistan" issue as "too special to concern most of our readers."[52] It illustrated a broader structural limit on Afghan foreign policy. Without some kind of structural insecurity in global order, Kabul could not interest foreigners in frittering money away on Afghanistan. "Pashtunistan" alone aroused confusion, not attention.

Throughout this period, Zabuli, who had returned to Kabul in 1946, sought to consolidate his power independent of the Royal Family. He founded and bankrolled several political parties in order to organize the educated classes.[53]

[46] *Iṣlāḥ*, May 21, 1947.
[47] Irland Jansson, "India, Pakistan, or Pakhtunistan: the Nationalist Movements in the North-West Frontier Province, 1937–47," (PhD Dissertation, University of Uppsala, 1981), 211–2.
[48] *Iṣlāḥ*, July 6, 1947.
[49] *Iṣlāḥ*, July 3, 1949.
[50] *Iṣlāḥ*, October 29, 1949.
[51] Rahman Pajwak, Letter to Jerry Talmer, October 10, 1949, 1, Item 3510, Box 17, *The Nation* Records, Houghton Library, Harvard University.
[52] Jerry Tallmer, Letter to Rahman Pajwak, September 30, 1949, Item 3510, Box 17, *The Nation* Records, Houghton Library, Harvard University.
[53] Bezhan, "The Second World War and Political Dynamics in Afghanistan," 185.

Knowing that royals would oppose his appointment as Prime Minister, Zabuli created four super-ministries that diluted the power of any challengers.[54] One September 1947 report from the Ministry of the National Economy described his policy plan. Afghanistan had to expand industries ripe for import substitution and secure foreign investment in extractive industries.[55] In the meantime, Kabul signed a five-year contract with the American engineering firm Morrison-Knudsen to build canals, dams, and roads in southern Afghanistan, paying the $20 million bill with savings it had hoarded during the war.[56] Zabuli also sought an economic *modus vivendi* with Karachi. In late 1947, leading Afghan ministers and ANB executives visited Pakistan to advocate for a coordinated economic policy.[57] In the summer of 1948, during a stopover in London, Zabuli hinted that Afghanistan would focus only on artisanal industries and food processing while the Pakistanis industrialized. Kabul would, he added, look favorably on a USSR–Afghanistan–Pakistan trade transit agreement.[58]

But Zabuli's policies were too clever by a hair. Officials at Zabuli's Ministry for the National Economy were frank about the problems confronting Kabul.[59] "If we take into account," they noted, "the fact that our country is an agrarian country and all of its needs must be satisfied through imports from without, as well as the fact that [Afghanistan] is located a great distance away from maritime routes, then it is clear that at the present moment we will have to pay 3–4 times as much for industrial goods and their import than we paid for them in the prewar period. One must also add the agricultural position of our country has dramatically worsened as a result of the recent years." The report turned to the core problem: "It may suffice to mention that India represented the most important export and import market for us; but after August 15 [1947], trade links and rail connections were cut between India and Pakistan. As a result, over the course of the last eight months, the scale of our country's import and export trade sharply declined." In southern Afghanistan, likewise, Morrison-Knudsen's costs had doubled, prompting Zabuli to accept

---

54 As Bezhan notes, "Zabuli had become so powerful that the prime minister could not do anything without his permission, even outside his formal responsibilities." Sayyid Rishtia, *Khātirāt-i Siyāsi-yi Sayyid Qāsim Rishtiyā, 1311 tā 1371* (Virginia: 1997), 85.

55 "Predlozheniie ministerstva narodnogo khoziaĭstva i utverzhdeniie ego," translated from *Iṣlāḥ*, 15–17 September 1947, in AVP RF, f. 71 (Referentury po Afganistanu), op. 35, p. 53, d.10, l. 7.

56 A. Poliak and E. Nukhovich, "Dva podkhoda k pomoshchi slaborazvitym stranam. Na primere Afganistana," *Mirovaia ekonomika i mezhdunarodnye otnosheniia* 1960 (2), 89.

57 "Rabota Ministerstva natsional'noĭ ekonomiki," AVP RF f. 159 (Referentur po Afganistanu), op. 37A, folder 72 (Informatsiia o vnutropoliticheskom polozhenii v strane) [1948], d. 1, ll.11–37.

58 *Dawn*, July 4, 1948, in AVP RF f. 159, op. 37A, folder 72 [1948], d. 1, ll. 2–3.

59 "Rabota Ministerstva natsional'noĭ ekonomiki," AVP RF f. 159 (Referentura po Afganistanu), op. 37A, folder 72 (Informatsiia o vnutropoliticheskom polozhenii v strane) [1948], d. 1, ll.11–37.

a $21 million loan at 3.5% annual interest from the U.S. Import–Export Bank.[60]

Zabuli's kowtowing to foreigners emboldened his rivals. Already in 1949, American diplomats had noted that Prince Naim and Daoud were wary of Zabuli's plan to rule indirectly through one of their Prime Ministerships.[61] Now, however, the Musahibans had a chance to remove him entirely. In 1950, Prime Minister Shah Mahmud Khan sacked Zabuli over a foreign exchange scandal, paving the way for Daoud (Khan's nephew) to assume the Prime Ministership.[62] The Kabuli government stripped ANB of its monopolies and established an Administration of Government Monopolies.[63] ANB remained Afghanistan's largest commercial bank and controlled key export markets, but the rise of Daoud to the Prime Ministry in September 1953 led to a "guided economy." Five years earlier, American anthropologist Louis Dupree had bemoaned "the futility of semi-Westernization" demanded an Afghan Atatürk to impose decisive reform.[64] With Daoud in power, however, Afghanistan seemingly stood at the brink of following the Turkish road to modernity.

Yet Kabul remained a long way away from Ankara. The Afghan state existed to keep its people at arm's length, not to transform them. "The Afghan bureaucrats do not love their people," noted Louis Dupree one day after visiting a Ministry. "I saw several examples of this while waiting for the chits. Naturally I was called to the front of the line as soon as I appeared – a courtesy gesture. One Afghan fella with a handful of papers, all in order, but then gave the clerk some lip and then saw his ream of signed and sealed papers torn to shreds before his eyes–o well another week of paper trotting should put him back where he was. He blew his stack and was tossed out on his ear by a couple of cops. The whole procedure went on outside the building. Never like those scummy peasants inside our pretty white washed gov't buildings."[65] Broke, weak, and without a social base, Daoud's Afghan state unable to mobilize its population. And Kabul's regional geopolitical situation was less favorable than at any time since 1919.

The one lever that Daoud and his regime possessed, however, was "Pashtunistan." Similarly to five years prior, diplomats presented "Pakhtunistan" as an established fact. A briefing provided by the Afghan Embassy in Washington, D.C. noted that Afghanistan was "bounded by Russian Turkestan on the north, by Pakhtunistan (small and newly formed) on the east, and by Iran on the

[60] Poliak and Nukhovich, "Dva podkhoda k pomoshchi," 89; Ghulam Farouq, "Conclusions and Suggestions" (1980), Dick Scott Archive (hereafter abbreviated as DSA).

[61] US State Department, "Memorandum of Conversation: Dr Raouf of Afghan–American Trading Company," American Embassy in Kabul, September 15 (1949), 2–3.

[62] Donald Wilber, *Afghanistan: Its People, Its Society, Its Culture* (New Haven: HRAF Press, 1962), 188; Bezhan, 186; K. Khalili, *Yāddāshthā-yi astād-i Khalili: Maqālāmā beh dakhtarash Mary* (Virginia, Herndon: All Prints, 2010), 339–43.

[63] Gurevich, *Ocherk istorii torgovogo kapitala Afganistana*, 86–7.

[64] Dupree, Field Diary, December 18, 1950, 250.

[65] Dupree, Field Diary, September 5, 1950, 18.

south."[66] "The Afghans," the same report continued in blurry language, "are divided into two groups, the first of which live within the political boundary of Afghanistan, and are 12 million. The second group live beyond the Durand Line, up to the Indus River in Pakistan, and they are the same people from a common stock with the first group." Daoud renamed the roundabout in central Kabul "Pashtunistan Square." Flags of Pashtunistan that bore a suspicious resemblance to the Afghan flag began to appear. Pashtunistan Day became an official holiday. Pakistan launched another blockade in 1955, but an Afghan *loya jirgah* declared that "it does not in any way regard the areas of Pashtunistan as part of the territory of Pakistan, unless and until the people of Pashtunistan desire it and consent thereto."[67]

To anyone familiar with Daoud's Pashto "credentials," the idea of "Pashtunistan" was suspect. "Pashtunistan" was a Potemkin nation-state packaged and sold by a Persian-speaking dynasty that exhibited few of the features of "the charter of Pashtun identity and social behavior."[68] Consider the experience of Mohammad Jamil Hanifi, then a graduate of Kabuli élite schooling. In spite of all of the Royal Government's agitation for the Pashtunistan issue, Hanifi "does not recall a single exposure to a map of Afghanistan during his schooling in the 1940s and 1950s."[69] Nor was this merely selection bias: "there is," writes Hanifi's son, "no map of Afghanistan in a prominent national encyclopedia published in 1955, nor is there any reference to Pashto or Pashtuns in that important public reference work." When, later, Hanifi was required to meet with Zahir Shah, he "was instructed by his Persianate secretariat to not speak in Pashtu with his majesty because he was 'tired' that afternoon! King Zahir spoke Farsi and some French, learned during his father's stay in France during the late 1920s."[70] Pashtunistan, in short, was "an urban Kabuli product built upon the illusion of Pashtun 'ethnic' domination of Afghanistan that also channels how the Durand Line is historically interpreted."[71]

Absent global insecurities, however, "Pashtunistan" was a marketing strategy without an audience. No one lesser than Louis Dupree was perplexed, writing in his diary that Afghans should "cut the emotional shit about Pushtoonistan & put it on an economic basis!"[72] Yet Dupree's earlier diary entries proved

---

[66] "General Information on Modern Afghanistan," Royal Afghan Embassy (Washington), September 1953.

[67] *Iṣlāḥ*, November 21, 1955.

[68] Hanifi, "Vending Distorted Afghanistan," 264.

[69] Hanifi, "Mapping Afghanistan," 11; Ariana Encyclopedia Society, Afghanistan.

[70] Hanifi, "Vending Distorted Afghanistan," 265.

[71] Hanifi, "Mapping Afghanistan," 12. The point, it bears stressing, is not whether the Musahibans were phonies or not. Irredentist movements, from early twentieth-century Irish nationalists to Kurdish nationalists in Turkey, have frequently been led by figures that did not exhibit the full "charter" of national identity, including native command of a language. The focus here is, instead, the extent to which the performance of Pashtun state domination encouraged perceptions of Pashtun nationalism as an inherent "problem" of Afghan statehood.

[72] Dupree, Field Diary, December 19, 1950, 250.

him wrong. Three months earlier, he had written "the USA should covertly support the Pushtoonistan movement, because the Tajiks, Uzbeks, and Turcomans
are coming indirectly under the influence of their brethren to the north."[73] After
all, he scribbled, "the *Ruskis* are obviously sending Tajiks down to the Tajiks,
Uzbeks to the Uzbeks, etc., and are being told of the wondrous religious and
ethnic freedoms in the USSR brotherhood." Here was the entire logic of Kabul's
Pashtunistan strategy: by filtering the colors of Eurasian identity politics into
the black-or-white polarity of the Cold War, Afghan élites could escape the
grim economics of arid Central Asia and tap into the global capital streams
of a postimperial moment. Rather than *separating* Afghanistan from imperial
resources, the Durand Line could finally *connect* it with them.

Cold War Global Projects

"Before you flies the state flag of Afghanistan, our southern neighbor and
friend," begins the 1957 Soviet film *Afghanistan*, one trickle in a flood of
Afghanistan-related movies that Moscow studios churned out in the late
1950s.[74] "The black band," the narration continues, "recalls the foreign yoke,
the red band blood spilled for the cause of freedom, while the green promises
the fulfillment of [the country's proud hopes]." Cue a wipe cut to a map of
Afghanistan. We learn that "the mountainous spine of the Hindu Kush cov-
ers four-fifths of Afghanistan with its spurs. Like a wall with jagged tow-
ers, the mountains have separated the country from the rest of the world
for centuries." But as another film emphasized, Soviet aid had transformed
Afghanistan. "Everywhere signs of change can be seen. You can find them in
these dams that stand over wild rivers, in the power lines which climb farther
and farther up the slopes of the mountains, in the first furnaces of the new
industry which the country had never known earlier."[75] Afghanistan remained
backwards, the film implied, but thanks to Soviet help, Afghans, too, could have
modernity.

Of course, the story that Soviet filmmakers spun took creative liberties. Mod-
ernizers like Zabuli had designs of their own that differed from the Soviet
project. And forty years of Soviet–Afghan relations had shown that there was
nothing inevitable about Soviet aid. Indeed, the quest to smooth rough-hewn
Afghanistan into an isomorph of the USSR began in the wake of American
missteps. As of the late 1940s, Helmand was derided as an engineering disaster and waste of money; seventy percent of the project costs had been spent
on wages for Americans.[76] In 1953, American Secretary of State John Foster

73 Ibid., September 23, 1950, 119.
74 Rossiĭskiĭ Gosudarstvennyĭ Arkhiv Literatury i Iskusstva (RGALI), f. 2487, op. 1, d. 138, l.5.
75 RGALI, f. 2487, op. 1, d. 496 ("'N.S. Khrushchëv v Afganistane.' Diktorskiĭ tekst V.F. Belikova
    i annotatsiia k fil'mu"), l. 2.
76 Poliak and Nukhovich, "Dva podkhoda k pomoshchi," 88–90.

Dulles further strained relations by inviting Karachi to join not one but two multilateral military alliance systems for Southeast Asia and the Middle East, the Southeast Asia Treaty Organization and the Central Treaty Organization (CENTO).[77] Moscow countered in January 1954, offering Kabul an aid package of three million rubles over eight years, and with three percent interest. It was modest compared to the USSR's thirty-year aid deal with China, but far more generous than anything America had offered.

But the Musahibans needed military aid – moth-eaten German equipment was increasingly inadequate to threaten Pakistan. Afghan diplomats petitioned to join CENTO, but when Foreign Minister Muhammad Naim visited Washington in October 1954, Dulles dismissed him with a note that read: "After careful consideration, extending military aid to Afghanistan would create problems not offset by the strength it would generate. Instead of asking for arms, Afghanistan should settle the Pushtunistan dispute with Pakistan."[78] Adding insult to injury, Dulles forwarded the note to the Pakistani Ambassador. Outraged, Daoud agreed to a January 1955 Soviet offer to train and equip his officer corps.[79] Eleven months later, Khrushchëv and Soviet Premier Nikolaï Bulganin capped a winter trip to India and Burma with a surprise December 15, 1955, visit to Kabul, where, flanked by Afghan soldiers in *Wehrmacht* uniforms, they guaranteed Afghanistan 150 million rubles a year in aid and transit rights through the USSR.[80] It was a diplomatic coup fit for the movies.

But this was not all to Khrushchëv's and Bulganin's visit. Toasting Daoud at a state dinner on December 16, Bulganin stressed the Soviet position on "Pashtunistan": "we sympathize with Afghanistan with respect to its policy on the Pakhtunistan Question. The Soviet Union supports a just solution to the Pakhtunistan problem, which will not be possible without consideration of the vital interests of the people of Pakhtunistan."[81] After returning to Moscow, Bulganin drove the Soviet Union's position home in a speech to the USSR Supreme Soviet, calling "Pashtunistan" "a country that is settled by Afghan tribes."[82] Bulganin's rhetoric was riddled with unclarities on the relationship between the terms "Pashtun," "Pakhtun," and "Afghan," and what that relationship meant for the legitimacy of a government in Kabul claiming to speak for Pashtuns on

77 Michael Barry, *Kabul's Long Shadows: Historical Perspectives* (Princeton: Liechtenstein Institute on Self-Determination, 2011), 29.

78 Copy of text communicated to former US Ambassador to Kabul, Leon Poullada, by Prince Naim in an interview in Kabul on December 12, 1976, cited in Barry, 29–30.

79 Barry, 30.

80 For the full text of the agreement, see "Prilozheniie," *Mezhdunarodnaia Zhizn'* 1 (1956), 82–3.

81 "Die Rede Marschall Bulganins anläßlich des Banketts von Ministerpräsident Sardar Mohammad Daoud," in *Nachrichten aus Afghanistan*, Vol. 5 (Bonn: Afghan Embassy, 1956) (January 2), 10, in AV Neues Amt B12/912 (Ideologische Einflüsse in der Innenpolitik Afghanistans 1955–1958), PA/AA.

82 Inayatullah Baloch, "Afghanistan-Paschtunistan-Belutschistan," in *Deutsche Außenpolitik* 3/80, 287, BSTU MfS HA II 27370.

the eastern side of the Durand Line. From Kabul's point of view, however, this was precisely the point. After a decade of frustration, Kabul had succeeded at exporting the irresolvable contradictions of its stance on "Pashtunistan" into the foreign aid apparatus of one of the superpowers, courtesy of the exogenous geopolitical pressures of the Cold War. From now on, Pashtun nationalism would be viewed "as an inherent 'problem' of the Afghan state structure" that had to be managed – or exploited – according to broader geopolitical dictates.[83]

Soviet technical advisers soon arrived to build an asphalt factory in Kabul and pave the capital's roads.[84] Based in Tehran as an interpreter, Georgiĭ Ezhov received his assignment and flew to Tashkent, expecting to board another flight to Kabul. But the plane was grounded: the landing strip outside of Kabul was snowed over.[85] Ezhov and family languished in Tashkent for a week. Finally, the skies were clear – to Jalalabad, the former Afghan summer capital. "When I boarded the small propeller airplane," Ezhov explained, "it was still a cold Tashkent spring – five degrees [Celsius] maximum. I had to wear a heavy jacket. I sat down on this 15-passenger plane, we flew for two hours, and when they opened the doors, I felt 30-degree air, subtropical, engulf me. The 'airport' there was only a dirt strip and a few tents for passengers." Fixers drove Ezhov, his wife, and their children up a rugged dirt road to the capital. But conditions were spartan. "No *tvorog*. No milk. No *smetana*. No sausage," reflected Ezhov. All there was with which to feed his infant son was local *nān*, mutton, and milk of suspect origin delivered in recycled benzene canisters. Salvation arrived in the form of a new Ambassador, Sergeĭ Antonov, whose ties as the former Deputy Minister for Meat and Milk Production secured better dairy. Rumors circulated that Antonov had even negotiated special Soviet-only access to the Afghan Royal pasture of Dutch, German, and Belgian cows.

Conditions in the ministries did little to dispel stereotypes of "backwardness." When Ezhov arrived in the capital, most of the bureaucracy was housed in the Dār al-Amān Palace, built for Amanullah by German engineers in the 1920s and about six miles southwest of the city center. A German-built railroad connecting Dār al-Amān with the city center had been ripped up, but two parallel rows of trees still lined the path. While Ezhov wore a white undershirt in the mornings to avoid soiling his suit during the drive, after a day of translating Russian financialese into Persian, he would promenade under the trees. Conditions in the Ministries themselves were less congenial. The Germans had installed steam heating, but wood-burning stoves generated most of the building's heat – and smoke. Bureaucrats' servants ran papers, brewed tea, and took visitors' coats. Afghans of ability and conviction administered above the chaos.

---

[83] Hanifi, "Mapping Afghanistan," 17.
[84] "Perechen' osnovnykh ob"ektov i rabot, po kotorym vypolnenie obiazatel'stv SSSR po okazaniiu tekhnicheskogo Afganistanu zaversheno," Unpublished Document, Private Archive of Valeriĭ Ivanov.
[85] Author Interview, Georgiĭ Ezhov, Moscow, Russian Federation, April 15, 2013.

'Abd al-Hai 'Aziz, the Secretary of the National Economy, spoke an implausible twelve languages, including Japanese; one day, when 'Aziz noticed a copy of Rudyard Kipling's *The Jungle Book* on Ezhov's desk (a gift for his family), he ordered Ezhov to put it away before launching into an exhaustive catalog of British crimes. The Afghan state had talent and rudimentary organization, but was still far from an iron cage, much less the Soviet country of steel.

Then again, why should it have been otherwise? Colonial intrigue, Soviet analysts agreed, had left Afghanistan in an "objectively" backward state. Backwardness was less a cultural phenomenon than a feature of the imperialist global system in which Afghanistan had been brutally exploited. "The policy of imperialist great powers," explained one Soviet economist, "directed toward the preservation of the feudal fragmentation of Afghanistan and the exploitation of the country as an agrarian and natural resource base and market for the sale of their goods, hindered the development of the productive forces of the country for many decades."[86] British imperialists and German fascists alike had sought only to turn Afghanistan into a dumping ground for their exports, a source of mineral resources, and a military client state. The Soviet Union, however, would be different.

There was only one problem, Soviet analysts stressed: Afghanistan had fallen under the influence of Western imperialism once again. "In the postwar years," explained the report, "the expansion of the USA in Afghanistan was greatly strengthened. Under the guise of providing various kinds of 'aid'–financial, technical, and the extension of loans on one-sided terms unfair to Afghanistan – the USA penetrated into the most important branches of the national economy of the country." The Soviet Union's task, then, was to build import-substitution industries for Kabul – development and antiimperialism in one fell stroke. While creating the material infrastructure of industrial modernity, moreover, Moscow had to encourage trade unions and laws protecting workers' rights. States – Afghanistan as much as Guinea – could not embody a global socialist condition overnight; rather, Moscow had to guide monarchies, bourgeois democracies, and postcolonies toward this *telos*.

The projects touted by the screenwriters at Moscow film studios soon filled the backlots, covered up the mud, and dammed the waters of the Afghan capital. Having completed the asphalt plant and roads, specialists built Kabul a bakery, a grain elevator, and a cement factory. Engineers built an equipment repair station in Jangalak, just to the south of the capital. Advisers installed port facilities on the Amu-Darya river at Hairaton, while work began on the Jalalabad Irrigation Complex in the east of the country in 1956.[87] In September

---

[86] G. Prokhorov, "Obzor ekonomiki Afganistana za 1955 god," (September 6, 1956), RGAE f. 365, op.2, d.1664, l. 18.

[87] L. Borokhovskiĭ, "Stroitel'stvo khlebokombinata v Kabule," *Mukomol'no-elevatornaia promyshlennost'* 3 (1956), 6–7; Author Interview, Abdulwahob Wahidov, Samarkand, Uzbekistan, September 21, 2012.

1956, Soviet economists and planners submitted a Five-Year Plan.[88] In 1961, Soviet nuclear scientists discussed the possibility of uranium enrichment and an Afghan nuclear power program.[89] Cotton experts from Uzbekistan studied how Afghanistan could grow more "white gold."[90] A Soviet-sponsored university, Kabul Polytechnic, admitted its first students in 1963. Soviet-style *mikroraĭons* of five-story apartment blocks became the capital's most desirable housing. The City of Moscow even funded the construction of the first such apartment block through a levy on its own residents.[91] In 1964, Soviet and Eastern Bloc engineers completed the Salang Tunnel (built at a higher elevation than any other in the world), which connected Kabul with the north.[92] Soviet modernity was everywhere: in the dwellings in which Afghans élites lived, in the ideas with which they wrestled, in the bread that they fed to their Soviet-trained Army recruits (no one would purchase the plywood-like bread on the open market, much preferring indigenous baked goods).

Coordinating everything was the State Committee for Foreign Economic Ties (GKES), an institution that mediated between foreign governments and Soviet All-Union Ministries.[93] "Our goal is clear," said the agency's leader in a presentation to the CPSU Central Committee. "We strive to help underdeveloped countries ensure their economic independence, more quickly stand on their own two feet, create a modern national industry, more fully utilize their natural resources, lift agricultural production and so contribute to improving the lives of the people of these countries."[94]

But if the Soviets' operative words were "economic independence," "national industry," and "their natural resources," American Cold Warriors insisted that the USSR was engaged in a bid for hegemony.[95] Afghan leaders'

---

[88] "Finansovoe polozheniie Afganistana," (October 1959), RGAE f. 365, op.2, d. 1987, l. 1.

[89] "Materialy o predvaritel'nykh peregovorakh delegatsii sovetskikh ekspertov s afganskoĭ storonoĭ ob okazanii Afganistanu nachno-tekhnicheskoĭ pomoshchi v oblasti mirnogo izpol'zovaniia atomnoĭ energii i geologorazvedochnykh rabotakh na uran (doklady, spravki, zapisi besed)," RGAE f. 365, op. 2, d. 1397.

[90] "Pomoshch' tashkentskogo uchënogo afganskim agranomam," *Tashkentskaia Pravda*, September 18, 1957; "XIV sovetsko-afganskaia konferentsiia' (po bor'be s saranchoĭ i vreditel'iami khlopatchika. Moskva Okt. 1957 g.)," *Zashchita rasteniĭ ot vrediteleĭ i bolezneĭ* 1 (1958), 57.

[91] Author Interview, Vasiliĭ Kravtsov, Moscow, Russian Federation, October 23, 2012.

[92] A. Biriukov, "Doroga Salang," *Ogonëk* 1960 (9): 22–3.

[93] Author Interview, Valeriĭ Ivanov, Ignatovo, Russian Federation, November 2, 2012.

[94] "Zapiski i spravki gosudarstvennogo komiteta SM SSSR po vneshnym ekonomicheskim sviaziam, Goskomiteta po kul'turnym sviaziam s zarubezhnymmi stranami i po voprosam truda i zarplaty o nauchno-tekhnicheskom i kul'turnom sotrudnichestve SSSR s VNR, PNR, SshA, OAR i dr. stranami, ob ekonomicheskom i tekhnicheskom sotrudnichestve Sovetskogo Soiuza so slaborazvitym v ekonomicheskom otnoshenii stranami i ob ekonomicheskoĭ i tekhnicheskoĭ pomoschi SShA slaborazvitym v ekonomicheskom otnoshenii stranami, o sovetsko-indoneĭskom ekonomicheskom sotrudnichestve," RGANI f.5 (Tsentral'nyĭ Komitet KPSS), op. 30, d. 305, l. 120.

[95] Robert Rakove, *Kennedy, Johnson, and the Nonaligned World* (Cambridge: Cambridge University Press, 2012), 6.

insistence on their nonaligned stance only confirmed Eisenhower and Dulles' opinion of Kabul's naïveté. Washington continued its investments in the country: the Helmand Valley Project, the southern half of Afghanistan's ring road, industrial parks in Kabul, and graduate scholarships for Afghan students. All of these had their positive effect. An unscientific word association survey conducted among Afghan students in 1962 found that youth associated the United States with President Kennedy, "many factories," and "standard of living."[96] These were hardly embarrassing results, especially compared to "advanced technology," Khrushchëv, and Communism for the Soviet Union.[97] But strolling the (Soviet-paved) streets of Kabul, one could get the impression that the Soviet Union built things and the United States did not. As one former Soviet adviser gloated: "Where is the quarter of Kabul that the City of Washington sponsored?"[98] West German advisers in Kabul concurred: "The Soviet Union has raised its contribution to the industrialization of Afghanistan in a way that could not have been expected. [...] Without adequate provision of aid, Afghanistan will eventually be lost for the West."[99]

American policymakers recognized the need for a more nuanced policy. In 1957, Robert M. McClintock, a former ambassador to Cambodia, argued that Washington had grown too dependent upon alliance systems.[100] Might not tacit support to neutralist states be advantageous to dealing with unreliable allies?[101] In that same year, the junior Senator from Massachusetts, one John F. Kennedy, wrote approvingly of social scientist Walt Rostow's interest in the Indian planning experience.[102] For both McClintock and Kennedy, the South Asian giant merited especial interest as "a centerpiece of the 'middle zone' of uncommitted nations extending from Casablanca to Djakarta," and the most obvious "'broker' middle state" in the Cold War.[103] But the India argument also applied to other nonaligned Asian states: American support for governmental interventions into states and economies was "a realistic response to the nature of the societies where a sustained rate of economic development was sought in the American interest."[104] Under American tutelage, countries could

---

[96] Louis Dupree, "Landlocked Images: Snap Responses to an Informal Questionnaire," *American Universities Field Staff Reports Service*, South Asia Series VI(5) (June 1962), 14.

[97] Ibid., 21.

[98] Author Interview, Vasiliĭ Kravtsov, Moscow, Russian Federation, October 23, 2012.

[99] Kurt Hendrikson, "Vermerk. Betr: Intensivierung der deutschen Enwicklungshilfe an Afghanistan," (June 12, 1960) in AV Neues Amt–1884 (Beratergruppe Dr Hendrikson für das afghanische Planungsministerium), PA/AA.

[100] Rakove, *Kennedy, Johnson, and the Nonaligned World,* 24.

[101] Memorandum, Robert McClintock to Robert Bowie, January 25, 1957, RG-59, Records of the Policy Planning Staff, 1957–1961, PPC-123, "Neutralism" folder, US National Archives.

[102] John F. Kennedy, "A Democrat Looks at Foreign Policy," *Foreign Affairs* 36(1) (October 1957), 44–59.

[103] Rakove, *Kennedy, Johnson, and the Nonaligned World,* 33.

[104] Walt Whitman Rostow, *The Process of Economic Growth* (New York: W.W. Norton, 1952), 254.

become the high-wage, productive societies without fundamental disagreements between labor and capital that the United States imagined itself to be. A global "politics of productivity" would "supersede class conflict with economic growth."[105]

India captured the imagination, but no country benefited more from American globalism more than West Germany. After renewing relations with Moscow in September 1955, Chancellor Konrad Adenauer sought to avoid the impression that the diplomatic representation of both the Federal Republic of Germany and the German Democratic Republic in Moscow implied that Third World countries, too, could recognize both Bonn and Berlin. West Germany developed a policy later known as the Hallstein Doctrine: states that recognized Berlin would lose out on West German engagement.[106] Nor was it prestige alone that was at stake. The loss of Silesia, Pomerania, and East Prussia had robbed the Federal Republic of its richest agricultural zones, forcing Bonn to import foreign foodstuffs while also rebuilding its industry.[107] Any and all export markets mattered. Soon, the devaluation of the *Deutschmark* lent Bonn with a structural export advantage, while the "Korea Boom" and American invitations to build infrastructure at foreign military bases helped engineering and construction firms alike.[108] In 1953, West German firms won a bid to construct a steel plant in Rourkela, India, the "first large investment project of German business in the Third World."[109] In January 1958, Bonn dispatched Kurt Hendrikson, an auditor, to provide services to the Royal Government of Afghanistan.[110] In light of "years of friendly-to-neutral relations," Hendrikson remarked, "Germans are the best-equipped of all Western nations to stand with their cultural and economic measures in the foreground of the contest with the East." By 1960, West Germany provided Afghanistan with 20 million *Deutschmarks* annually, making it the third largest donor to Kabul after Moscow and Washington.[111]

---

[105] Charles S. Maier, "The Politics of Productivity," *International Organization* 31(4) (1977), 629.

[106] Bastian Hein, *Die Westdeutschen und die Dritte Welt: Entwicklungspolitik und Entwicklungsdienste zwischen Reform und Revolte, 1959–1974* (Munich: R. Oldenbourg Verlag, 2006), 21–2.

[107] Ibid., 26. For more on the constraints facing the postwar German export trade, see Jürgen Bellers, *Außenwirtschaftpolitik der Bundesrepublik Deutschland 1949–1989* (Münster: 1990).

[108] Hein, 26–7; Ulrich Damm, *Die Bundesrepublik Deutschland und die Entwicklungsländer. Versuch einer Darstellung der politischen Beziehungen der Bundesrepublik Deutschland zu den Entwicklungsländern unter besonderer Berücksichtigung der Entwicklungshilfe* (Coburg: Graphischer Betrieb H. Biehl, 1965), 25, 31–33, 43–4, 55–9.

[109] Klaus Bodemer, *Entwicklungshilfepraxis – Politik für wen? Ideologie und Vergabepraxis der deutschen Entwicklungshilfe in der ersten Dekade* (Munich: 1974), 29.

[110] Kurt Hendrikson, "Vermerk für Herrn Dr. Peckert," April 5, 1968, in AV Neues Amt–1884 (Beratergruppe Dr Hendrikson für das afghanische Planungsministerium), PA/AA.

[111] Kurt Hendrikson, "Vermerk. Betr: Intensivierung der deutschen Enwicklungshilfe an Afghanistan," June 12, 1960, in AV Neues Amt–1884 (Beratergruppe Dr Hendrikson für das afghanische Planungsministerium), PA/AA.

Even as a Federal Ministry for Economic Cooperation was founded in 1961 to consolidate Bonn's policies, however, Moscow seemed unstoppable. Hans Hellhoff, Siemens' Afghanistan country director, summarized the situation in a 1962 letter.[112] Bonn had, Hellhoff argued, to "maintain the friendship we have had for years and decades with countries" like Afghanistan by countering "the economic offensive of the Eastern states." American and German complacency had harmed Western interests and left Kabul open to Soviet entreaties. "The result," wrote Hellhoff, "was that since [1955] no major assignment for an installation went to Germany, while the Russians tackled the construction of several hydro-power stations – projects that prior had been constructed exclusively by Siemens." This was brutal. "Every large assignment lost to the East is the same as a lost battle," wrote Hellhoff.

Hellhoff's parallel of Afghanistan to the Eastern Front was unfortunate, but it bespoke how the place of Afghanistan in the global mind had changed. A mere five years earlier, Daoud had failed to make Afghanistan relevant. Attempts to win international support for "Pashtunistan" were met with miscomprehension. Now, however, thanks to Dulles' blunders, Soviet opportunism, and the perception that the Cold War had to be fought on a global scale, Afghanistan mattered. Yet in an ominous shift, Soviet engagement began to lend bone, flesh, and brain to the phantasm of Pashtun state domination projected onto a nation-state. Surplus male bodies from eastern Afghanistan received military and ideological training from Moscow. Romantic nationalists like Taraki received dotage from Soviet mentors. And US support for Pakistan gave Daoud grist to beat the war drum at home. Afghanistan and "Pashtunistan" had become enmeshed and transformed *by* the Cold War, even without yet being a major theater *in* it.

American globalism could not but involve formerly irrelevant Afghanistan. Part of the reason, after all, why Americans had elected a youthful, new 43-year-old President was "the belief, diffuse at the time, that the possibilities available to the United States were almost unlimited."[113] "There was practically nothing the country could not do if it wanted to do it," went the zeitgeist.[114] Soon, calls electrified the exchange boards connecting New Dealer networks, seeking to deploy expertise to shape the world according to American desires. Kennedy assembled a star team: "crisis managers" like former Harvard Dean McGeorge Bundy and former CIA staffer Robert Komer directed policy on a day-to-day level.[115] Idea men like Walt Rostow lent coherence to the administration's developmental vision. Liberals like former Connecticut Governor

---

[112] Hans Hellhoff, Letter (October 10, 1962), Folder Six: "Afghanistan/Allgemeines," B213/2791, Bundesarchiv Koblenz.

[113] Mario del Pero, *The Eccentric Realist: Henry Kissinger and the Shaping of American Foreign Policy* (Ithaca: Cornell University Press, 2010), 20.

[114] Robert Lovell, quoted in John Lewis Gaddis, *Strategies of Containment: A Critical Appraisal of Postwar American National Security Policy* (New York: Oxford University Press, 1982), 94.

[115] Rakove, *Kennedy, Johnson, and the Nonaligned World*, 36.

FIGURE 4. "Hydroelectric power plant Naglu on Kabul River built in collaboration with USSR. Republic of Afghanistan."
Source: Photographed by A. Goryachev, 1974. Courtesy of RIA Novosti.

Chester Bowles served as Ambassadors in key theaters.[116] In the summer of 1961, calls reached Robert Nathan and Arthur Paul, two men whose accounts help us reconstruct the tensions of Afghanistan's developmental moment.[117] Reporting to appointees like Bowles and career Foreign Service Officers like

---

[116] Ibid., 45–7. For Bowles' work on American policy in the Third World, see *The New Dimensions of Peace* (New York: Harper, 1955); *American Politics in a Revolutionary World* (Cambridge: Harvard University Press, 1956); *Africa's Challenge to America* (Berkeley: University of California Press, 1956); *Ideas, People and Peace* (New York: Harper, 1958).

[117] "Economic Advisory Services Provided to the Ministry of Planning, Royal Government of Afghanistan, September 1961 to June 1972, Final Report. Submitted to the Royal Government of Afghanistan and U.S. Agency for International Development by Robert R. Nathan

Henry Byroade (the U.S. Ambassador to Afghanistan from 1959 to 1962), Nathan and Paul became the face of American globalism in its battle for the Afghan state.

Together, Nathan's and Paul's careers provide a neat portrait of the assumptions that shaped American thinking about the state and economy at the height of the American "empire of production."[118] Paul hailed from an old Philadelphia family not far from the world that his Princeton classmate F. Scott Fitzgerald would immortalize.[119] Throughout the 1920s, he worked as the Secretary, Treasurer, and, eventually, Vice-President of Dexdale Hosiery Mills, a thriving textile business in Lansdale, Pennsylvania.[120] Nathan was a second-generation Russian–American Jew from Ohio, but he, too, soon dwelled among the spires and gargoyles of the Ivy League when, in spite of *numerus clausus* restrictions, he gained admission to the University of Pennsylvania. "Economics" did not exist as a formal discipline, so Nathan cobbled together an education in business, statistics, and mathematics. Working with another Russian–American Jew, Simon Kuznets, Nathan grew interested in the concept of household income and developed novel sampling techniques. Nathan hired area women as "enumerators" to collect "unemployment numbers in Philadelphia by composition by age, and by jobs and duration, and so forth, of unemployment."[121] As Paul exported pantyhose and Nathan measured economic activity, both men's ties with industrial production and statistics thickened.

When stock markets collapsed and the Roosevelt Administration needed experts, both men came into contact with Washington. Paul already had social contacts into the world of New Deal Washington through his second marriage to Adeline van Nostrund Hitch, a Dalcroze dance instructor and a member of the extended Delano family.[122] And in 1933–4, the Farm Security Administration "decided that rehabilitation of marginal farm families was a sound method of rural reconstruction."[123] Dexdale submitted a proposal to manage five "homestead" sites in Appalachia and the South, where farmers were to work at Dexdale-operated mills financed through federal loans.[124] Later, the

Associates, Inc., Washington, DC," July 1972, vii; Arthur Paul Journals (APJ), 1–3, Arthur Paul Collection, Criss Library, Omaha, Nebraska.

[118] Charles S. Maier, *Among Empires: American Ascendency and Its Predecessors* (Cambridge, MA: Harvard University Press, 2006).

[119] Author Interview, Leslie Symington, Oxford, United Kingdom, October 21, 2011; Author Correspondence, Leslie Symington, May 10, 2015.

[120] "Government Agency Enters Hosiery Manufacturing Field," *Reading Eagle*, September 3, 1938, 1, 12.

[121] Robert R. Nathan, Oral Interview, Conducted on June 22, 1989 by Niel M. Johnson, Harry S. Truman Library, available online at: www.trumanlibrary.org/oralhist/nathanrr.htm.

[122] Author Correspondence, Leslie Symington, May 10, 2015.

[123] "Five Government Homestead Mills," *Textile World* (April 1941), 70.

[124] "Government Agency Enters Hosiery Manufacturing Field." The homestead projects became extremely controversial and the objects of criticism from both Northern and Southern unions

Foreign Economic Administration hired him to "manage a number of South American economic development projects that were related to the needs of the U.S. Government for strategic raw material."[125] After the war, Paul, a former American delegate to the International Labor Organization, served as Director of the Office of International Trade under Secretaries of Commerce Henry Wallace and Averell Harriman.[126] Nathan, meanwhile, followed Kuznets to Washington, where war lent new urgency to the task of creating national income figures. Employed by the Department of War, Nathan calculated how much of certain strategic materials American enterprises could produce under "total mobilization." Nathan squared these production limits with Allied demands for materiel. The exercise, the first to model the American "national economy," convinced American leadership to defer an invasion of Europe from 1943 to 1944.[127] A consulting business that worked everywhere from Israel to South Korea to New Jersey followed. War had transformed parochial knowledge about supply chains for silk stockings, or the median income of Main Line matrons, into the intellectual ingredients for the making of states and economies.

After a decade back in the private sector, during the 1959–60 academic year, Paul came as a visiting fellow to Princeton's Woodrow Wilson School, researching India's First and Second Five-Year Plans under the auspices of the Lockwood–Patterson Seminar, which explored "problems of economic development" in "underdeveloped countries."[128] In the spring semester of 1960, Gardner Patterson, the Dean of the Wilson School, "asked whether [Paul] would be interested in working in Afghanistan for a year or two."[129] Kabul, Patterson explained, "wanted an economic adviser and had asked the Asia

and corporations as an example of unfair competition. At least one point, they were even compared to Soviet enterprises, and for a period in 1938, the U.S. Comptroller-General refused to fund the FSA loans to Dexdale's hosiery plants. However, the plants, which were defended on the grounds of providing superior production to the "master-slave" system of Hitler's Europe, eventually entered operation and produced hundreds of thousands of stockings. Three of the plants were eventually sold to Dexdale and two other textile firms for $1,200,000. For the comparison to the Soviet Union, see "Sovietizing the U.S.A.," *The Hosiery Examiner*, October 1938. On the denial of FSA funds, see "F.S.A. Factory Loans Declared Illegal," *New York Times*, December 19, 1938. For the defense of the scheme, see Milo Perkins, Letter to Arthur Paul (December 23, 1941), Personal Archive of Leslie Symington. On the sale of the plants, see "[?] Sells 3 Hosiery Mills," *New York Times*, June 14, 1945. While connections between New Deal-era emergency aid programs and Cold War development is not my focus here, there are obvious echoes between Paul's story and that of David Ekbladh's *The Great American Mission: Modernization and the Construction of an American World Order* (Princeton: Princeton University Press, 2011), 40–76.

[125] APJ, Introduction, 3.

[126] Résumé of Arthur Paul, Personal Archive of Leslie Symington.

[127] Jim Lacey, *Keep From All Thoughtful Men: How U.S. Economists Won World War II* (Annapolis: Naval Institute Press, 2011).

[128] APJ, Introduction, 2–3.

[129] Ibid., 1.

Foundation to help it find someone who was suitable for the job." A team of Soviet economists was working for the Ministry of Planning, but the Afghans wanted a Western economist in the Ministry of Commerce. Soviet economists would develop the country's Second Five-Year Plan, but Paul, if he accepted, "could work on some of the more immediate economic problems in the country." Paul was inclined to accept: he found the contemporary literature on development insufficient, and "the idea of studying development in a smaller and more primitive area [than India] had an appeal."[130] After reading more, meeting with Afghan diplomats, and attending briefings in Washington, Paul took the job. A year later, in 1961, Nathan's consulting firm was hired to conduct a survey on the kinds of consulting services the Afghan government might need; predictably, the International Cooperation Association (the predecessor to the United States Agency for International Development, USAID) soon hired Nathan Associates to send four economists to Kabul to provide assistance.[131] USAID perpetually extended the contract until June 1972.

The competition between the empire of planning and the empire of production had begun. And yet while ideology seemingly divided Soviets and Americans, there was a curious symmetry between the two, for both had engaged Third World nation-states in mirrored global projects. For wizards of production like Nathan and Paul, states had to advance as quickly as possible toward domestic productivity and participation in a liberalized global economy. "The leitmotif of American foreign policy" was "to reconstruct the American experience in other parts of the world."[132] Eventually, nation-states could find their niches as productive, harmonious market societies that were isomorphs of the global market. Factors that halted this march were not "objective" factors of History, but rather only hiccups as America's internationalist rules swallowed the planet. The Soviets, in contrast, cared about the democratization of the means of production. The "objective" logic of History was the subordination of the economic to the political. The point was not to *produce* more so as to discourage conflict between labor and capital, but rather for the Third World nation-state to develop its own industrial proletariat, play host to anticapitalist revolution, and become a classless society that would approximate the future of the entire planet. The politics of the nation-state was the politics of the planet in miniature.

Both global projects had their blind spots. American advisers never convincingly stated how economically marginal regions of the planet like Afghanistan could participate in the global economy. As American, German, and, soon,

---

[130] Arthur Lewis, *Theory of Economic Growth* (London: Allen & Unwin, 1955).

[131] "Economic Advisory Services Provided to the Ministry of Planning, Royal Government of Afghanistan, September 1961 to June 1972, Final Report. Submitted to the Royal Government of Afghanistan and U.S. Agency for International Development by Robert R. Nathan Associates, Inc., Washington," July 1972, vii.

[132] Stephen Krasner, *Structural Conflict: The Third World Against Global Liberalism* (Berkeley: University of California Press, 1985), 23.

Japanese and South Korean products saturated international markets, the crisis of overproduction seemed closer than ever. The model of dynamic client states purchasing American debt for the privilege of their middle classes holding the jobs that Americans "had collectively held during the preceding generation" could obviously not apply to the whole planet.[133] The Soviets faced a similar problem: even if the proletariat controlled the means of production, in a world still dominated by the hyper-productive Americans, Germans, and Japanese, there was no place for Guinean belts or Afghan bread to go other than as a kind of tribute in reverse into the Soviet Union. As long as imperialism persisted, the Soviet Union seemingly had little choice but to subsidize the crisis of subaltern overproduction that Soviet aid incentivized. Until the global economy gave way to a true international socialist system, the Soviet Union had to stand in as the core of a ramshackle global socialist economy that was less productive than its American competitor.

Whether these global projects were suited for Afghanistan had never been the point. The Afghan state had, contrary to ideologies that stressed territorial national economies as the *telos* of the nation-state, survived in an environment of empires and loose borders. Yet Partition had aborted this world. Border closures were common, and Pakistan Railways refused wagons for Afghan goods to enter Pakistan; the transit of goods to India was, needless to say, anathema.[134] Reconciling postcolonial sovereignty with the freedom of trade seemed impossible. As Afghan newspapers argued, "in 1947, when Pakistan appeared, the whole world had found any number of ways [to export goods]. Not only the ports of Italy were open to Switzerland, but in all the corners of the globe the full right of freedom of transit for countries which lack access to the sea was recognized."

Yet as contemporary jurists had noted, the "right to transit" was not so clear.[135] Some countries, like Afghanistan or West Germany's Berlin enclave, only possessed one "transitable" country for sea access.[136] "In these circumstances," wrote one scholar, "it appears probable that the correct way in which to frame the concept of a 'way of necessity' in international law is to say that the transit State is bound to accord such facilities as the exercise by the administering authority of its right in the enclaved area, including the maintenance of 'peace, order and good government,' may warrant."[137]

But almost any interpretation of either principle bore explosive political implications. If Pakistani transit really was a "way of necessity" for Kabul, it followed then Islamabad ought to let India-bound Afghan goods traverse

---

[133] Maier, *Among Empires*, 268.

[134] "Tranzit Afganistana i velikodushie Pakistana," *Anis*, September 17, 1961, in AVP RF f. 71, op. 51, *papka* 70, d. 11.

[135] Hersch Lauterpacht, "Freedom of Transit in International Law," *Transactions of the Grotius Society* 44 (1958), 313–56.

[136] Ibid., 336–7.

[137] Ibid., 332.

Pakistani territory unencumbered. But if Islamabad refused to allow this, this implied that "peace, order, and good government" for Pakistan demanded permanent economic war with Afghanistan. One could argue that Pakistan was not, in fact, a "way of necessity," since Kabul could export via the USSR. But that would imply deeper relations with Moscow. Self-determination and territoriality had clashed, but as foreigners sought to shape Afghanistan into their respective global projects, the details mattered little. It was time to make the square peg of development fit into the round hole of Afghanistan.

Money: Financing Afghan Statehood in Kabul

Such concerns about the applicability of developmental models to Afghanistan, however, were far from the minds of the advisers now descending upon Kabul. After a briefing in New Delhi, Paul boarded an unpressurized DC-3 Afghan Ariana Airlines flight to Kabul.[138] Soviet engineers had built a tarmac at Bagram, north of the capital, permitting a less roundabout arrival than Ezhov's five years earlier. Even then, only "tents and wooden sheds" greeted Paul as he descended from the plane. The Asia Foundation's representative in Kabul met Paul and treated him to a can of beer – his last for a while, he joked – before driving him into the capital. Nathan arrived roughly a year later.[139] An expanded West German group had already been in Kabul for a year, he explained, helping the Afghan government write its Five-Year Plans while lead adviser Kurt Hendrikson helped Afghan industrial enterprises reform their accounting systems.[140]

But Americans were about to learn what their Soviet counterparts already knew: the Afghan "national economy" was something quite distant from the ideal. In a May 1960 report, the Deputy Director of GKES in Kabul highlighted the challenges.[141] He began with the good news: Soviet–Afghan relations were strong coming off of Khrushchëv's March 1960 visit to Kabul. Soviet enterprises had trained Afghan specialists. But Kabul's state finances were "in a tense state. The budget comes with a significant deficit that is covered by foreign loans and aid."[142] The adviser attached a chart underscoring his point. The real problem, he emphasized, was less the structural budget deficits; the government covered them by raising prices for products on which it held a monopoly. More concerning was that the table was the *only* information available on Afghan state finances.

---

[138] APJ, Saturday, June 4, 1960.
[139] Robert R. Nathan, Diary Entry, May 19, 1961, Robert R. Nathan Papers, Division of Rare and Manuscript Collections, Cornell University Library, Box 1, Folder 20. All entries from this collection are hereafter abbreviated as RRNP.
[140] *Işlāh*, August 3, 1967.
[141] A. Matalasov (Deputy Director of GKES in Afghanistan), Overview of Afghan National Economy, RGAE f. 365, op.2, d. 1987, ll.58–70.
[142] Ibid., 68–9.

TABLE 1. *Afghanistan's "tense" finances. From A. Matalasov (Deputy Director of GKES in Afghanistan), Overview of Afghan National Economy, RGAE f. 365, op.2, d. 1987, l. 69*

Financial Year	1957–8	1958–9	1959–60
Revenues (millions of *afghānis*)	1,593	1,934	1,428
Expenditures (millions of *afghānis*)	(2,113)	(2,455)	(3,388)
Deficit (millions of *afghānis*)	(520)	(521)	(960)
Foreign Loans and Aid (millions of *afghānis*)	520	521	960

But economists needed statistics. A group from the University of Chicago's School of Public Administration had been in the Ministry of Finance since 1957, attempting to reform the accounting system, but after three years they had "not yet got their hands on the raw material they need in order to help produce proper financial records."[143] The lack of statistics was maddening. Later, V. Strigin, the Soviet statistical adviser in the Ministry of Planning, noted that Kabul had never organized a centralized collection of statistics. No one knew how much, exactly, had been invested into the country.[144] Strigin had urged the Ministry of Planning to standardize statistics across Ministries, but because each Ministry had generated its own statistics autonomously during the Second Five-Year Plan, Strigin also had to retroactively cross-standardize data.[145] Concretely, this meant synchronizing the reams of data produced by twenty-five statistical departments across different Ministries and Departments, each of which typically employed four or five Afghan statisticians.[146] During the 1960s, however, said statisticians been retrained *again* by visiting teams from the Soviet Central Statistical Administration, making the cross-standardization problem more byzantine still.[147] Shared frustrations demonstrated common truths: Americans, Soviets, and Germans all needed data, precious data, to mold the national economy.

Yet where statisticians had made the economy legible, economists cringed at what they found. Soviet financial advisers rationalized the Afghan income tax code, lowering the lower end rates, increasing the top marginal rate to 60 percent, and raising corporate tax rates.[148] The Afghan state, they emphasized,

---

[143] APJ, June 6, 1960, 22.

[144] V. Strigin (Adviser for Statistics), "Otchët o rabote sovetnika po statistike Ministerstva planirovaniia Afganistana za 1 polugodiie 1967 goda," (June 1967), RGAE f. 365, op.2, d.2669, l. 22.

[145] Ibid., l. 23.

[146] V. Strigin, "O sostoianii i merakh po dal'neĭshemu sovershenstvovaniiu statistiki v Afganistane," (September 25, 1967), RGAE f. 365, op.2, d.2669, ll. 75–88.

[147] V. Strigin, Proposal to Ministry of Planning of the Royal Government of Afghanistan (Summer 1967), RGAE f. 365, op.2, d.2669.

[148] "Finansovoe polozheniie Afganistana," (October 1959), RGAE f. 365, op.2, d. 1987, l. 33.

needed more capital; "laborers" were taxed enough.[149] Still, they conceded, "the financial position of the country will remain – in all likelihood for the long term – tense insofar as foreign loans and credits will absorb a significant part of the currency reserves of the country. The Afghans, moreover, are not currently in a position to increase [those foreign exchange reserves]."[150] Nathan thought that government wages ought to be doubled, but any such increase would spike inflation. Policymakers could invest more in private industry, spurred by an expansionary monetary policy. But "because of the expansionist fiscal policy [...] it has been necessary for the Central Bank to be exceedingly restrictive on credit extension."[151] Theoretically, Kabul ought to have collected more taxes and expanded the money supply, but instead it had depleted its foreign currency reserves, induced inflation, and "run out of borrowing capacity at the IMF." At the Ministry of Commerce, Paul encountered a byzantine system of exit and reentry permits for foreign traders, "'made to order' as a source of corruption."[152] A multiple exchange rate system collected some customs revenue but discouraged capital investment and spurred a balance-of-payments crisis.[153] Nothing – nothing, that is, but the rising waters of the Cold War – could keep Afghanistan's fiscal ark afloat.

What had first bedeviled the Soviets, and now confounded Nathan and Paul, was less a failed state than one that failed to conform to Cold War monoeconomics. Nathan's and Paul's American training had lent them American intuitions for what national economies were supposed to accomplish.[154] In the United States, income taxes had long surpassed tariffs as a source of revenue, and memories of the 1930 Smoot–Hawley Tariff led consultants to support free trade. But support for free trade just as likely derived from the fact that the mid-century United States generated more than a third of global output. In an American century, states, it stood to reason, ought to look more American.[155] But this was of course unrealistic. The issue was not, as Nathan despaired, that tribal, "ascription-oriented" Afghan culture prevented the development of a modern state.[156] Rather, Afghanistan's fiscal destiny was its borders, and, more specifically, how Partition had transformed the historic financial core of an Afghan state into Pakistani territory. Even Paul conceded that the multiple

---

[149] Ibid., 1.
[150] Ibid., 69–70.
[151] Ibid.; RRNP, March 8, 1965.
[152] APJ, June 11, 1960, 40.
[153] APJ, June 16, 1960, 59.
[154] Maier, "The Politics of Productivity," 609–18.
[155] Data from the World Bank, available online at http://data.worldbank.org.
[156] Robert R. Nathan Associates, "Economic Advisory Services Provided to the Ministry of Planning, Royal Government of Afghanistan, September 1961 to June 1972, Final Report. Submitted to the Royal Government of Afghanistan and U.S. Agency for International Development by Robert R. Nathan Associates, Inc., Washington," June 1972, 2; RRNP, May 5, 1966. In mentioning "ascription-oriented" culture, Nathan was citing Ralph Linton, *The Study of Man: An Introduction* (New York: D. Appleton-Century, 1936).

exchange rate system was a rational adaption for a country where duty collection on the border was impracticable. Nor were Afghan technocrats blind. "It is no secret," wrote an Afghan planner in 1948, "that the customs policy of our country over the course of the last seventy years was based not on the demands of the national economy, but on the interests of government revenues."[157] The patchwork fiscal-administrative state that Nathan and Paul critiqued was but an ingenious *ad hoc* solution to the crisis of 1947. The fact that foreigners were in Afghanistan in the first place, pumping money into the state while diagnosing its shortcomings, represented not the failure, but the success of Afghan policy.

Once again, however, the structural bipolarity of the Cold War made disciplining the Afghan economy impossible. Working simultaneously in Kabul with Nathan and Paul was the team of Soviet Gosplan economists present in Kabul since the late 1950s.[158] They did little to dispel American fears about a Soviet aid "offensive" in their initial encounters with their Cold War rivals. At his first joint meeting with the Gosplan team, Paul was aghast to see the Soviets harping on the need to meet unrealistic export targets that would "create enough tension, stress, and strain. Several times the senior members of the group," wrote Paul, "told me that the Russian people have achieved 'the impossible' because high targets had been set by the planners." But unrealistic assumptions about exports meant understating planned deficits and inflation. Predictably, interest rates rose. And as long as the Afghan government delayed reforming the exchange rate, businessmen withheld investment. In 1964, Nathan convinced his Afghan colleagues to devalue the exchange rate from 20 *afghānis* (the Afghan currency) to the dollar to 45:1, closer to the market rate of 50:1.[159] Kabul lowered duties on Afghanistan's principal exports and forced foreign importers to purchase goods at the official exchange rate. Finally, it hiked import tariffs to reflect the new, higher prices. The reforms slashed budget deficits by twenty percent in 1963-4, then by another twenty-six percent in 1964-5. But because the Nathan team could not carry out further tax reform, inflation and foreign currency shortages continued to plague the government.

As a result, Afghanistan crept into an embrace with the Soviet Union. When Paul spoke with the head of a wool export business "that handles perhaps forty percent of all of Afghanistan's wool trade," the former textile manager observed how the enterprise "goes along on its own inertia" and how the owner "shies away from any proposals for change. Most Afghans' raw wool goes to Russia, where it is washed and processed in plants on the other side of the border,

---

[157] "Rabota Ministerstva natsional'noĭ ekonomiki" (1948), AVP RF f. 159 (Referentura po Afganistanu), op. 37A, folder 72, d. 1, ll.11–37.
[158] RRNP, May 12, 1962.
[159] Robert R. Nathan Associates, "Economic Advisory Services Provided to the Ministry of Planning, Royal Government of Afghanistan, September 1961 to June 1972, Final Report. Submitted to the Royal Government of Afghanistan and U.S. Agency for International Development by Robert R. Nathan Associates, Inc., Washington," June 1972, 94.

near Tashkent." The manager brushed off any ideas for processing the wool in Afghanistan and taking advantage of the low cost of labor.[160] Likewise, in a 1962 meeting with a senior Afghan minister, Paul learned that Kabul had accrued huge debts to Moscow "because of the way in which the USSR has saved part of this year's crop of fresh fruits which cannot be shipped to the usual markets in India and Pakistan because of the closed border."[161] As grapes threatened to rot in Kabul and Qandahar warehouses, Moscow arranged for a daily airlift of ten planes' worth of fresh and dried fruits to Tashkent, where they were processed for onward sale in Soviet markets. Paul sighed: "This shows how badly the new raisin cleaning plant is needed. It would enable Afghanistan to sell dried fruits in the European markets for convertible currency and to use the proceeds in whatever way the country wants." Rather than making capital improvements, Afghan businessmen preferred Soviet subsidies.

Undaunted, Paul encouraged his Afghan interlocutors to embrace a more catholic trade policy. In the summer of 1962, Paul accompanied Ministry of Commerce officials to potential export markets and discussed setting up an Egyptian- and German-run grading operation for Afghan cotton with Zabuli's representatives in Hamburg.[162] By helping Afghan entrepreneurs implement the improvements in industrial management he knew well (Dexdale's panty-hose plant had been transformed into a parachutes, aircraft gear, and rocket nose cone factory during the war), Paul sought to integrate Afghanistan into the international economy.[163] He linked "his" Afghans with officials from Burmah-Shell, who wanted to "acquire petroleum supplies from the Persian Gulf via Karachi and thence by rail to the Afghan border near Qandahar."[164] The American International Cooperation Administration (then the country's main foreign aid institution) was even willing to improve the roadway for more petroleum deliveries. But Kabul had no convertible currency to pay these corporations. And as Afghan élites understood, Asia was no emerging market. One Afghan banker reflected at a 1961 Bangkok summit that "the five largest countries of Asia – Burma, India, Pakistan, Ceylon, and Indonesia – can today purchase 400 million dollars less of industrial goods than they could thirty years ago."[165] Combined with the decline in terms of trade that commodities exporters like Afghanistan experienced during the 1960s, Afghan businesses were rational in forgoing capital investment to sell at Soviet importers' inflated prices.

[160] APJ, September 4, 1960, 166.

[161] APJ, September 22, 1962, 998.

[162] Paul and the Afghans visited Egypt, Sudan, Kenya, Tanganyika, Greece, Italy, France, the UK, the Netherlands, West Germany, Denmark, Sweden, Finland, and Austria.

[163] Author Interview, Leslie Symington, Oxford, United Kingdom, October 21, 2011.

[164] APJ, September 10, 1960, 174.

[165] "Obzor razvitiia torgovlia i torgovaia politika (Rech' direktora Mukhameda Akbara Omara na 4 sessii torgovogo komiteta v Bangkoke)," *Anis*, February 3, 1961, in AVP RF, f. 71, op. 57, *papka* 70, d. 10, l. 19.

Soon, then, what statistics trade analysts could compile testified to the growing economic influence of the Soviet Union in the Afghan economy. In June 1969, a British diplomat compiled a table of economic data on Kabul's export and import partners. The Soviet Union, his research showed, had gone from supplying thirty-eight percent of imports in 1957 to sixty-three percent in 1963. Western exporters and Japan supplied only a third of Afghanistan's total imports, and Indian exports to Afghanistan had collapsed by half since 1957. Export statistics were almost as grim. Before Soviet routes became Afghanistan's only real outlet, Western economies consumed fifty percent of Afghanistan's exports, as compared to twenty-five percent for the USSR. In 1963, the two blocs stood at parity.[166] By 1970, total Soviet trade accounted for forty percent of total trade turnover, one reason why Western reports fretted over Soviet domination.

Yet between Dulles' missteps, a surge in US military aid to Pakistan, CIA espionage flights from Peshawar, and the grave state of relations with Pakistan, neither Moscow nor Kabul lacked for reasons to collaborate.[167] Rather than rushing to conclusions about Moscow's apocryphal aims of obtaining a warm-water port in the Persian Gulf, it is important to stress the actual diplomatic context. On May 30, 1953 (weeks after Stalin's death), Moscow dropped its pretensions to territories in eastern Turkey and access to the Bosphorus, while in the spring of 1956, Khrushchëv hosted the Shah of Iran in Moscow, where the Soviet leader "frankly admitted past mistakes (attributed to Stalin) in their policy towards Iran. [He] appeared genuinely anxious to turn over a new leaf."[168] The point was to seek détente with governments from Islamabad to Ankara and provide cautious patronage to the Communist Parties of the region (themselves mostly scattered by the 1970s – Afghanistan being the exception that proved the rule).[169] As one Soviet policy analyst emphasized, if Moscow had really been interested in warm water ports, it would have later supported Hafizullāh Amin ("the most rapid proponent of Afghanistan having access to the Indian Ocean"), not killed him.[170] Ironically, noted Soviet policy analyst Brutents, "the idea of 'access to warm waters' I heard only once: from the First Secretary of the Communist Party of Uzbekistan, when we spoke on board a plane traveling to Algiers. Even he, I think, borrowed the idea from the American press."

---

[166] According to Afghan statistics, in 1923, the USSR had accounted for only seven percent of Afghanistan's total trade balance. See Soviet Embassy in Kabul, Summary of Untitled Pamphlet Written by 'Abd al-Hai Aziz for the Afghan Press Ministry, in AVP RF, f. 71, op. 57, *papka* 70, d. 10, n.p.

[167] U.S.–Pakistan aid data from "Sixty years of US Aid to Pakistan: Get the Data," *The Guardian Datablog*.

[168] Communiqué from British Embassy Moscow to Foreign Office, July 12, 1956, PREM (Records of the Prime Minister's Office) 1535, National Archives.

[169] Author Interview, Vasilĭ Kravtsov, November 15, 2012; Author Interview, Valerĭ Ivanov, Ignatovo, Russian Federation, November 2, 2012.

[170] Brutents, *Tridtsat' let na staroĭ ploshchadi*, 481.

It is only in light of such facts that the complaints of Soviet officials from Kabul in the mid 1960s become legible. Rather than priding themselves on having "won" Afghanistan, advisers despaired over the complacency in all things economic that their policies had encouraged in the Afghans. In an April 1966 meeting with Soviet economists, Bob Nathan asked them whether the Third Five-Year Plan should favor state-run enterprises or private businesses. "This would depend on the industry," replied one, "but by and large [he] felt that the managers of government-owned enterprises were not sufficiently 'commercially oriented' and that they ought to be more business minded in their tasks."[171] Mechanized large-scale farming, a staple of previous Soviet proposals, never came up. Other Soviet economists underscored the importance of "mobilizing private capital and encouraging private investment." Echoing Paul, they argued that small farmers needed "material incentives" to improve the quality of their produce. Soviet commodity purchase agreements had led to rash purchases of low-quality goods that rotted and rusted in warehouses.[172] Further, the Soviet export boom had exposed institutional contradictions: since GKES was only a coordinating bureaucracy, it possessed few options to pressure individual Soviet factories or oil- or lumber-producing *sovnarkhozy* (regional production complexes in the USSR) to improve their export goods.[173] Hence, as Nathan wrote, "the market here has not tended to absorb Russian consumer goods readily. The people prefer American goods and I am convinced that far more American goods could be absorbed."[174] But managers of Soviet enterprises bristled at foreigners' complaints that Soviet wares were substandard.[175] Rejecting free trade, Moscow allied with the states that had the least to gain from economic globalization, built the material infrastructure of economic nationalism for them, and then bemoaned its own role as a purchaser of last resort.

Nor were these isolated episodes of Americans hearing what they wanted to hear. In closed meetings, Gosplan economists saw themselves as exploited by the Afghans. At a 1968 conference, one K. Kondrat'ev explained the problem. Trade had grown in recent years. The Soviet Union was by far Afghanistan's largest trade partner, soaking up twenty-five percent of the country's exports and supplying half of all imports.[176] Even if Soviet refrigerators and shoes

[171] RRNP, May 3, 1966.

[172] Attwood, *The Reds and the Blacks: A Personal Adventure–Two Tours on Duty in Revolutionary Africa as Kennedy's Ambassador to Guinea and Johnson's to Kenya*, 72; Masov, *A Distant Front in the Cold War: The USSR in West Africa and the Congo*, 211.

[173] Oscar Sánchez-Sibony, "Red Globalization: The Political Economy of Soviet Foreign Relations in the 1950s and 60s" (PhD Dissertation, The University of Chicago, 2010), 217–33.

[174] GARF, f. 5446 (Sovet ministrov SSSR), op. 1, d. 687, l. 5; RRNP, November 11, 1965.

[175] RGAE, f. 4372 (Gosplan SSSR), op. 62, d. 462, l. 15–16.

[176] K. Kondrat'ev, "O sostoianii vneshneĭ torgovli Sovetskogo Soiuza s Afganistanom," in "Materialy pervoĭ ekonomicheskoĭ konferentsii sovetskikh spetsialistov, rabotaiushchikh v Afganistane," (October 24–25, 1968), RGAE f. 365, op.2, d. 2739, l. 290.

had a suspicious habit of turning up at bazaars in Karachi, the USSR supplied eighty percent of all of Afghanistan's energy imports, seventy percent of its automobiles and auto parts, ninety-five percent of its sugar imports, and so on.[177] Because, however, Moscow had neither revised a 1950 trade agreement nor offered to Afghanistan most favored nation status, the Afghan Ministry of Trade imposed regulations that dictated both the quantity of goods and the Afghan firms from which Soviet purchasers had to obtain wares.[178] Nor did Afghanistan force the same terms on Western purchasers. No wonder Paul's wool trader had been so complacent.

Kondrat'ev probed further. Moscow had extended considerable credit to Kabul and wanted it repaid. But how? Kondat'ev conceded that "the export resources of Afghanistan consist exclusively of goods of agricultural production."[179] Without a surge in Afghan industrial output, trade would stagnate. "Afghanistan is, obviously, not going to find [new goods to export]," continued the economist, "but Soviet specialists can provide help with this question." Energy seemed promising "insofar as Afghan exports of gas to the USSR are projected to rise from $19.2 million in 1967 to $20 million in 1971. But even this is not enough insofar as the entire revenue stream from the gas will have to go to the repayment of credits provided to Afghanistan by GKES. There are simply no further means for Afghanistan to purchase Soviet goods. The real task of Soviet specialists is to find new sources [of exports], new goods for export to the USSR that our national economy will be interested in." Kondrat'ev cited Iran, from which the USSR imported lead and zinc ore, as a model, and noted that improvements to the port at Hairaton could boost trade.[180] But it seemed as if Soviet geologists and petroleum engineers would have to strip mine the entire Afghan substratum if they ever hoped to recoup earlier loans. Indebtedness, talk of concessions, the notion of Afghanistan as objectively backwards – did this not all sound familiar to Soviet economists' original criticisms of Western "imperialist" aid?

Perhaps there were not "two approaches to help," as Soviet economists had once so proudly touted.[181] The collapse of an imperial world had forced a crash reinvention of Afghan statehood. The Cold War had lent Zahir Shah, Daoud, and Prince Naim a way to do so. But as mounting Soviet–American frustrations suggested, it was not clear what backwards, undeveloped, landlocked countries could do to attract permanent financing from the superpowers. In the absence of the Cold War, only surplus population itself – higher counts of the current or prospective number of hungry, sick, or dead people in Third World

[177] Ibid.; Author Interview, Georgiï Ezhov, Moscow, Russian Federation, April 15, 2013.
[178] Ibid., 291.
[179] Ibid., 293.
[180] Ibid., 294.
[181] Vladimir Plastun and Vladimir Andrianov, *Nadzhibulla. Afganistan v tiskakh geopolitiki* (Moscow: Agenstvo "sokrat," 1998), 182.

nation-states – could justify funding. The symmetry of not only of the American and Soviet global projects, but also of their failures, testified to the limits of the politics of productivity in a postcolonial epoch.

And yet Moscow's forms of aid injected radically new ideas, professions, and expectations into Afghan society. In 1948, an Afghan pilot, Rahman, who had studied in the Soviet Union, returned to Kabul married to not just a Russian woman but also a Marxist vision of the future. Maintaining ties with the Soviet Embassy, Rahman spread political literature among student circles at Kabul University, circles that included a young Babrak Karmal.[182] Not long after its founding in January 1965, the PDPA, noted Karen Brutents, "wasn't doing a bad job in learning the 'technique' and 'technology' of the activity of a Communist Party: their people gradually penetrated various administrative structures, government agencies, and the army in particular."[183] Even if Kabul's Soviet-trained army officers were not about to overthrow their monarch and build socialism, geopolitics demanded maintaining Afghanistan as an ally.[184] The PDPA only figured into very long-term planning. Vladimir Plastun, later the Second Secretary at the Soviet Embassy, noted that the April Revolution "came like a bolt from the blue to Soviet specialists in Kabul; they had 'overslept' events. The leaders of the PDPA hid their plans on the overthrow of Daoud from the Soviets and didn't even consult [with us] on it, since they were certain of a negative answer from Moscow as to their ideas."[185]

In the meantime, then the situation was more ambiguous than "Sovietization." Aid and the Cold War conspired to create islands of infrastructure and modernity across Afghanistan.[186] The Afghan state had been impotent to realize infrastructure in the past, but foreigners were not. Foreigners understood materials like water, oil, and wood that could be mastered to build the "national economy." Soon, foreigners and Afghans would together work changes on the land. In the river basins of Helmand, snow from the Hindu Kush would hydrate a hydraulic civilization that nomads and landless farmers would settle. In the oil- and gas-rich northern lowlands, reservoirs of petrified sunlight would be unleashed to create an industrial civilization. In the east, the cedar trees of Paktia would sacrifice their lives for the sake not of Karachi merchants, but for a national Afghan market. The foreigners in the Afghan capital had struggled to find the state, but maybe this was because Kabul had not yet mastered the resources within its own borders. Dreams of the developmental state and the national economy could not wait for objections about the weakness of the

---

[182] Ibid., 22.
[183] Brutents, 453.
[184] Ibid., 475.
[185] Plastun and Andrianov, 33.
[186] Author Interview, Valeriĭ Ivanov, Ignatovo, Russian Federation, November 2, 2012; Author Interview, Georgiĭ Ezhov, Moscow, Russian Federation, April 15, 2013.

Afghan state. Advisers had arrived to impose an economic dream on brackish, oily, knotty reality.

Water: American Hydrology in Helmand

Few of the Afghan borderlands whose ecology and economy were to be molded by foreigners had a longer history of interventions than the Helmand and Arghandab River watershed in southern Afghanistan. Hearsay had it that "Pashtun groups settled in the Helmand region through land granted by Ahmad Shah in his attempts to unify his young nation in the mid to late 1700s."[187] But serious efforts to turn ecological caprice into demographic fortune began in 1910–14, when Kabul "began to develop parts of an old canal system to be known as the Seraj Canal."[188] Soviet refugees were among the first to be settled in the reclaimed lands.[189] In the 1930s, German and Japanese engineers extended both the Seraj Canal and another old waterway, later renamed the Boghra Canal. By 1946, 25 kilometers of canals carried water.

But when Kabul chose to extend the canal system after the Second World War, it turned to Morrison-Knudsen, an American construction company, to do so. The choice was not obvious given the legacy of Afghan–American relations. True, adventurers like Joseph Harlan had lived in Afghanistan in the late nineteenth century, and the Emir Habibullah had even employed a former engineer for General Electric to oversee the construction of a hydroelectric plant at Jabal Serāj in the first decade of the twentieth century.[190] But when an official Afghan delegation sought diplomatic recognition from Washington in the summer of 1921, officials rebuffed them. State Department Orientologist Wallace Murray saw Afghanistan as "doubtless the most fanatic, hostile country in the world today" and implored Secretary of State Charles Evans Hughes not to recognize Kabul. Hughes wrote to President Harding, arguing that London would disapprove of recognition, since "Afghanistan, although ostensibly independent, was still within the British 'sphere of political influence.'"[191] (Such niceties did not stop Lenin from receiving the same Afghan delegation in

---

[187] Dick Scott, "Tribal and Ethnic Groups in the Helmand Valley," Afghanistan Council of the Asia Society, Occasional Paper #21 (Spring 1980), 3. DSA.

[188] Frydoon Sharzai, Ghulam Farouq, and Dick Scott, "1975 Farm Economic Survey of the Helmand Valley," 7, DSA.

[189] Scott, "Tribal and Ethnic Groups in the Helmand Valley."

[190] Jewett's wife assembled a documentary collection of her husband's time in Afghanistan, published as *An American Engineer in Afghanistan* (Minneapolis: University of Minneapolis Press, 1948).

[191] Wallace Murray, "NEA Memorandum of Conversation," US National Archives File 890h.00/122 (1930), quoted in Abdul-Qayum Mohmand, "American Foreign Policy Toward Afghanistan: 1919–2001" (PhD Dissertation, University of Utah, 2001), 52; Charles E. Hughes, "The Secretary of State to President Harding," *Papers Relating to the Foreign Relations of the United States 1920/1* (Washington, 1936), 258.

the Kremlin, where he extended diplomatic recognition to Kabul.)[192] Hughes and Harding received Afghan representative Mohammad Wali Khan but gave him only a personal letter and no guarantees of recognition.[193] All the same, a small American community thrived in Kabul. Ernest Fox, an American geologist, searched for gold in Badakhshan; English-language teachers forged a generation of Afghan élites who would pursue their higher education at Columbia University's Teachers' College and the University of Wyoming.[194] Only in January 1942, when Hitler threatened, did the former American chargé d'affaires in Tehran open an Embassy in Kabul.

By 1946, then, early misunderstandings seemed like water under the bridge. The tasks Kabul presented to Morrison-Knudsen appeared straightforward: upgrade the Boghra Canal with a diversion dam in order to water the desert in Nad-i 'Ali and Marja; build diversion structures on the Boghra to feed a second canal, the Shamalan; and build "road improvements between Chaman and Qandahar."[195] Yet the canals went over budget. The Boghra sprung leaks. The areas around the Boghra Canal and Shamalan extension lacked proper drainage. As we saw earlier, in 1949, the Afghan government turned to the U.S. Import–Export Bank to fund a second contract. More Morrison-Knudsen engineers arrived in the south to fix the canals and build two new dams. In 1952, Kabul founded the Helmand Valley Authority (HVA), a government agency, to oversee development in, and resettlement to, the region.

The alphabet soup concealed an interesting story of nation-building. HVA's Charter explicitly identified the resettlement of nomadic Afghans to newly irrigated farmlands as a key goal.[196] This was no marginal project: in southern Afghanistan, nomads based in the Registan and Dasht-i Margo migrated in search of oases, or out of Afghanistan altogether during times of drought. In eastern Afghanistan, meanwhile, nomadic Pashtuns shuttled between Afghanistan and Pakistan to graze their herds.[197] Nation-building demanded nomad-breaking, however, and so Kabul resolved to resettle many eastern Pashtuns to Nad-i 'Ali in the early 1950s. By concentrating the waters

---

[192] M.M. Yaftali, "Pis'mo Mirzy Mukhammed Yaftali o ego vstrechakh s V.I. Leninym i o ego poezde v Rossiiu" (September 28, 1957), in AVP RF f. 159, op. 69d, d. 88, *papka* 2, l. 10–10a.

[193] Mohammad Wali and his team visited Turkey, Iran, the Soviet Union, and several European countries prior to their arrival in the United States.

[194] "Remembering the Past: The Early Years of U.S.–Afghan Relations," *In Small Things Remembered*, Online Exhibition, available online at: www.meridian.org/insmallthing sremembered/about-the-exhibition/remembering-the-past-the-early-years-of-u-s-afghan-relations.

[195] Frydoon Sharzai, Ghulam Farouq, and Dick Scott, "1975 Farm Economic Survey of the Helmand Valley," 8, DSA.

[196] Quoted in Frank E. Patterson (U.S. Technical Cooperation Service), "Report on the Site Selection for the Permanent Administrative Center of the Helmand Valley Authority" (March 5, 1953), 2, DSA.

[197] Klaus Ferdinand, *Preliminary Notes on Hazara Culture* (Copenhagen, 1959); Ibid., "Nomad Expansion and Commerce in Central Afghanistan," *Folk* 4 (1962), 123–59.

of a transnational river in the deserts of southern Afghanistan, the HVA could parch transnational pastors' worlds, concentrate populations around hydraulic infrastructure, and secure the buy-in of hydrologically minded Americans, too.

This last point is no exaggeration. When Paul S. Jones, a Morrison-Knudsen engineer, traveled to Helmand in 1950–51, he saw himself as part of a mission to export freedom.[198] Just as hydrological expertise had civilized the Great West, so, too, could it tame Asia. Helmand, he imagined, had once thrived under Darius and Alexander, but drought had destroyed its ancient civilizations. Now, explained Jones:

It now so happens that 2,250 years later – in these years of the 1950's AD – another 'conquest' has begun…this time in reverse.

THE CONQUERER: His Majesty, the King of Afghanistan, and his Government.
THE ARMY: M-K-A Inc., with its thousands of Afghan workers.
THE ENEMY: a recalcitrant Nature.
CAUSE OF WAR: Nature's enforcement of its decree that a vast region be doomed to
    drought forever.
FIELD OF BATTLE: the Arghandab and Helmand River valleys and Sistan basin.[199]

Jones' ignorance empowered solipsistic remappings of the Great West onto the Afghan south. Afghanistan was a "new frontier"; the Pashtun nomads he saw, "the Afghan version of the American covered wagon days and the settlement of our western irrigation projects."[200] But Pashtuns, Jones added, were also "wild and carefree like the original North American Indian, and well-to-do with their valuable flocks."[201] In conversations with an Afghan engineer about the future of the HVA, Jones projected his Western life onto Afghanistan: "farm units, villages, schools, hospitals, recreation centers, industry, improved agriculture, electric power, stock-raising – a wealth of productive uninhabited land – enough for all Afghans who want it on a basis similar to the American irrigation reclamation project plan – and water to irrigate it from the Helmand, a veritable Colorado River with its many tributaries."[202]

Jones' musings crystallized contemporary American views of the developing world. Americans of his generation invested hydrological "transformation with a variety of metaphorical meanings […] waterlands were a screen on to which a changing society projected its hopes and fears."[203] They had good reason to, for institutions like the Department of the Interior and the Department of

---

[198] Paul S. Jones, *Afghanistan Venture: Discovering the Afghan People: The Life, Contacts and Adventures of an American Civil Engineer During His Two Year Sojourn in the Kingdom of Afghanistan* (San Antonio: Naylor Co., 1956), 95.
[199] Ibid., 129–30.
[200] Ibid., 95, 214.
[201] Ibid., 220.
[202] Ibid., 79.
[203] David Blackbourn, *The Conquest of Nature: Water, Landscape and the Making of Modern Germany* (London: Pimlico, 2007), 18.

Agriculture and schemes like the Homestead Act, the Desert Land Act, and the Mineral Leasing Act had indeed "reclaimed" Jones' Western landscapes. Millions of Americans settled west of the Mississippi, human gusts in the sails of Manifest Destiny. In California, private water companies and public projects tapped the Colorado River and the Sierra Nevada to make Jones' home, the Central Valley, the most productive agricultural region in the world. Together, settler colonialism and hydrological ingenuity formed liberty's surest guardian. Helmand could look forward, as California once had, to seeing orchards where deserts had once stood – even without the institutions and terror that made an Anglophone settler world. After all, the Californian dams dried up rivers, devastated fish populations, and submerged Native American settlements forever. Ironically, however, the submerging of indigenous sites – and the hydro-ignorance it enabled – endowed Jones with the confidence to use water to recover "lost" civilizations.

All of this made Americans useful idiots for entrepreneurial Afghans. In a disastrous twist, however, the idea of "Pashtunistan" would warp foreigners' understandings of the Afghan state. Between Khruschëv's endorsement of Kabul's position and the Afghan state's aggressive marketing of Pashtun state domination, American analysts and figures like Jones resigned themselves to Pashtun nationalism as an inbuilt feature of Afghan statehood.[204] The truth was more complicated: an underfunded and underimagined postcolonial Afghan state had simply repeated core colonial tropes (Aryanism, *jihād*, Pashtun domination) as key markers of national identity. Like their Soviet counterparts, however, American Orientologists like Louis Dupree and Donald Wilber were poorly equipped to challenge such claims. As a result, the aid bureaucracy plowed millions of dollars into a Pashtun resettlement scheme, fearful of being outflanked by Moscow as a champion of Afghan national aspirations. The colonially constructed battleship of Pashtun domination of Afghanistan – a "Pashtun state" also threatened by Pashtuns – had found safe harbor in the waters of the Cold War, in the rivulets of the Helmand.

The quest to remake the south was on. In 1953, HVA authorities planned the development of a permanent regional administrative seat, as its offices were dispersed between Qandahar, Girishk, and Nad-i 'Ali.[205] They turned to the U.S. Technical Cooperation Service to recommend where HVA could unify its administrative functions in a model city. American spatial planning engineers had to evaluate not the actually existing population of the region, but rather the projected needs of the population that would be resettled to the region. Centralizing everything in Girishk was mooted, but dismissed because of the

204 Dennis Kux, *The United States and Pakistan, 1947–2000: Disenchanted Allies* (Washington: Johns Hopkins University Press, 2001), 77–9.
205 Quoted in Frank E. Patterson (U.S. Technical Cooperation Service), "Report on the Site Selection for the Permanent Administrative Center of the Helmand Valley Authority" (March 5, 1953), 3, DSA.

city's high water table, poor drainage, and distance from project sites.[206] The Service settled on an uninhabited site called "Lashkaari Bazaar," favorable because of its soil, drainage, and cool weather. Coincidently, the site lay near a series of ruined *karezes* and canals. "It is apparent that the Afghans of 1000 years ago were logical planners and engineers," gloated a report, "and recognized the excellence of the situation between the Arghandab and Helmand Rivers. [...] It is fitting, therefore, that this area should once again become the economic and cultural center of a resurgent civilization."[207] Lashkaari Bazaar became a Stepford town, dotted with an archaeological museum, a library, and a cinema, and the town was itself dubbed "America-in-Asia."[208]

Thus the basis was laid for mass resettlement. From 1953 to 1973, the HVA resettled 5,486 families, or an average of one every day.[209] Yet resettlement was "chunky." HVA resettled families in groups of 50–100 at a time, categorized by tribe or ethnic group. Describing the resettlement as "Pashtunization" obscured ethnic Pashtun subgroups resettled across the south.[210] In Nad-i 'Ali (est. 1954), for example, the population was 34% Kharoti, 9% Arab, 8% Kakar, 6% Achakzai, 5% Nurzai, and 5% Baluch. And even this ignored nineteen other self-identified ethnic groups. Intersettlement diversity was even greater. Some sites, like Marja (est. 1959), were relatively homogeneous, with twenty-six percent of respondents identifying as Nurzai and eighteen percent as Alikozai Pashtuns.[211] Around the Shamalan Canal, it was 52% Barakzai, 14% Popolzai, and 8% Nurzai. Waves of resettlement had deposited human flotsam and jetsam upon a landscape already populated by 30,000 souls.[212]

Soon, U.S. Federal institutions replaced Morrison-Knudsen, which wound up operations in the late 1950s. In 1960, the ICA selected the U.S. Bureau of Reclamation to consult with HVA, underscoring the isomorphic mapping of the Great West onto the Middle East.[213] But the first Reclamation consultants "found very few agricultural statistics or data pertaining to the Helmand Valley."[214] "Once the Bureau of Reclamation took over in 1960," said one Helmand veteran, "their main question was, 'how can we increase the outputs

---

[206] Ibid., 10.

[207] Ibid., 14.

[208] Ibid., Appendix, Plate V: "Typical Street Sections"; Arnold Toynbee, *Between Oxus and Jumna* (New York, 1961), 12.

[209] Dick Scott, "Tribal and Ethnic Groups in the Helmand Valley," Afghanistan Council of the Asia Society, Occasional Paper #21 (Spring 1980), 3. DSA.

[210] Among those resettled, noted Scott, Pashtun subgroupings were "at least as significant a political identification [...] as is being Turkmen, Uzbek, or Hazara."

[211] Ibid., 9.

[212] Ibid., 11, "Map No. II. Shamalan region with Ethnic Groups" and 13, "Map No. III. Cadastral Map. North Shamalan. Barakzai Holdings by Sub-Tribe."

[213] Dick Scott, "The Shamalan Land Project: An Introduction," 16, DSA.

[214] Ira M. Stevens (Agricultural Economist for U.S. Bureau of Reclamation), Enclosure to I.M. Stevens and J.K. Tarzi, *Economics of Agricultural Production in Helmand Valley, Afghanistan* (1965), DSA.

and the quality of life for Afghan farmers already in the area?'"[215] HVA, in contrast, obsessed over resettlement. Farm evaluations counted, but only insofar as their findings could boost farm yields, allow greater population density, and thus facilitate more settlements. Rumors of poor soil quality and drainage persisted, but there was no way to confirm them without sending researchers out into the field.

Hence, in early 1963, an American agricultural economist and an Afghan agricultural economist, Ira Stevens and Kamaluddin Tarzi, began interviewing families on crop yields. HVA channeled the pair's work through provincial *hākims* (district governors) and Helmand Valley Extension Offices, which "supplied the names and populations of all villages under its jurisdiction."[216] Stevens and Tarzi chose a representative sample of small, medium, and large villages and traveled to their sites to meet village chiefs, who then prepared a list of selected farmers. The researchers then "chose the names of farmers to be interviewed from lists supplied by the village chief. These names were chosen at random and farmers were usually called to come to the village chief's home where we interviewed them." Unaccountable bureaucratic and tribal power determined who would be interviewed.

Soon, however, Stevens and Tarzi challenged the survey's methodology. They spontaneously contacted farmers at home or in the fields, eliminating "some of the bias we seemed to have been getting." Over 1963 and 1964, the two interviewed 495 Afghans – primarily landowners, but also sharecroppers and village chiefs – to learn what crops they cultivated, their family size, their average sell price, and, crucially, their yields. But the results were mixed. True, some farmers reported yield increases of up to fifty percent compared to a decade prior.[217] More, however, saw yields drop by as much as two-thirds. Peeved, HVA reassigned the researchers "to find and examine the opinions" (not the reasons) "farmers gave for yields being higher or lower." In Marja and Nad-i 'Ali, the farmers complained that "the soil is basically poor, lacking in fertility." Early growing seasons had been productive, but crop quality and output declined year after year.[218] In other areas, the cotton that HVA forced farmers to grow at below-market prices exhausted the soil.

In what was to become a set piece, the ensuing report blamed Helmand farmers for their low yields. "Many farming practices have not changed very much in Helmand Valley over the centuries," commented the subtitle of a photograph of a rail-thin peasant sowing wheat seed by hand.[219] A photograph of a clay pot supplied confirmation: while most farmers "said this storage was

[215] Author Interview, Dick Scott, October 5, 2012, conducted via telephone from Tashkent, Uzbekistan.

[216] I.M. Stevens and J.K. Tarzi, *Economics of Agricultural Production in Helmand Valley, Afghanistan* (1965), 1, DSA.

[217] Ibid., 29.

[218] Ibid., 30.

[219] Ibid., Figure 10, Page 22.

adequate, there was some loss from insects and rodents."[220] Even as a majority of farmers "said they did not need more or better roads," the report insisted that transportation infrastructure was inadequate.[221] Documentary photography showed their folly, contrasting a sleek paved highway with a turbaned man walking along the shoulder with an overburdened mule. "As the country develops," captions explained matter-of-factly, "better roads will be needed." Unhygienic, reactionary farmers, the report implied, would not.

Even as problems mounted, the development machine churned out copy that championed the project in glowing terms.[222] In 1967, USAID's Assistant Director for the region tasked the wife of a Bureau of Reclamation official with a history of the region.[223] The text, later approved as official canon, explained that the Helmand Valley initiative "corresponds to the Salt River Project in Arizona."[224] "The Green Revolution that is sweeping Asia has reached the Helmand-Arghandab Valley," the report explained, rendering Afghanistan "a nation ready to accept a position of responsibility in the world."[225] The history unintentionally distilled the zeitgeist in another paragraph: "progress in agricultural production is evident from close observation in Helmand Valley," even if "the exact amount of progress cannot be measured because accurate production statistics are not available."[226]

But even if the soils furnished dwindling amounts of cotton or wheat, they had to be coaxed to sprout the social scientist's cash crop, data. As Stevens and Tarzi were completing their farmer interviews, HAVA (since renamed to include not only the Helmand but also the Arghandab River watershed, hence the "A") approached Reclamation "to select an area for immediate study."[227] Reclamation settled upon the Shamalan, a flood plain in whose north a test area of roughly 200 acres was to be cleared of farmers, leveled, and stripped of trees, houses, vineyards, and orchards. The site would then be covered with ultra-high-yield soils that would then be redistributed in rationalized model plots to the displaced farmers.[228] A lateral canal branching from the main Shamalan Canal would deliver water south, permitting further resettlement. Data, generated through further farmer surveys, would theoretically justify the extension of the model to the entire region. And if Afghans wanted this? Farmers, one report stressed, simply had to be informed of the "methods of modern

---

[220] Ibid., Figure 8, 20.

[221] Ibid., 39.

[222] Mildred Caudill, *Helmand-Arghandab Valley: Yesterday, Today, Tomorrow* (Lashkar Gah: Afghanistan, 1969).

[223] Ibid., Foreword.

[224] Ibid., 1.

[225] Ibid., 9, 33.

[226] Ibid., 1.

[227] "Shamalan Unit Draft Feasibility Report" (September 1967), 16, DSA.

[228] Dick Scott, "The Shamalan Land Development Project: An Introduction," DSA.

agriculture and irrigation practices."[229] A fresh armada bulldozers and scrapers replaced the rusting Morrison-Knudsen equipment to scrape bumpkins off the floodplains.[230]

USAID consultants had once again enabled Afghan bureaucratic power. In an August 1970 memorandum, one AID official warned that "HAVA has not organized a systematic campaign" to win the support of the locals for the project.[231] Yet the officer's proposed solutions just reinforced antidemocratic precedents. Afghan state representatives had to lobby local *khāns* and identify farmers "aware of the need for change and more willing to accept change than are the mass of people."[232] Agricultural extension agents from the central government in Kabul had to produce "from each village a list of ten or twenty people who have proven themselves receptive to new ideas."[233] "The decision to support or not support the project," bluntly acknowledged the AID administrator, "will not be made by the mass of the people. This decision will be made for them by the leaders."[234]

When a young USAID analyst, Richard "Dick" Scott, arrived in Afghanistan fresh in early 1971, he discovered, to his horror, that USAID barely informed the Shamalan villagers of the project.[235] Some farmers had been compensated for losses of crops or land already inflicted, but HAVA had no formal reimbursement policy.[236] The tone of a September 1972 meeting between a HAVA Land Committee and several villagers captured much. While villagers had come to the meeting spot an hour prior to the scheduled start, HAVA and central government officials arrived an hour late.[237] A government tax collector spoke only Persian and was ignored by the Pashto-speaking audience. Finally, when the representative of the Land Committee finally arrived, he "was informed that his Pushto was not the same as [the farmers'] and that he should say no more." Only to HAVA and AID was it a surprise when locals met American bulldozers with rifles.[238] By the autumn of 1972, the Governor of Helmand Province had

---

[229] Ibid., iv.
[230] Scott, "The Shamalan Land Development Project: An Introduction"; Author Interview, Dick Scott, October 5, 2012, conducted via telephone from Tashkent, Uzbekistan.
[231] Charles Husick, "Organization of Political Effort in Support of the Shamalan" (August 3, 1970), 1, DSA.
[232] Ibid., 2–3.
[233] Ibid., 3.
[234] Ibid., 4.
[235] Dick Richard B. Scott, "The North Shamalan: A Survey of Land and People" (August 1971), 6, DSA.
[236] Dick Richard B. Scott and Cecil Uyehara, "Another Visit to the North Shamalan" (May 29, 1972), DSA.
[237] Richard B. Scott, "The Beginning of the Crunch: A Statement and Analysis of Present Village Attitudes in the North Shamalan" (November 8, 1973), 7, DSA.
[238] Cynthia Clapp-Wincek, "The Helmand Valley Project in Afghanistan" (AID Evaluation Special Study No. 18) (December 1983), 7, DSA.

grown skeptical of ever-rising costs; authorities ditched the North Shamalan project.[239] Builders completed the canal itself, but the dream motivating the Shamalan had evaporated.

By the early 1970s, then, the American presence in the region stood in question. A year after Daoud's 1973 coup, USAID shuttered its activity in the south.[240] Panic ensued: would American funding stop? When Henry Kissinger visited Kabul in November 1974, Daoud's brother, Naim, stressed that Helmand was a long-term project and that Kabul needed another decade of commitment from Washington.[241] Kissinger bemoaned the "many frustrated missionaries who can't resist reforming everyone," but agreed to "send some senior official from AID out here to whom you can make specific requests." Kabul soon got the cash it needed to accelerate resettlements.[242]

And yet changes to Daoud's cotton policy would transform the region's economy more than Americans ever could. Under Zahir Shah's rule, British aid agencies had built a cotton gin near Bost, but farmers devoted less than five percent of their land to the crop.[243] The reason why was simple: Kabul forced farmers to sell their crops at an artificially low price, allowing the state to reap a handsome profit for itself on world cotton markets. Daoud, however, liberalized Afghanistan's cotton policy. Farmers received free fertilizer and seeds and a guaranteed price tied to world market rates. Soon, farmers devoted forty percent of their fields to "white gold." The cotton gin became so crowded that backlogs of a year were not uncommon. Kabul lobbied London for another cotton gin in Girishk. Yet without specialized fertilizers, cotton degraded soil quality more quickly than subsistence crops. Within two years, "yields had stagnated because of the decreased soil quality due to the salinity, sodicity, and drainage problems."[244]

Here was the chance for USAID to intervene. In 1975, the Ministry of Planning pressed AID to construct drains in four select areas: Nad-i 'Ali, Marja, Darweshan, and the Shamalan.[245] Skeptical, however, AID officials suggested beginning with a test project of 120 kilometers of drains financed by AID,

[239] Richard B. Scott, "The Beginning of the Crunch: A Statement and Analysis of Present Village Attitudes in the North Shamalan" (November 8, 1973), 9, DSA; Author Interview, Dick Scott, October 5, 2012.
[240] Cynthia Clapp-Wincek, "The Helmand Valley Project in Afghanistan," 5.
[241] Memorandum of Conversation, Friday, November 1, 1974, in *FRUS 1967–1976*, Vol. E-8, Documents on South Asia, 1973–1976.
[242] Dick Scott, "Tribal and Ethnic Groups in the Helmand Valley," Afghanistan Council of the Asia Society, Occasional Paper #21 (Spring 1980), 3. DSA.
[243] Author Interview, Dick Scott, October 5, 2012. London took on a leading role because U.S. government regulations imposed by the American cotton lobby forbade USAID from promoting overseas cotton production.
[244] Clapp-Wincek, "The Helmand Valley Project in Afghanistan," 13.
[245] A.A. Ferogh (Afghan Deputy Minister of Planning), Letter to Vincent H. Brown (Director of USAID Mission Kabul), February 12, 1975, in "Project Paper: Central Helmand Drainage," USAID Office Kabul (April 8, 1975), DSA.

overseen by the United States Soil Conservation Service, and implemented by HAVA.[246] Framed as a minimalist approach, this still meant moving thousands of tons of soil. HAVA had not only to deepen existing canals, but also to construct dozens of kilometers of drainage ditches leading into those canals.[247] AID suggested that if all went well, a second phase of the project could begin in late 1976. Dick Scott, however, was skeptical. None of HAVA's behavior suggested that it would "deal fairly with the farmers in these matters [of irrigation], nor use other than purely authoritarian methods to accomplish project ends."[248] In a remark telling of discursive shifts to come, Scott added that one could not trust Helmand's Governor, a former military officer "of the Muslim world and trained by Russia" unlikely to "be aware of the need for or sensitive of basic human rights that should be part of any USAID project."[249]

The test phase confirmed Scott's fears. In Zargun Qala, a village near Nad-i 'Ali, builders planned to extend and deepen a seven-meter wide drain, but HAVA deployed Shamalan-era bulldozers and drag lines to do so, "damaging large areas of farm land."[250] And because HAVA had to dig irrigation ditches to feed the canal, farmers whose land bordered the drain were ruined for the spring 1976 planting season.[251] Many of the forced migrants in Nad-i 'Ali felt powerless to oppose HAVA, but "these projects are strongly identified by the farmers as American projects."[252] All the while, resettlement to the region accelerated. But if the 1950s settlers had received twenty-seven *jeribs* (about thirteen acres), the Daoud-era wave of forced migrants, however, received twelve *jeribs* and "virtually no other assistance or training."[253] The formerly landless farmers were "generally happy or at least uncomplaining with their immediate condition," Scott noted, but "with the Muslim rules of inheritance of equal division of property among the sons the next generation will certainly be at sub-subsistence level which suggests perhaps urban migration, a downward drift into sharecropping or seasonal farm labor."[254]

USAID's Kabul office had initially endorsed the drainage project because it seemed unpolitical. It seemed easy. And where USAID had provided drainage,

---

[246] Richard Scott, undated 1975 memorandum to Ernest J. Barbour, "Comments on 'Central Helmand Drainage and Irrigation Improvement: Helmand-Arghandab Valley' Project Paper, and the Social Context Within Which the Project Must Function," DSA.

[247] Ibid., 25–6.

[248] Richard Scott, Memorandum to Ernest J. Barbour, "Comments on 'Central Helmand Drainage and Irrigation Improvement: Helmand-Arghandab Valley' Project Paper, and the Social Context Within Which the Project Must Function," (1975) 2, DSA.

[249] Ibid., 2.

[250] Ibid., 1.

[251] Ibid., 2.

[252] Ibid., 3.

[253] Richard B. Scott, Memorandum to Charles A. Johnson, "HAVA Priority of Land Settlement and Potential AID Project Development in Land Improvement and Drainage" (March 6, 1976), 3, DSA.

[254] Ibid., 4.

"net incomes rose to two or three times the incomes prior to the project."[255] But the extreme cautiousness of the project raised the question of what, exactly, America's strategy was in Helmand. AID had initially engaged itself with the region out of a desire to secure American influence in Afghanistan. More specifically, however, Americans had sought to embed the Afghan state's supposedly inherent Pashtun nationalist strivings in a framework of agricultural freeholding that promised to domesticated "wild" resettled eastern Pashtuns. Never questioning the logic of the Cold War or the Afghan state's colonial epistemology, Americans became complicit in a violent campaign of forced migration that turned Helmand into a dust bowl of intra-Pashtun disputes.

American dreams of transforming the Afghan South into the American West had evaporated like water in the desert. Yet Americans were not the only ones to see oases where there stood only mirages. Water was not the only resource to be mastered if Afghanistan was to become a territorial state with a national economy. The waters of the Helmand and Arghandab Rivers could make the fields of the Shamalan bloom, but would not agriculture merely condemn Afghanistan to centuries more of dependence? Was not heavy industry the only way out of dependence? American-paved highways may have snaked through the hydraulic civilization in the south, but for much of the development decade it seemed as if routes slithering through Moscow's tunnels to the country's north led to modernity. What if it was not hydro-freedom, but carbon socialism, that embodied the future?

Oil and Gas: Soviet Petroleum Expertise in Afghan Turkestan

It was impossible to visit Afghanistan during the Cold War and not be struck by the magnitude of Soviet aid. When Georgiĭ Ezhov retraced the trail of his initial mid 1950s journey to Afghanistan in the mid 1960s, the changes in a mere decade were striking. Not only was the Jalalabad runway now paved thanks to Soviet aid, but in the lowlands surrounding the Kabul and Laghman Rivers, an army of Soviet engineers was building state farms and a hub for Afghanistan's fruit industry. "This was a huge project," Ezhov recalled.[256] Azerbaijani scientists who had perfected olive species in Abkhazia transplanted their specimens to test sites in the valley.[257] "There were huge rocks in the ground," remembered Ezhov, "that had to be hauled out and ground down, and after that they transplanted several thousand tons of dirt from Uzbekistan to Afghanistan to provide thirty centimeters of topsoil covering several thousand hectares. Not a small task. They brought in a special machine from Armenia that could chew up rocks and turn them into gravel, but with these Afghan boulders it broke within a day or two." Uzbek dirt soon yielded Afghan bitter oranges, pomegranates,

[255] Clapp-Wincek, "The Helmand Valley Project in Afghanistan," 13.
[256] Author Interview, Georgiĭ Ezhov, Moscow, Russian Federation, April 15, 2013.
[257] Leon Sudzhan, "Olivkovaia vetv'," *Vokrug sveta* 8 (1987).

figs, and olives. E. Zhilin, an agricultural engineer who oversaw operations in the valley, recalled his time in Jalalabad to Uzbek readers Soviet journalists.[258] Recalling a screening of *Nangarhar's New Day* in a makeshift theater in Jalalabad, Zhilin noted that "the shots from this film vividly and convincingly convey the change that the Soviet people have brought here. The former camel minder now drives a tractor. Women now work as seed planters. The former shepherd now monitors the readings from the hydro-electric dam from a remote station." Stacked around the Afghan moviegoers, Zhilin boasted, were crates stamped "AFGHANISTAN. EXPORT."

Granted, Pakistani blockades halted exports to the east, but if one traveled west, toward Kabul, the Soviet presence was unmissable. Returning from an overnight visit to the Laghman Valley, Bob Nathan observed the Soviet-built 24,000-kilowatt Sarobi dam.[259] At one point along the road, Nathan saw "a busload of perhaps fifteen Russians stopped for water. They looked sturdy, dressed for work, though neatly."[260] Another Soviet dam, the Naghlu, generated a forbidding half of Afghanistan's hydroelectric energy.[261] Of course, the view of Soviet infiltration was different when viewed from the eastern side of the Iron Curtain. Prior to traveling abroad, recalled Afghanistan expert Viktor Korgun, he had to pass a battery of "political literacy" tests where instructors drilled him on the names of heads of Communist Parties in Third World countries. "You're the face, the representative, of the leading socialist country in the world," the proctor reminded Korgun. "Once you get there, tell Afghans how wonderful it is!"[262] Once in Kabul, rules barred Soviet diplomats from spending free time with locals; Korgun flaunted them and discovered the country. "The 1960s were a magical time in Afghanistan," he recalled.

Were one to continue north from the capital on the Soviet-built highway, the parade of infrastructure continued. At Bagram, Soviet engineers were busy building a military base for the Afghan National Air Force; further north loomed the Salang Tunnel.[263] North of the tunnel, in Pul-i Khumri, a Soviet-built dam powered textile plants, while Soviet aid had transformed the fields around Baghlan into the hub of the Afghan cotton industry.[264] One Polish engineer, entering the director's offices of the Baghlan sugar factory, encountered "a woman of rare beauty dressed in European clothing. Splendid black

[258] E. Zhilin, "Plody na kamniakh. O pomoshchi spetsialistov Uzbekistana stroiteliam Afganistana," *Tashkentskaia Pravda*, November 23, 1973.

[259] RRNP, May 25, 1961.

[260] RRNP, May 26, 1961.

[261] *Avtoreferat* for Zokira Wakhidi, "Strukturnye preobrazovaniia natsional'noĭ ekonomiki respubliki Afganistan v 80–e gody," (*Kandidat nauk* Dissertation, G.V. Plekhanov Institute for the National Economy, 1990), 20.

[262] Author Interview, Viktor Korgun, October 15, 2012, Moscow, Russian Federation.

[263] Paul Robinson and Jay Dixon, *Aiding Afghanistan: A History of Soviet Assistance to a Developing Country* (London: Hurst, 2013), 60.

[264] Wakhidi, "Strukturnye preobrazovaniia," 20.

hair framed her dark-complexioned face on which only her eyes were seen. The impression was so staggering that I wanted to take a step back." The Pole attempted a few words in pidgin Persian, but the woman interrupted, suggesting they converse in English, French, or German. "Here in front of me," the Pole reflected, "sat a modern Afghan woman." What better proof of a functioning state was there?

But the river valleys that fed the cotton mills had a dark past, one that was more entangled with the Soviet Union than advisers would have liked to recall. Like the meadows of southern Afghanistan, these lands had a history as a Pashtun settler colony. The Soviet–Afghan border dated to the 1880s, when Anglo-Russian competition prompted the drawing of an "ethnographical frontier" that would "prevent the constant occurrence of the difficulties between neighbors which would inevitably result from the separation of populations of the same race."[265] British authors saw the 630-kilometer border as "only an arbitrary line based on the circumstances of the moment rather than on any permanent and natural basis" that could not "be expected to be permanent."[266] But the idea of an ethnic line proved more durable than the British expected. 'Abd al-Rahmān Khan began resettling Pashtuns into northwestern Afghanistan, displacing local Turkmen shepherds; when a Russian adventurer traveled the region in the early 1880s, he noted that Turkmen residents "approached me with a request about being taken up into Russian rule," fearing that "the Afghans would attack their families."[267] In 1885, Tsarist officials signed a decree ratifying "[the Turkmens'] wish [...] to be subjects of the White Tsar, in the hope of preserving their yurts and estates and freeing themselves from the cruelties of the Afghans."[268]

The terror frozen in these voices, now preserved in Turkmen state archives, reflected the violence unleashed once the frontier defined sovereign state space that 'Abd al-Rahmān Khan then dominated. Throughout the 1880s, 'Abd al-Rahmān sought to diminish his cousin, Ishaq Khan, sovereign over much of northern Afghanistan and a pretender to the throne.[269] When governorships opened up in Qandahar and Herat in 1881, 'Abd al-Rahmān denied them to Ishaq Khan's sons. Three years later, after 'Abd al-Rahmān's sack of the Uzbek Khanate of Meymana, he rejected Ishaq's claim to the territory. And when, in August 1888, Ishaq Khan declared himself Emir, 'Abd al-Rahmān dispatched an army to the north. Ishaq's forces dissolved upon false reports of defections, granting 'Abd al-Rahmān dominion over the region. 'Abd al-Rahmān, moreover, completed this conquest following victories against rival Ghilzai

[265] *Journal de St Petersburg*, February 26, 1885, quoted in *North Otago Times*, Tuesday, May 5, 1885, 3.

[266] C.E. Yate, *Northern Afghanistan, or Letters from the Afghan Boundary Commission* (Edinburgh and London, 1888), 178f.

[267] P.M. Lessar, *Iugo-Zapadnaia Turkmeniia (zemlia sarykov i salyrov)* (St. Petersburg, 1885), 45.

[268] "O priniatii v russkoe poddanstvo Pendinskikh sarykov 22 avg. 1885g. Proshenie ot imeni vsego naroda," *Tsentral'nyĭ gosudarstvennyĭ arkhiv Turkmenistana*, f.1, op.2, d.9661, l.2.

[269] Barfield, *Afghanistan*, 149.

Pashtuns, 18,000 families of whom he had deported from eastern Afghanistan to "reclaimed" lands in the north, creating an archipelago of Pashtun "winners" overlaying a base of non-Pashtun "losers."[270] A pattern was emerging. Under Amanullah, Afghan law formally bestowed upon the population of Kabul and of "governments to the east and south" the right to settle northern lands. The law promised fair compensation in the event of property disputes, but Pashtun settlers confiscated the lands up to the doorway of non-Pashtun peasants' homes, "compensating" them with barren lands miles away. Soon, the farmer's total property holdings were untenable as distributed. Pashtuns intimidated the farmer into selling his house at below-market rates, and then granted the house to settlers. Bitterness curdled in the hearts of the dispossessed who were driven off their fathers' land, deprived of legal recourse, and told: "You – you're an *Afghan*."[271]

At the same time, the emergence of the Soviet Union changed the meaning of the frontier. Moscow recognized Afghanistan's independence, but Amanullah gave refuge to anti-Bolshevik raiders expelled from the Emirate of Bukhara and the Khanate of Khiva. Only did the 1921 Soviet–Afghan Friendship Treaty firmly establish the border as a line of noninterference, though still recognizing Afghanistan's claim to "all of the lands in the frontier zone and which had belonged to Afghanistan in the past century."[272] The Treaty did not specify where, exactly, the "frontier zone" was, but it did leave open the possibility of ceding said territory to Afghanistan in the event of a popular referendum. Yet Soviet ethnographers had soon turned Bukhara and Khiva into cartographic whispers, as both were dissolved into an Uzbek SSR.

The birth pangs of a new Central Asia created a massive transnational refugee crisis. As Bolsheviks took power, Turkmen nomads fled into north-western Afghanistan. In the Tajik ASSR, 300,000 people (forty percent of the ASSR's population) fled to Afghanistan in two years.[273] Moscow, responding, granted land to Afghan illegal immigrants who had arrived in the Soviet Union, while also resettling "mountain Tajiks" from "rebellious" mountain regions to colonies abutting the Amu-Darya River.[274] From 1922 to 1933, Moscow resettled an additional 10,000 Soviet households to southern Tajikistan.[275]

---

[270] Khadiia Khashimbekov, *Uzbeki severnogo Afganistana* (Moscow: Institut vostokovedeniia, 1994), 10–11.

[271] Author Interview.

[272] "Ma'āhadeh-yi fimābin-i Afghānistān va Rus," February 21, 1921, in *Manāsabāt-i Afghānistān va Atahād-i Shuruvi Dar Sālhā-yi 1919–1969* (Kabul, 1969), 17.

[273] Tsentralnyĭ Gosudarstvennyĭ Arkhiv Respubliki Tadzhikistana (TsGA RT), f. 19 (Gosplan TASSR), op. 1, d. 307, "Voprosy pereseleniia," l. 105.

[274] Martin, *The Affirmative Action Empire: Nations and Nationalism in the Soviet Union, 1923–1939*, 832.

[275] Botakoz Kassymbekova, "Humans as Territory: Forced Resettlement and the Making of Soviet Tajikistan, 1920–1938." *Central Asian Survey* 30 (3–4), 357; "Otchët Uchreditel'nogo S"ezda KP(b) Tadzhikistana," RGASPI, f. 17, op. 28, d. 20, l. 119.

Bolshevik commissars marched "settlers" from their homes without food, and the resettlement sites lacked food, potable water, and shelter.[276] Highland populations became sick and died in the malarial lowlands. By 1932, another 300,000 people (a third of the Tajik SSR's remaining population) had become infected with malaria.[277] To contain the epidemic, Soviet medical specialists ran "medical points" in Mazar-i Sharif and Herat, part of a larger network stretching from Persia to Xinjiang.[278]

One Central Asian world was born; another was dying. After battling anti-Bolshevik *basmachi* based in the eastern reaches of the Tajik SSR, the Soviets deployed air power to drive the rebels into Afghanistan.[279] Yet the *basmachi* did not give in. A year after eastern Pashtuns overthrew Amanullah and replaced him with a figurehead bandit, Habibullah Kalakani, the *basmachi* commander Ibragim Bek launched a campaign based out of northern Afghanistan, devoted to the "overthrow of the Afghan regime and the formation of an independent Uzbek and Tajik state in the regions of Kattagan and Badakhshan."[280] Bek's armies fought Afghan government forces to an initial draw, but in early 1931, Kabul smashed Bek's armies and drove the rebel back into Tajikistan, where he was soon captured and killed.

Nationalized bodies and cottonseed soon overwhelmed the land. Under Zabuli, Kabul ordered the construction of a 10-kilometer-long canal in Qala-i Zal and divided the lands between local construction brigades and Pashtun settlers.[281] As cotton and sugar beet production expanded, another 600 Pashtun households were resettled to Baghlan.[282] Iranian sugar beets, Soviet cotton, German capital, and Pashtun bodies met in this workshop of capitalism and ethnic domination. Similar developments were apace in the Soviet Union. In Tajikistan, the Great Purges gave planners room to adopt more extreme resettlement measures.[283] If the first wave of resettlements had shifted "Tajiks" to "Uzbek" lowlands, a second wave of resettlements from 1936 to 1938 moved 4,623 households from *northern* Tajikistan and the Uzbek SSR, plus 200

[276] Kassymbekova, 358–359. For more on other Soviet deportations, see Norman Naimark, *Fires of Hatred: Ethnic Cleansing in Twentieth-Century Europe* (Cambridge, MA: Harvard University Press, 2001), 85–107.
[277] Hirsch, *Empire of Nations: Ethnographic Knowledge and the Making of the Soviet Union,* Chapter 6.
[278] GARF, f. A482 (Minzdrav RSFSR), op.31, d. 529 and 530. For other files on this project, see d. 531–7.
[279] William S. Ritter, "Revolt in the Mountains: Fuzail Maksum and the Occupation of Garm, Spring 1929," *Journal of Contemporary History* 25 (July 1990), 549.
[280] Quoted in Iu.V. Gankovskiĭ, "Ibragim-bek Lokaĭ (1889–1932)," *Aziia i Afrika segodnia* (1994), 60–3.
[281] Aleksandr Davydov, *Razvitiie kapitalisticheskikh otnosheniĭ v zemledelii Afganistana* (Moscow: Nauka, 1962), 68–9.
[282] Okimbekov, 130; Sh. Zaripov, *Proizvoditel'nye sily sel'skogo khoziaĭstva sovremennogo Afganistana* (1972), 111.
[283] TsGA RT, f.1, d. 986, l. 88–90, Untitled Speech, November 7, 1937.

Russian households, to the cotton belt.[284] Plans were more modest in 1937, when the Republican Ministry of the National Economy intended to resettle 2,000 households, but the pattern was the same.[285] Redefined in life as "Uzbeks" or "Russians," Soviet citizens arrived in the fens of the Amu-Darya to perish as "Tajiks."

In private, Soviet planners were frank about the catastrophe. Those lands abutting Afghanistan were well maintained, but the Potemkin border masked mass murder. Most settlers inhabited ruined "brick yurts" built before 1937; less than ten percent of households had passable dwellings.[286] Of 20,000 households resettled to the area since 1932, 11,070 abandoned their sites.[287] All the same, the last prewar resettlement plan envisioned a fourfold increase in the number of households to be resettled from northern Tajikistan and Gharm to the south.[288] Before war aborted these plans, Soviet power had resettled 61,000 *households* into southern Tajikistan.[289] At least a fifth of Tajikistan's 1939 population was a forced migrant. To the dispossessed south of the river, however, the resettlement projects *appeared* like a successful alternative modernity to that offered by the Kabuli state. Afghanistan's north and the Tajik SSR's south mirrored one another more than Kabul or Dushanbe would have admitted. Both represented crash projects to build Pashtun- and Tajik-dominated subunits of their respective countries, albeit often using outsiders' bodies to accomplish the somatic work of agro-industrial modernity.

Partition in South Asia only further accelerated the Afghan settler colonialist project. Having lost its "phantom limb" to the British Raj, Kabul seemed hellbent on stitching Uzbek and Tajik homelands to the trunk of a Pashtun state.[290] The 1921 Soviet–Afghan Friendship Treaty had tantalizingly reserved for Afghanistan the right to claim lands *north* of the Amu-Darya, but in a 1946 renegotiation of the Soviet–Afghan Friendship Treaty, Kabul ceded all claims to Soviet lands. The lack of fanfare with which Kabul symbolically signed away millions of Tajiks and Uzbeks to permanent Soviet domination contrasted with the hysteria it attached to "Pashtunistan." "Everyone in Afghanistan has a relative who lives beyond the borders of the country," reflected one Afghan Turkmen. "The difference was, we were cut off from ours."[291]

---

[284] TsGA RT, f. 18, op. 1, d. 1378, l. 90, "Spravka o vesennem pereselenii 1936 g. i osedanii pereselentsev v Vakhshoĭ doline Tadzhikskoĭ SSR, po sostoianiu na 15/IX-36g."

[285] TsGA RT, f. 18, op. 1, d. 1624, "Postanovlenie SNK TSSR, dokladnye zapiski i perepiska o pereselenii v vakhshkuiu dolinu," l. 48, "Ob utverzhdenii plana pereselenii v raĭony Vakhskoĭ doliny na 1937 god," (April 1937).

[286] TsGA RT, f.18, op.2, d. 10, l. 33, "Zakliuchenie Komissii Narkomzema SSSR po obosledovaniiu sostoianiia pereselencheskogo dela v Tadzhikskoĭ SSR." l. 36.

[287] Ibid., l. 34.

[288] Ibid., l. 71.

[289] TsGA RT, f. 18, op. 2, d.10 (Plan pereseleniia na 1940 god v Tadzhikskoĭ SSR), l.17, "Kartochka No. 1 – Pereseleniie."

[290] Barfield, *Afghanistan*, 48.

[291] Author Interview, January 2014. The person interviewed on this subject has requested to remain anonymous.

But no matter: Soviet gas and petroleum engineers soon arrived to transform the north, scouring the soil for something, anything, with which Kabul could pay back its arrears. The area had an abortive history of resource extraction. Shortly after establishing diplomatic relations with Washington, in November 1936, the Afghan government "granted her first concession to the American Inland Exploration Company (AIEC)" to prospect for oil.[292] AIEC, however, unilaterally canceled a contract in 1938, arguing that "the exploitation of these areas have been rendered uneconomic by the recent discovery of oil in important quantities on the Arabian mainland near the Persian Gulf coast."[293] For the time being, Afghan oil imports flowed from Western oil companies via the Subcontinent.[294] Interwar attempts at an oil deal with Moscow went nowhere: the costs were too high, Afghan oil too pure, and the Soviets' investment rights too uncertain. Moscow wanted guarantees that Kabul would never grant concessions to Washington, Berlin, or London.[295]

But the Cold War changed both sides' calculations; when Pakistan blockaded Afghanistan in 1950, Moscow offered oil prospecting services *gratis*. The fact that, by the mid 1960s, Soviet economists were harping on the need to redeem trade credits provided further reason to drill. A range of agreements turned the region into a drilling site, with funding contingent on the nonadmission of American oil experts.[296] By 1960, drillers hit pay dirt in Aq Shah.[297] The quest for oil took place alongside a gas hunt. Russian geologists had sought gas in northern Afghanistan since at least 1841, but after Kabul agreed in 1963 to future deliveries of natural gas, Moscow extended $39 million to fund exploration. Soon, Soviet geologists were probing the gas fields of Sheberghan, where discoveries permitted the construction of a gas pipeline to the Turkmen SSR.[298] A 1967 agreement foresaw 58 billion cubic meters of gas deliveries over the next two decades. (For comparison, a blockbuster 2014 gas deal between China and Russia was for 38 billion cubic meters over thirty years – a third as much "velocity.") In 1967, too, the pipeline connecting the fields with Turkmenistan opened. A gas extraction facility followed.[299] Moscow built a petroleum sciences technical college near Mazar-i Sharif, training Afghan cadre to run extraction

---

[292] Mohmand, "American Foreign Policy Toward Afghanistan: 1919–2001," 64.

[293] Wallace Murray, "Memorandum by the Chief of the Division of Near Eastern Affairs (Murray)," *Foreign Relations of the United States, Diplomatic Paper 1938/II* (Washington, 1955), 753.

[294] Arthur Jay Klinghoffer, *The Soviet Union & International Oil Politics* (New York: Columbia University Press, 1977), 234.

[295] Zābali, 35.

[296] B.A. Tkhostov, "Afganistan (O geologicheskom stroenii i perspektivakh neftenosnosti severnoĭ Afganistana. Zametki sovetskogo geologa)," *Geologiia nefti* 9 (1957), 61–4.

[297] Klinghoffer, 235.

[298] Tkhostov, B.A. "Afganistan," 61.

[299] "Spravka o pervoocherenykh ob"ektakh ekonomiki Afganistana trebuiushchikh vosstanovleniia ili rekonstruktsii v tseliakh obespecheniia pod"ema ekonomiki DRA," Personal Archive of Valeriĭ Ivanov.

facilities. Afghan gas helped Soviet enterprises, too, since it "entered a pipeline to gas-deficient areas of the Russian republic." Moscow froze oil prices for sales to Afghanistan at 1973 levels, and at a June 1974 summit Brezhnev and Daoud settled on gas prices far below world market rates.[300]

The discoveries must have relieved the GKES economists who wondered whether they would ever find something worth convertible currency in Afghanistan. But carbon in the north thickened domestic and international political economies differently than did water in the south. Gas allowed Kabul to shore up its state finances in a way it could not by channeling water. Pipelines became umbilical cords between states in a way not true for rivers, which had to be dammed and canalized in order to concentrate arable land and national energies inside the territory of the nation-state – and to destroy nomadic "shadow nations" in between them. Carbon may have provided breathing room on the Chicago-disciplined ledgers, but as any dung-burning Afghan could attest, the key link was between the Soviet and Afghan states, not between the Afghan state and nation. Water encouraged one to move and transport populations on the land; carbon, to trace numbers on a spreadsheet.

Soon, Soviet petroleum expertise reorganized oil and gas into the foundations of carbon socialism.[301] Soviet advisers and their Tajik translators moved into apartments in Mazar-i Sharif, where housing and consumer goods were superior to those in the USSR itself.[302] A complex near Sheberghan housed a swimming pool and frequent cultural events. Some were unplanned: in 1978, after several years of excavations, a joint Soviet–Afghan team of archaeologists discovered several thousand pieces of gold jewelry at Talā Tepheh ("Gold Hill"), the so-called "Bactrian Gold," thought to belong to ancient Scythians. Lead archaeologist Viktor Sarianidi invited Soviet advisers to the site to touch the treasure before the pieces were carted off to the Kabul Museum. Pleasures less innocent also abounded. Abdurrakim Samodov, a Tajik translator who worked in Mazar-i Sharif from 1974 to 1979, recalled that "some Soviet women–not all, I repeat, some–behaved themselves in a very uncultured way ... you can understand what I mean by that." Samodov, married, kept to his Afghan interlocutors, who ironically questioned him about Soviet marriage norms and Islam in the Soviet Union. Asked whether he considered Afghans "true" Muslims, Samodov replied: "Of course! How could they not be?" Yet Samodov's own reflections suggested how negotiated Soviet Muslimness was. "As a Tajik, of course I was a Muslim." Only in comparison to the Afghans did he feel "somehow, somewhere, an insufficient Muslim."

Small encounters like these remind us of the cultural and intellectual gulf that spanned lands once common. Central Asian SSRs like Tajikistan and Uzbekistan derived their legitimacy from not only the infrastructure that advisers like

---

[300] Klinghoffer, 234, 236.
[301] Mitchell, "Carbon Democracy," in *Economy and Society* 38(3) (August 2009), 401.
[302] Author Interview, Abdulrakim Samodov, Dushanbe, Tajikistan, July 19, 2012.

Samodov cloned abroad but also the "house of lies" regulating the study of indigenous history, literature, and religion.[303] Central Asian regimes enforced a forgetting of the pre-Soviet past clouded through Latinization, Cyrillicization, and purges. Postwar intellectuals wrote of how denizens of these "national republics" had become *manqurts* – people who had lost any sense of their past and hence ideal slaves. Said the Uzbek intellectual Shukrullo: "My family buried all of their books in cloth sacks in our fruit garden. When I wanted to unearth them in 1965, I found only decay and cried [...] In our generation a mental constitution arose whereby man was no longer supposed to feel any need to learn history. One was supposed to struggle to forget the entire past, religion and history together." This mentality helped maintain a psychic distance between Soviet Central Asia and Afghanistan wider than the river's breadth. Men like Samodov felt a residual sense of "Muslimness," albeit one clouded by a shame and inadequacy before "real" Muslims that hindered solidarity. The Amu-Darya, the "natural" border between amnesia and inadequacy, took on mythic significance. Mnemonic interventions enforced mental linkages between cities as distant as Termez and Moscow: one Soviet traveler's first impression upon reaching the southernmost city in Uzbekistan after an Afghan voyage was "the December sun [that] shines like in Moscow in summer."[304]

All the same, friendships forged a shared Soviet–Afghan world. While living in Mazar-i Sharif, Samodov befriended an Afghan film director and was invited to his home, where he met not only the director's wife but also all thirteen members of his family, all living under one roof. After a feast with them, Samodov felt compelled to invite the director and his wife to his home for dinner. He obtained permission from Soviet authorities, then, when the evening came, awaited the couple with his wife. The buzzer rang, but Samodov opened the door to *fifteen* people – the couple and the family – who had arrived at their shoebox-sized apartment. Samodov's wife slipped into the kitchen to stretch the meal; Samodov bought time. "In Mazar," he recalled, "there was a store there for Soviet citizens. You could get one bottle of spirits a month, and so even though I was not a great drinker, I got the bottle every month to save it up. [...] So by the time the director and his family came over, we had accumulated, let's say, several bottles of cognac. My wife made it work with the food, somehow, but meanwhile I invited them to drink. They refused at first, since they were Muslims. But I insisted: 'You are no longer on the territory of Afghanistan. In our apartment, you're on the territory of the Soviet Union. Have a drink!'" The guests relented: "even the young girls drank." But when Samodov's name reached the top of an apartment queue back home in the summer of 1978, "I had to decide: do I want an apartment or Afghanistan?" Prior to his departure,

303 Ingeborg Baldauf, Afterword to Shukrullo, *Die ohne Leichentuch Begrabenen* (translation of *Kafansiz ko'milganlar*), trans. Ingeborg Baldauf (Wiesbaden: Reichert Verlag, 2005), 178.
304 Nikolaï Tikhonov, "Vozvrashcheniie," *Oktiabr'* 1 (1957), 101.

his Afghan friends presented him with an Italian typewriter and an Afghan rug as parting gifts. Soviet customs guards fleeced Samodov of his rubles, but not of the material trinkets and memories gained in a border world.

Granted, the border world of carbon socialism was an intensely gendered one. The wives of Soviet builders often came as such – Stepford Soviets, not independent professionals. Soviet aid projects bound men and women into nuclear family units, shipped whither their husband's job called. In a world of workers, women came second.[305] Then again, there was no shortage of jobs that fulfilled all of the sooty, sweaty, and gendered stereotypes of the proletarian. A Soviet-constructed river port at Sherkhan never handled less than half of Afghanistan's overall trade, while in its peak years (1966–8) it handled more than seventy percent of Afghanistan's commerce.[306] A Soviet-built cement plant in Pul-i Khumri, the country's largest, put out 400 tons of cement a day starting in 1962.[307] Soviet machinery turned a coal mine in Karkar into the country's main source of coal.[308] The fertilizer plant built in Mazar-i Sharif tripled the efficiency of sugar beet cultivation.[309]

Such projects captured the essence of the Soviet project: industrial production forged mass politics and proletarian identity. Modernity meant the swelling of national space with industrial enterprises, most often ones associated with the concentration of labor around raw materials or the industrial sites to transform them. One Russian phrase used to describe Soviet developmental projects captured it all: the gasworks in Shehberghan, or the fertilizer plant in Mazar-i Sharif, were *vvedennye v ekspluatatsiiu promyshlennye ob"ekty*, "objects brought into exploitation." Development inscribed industrial objects into a national grid; once embedded, these "objects" could then "exploit" the natural world, rather than abetting capitalist exploitation. Production was everything, as Ezhov discovered: Antonov, the Ambassador beloved for his ability to secure fresh milk, was the Minister of Dairy and Meat Products not only before but also *after* his diplomatic assignment. There was no contradiction in transitioning from overseeing curd cheese production to diplomacy; democratizing the means of production and fighting the Cold War were the same arena for justice in which the Soviet Union existed. Industrial production, fueled by carbon combustion, fueled this Soviet project at home and in the Third World.

[305] Geoff Eley, *Making Democracy Social: A History of the Left in Europe* (Oxford: Oxford University Press, 2002), 23.

[306] E.R. Makmudov, *Transport sovremennogo Afghanistana. Nekotorye ekonomicheskie problemy* (Moscow: Nauka, 1983), 69.

[307] Okimbekov, 158. See also Georgiĭ Ezhov, "Razvitiie ekonomiki Afganistana v period pervogo piatiletnego plana (1956/7–1960/61)" (*Kandidat nauk* dissertation, Moscow State University, 1968), 216.

[308] Ibid., 165. See also Ezhov, "Razvitiie ekonomiki Afganistana v period pervogo piatiletnego plana (1956/7–1960/61)," 149.

[309] Okimbekov, "Problemy ekonomicheskogo i sotsial'nogo razvitiia severo-vostoka Afganistana," Table A.

Everywhere, the motivating images remained coal shafts, laboring masculine bodies, and sausage casings.

But industry drove imagination as much as ideology drove industry. Soviet development created a material world in which Afghans could imagine themselves as "proletarians." One Amanullah Ostowar, later a prominent Leftist, attended Kabul Polytechnic University before receiving further training at the Mazar-i Sharif fertilizer plant and further higher education in Romania.[310] What was his life if not a study in "proletarian internationalism"? The memoirs of the Hazara Communist Sultan, 'Ali Kishtmand furnish another example. In 1967, Kishtmand noted, "the leadership of the Party (Parchamists) executed a march composing more than 350 bodies of the workers and employees of the oil and gas processing facilities of the north who had been introduced to the victorious and epochal march. This action qualified as one of exceptional importance in the workers' movement of the country. The workers participating in the march came from Shiberghan to Mazar-i Sharif, then from Pul-i Khumri to the Salang Pass, over a distance of more than three hundred kilometers. They carried written placards, poems, and posters, among them the famous 'Chain-breaking Worker' poster. As the protesters went through the cities and through the populated areas, they explained their reasons and explained themselves along the protest route."[311] Here, seemingly, was the Soviet global project translated to the scale of the nation-state: industry created factory floor jobs, factory floor jobs forged class consciousness, and class consciousness motivated revolution.

The march continued: "We don't have any pressing needs [said the protesters]. Wherever we're wanted, we'll go." When authorities in Jowzjan tried to arrest marchers on charges of "instigation," they fought back, yelling "we *are* the true instigators. We're the ones with sunburns and hungry stomachs!" And yet Kishtmand's telling of the story revealed more about himself than the prospects for Afghan socialism: just as the march approached the Soviet-built Salang Tunnel, Soviet-trained officers halted the marchers with AK-47s and forced them to turn around. The Soviet global project had inspired many national equivalents to Kishtmand – Leftist parvenus who found inspiration in Moscow. But true working classes were few and far between. Despotic Third World leaders were skilled at hijacking military aid to fortify nonsocialist authoritarian regimes that killed workers. At a moment when the Left outside of the Eastern Bloc was shifting its revolutionary hopes away from the worker and to the peasant, or, failing that, the student, Third World Marxists like Kishtmand constituted only an alienated, deluded, isolated Left whose chances of seizing power through a Leninist coup seemed trivial.

[310] Khashimbekov, *Uzbeki severnogo Afganistana*, 35.
[311] Sultan 'Ali Kishtmand, *Yāddāshthā-yi siyāsi va ruydādhā-yi tārikhi: khāṭirāt-i shakhṣi bā burah'hā'i az tārikh-i siyāsi-i mu'āṣir-i Afghānistān* (Tehran: Najib-i Kabir, 2002), Vol. 1 & 2, 204–6.

Yet the combination of racial capitalism and Marxist–Leninist ideology was like putting flame to oil. As ultra-nationalists in the Khalq ("Masses") wing of the PDPA knew better than anyone, Kabul's deployment of the myth of Pashtun state domination had transformed the burden of colonial cartography into an asset. But such Pashtun chauvinists also knew better than anyone that none of Kabul's moves toward expansive civic identity in the 1960s – appointing a non-Pashtun as Prime Minister in 1963, making nods to minority linguistic communities in the 1964 Constitution, or introducing radio broadcasting in languages other than Persian or Pashto – were what genuine radical nationalists did.[312] The other wing of the Party, Parcham ("Banner"), was more realistic, representing as it did the Persian-speaking Kabuli intelligentsia. In the mid 1970s, for example, Parcham even proposed dividing Afghanistan into five autonomous administrative units as well as autonomous Nuristani, Hazara, and Baluch districts inside of other ethnicities' provinces.[313] But Khalq rejected the idea. Having reinterpreted the Musahibans' performance of Pashtun state domination as a desiradatum rather than as a means to channel imperial resources to Kabul, the Afghan Left had become the vector for a combination of socialism and eliminationist nationalism that would be ruinous anywhere, but especially so in agrarian, multiethnic Afghanistan.

Khalq's intransigence prompted non-Pashtun Leftists to form their own underground parties. In 1968, two PDPA leaders, Tahir Badakhshi, who hailed from Badakhshan, and Ghulam Dastagir Panjsheri, a Tajik from the Panjshir Valley, formed National Oppression, a Marxist–Leninist group that advocated for an "independent Turkestan" free of Pashtun domination.[314] Panjsheri, along with the aforementioned Amanullah Ostowar, later founded a new organization, the Group of Labor, that fused Marxist–Leninism with nationalism. The PDPA's Pashtun nationalism actually made it a counterrevolutionary organization, argued Panjsheri. The laborers among national minorities had to lead, since they were doubly alienated as proletarians and ethnic minorities. As a result, the Group remained miniscule: it had only 3,000 members, compared to 17,846 for the PDPA in August 1980.[315] Indeed, facts on the ground in the north suggested that "the process of mixing of ethnicities had begun long ago," but to revolutionaries, this was hardly an excuse to maintain an unjust

---

[312] Vladimir Basov, "Natsional'nyĭ vopros v politicheskoĭ bor'be v dorevoliutsionnom Afganistane," in V.V. Basov, *Natsional'noe i plemennoe v Afganistane. K ponimaniiu nevoennykh istokov afganskogo krizisa,* ed. V.B. Kravtsov (Moscow: Nauchno-issledovatel'skiĭ tsentr FSKN Rossii, 2011), 56; 1964 Constitution of Afghanistan, Article 1; Edward Allworth, Handwritten Note, "Afghanistan. Manuscripts and Notes" Folder, Edward Allworth Papers, New York Public Library. The same folder contains a fascinating interview with the Afghan–Uzbek author Faizullah Aymoq on the state of Afghan Uzbek literature. See: "Robert Barret-Faĭzulla Aĭmokdan olgan interviusi" (August 25, 1976).

[313] Ibid., 62–3.

[314] Ibid., 64.

[315] Basov, 67, 146.

system.[316] To these rebels, everything seemed to be building toward a crisis point: in the mid 1970s, Daoud flirted with the idea of redirecting the waters of the Kunduz River to feed a massive 300-kilometer-long canal parallel to the Amu-Darya River that would water a northern tier of Pashtun latifundia along the Afghan–Soviet frontier.[317] As Georgiĭ Ezhov recalled, "by the 1970s, it appeared that some critical moment was approaching for the country – we just didn't know what, precisely, was the problem."[318]

Ezhov's background blinded him to the answer: Soviet aid both facilitated Pashtun settler colonialism and anchored radical opposition to the same project. Maximally decontextualized and transformed into rubles on balance sheets, fossilized algae and zooplankton sacrificed themselves as oil to finance debts accrued from earlier Soviet infrastructure development. Yet the violent transformation of the lands north of the Amu-Darya supplied new imaginaries of opposition to the Afghan Left. Admiration fused with confusion and confusion with despair, as members of the Soviet-sponsored Left dreamed of a national future modeled after the USSR. When a normally taciturn Babrak Karmal, arrived at Georgiĭ Ezhov's Kabul villa in the early 1960s, he opened up. "Karmal loved to drink," Ezhov recalled. "He would even take several drinks without snacks in between. After two, say, three, glasses, he would be totally forthright. He'd plead: 'Why not take on Afghanistan as a sixteenth republic? The Afghan Soviet Socialist Republic.'" "Sorry," Ezhov replied, "we already have enough." As Ezhov explained, "if you had wanted to carry out revolution in a country with a population that was 99 percent illiterate, 99 percent peasants, well, then, perhaps Maoism, perhaps. But socialism? To stage a socialist revolution without people knowing the principles of socialism, this is not going to work. And when they did attempt to do this, of course, everything was done childishly."

And yet how could the Soviet example not have impressed? Leninist nationalities policy had averted internecine warfare of the kind that devastated Katanga, Biafra, East Pakistan, and East Timor. In a world dogged by rapacious multinational corporations, Moscow built capital-intensive infrastructure and donated it to the state. And the energy industry in both the Soviet Union and Afghanistan seemed to have dodged the challenges that dogged other energy-producing regions around the world. In capitalist economies, the shift to more mobile, capital-intensive forms of energy extraction such as oil threatened "carbon democracy."[319] But carbon had provided a new lease on life for the petri dishes of socialism. Carbon fueled new grain elevators, mills, bread factories: stops in the social contract of cradle-to-grave industrial employment.[320]

---

[316] Ibid., 75.
[317] Author Interview, January 2014. The person interviewed on this subject has requested to remain anonymous.
[318] Author Interview, Georgiĭ Ezhov, Moscow, Russian Federation, April 15, 2013.
[319] Mitchell, "Carbon Democracy," 408.
[320] "Spravka o pervoocherenykh ob"ektakh ekonomiki Afganistana trebuiushchikh vosstanovleniia ili rekonstruktsii v tseliakh obespecheniia pod"ema ekonomiki DRA."

Carbon supplied Kabul with more than a third of state revenues. Shifts in energy may have betrayed British coal miners, but carbon had made a shared world of real existing workers, machines, and industry.

Yet this methane civilization rested on several unwinding assumptions about the marriage between socialism and carbon extraction. Several of them appeared particularly fragile nowhere else than the Soviet Union itself. There, Baku, the original home of the Russian oil industry, Groznyĭ, in Chechnya, 300 miles north, or Maĭkop, near the Black Sea, had provided a powerful set of images for what Afghanistan could become. Yet such cities were actually in decline. In Baku, "even in 1966, the postwar peak, Azerbaijani oil output was unable to equal the 22.2 million tons pumped in 1940."[321] In the Volga-Urals fields, production declined after the mid 1960s.[322] Only the discovery of "super-giant" fields in western Siberia allowed Soviet oil production to continue growing. By the 1970s, Siberian drilling in Tiumen', Nizhnevartovsk, and Tarko-Sale, not the shores of the Caspian or the Volga, represented the future of carbon socialism.[323]

Such shifts threatened the Soviet social contract. The fields in western Siberia still employed 200,000 souls by 1983, but the workplace had changed.[324] In the mid 1970s, the so-called "expedition method," whereby a drilling crew would be flown in from outside of Siberia for two weeks to operate, became popular in Tiumen'. By the mid 1980s, it "accounted for forty percent of all drilling and twenty-five percent of well repairs and maintenance."[325] Yet this system rested upon an idea of labor as a variable expense that could be shifted thousands of miles to follow capital, not a fixed expense tied to specific sites. Tellingly, when gas workers at a giant field attempted to resettle their wives and children there from a nearby town, Party officials forcibly resettled them back.[326]

Shifts in production, as Marxists understood, forged shifts in mentalities. Early Western observers of the coal industry had noted how "the very geography of the working places inside a mine" fostered social democratic sentiments among miners.[327] Residents of Siberia understood this better than anyone: they rebelled against the use of "expedition method" in their home districts. "Human values cannot always be translated into the language of economic categories," argued the First Party Secretary of the Yamal-Nenets District

[321] Marshall L. Goldman, *The Enigma of Soviet Petroleum: Half-Full or Half-Empty?* (London: George Allen & Unwin, 1980), 34.

[322] Ibid., 34; Robert W. Campbell, *Trends in the Soviet Oil and Gas Industry* (Baltimore: Johns Hopkins University Press, 1976), 27.

[323] M.M Brenner, *Ekonomika geologorazvedochnykh rabot na neft' i gaz v SSSR* (Moscow: Nedra, 1979), 90.

[324] Alekseĭ Khaĭtun, *Ekspeditsionno–vakhtovoe stroitel'stvo v Zapadnoĭ Sibiri* (Leningrad: Stroĭizdat, 1982), 22.

[325] Iu. Belanov and V. Kremer, "Trudnaia neft'," *Sotsialisticheskaia industriia*, August 7, 1985.

[326] Thane Gustafson, *Crisis Amid Plenty: The Politics of Soviet Energy Under Brezhnev and Gorbachev* (Princeton: Princeton University Press, 1989), 176.

[327] Carter Goodrich, *The Miner's Freedom: A Study of the Working Life in a Changing Industry* (Boston: Marshall Jones & Co., 1925), 19; Mitchell, "Carbon Democracy," 404.

in an interview with *Pravda*.[328] "The temporary worker often has a mentality that is alien to society, a consumer-minded approach to the job, and a plundering attitude toward nature." He may have been right, but such local communities struggled to articulate how Moscow could justify massive outlays into sedentary carbon communities at a time when the savings of the "expedition method" and a shift toward conservation in Soviet energy policy pushed against him.

The resources, it appeared, through which one imagined an Afghan state mattered greatly for the concepts and categories one used. Water led one to think in terms of population densities and local political economies. Water, sunlight, and topsoil could be transformed into calories that could sustain and anchor a sedentary population. Energy-dense but inedible oil and gas invited one to transform trapped sunlight into the joules that could power industrial transformation and proletarian consciousness. Worker's consciousness may have been illusory, even dangerous, but to Soviet economists it meant security. Transformed into gas and oil and packed into Soviet-built pipelines, carbon could become the rubles over which GKES economists had fretted so. Gas and oil, moreover, unambiguously belonged to the Afghan nation-state. No one seriously contended that the waters of the Helmand or the gas beneath Sheberghan belonged to others. In both cases, however, particularly national dreams of homesteading or socialist development intersected catastrophically with the capacities of the Afghan state, generating contradictions that more developmental aid was unlikely to resolve.

But perhaps wood was different. Perhaps the cedar forests of Paktia Province, eagerly felled by loggers and transported to Pakistan, were different. Given Paktia's location along the Durand Line and its broader symbolism for the transborder exchanges that had hindered an Afghan national market for centuries, it represented a dramatic test for the developmental imagination. But perhaps a different approach was needed, too. Americans and Soviets had struggled alike to translate global projects to the scale of the nation-state, but perhaps that merely reflected the arrogance of superpower social science. Perhaps a more modest partner – the West Germans, for example – could deliver where the Soviets and Americans had not. Not only had West German teams been present in Kabul for nearly as long as the Soviets; more than that, the Germans were known for their long tradition of forest management. Could West German foresters bring their expertise to bear on the wild woods of Paktia? Could the national economy triumph in a transnational Pashtun frontier?

Wood: West German Forestry in Paktia

However much a closer look at Soviet projects in the north revealed chinks in the armor, Moscow's "aid offensive" looked impressive to contemporaries. Helmand was a white elephant, and while Bonn had provided twenty-four million

---

[328] K. Mironov, "U istokov gazovykh rek," *Pravda*, April 17, 1981.

dollars of aid by 1970, Afghanistan's thirst was unslakable. Beyond the twenty-four million dollars in disbursed aid, Afghans had submitted a "wish list" for fifty-six million dollars' worth of additional projects. Paying the bill might have been justified if it meant privileged political access in Kabul, but with Soviet dams around seemingly every river bend, Moscow seemed prepared to build projects on a scale that West Germany could not justify matching. Indeed, given Afghanistan's location, there was little obvious strategic rationale for Bonn to outspend the Soviets.

But perhaps small was beautiful. Perhaps if Bonn focused more on provincial development, it could prove the West to be more than the equal of the Soviets.[329] So, at least, argued Bob Nathan to lead German adviser Kurt Hendrikson in the fall of 1961.[330] Hendrikson soon contacted Klaus Lampe, a development coordinator in Bonn, who assembled a team of agronomists, civil engineers, husbandry experts, road engineers, and architects.[331] Five years of feasibility studies followed: where to station a regional development project? The Germans were hardly alone: the United Nations had implemented an implausible wine-growing program for peasants in Parwan Province. The Asian Development Bank and Paris were at work on projects in Kunduz and Baghlan Provinces. The World Bank and the UN ran a joint project in Kunar; the People's Republic of China ran another one in Parwan Province. Provincial, it seemed, was beautiful.

Initial studies suggested Paktia Province in eastern Afghanistan as a suitable test site. The region's ecology was unique, as Paktia contained some of the country's few forests. One German forester explained: "The natural forests of Afghanistan are, owing to the extremely dry climate, restricted to the Safid Kuh range of the Hindu Kush that separates Afghanistan from Pakistan and remains influenced by the Indian monsoon climate. There, in an altitude range of between 1,800 and 3,200 meters that is still nonetheless dominated by strips of rock and scree, are mixed reserves of some 80% Himalayan cedar and spruce, fir and pine."[332] Locals prized Himalayan cedar (*Cedrus deodara*) in particular, but, continued the forest expert, "the province is especially difficult, since its freedom-loving population possesses political privileges and has closed itself off long ago against all foreign influence. [...] All of the woodlands are owned

329 Christoph Häselbarth, "Ein Landwirtschafts- und Provinzentwicklungsprogramm in Afghanistan unter Leitung von Dr. Wakil, Minister ohne Portfolio im Kgl. Afghanischen Premierministerium" (January 24, 1972), B213/2797, Bundesarchiv Koblenz.

330 Author Interview, Christoph Häselbarth, Strittmatt, Germany, April 14, 2012. West German Embassy Kabul, "Wirtschaftliche Entwicklung der Provinz Paktia" (October 17, 1964), in AV Neues Amt 1.871 (Paktia [allgemein] auch Koordinierungsausschuss B), PA/AA.

331 Author Interview, Christoph Häselbarth, Strittmatt, Germany, April 14, 2012. West German Embassy Kabul, "Wirtschaftliche Entwicklung der Provinz Paktia" (October 17, 1964), in AV Neues Amt 1.871 (Paktia [allgemein] auch Koordinierungsausschuss B), PA/AA.

332 Thomas Voll, "Die forst- und holzwirtschaftliche Hilfe für Afghanistan," *Holz-Zentralblatt* 86 (1969), Fifth Folder: "Heft 15. Vom 23.6.1970," B213/2838, Bundesarchiv Koblenz.

by extended families and tribes. The formula for allocating forests is incredibly muddled and complicated and often leads to bloody arguments." This would have been an academic issue had Paktia lain five hundred miles to the west, but the fact that the Durand Line intersected the Safid Kuh range and the fact that the markets for these trees lay in Pakistan made Paktia a vital front in the quest for the national economy. Locals ignored the border as they engaged in the wood trade. Men felled trees, saddled the logs onto mules, and shipped the wood to Pakistani sawmills and markets. "Since a few years ago," explained one forester, "a high price has been paid for cedar wood in the neighboring 'forest-poor' but more industrially developed regions of Pakistan. This has led to massive deforestations and to the desertification of many high-altitude forests. Trees are felled exclusively with the ax, prepared as timber with significant waste, and brought across the border in long camel caravans."[333] Locals' engagement with Pakistani markets threatened to destroy Paktia's woods. "The demand on the Afghan wood market is low, in light of the modest home-building culture. In contrast, exports to Pakistan are constantly increasing." By 1968, upward of a thousand camels, each carrying one cubic meter of timber, crossed the border daily.[334] One report estimated that the timber industry provided livelihoods for 200,000 people and $2.5 million in revenues.[335] Yet "with such exploitation apace," went the German analysis, "we can count on the annihilation of the remaining 35,000 hectares of woodlands in the foreseeable future. At the same time, the population density, and, with it, the need for firewood and pasture is increasing."[336] All these factors combined threatened a desertification of the region.

These economic facts posed political questions. As a 1963 report from the West German Embassy in Kabul noted, Afghanistan had long demanded the "release" of Pashtun territories "for the to-be-founded new state of Pashtunistan." The Embassy was skeptical, but added that "it would be unfortunate for Afghanistan to turn this already questionable demand into something worthy of ridicule if it turned out that Afghanistan cannot administer and develop its own Pashtun territories." In short, concluded the report, "the Paktia problem is no fashionable idea of a few politicians, as is so often the case in developing countries, but rather a political and economic problem of great importance

---

[333] Ibid.
[334] For longer-term echoes, consider Shah Mahmoud Hanifi, "Comparing Camels in Afghanistan and Australia: Industry and Nationalism During the Long Nineteenth Century," in *Camel Cultures: Historical Traditions, Present Threats, and Future Prospects*, ed. Ed Emery (London: SOAS, 2013).
[335] West Germany Embassy Kabul, "Entwicklungspläne der afghanischen Regierung in der Provinz Paktia" (July 17, 1963), 3, AV Neues Amt 1.871 (Paktia [allgemein] auch Koordinierungsausschuss B), PA/AA.
[336] Thomas Voll, "Die forst- und holzwirtschaftliche Hilfe für Afghanistan," *Holz-Zentralblatt* 86 (1969), Fifth Folder: "Heft 15. Vom 23.6.1970," B213/2838, Bundesarchiv Koblenz.

whose management justifies the deployment of considerable resources."[337] The Afghans had, moreover, directly asked Bonn to direct the rural development plan for the region.[338] Bonn had to step in, not only to maintain its own prestige, but also to respond to Polish and Yugoslav commitments ($18 million) in Paktia.

Once more, the Cold War and the idea of "Pashtunistan" were conspiring together. Eastern Bloc aid triggered a panic that Kabul's reframing of the Durand Line only amplified. Suddenly, rather than asking why they needed to be in Paktia in the first place, Germans were neatly supporting the politics of "Pashtunistan." A familiar pattern repeated itself. Afghanistan, the Germans' interlocutors explained, was a Pashtun-dominated state, which was why it sought to help "its" Pashtuns. But Afghanistan was also a failed state under threat of destruction from Pashtuns. Afghan interlocutors once again conjured forth the ghosts of 1929 to unify two intellectually contradictory, but practically constitutive, claims. Without scientific management of the forests, Paktia would become a "moonscape." Unemployed foresters and goat shepherds would launch a "hunger march of a half million Pashtun warriors on Kabul," a nightmare that had to be "intercepted."[339] Genuine Mohammadzai angst toward "wild" Ghilzai Pashtuns and conscious projection of these fears onto foreigners justified more money, more expertise. Kabul had to reconfigure the entire economy of a region on the verge of ecological collapse, even while knowing that neither markets nor nature justified optimism. It had to destroy a real existing Pashtun world to save the dream of another.

Soon, ideas of territorial economic space and German "sustainability" arrived in Paktia. In 1964, Kabul created a Paktia Development Authority, analogous to HVA in the south. That autumn, a fact-finding mission arrived; two years later, the first teams of agricultural and forest advisers settled into Khost, the provincial capital.[340] Most were involved in the Agricultural Project, a program that ran from 1966 to 1972 and the centerpiece of what became known as the Paktia Project.[341] Employing several hundred German experts, and over 10,000 Afghans as part-time workers, the Agricultural Project constructed irrigation canals, attempted to halt erosion, and introduced new agricultural techniques. In some model fields, experts set up test plots to establish which combinations of fertilizers and seeds produced the greatest yields. Courses in Khost "introduced" farmers to water pumps, tractors, and Western fertilizers. "In the far-flung province of Paktia," German newspapers bragged,

337 Ibid., 4.
338 Ibid., 2.
339 Ibid., 3.
340 The specialists included Eduard Mückenhausen, a specialist in pedology, Heinz Angerer, an irrigation specialist, and others. "Wirtschaftliche Entwicklung der Provinz Paktia," (October 17, 1964), in AV Neues Amt 1.871 (Paktia [allgemein] auch Koordinierungsausschuss B), PA/AA.
341 Author Interview, Christoph Häselbarth, Strittmatt, Germany, April 14, 2012. See also Nathan's discussion of the project in RRNP, July 28, 1971.

FIGURE 5. Development on exhibition. English- and Pashto-language signage greets visitors to an exhibition of the Paktia Development Authority, late 1960s.
Source: Courtesy of Christoph Häselbarth.

"there will soon be no money in being a medicine man. A fifteen-head German development group has begun systematic research of the region, and already today the local population prefers to go to the German doctor when they are ill. The old medicine woman will, along with her quaint amulet, roots, and animal bones, soon be only a relict of a lost era."[342]

Once again, Afghanistan had been entangled in global regimes of expertise. In 1970, Christoph Häselbarth, the lead German adviser, was invited to the University of the Negev in Beersheba, Israel, to learn afforestation techniques from Israeli experts. Häselbarth brought his new expertise back to Paktia, where, in the wake of droughts and overburdened traditional water management systems, he instituted a Food-for-Forests program. The Germans paid Afghans rations to set up plots of 225–400 square meters per tree and hand-dig small canals leading to wells in which they could plant saplings. During rainstorms or floods, water flowed through the rivulets into the wells, which themselves were filled with soil and stones to stabilize the specimens. The trees grew, and one or two years later, teams replanted the trees elsewhere. "If you look at Paktia today," said Häselbarth, "or most of Afghanistan for that matter, it looks like a

[342] *Frankfurter Allgemeine Zeitung*, April 27, 1968.

giant desert – basically, what Israel looked like in the Sixties. But within a year or two, it had become really quite green."[343]

Yet Häselbarth's comments overlooked the political mission that often informed afforestation. His reflections on Afghanistan and Israel obscured the morally ambiguous role that forests played in the post-1948 "redevelopment" of Palestine. The Jewish National Fund planted large forests over the ruins of Palestinian villages whose population had been expelled into Transjordan. Israeli institutions devised Hebrew place names for bulldozed sites. One 1963 short story by Israeli author A.B. Yehoshua captures the moral dilemma. On the last day of a young Israeli scout's assignment to watch a pine forest, an old Arab man burns down the forest, revealing a ruined Palestinian village "in its basic outlines as an abstract drawing, as all things past and buried."[344] Yehoshua was capturing a point not specific to Israel. Because trees were green, part of "the environment," it was all the more difficult to view these evergreen conifers as instruments of political ecology.

It would not be the only moment of political blindness. "You have no idea how long this all took," said Häselbarth, reviewing photographs of Pashtun farmers sitting in a circle. "We'd make a suggestion for anything – to build a school, to introduce a new kind of pepper or corn or any sort of vegetable, and they'd react very skeptically at first. Then they'd go off in their circles, sit and discuss it, often for hours on end while we just stood there. Finally, they'd come over and let us know, and often it would work out fine." Häselbarth gestured at photographs of locals posing with enormous vegetables. Being *volksnah* ("close to the people") involved risks. "We once tried to introduce a new species of corn," he noted, pointing to a photograph of two cornstalks, one much taller than the other. "It was imported from somewhere, Mexico or North America, I think. But at first they said they didn't want it. They made up excuses, said they had no need for more maize even though there were clearly problems with hunger." Häselbarth observed that the mere guarding of a semi-public good (cedar trees in a forest, or unfenced plots) made it more valuable in locals' eyes. He asked his Afghan colleagues to post a guard to be posted around the maize. "From there," explained Häselbarth, "it was simple to convince them to use the new corn. The mere fact of something being constantly robbed, or the threat that it would be stolen, made it more valuable."[345]

This intuition jived with others about the criminal nature of Pashtun farmers. "Every day in Khost," Häselbarth explained, "there were dozens of cases of blood revenge or disputes. Ninety-nine percent of them had to do with two things: water and land." But because West Germans "were viewed as

[343] Author Interview, Christoph Häselbarth, Strittmatt, Germany, April 14, 2012.

[344] A.B. Yehoshua, "Facing the Forests" (1962), in *Three Days and a Child* (New York: Doubleday & Company, 1970), 170.

[345] Author Interview, Christoph Häselbarth, Strittmatt, Germany, April 14, 2012.

nonpartisan observers to these conflicts, and because they thought we knew what we were talking about with land and water, tribal chiefs and affected parties often came to our offices in Khost to give us the details of a case and ask what we thought should be done in that case or the other." Some advisers went too far: particularly around 1968, Häselbarth recalled, "we received several [German] students who would talk constantly about how society had to be completely overthrown and rebuilt from the start. Most of those people didn't last too long in Paktia."

Yet Häselbarth's juxtaposition of technocracy with student radicalism glossed over the ambitions of the Agricultural Project. However, out-of-touch student activists sent to Paktia may have been, they had at least the virtue of presenting themselves as political beings, as part of an "extraparliamentary opposition" prepared to make public political and moral demands of the Federal Republic even if it shut them out of mainstream institutions. The most eloquent of radicals insisted on a respect for *existing* institutions and framed reform as a "long march through the institutions." "Permanent revolutionaries" ironically had to remain both political and democratic: credentialed, technocratic, but nondemocratic expertise played little role in their worldview. No wonder Häselbarth was so dismissive. If students were obsessed with the political, the guiding ethos of the Agricultural Project was to reframe politics (the stakes so visible in the long debates that *jirgahs* held) as economics. Politics was boring, exhausting, irrelevant: the *jirgahs* took place for hours "while we [experts] just stood there." When Häselbarth described the suggestions he made to local elders about new crops, his syntax revealed his conceptual universe. Villagers were the objects, not the subjects, of economies.

Foresters' interventions into the region's cedar stock proved no less fraught. In 1963, Kabul requested a study of Paktia's forests.[346] Two years later, German experts set up a "demonstration forest" in Mandaher in northeast Paktia. Teams took a complete inventory of the forest, trailblazed 20 kilometers of paths, and established a nursery housing native tree species and "specimens from the German stock of seed and plants." A forestry school, sawmill, and workshop for wood processing joined these institutions in 1968, allowing Mandaher to host hundreds of volunteer workers and Afghan civil servants during summer camps. Select Afghan Army officers and graduates of a local technical college received the chance to study forestry in West Germany, too. Yet mapping Paktia's forests only revealed how knotty the situation was. In May 1969, the Governor of Paktia Province lent the German team a helicopter to conduct an aerial survey of the entire Province. "The results," wrote the lead German forester to the Afghan Ministry of Planning, "are hopeless and crushing. Besides the state forest in Mandaher, which, from a bird's-eye view, looks like a forest oasis in the middle of the cut-down reserves, and a few scattered smaller remainders, from the point of view of forest management, all of

---

[346] Voll, "Die forst- und holzwirtschaftliche Hilfe für Afghanistan."

the other wooded surfaces of the province are exploited and annihilated."[347] The major forested areas of Paktia – Jaji, Mangal, Chadran, and Charuti – were totally depleted.[348] The conclusion was bleak: "the substance of Paktia's forests is reduced. The protective function of the forest for the soil and water is destroyed in large areas. Any further use of the region's woods as usual will mean eventual desertification."[349]

Kabul had, the experts suggested, to take radical action: it had to impose a total ban on logging for the four forest areas, with the exception of Mandaher, which could be "used sustainably (*nachhaltig*) according to the economic plan of the German Forest Group." It had to ban tribes from using the forest areas as pasture for their animals. It had to ban the export of wood to Pakistan. And it had to construct two sawmills in Paktia to cut wood more efficiently for domestic use. Unless the tribes delivered themselves unto the national economy, they had no future.

But on-the-ground surveys provided little ground for optimism. In October and November 1969, the Forest Group conducted a comprehensive survey of the state of the forests that made clear their precarious fate. Only three percent of Paktia's woods could be classified as areas that "could be directly transferred to a sustainable economy."[350] Two-thirds of the region's surface area might be restored to a sustainable state via triage, but the rest was destined to permanent decline. Outside of the government forest in Mandaher and in Waziri District (where threats of kidnapping deterred surveyors), Jaji District had the greatest percentage (55.6 percent) of forests that could be sustainably harvested or restored to a sustainable condition. Most old-growth cedar forests, meanwhile, were concentrated far away from the Pakistani border. But how? In the early 1960s, Kabul attempted to resettle the Lewani Pashtuns to the Gardez Valley, guaranteeing them land rights. But "the confrontation between the government and the members of the tribe about specific ownership rights and claims led overwhelmingly to demonstrative and wild logging operations, and the King soon ceased his efforts."[351] The myth of 1929 – an overzealous Afghan state prompting revolution from tribes in the east – loomed darkly. Kabul would proceed slowly.

The more fundamental problem, unspoken but ubiquitous, was social science itself. It was the idea of the territorial state as the basic unit of analysis. German foresters admitted that no one who lived alongside the Durand Line

[347] "Waldinventur der Provinz Paktia" (May 26, 1969), Fourth Folder: "Afghanistan – Heft 14," B213/2838, Bundesarchiv Koblenz.
[348] "Waldverwustung in Paktia/Afghanistan" (February 22, 1969), Fourth Folder: "Afghanistan– Heft 14," B213/2838, Bundesarchiv Koblenz.
[349] Ibid., 8.
[350] "Waldinventur der Provinz Paktia/Waldinventur" (January 1, 1970), B213/2838, Bundesarchiv Koblenz.
[351] "Die künftige Konzeption des Forstprojektes in Paktia/Afghanistan" (January 19, 1968), First Folder: "Afghanistan/Abkommen u. IRA-Vorlagen," B213/2838 Bundesarchiv Koblenz.

recognized it as a meaningful boundary; the Pashtun loggers whom they sought
to educate participated in larger markets centered around Karachi. Desertification was real, but understanding Paktia's forests demanded crossing a frontier epistemological as much as real. It demanded understanding how tribes in
Jaji or Mandral, for instance, interacted with merchants and sawmills in the
Pakistani Federally Administered Tribal Areas (FATA), the Northwest Frontier
Province, or points further south along the road to Karachi. Yet conducting
such transnational economic analysis was analytically impossible through the
lens of the national economy. It was hardly surprising, then, that instead of
seeing Paktia through the ambiguous border line so common on Afghan maps
of the period, they saw it through the thick, bold, constricting lines of borders
demanded by the national economy.

Paktia became an analytical "negative space" that drained resources from
Kabul, defined in terms of what it was not, rather than what it was.[352] German
foresters understood the transnational market interactions that defined Paktia,
but insisted that they could corral and reshape "irrational" human geographies
if only they explained themselves more clearly. As the German team argued
in response to criticism, Paktia was a long-term project.[353] "In the field of
forestry," wrote one forester, "in contrast to agriculture, visible successes can
only be awaited in the longer-term time span. The fact that centuries-long customs aren't given up in the space of a few years shouldn't surprise anyone
who comes from an industrial country and gets to know all of the traits of
a just-developing country: the coexistence or counterexistence of tribes with
their socioeconomic structures; their property relations which cannot be overlooked; their occasional tribal feuds; their taboos; their extensive and partly
nomadic forms of using the land; their way of thinking focused only on their
immediate needs."[354]

The Forest Group's inventory of Paktia's forests suggested, however, that
the team was interested less in understanding, and more in rereading, territory
in ways that erased alternative narratives. Moral or transnational economies
that did not conform to visions of an Afghan "national economy" simply had
to adapt. Understanding the woods of Paktia demanded reconceptualizing the
province in terms not of its social reality but rather in terms of the "natural"
structure of the economy as suggested by its physical geography. "Since describing the region in terms of tribal territories would not yield any sensible solution," noted the inventory's preface, "[our report conceptually] combines the
valley systems and regions whose flow of wood exports is forced into a common
direction by geographical particularities."[355] Human geographies were simply

352 Timothy Mitchell, *Rule of Experts: Egypt, Techno-Politics, Modernity* (Berkeley: University of
     California Press, 2002), 245.
353 Harry Hamm, "Pachtia in Afghanistan," *Frankfurter Allgemeine Zeitung*, January 24, 1970.
354 Herr von Hegel, "Forstwirtschaftliche Entwicklung in Paktia/Afghanistan," 2, B213/2838,
     Bundesarchiv Koblenz.
355 "Waldinventur der Provinz Paktia/Waldinventur" (January 1, 1970) 2, B213/2838 Bunde-
     sarchiv Koblenz.

written out of the group's report as "irrational." The Forest Group recognized that its concept of "natural" flows of wood to Afghan markets as determined by physical geography had no basis in reality. In their response to the newspaper article, however, representatives from Bonn argued that if the tribes could just think beyond an eternal present, they would see the Forest Group's "natural" geography. Still, "in light of [the tribes'] need to get all they can out of the woods as long as the reserves are there, and to use a momentary chance at gain until nothing is left, convincing them to think in terms of the tomorrow is rather difficult."[356]

The foresters never seemed to want to learn about the places they sought to transform. Their successes were limited. They halted exports of processed two-by-fours across select border locations, but this was meaningless across a "border" that did not really exist on the ground. As the borderlands demonstrated more vividly than anywhere else, Afghanistan was a space of economic flows, not an autarkic nation-state. Any clarity that the Durand Line lent to analyses of a "national economy" was illusory. The imposition of a territorial state order had forced Afghanistan into a bind. The old fiscal-administrative model of Afghanistan as a space of exchange no longer worked. Élites had imported experts who thought of the state as a territorially enclosed economic space. But neither the Afghan government, nor the Germans, could convince Afghans to think in terms of "natural" timber flows, a "rational" tomorrow, or a "national" market to which they had to contribute. Social science vision could talk, argue, and produce reports, but it could not see.

The Germans had grown skeptical about Paktia. One diplomat who visited the province admitted that the Paktia Project had failed. The foresters' geographical models made no sense: "Just as Paktia as a whole is separated from the rest of Afghanistan by tall mountains, several individual parts of the province are separated from one another by mountain chains. The Khost basin and the Chamkani Valley have their natural foreign markets in Pakistan."[357] Yet the diplomat quickly underscored that the failure was not theirs: "A more suitable region could have been found for regional development when the years-long planning process was undertaken." When Kurt Hendrikson spoke later that year with the Afghan Minister of Planning, he was told that a ban on wood exports was impossible. "The tribes are powerful, and the state administration is corrupt," succinctly explained the Minister.[358] A byzantine attempt to create a public–private corporation (with the central Kabuli government having a majority share) that would own all of Paktia's woods and pay the tribes dividends in exchange for severe restrictions on logging went nowhere.

---

[356] Voll, "Die forst- und holzwirtschaftliche Hilfe für Afghanistan."

[357] West German Embassy in Afghanistan, "Dienstreise nach Afghanistan in der Zeit vom 9.–23.6.1968," in AV Neues Amt 1.871–Paktia (allgemein) auch Koordinierungsausschuss B, PA/AA.

[358] Kurt Hendrikson, "Deutsche Technische Hilfe für Afghanistan. Hier: Meine Dienstreise in die Provinz Paktia" (August 12, 1968), 6, in AV Neues Amt 1.871 – Paktia (allgemein) auch Koordinierungsausschuss B, PA/AA.

A month later, the Afghan Foreign Ministry's political director spoke to the German Embassy of rebellions and violence between the Mangal and Jajis in Paktia; military intervention was not out of the question.[359] When Soviet-trained Afghan Army officers, many of whom came from the borderlands, over-threw Zahir Shah and installed his cousin Daoud as the country's new President in 1973, the Paktia Project shut down.

Yet the Germans had been right about one thing. "Afghanistan could have been green," lamented Häselbarth. "It could have had forests. It could have been like Israel." But much of the work that Häselbarth and the Forest Group put into replenishing the borderlands went for naught. Tribes did cut down Paktia's forests to the point of desertification, accelerating a regional meltdown.[360] Within a decade, moreover, what remained of the forests went up in flames. "When the Russians came," said Häselbarth, "they used napalm bombs on many of the trees we had planted. Partisans were hiding underneath the trees we had planted, and so they had to all be burnt down." Soon, the woody mate-riality of the borderlands would be lost entirely. "Everything was trucked out of Afghanistan," recalled one Afghan women's activist, "everything in the ground, and everything in the air. They cut down the trees to ship them to Karachi, and they captured the birds to sell them at bird markets in Saudi Arabia."[361] Paktia today boasts few forests, and those that remain are in decline. The data that German foresters collected bears witness to the folly of social science, true, but it also remains an unwitting timestamp to the age, diversity, and beauty of Paktia's forests during Afghanistan's developmental moment – a global moment, indeed, as endangered as *Cedrus deodara*.

Conclusion

Afghanistan had gone through an exhilarating journey. Following indepen-dence in 1919, the Royal Government had made Afghanistan commercially independent from Anglo-Indian commercial networks. Afghanistan survived in a world of empire, exploiting the tools that sovereignty provided to become a barometer between the British, the Soviets, and the Germans. Yet at the very moment when Kabul seemed to have achieved its goal, Partition reconfigured Central Asia into a world of territorial states where interwar strategies no longer worked. If Afghanistan's Persianate élite wanted to continue its project of glacial modernization and foreign subsidization, they would have to do so as a test subject for foreign visions of economic development and the territorial state. The only way to do so, it seemed, had been to appropriate old British

---

[359] West German Embassy in Afghanistan, "Stammesunruhen in Paktia" (September 7, 1968), in AV Neues Amt 1.871 – Paktia (allgemein) auch Koordinierungsausschuss B, PA/AA.

[360] Author Interview, Christoph Häselbarth, Strittmatt, Germany, April 12, 2012.

[361] Author Interview, Sakina Zyar, Oxford, United Kingdom, July 12, 2011.

Indian discourses of Pashtun nationalism for use by a Persianate state, all part of an effort to make obscure, irrelevant, ignored Afghanistan matter.

This plan failed, but the Cold War bailed Kabul out. Social scientists arrived. Ideas born in Philadelphia suburbs molded the Afghan state. Vaccines perfected in Moscow labs entered the veins of Afghan peasants through the syringes of American vaccinators. Images, images of German forests, Southwestern deserts, of oil derricks and male workers' bodies, impressed themselves upon Afghanistan. Shared worlds opened up. One spring day in 1970, a Peace Corps vaccinator sat down to write a letter to her parents back home to tell them about a young Afghan man she had befriended, indeed more than that. "Ahad has been a very big part of my life for the past half year or so," she wrote. "I must say truthfully he is the one person I could consider marrying." She hesitated. She crossed out the last three words and put pen to paper again: "the one person I *want to marry*."[362]

Lives had been transformed. Yet the great transformation that social science had promised never materialized. Afghans were surrounded by the hallmarks of foreign modernity, yet few saw any improvement in their own lives. Those Afghans who went to Germany, complained one veteran development worker, experienced one personal catastrophe after another. Afghans tended "to find a blond girlfriend in Germany, then try to stay in Germany or take the bride back home with them, get married, and sooner or later the marriage goes down the toilet."[363] Those who returned to Kabul came back with nothing but the desire for a "white collar job – for a desk with a telephone and a servant and the rejection of all 'dirty work.'" A Russian language teacher in Mazar-i Sharif who led a class discussion on space exploration was surprised to find that none of her students seemed interested in becoming cosmonauts. Why, she asked? The issue, she learned, was not that the students did not want to become cosmonauts *per se*, but rather "that they wanted to be Soviet cosmonauts since Afghanistan will never conquer outer space; Afghanistan is a poor country."[364] The postcolonial nation-state had become a prison.

Bob Nathan pondered the problem during a layover at the Qandahar airport, itself a testament to the future that never happened: jet travel had rendered irrelevant the original justification of using the airport for intra-Asian stopovers. Nathan stared at the modernist terminal, itself "moving along toward completion. It seems certain that it will be a landmark of bad planning and poor implementation. It will cost about $30 million and has no real justification. It was a bad political decision which will haunt our foreign aid program for years

---

[362] Lynn LaFroth, Letter to Parents, April 24, 1970, 2. Collection on Women Peace Corps Volunteers in Afghanistan's Smallpox Eradication Program, 1968–71 (Collection 2012–M2), Arthur and Elizabeth Schlesinger Library on the History of Women in America, Harvard University.

[363] "Vorschläge auf Grund meiner Erfahrungen in sieben Jahren in Entwicklungsländern" (May 25, 1970), Folder One: "Afghanistan/Allgemeines," B213/2727, Bundesarchiv Koblenz.

[364] GARF f. 9606 (Ministerstvo vysshego i srednego obrazovaniia), op. 11, d. 5909, l. 24–5.

to come."[365] There was, Nathan concluded, only one upside to the Qandahar white elephant. "There is talk of making it into a military airport. Not a bad idea so as to get it out of the sight of civilians. This was a really big blooper."

Nathan's words were prophetic. The idea of development itself was in free fall. For many Americans, the debacle in Vietnam discredited the idea that social science could tame the former colonial world. "Modernization" was out; "linkage," "détente," and "credibility," in. Washington leaned heavily on Islamabad; "no one has occupied the White House who is friendlier to Pakistan than me," said President Nixon in 1970.[366] Even before Nixon took office, however, America's foreign aid outlays as a percentage of GDP had halved since 1962; the State Department contemplated shuttering the Kabul Embassy.[367] As *Ostpolitik* eased East–West tensions, West Germany had fewer imperatives to involve itself in obscure Third World locations. All the same, Soviet advisers carried out projects in Afghanistan unabated.

To Pakistani eyes, however, Afghanistan remained a threat. The oases of development in Helmand, the north, and Paktia may have been mirages viewed up close, but from the vantage point of Pakistani élites, they were challenges. Kabul's insistent performance of "Pashtunistan" had changed the possible interpretations of the Durand Line, and after the 1971 Indo-Pakistani War cleaved Pakistan in two, Islamabad viewed the installation of a compliant regime in Kabul as a core national security interest. But in a world defined by territorial sovereignty, this goal seemed impossible. Ironically, it would take the intervention of the Soviet Union – the purest expression of a territorial politics – to enable Pakistan to overcome the limits sovereignty imposed. As the Soviet invasion displaced millions of refugees into Pakistani territory, international NGOs would enter the scene – first in Pakistan, where the refugees were, but then, because suffering knew no boundaries, into Afghanistan itself. The developmental moment was over. A new age had dawned. The utopias and dystopias generated by so many readings of lines on the maps were about to turn the space at the semantic core of "Pashtunistan" into a laboratory where new global projects would interact, with terrifying results for those caught in between.

---

[365] RRNP, May 7, 1962.

[366] Kux, *The United States and Pakistan*, 215.

[367] Daniel Sargent, *A Superpower Transformed: The Remaking of American Foreign Relations in the 1970s* (Oxford: Oxford University Press, 2015), 35; Author Interview, Dick Scott, conducted via telephone from Tashkent, Uzbekistan, October 5, 2012.

3

States of Exception, States of Humanity

What made categories such as "class" and "ideology" so powerful in an earlier age was the fact that these categories functioned as another name for the future – the future as a political question or as the term for the struggle to produce a meaningful life. Interrogating the future helps us to reflect critically on some figure of the present – the present not necessarily as a temporal unit inserted between the past and the future, but precisely as that vulnerable space, that precarious and elusive entry point through which a radically different temporal experience might make its appearance.[1]

Cyclones, famines, refugees; technotronic eras, future shock, population bombs; arcs of crisis, last utopias, ages of fracture: little wonder why "the general history of the 1970s is usually treated as one of disaster or even nervous breakdown."[2] Few regions of the planet seem to fit this narrative more tightly than Afghanistan's. To the west, Iran's petro-dictatorship collapsed with shocking alacrity. To the east, civil war and foreign intervention cleaved Pakistan in two. In Afghanistan, famines begat coups, coups begat more coups, and coups begat civil wars and revolutions from abroad. Reassuringly linear narratives of the nation-state in history were deracinated into counter-narratives of ethnic war, chiliastic Shi'a millenarianism, or class annihilation. Schizophrenic identities, schizoid economics, schizogenic nations: these, not development, were the watchwords of the day.

---

[1] Achille Mbembe, quoted in Jesse Weaver Shipley, Jean Comaroff and Achille Mbembe, "Africa in Theory: A Conversation Between Jean Comaroff and Achille Mbembe," *Anthropological Quarterly* 83:3 (Summer 2010), 673.

[2] Samuel Moyn, "The Return of the Prodigal: The 1970s as a Turning Point in Human Rights History," in *The Breakthrough: Human Rights in the 1970s*, eds. Samuel Moyn and Jan Eckel (Philadelphia: University of Pennsylvania Press, 2014), 3.

And yet "the 1970s" must be seen as more than just an era of breakdown, for the decade was also marked by a "move from the politics of the state to the morality of the globe."[3] True, states were failing, as the Bhola Cyclone showed at the decade's dawn. "The West Pakistani government didn't do anything," reflected one witness to the hurricane that deluged Bengal in November 1970.[4] But as emergencies overwhelmed states, humanitarian organizations sprouted up like mushrooms after a storm. Lent legitimacy by quiet but momentous changes in the global Left, the location of sovereignty was moving from states to individuals. No longer "politics among nations," but politics in spite of nations; no longer dependence theory, but interdependence; no longer territoriality, but postterritoriality – these were the key shifts of the age.

Any coherent explanation of events in Afghanistan must, therefore, locate them relative to global shifts. It must explain how the space formerly at the semantic core of "Pashtunistan" became a laboratory for new models of sovereignty, development, and humanitarianism. It must explain how some states, namely the Soviet Union and Pakistan, remained wedded to conventional norms of territoriality. But it also must weave into this familiar story the antipolitics of morality that rejected the legitimacy of national borders. Only through such a synthesis may one appreciate how Afghanistan could become the arena for two opposing global projects, namely real existing socialism and humanitarianism. The new Soviet global project destroyed states *within* borders; humanitarian actors *crossed* borders in order to challenge illiberal state functions altogether. Improvising out of the clash between these two global projects, however, Pakistan would exploit the ambiguity of the Durand Line to usher in a terrifying future for Afghanistan.

Afghanistan Today, Pakistan Tomorrow

"A country," wrote Rabindranath Tagore, "is not territorial, but ideational."[5] Few countries demonstrated this truth more than Pakistan. Muslim League activists had always been vague on the territory of a proposed Muslim homeland, and as late as the mid 1940s, they envisioned Pakistan as a vast archipelago across all of South Asia, not a unified territory. The territories that eventually did form Pakistan were hardly contiguous with former Muslim empires in South Asia, much less the Subcontinent's Muslim population, or even one another. Adding to the confusion, Jinnah and Iqbal proposed as a national language not Arabic, English, Punjabi, or Bengali, but Urdu, a language whose "home" lay between the two wings of Pakistan. "The forts of Agra and Fatepur

---

[3] Samuel Moyn, *The Last Utopia: Human Rights in History* (Cambridge, MA: Harvard University Press, 2012), 43.
[4] Eric Griffel, quoted in Gary Bass, *The Blood Telegram: Nixon, Kissinger, and a Forgotten Genocide* (New York: Knopf, 2013), 23.
[5] Rabindranath Tagore, *Rabindra-Racnabali* (Kolkata: Biśvabhāratī, 1995), 1.

Sikri are today in defeated ruins," wrote a Pakistani student in 1948, "destroyed not by age but by rapine and plunder. Their debris is a constant reminder of our defeat, a living symbol of our disintegration."[6] The audacity of Pakistan as a political idea stood in direct proportion to its territorial illogic. A state for Muslims in South Asia, but with fewer Muslims than India; a Muslim state, but torn from the premier sites of Mughal civilization; a territorial warren, but for a nonnational nation – little surprise that Pakistan "never possessed a stable form even in its own imaginaries."[7]

Yet Pakistan as *state* could not but be territorial, something that Pakistan's nationalist activists knew all too well. One usually remembers Partition as an event located in Bengal and the Punjab, but it also crystallized borders in Baluchistan and Pashtunistan, respectively. Many objected to the One Unit Scheme of 1955, an act of administrative fiat that distorted Baluchistan and Pashtunistan into the outline of "West Pakistan." Deprived of democratic elections, activists protested Jinnah's vision as "a picture full of irreconcilable elements, midriffbaring immigrant saris versus demure, indigenous Sindhi shalwar-kurtas, Urdu versus Punjabi, now versus then: a miracle that went wrong."[8] Baluch leader Ghaus Bux Bizenjo argued that "we have a distinct culture like Afghanistan and Iran, and if the mere fact that we are Muslims requires us to amalgamate with Pakistan, then Afghanistan and Iran should also be amalgamated with Pakistan ... They say we must join Pakistan for economic reasons. Yet we have minerals, we have petroleum, and we have ports. The question is, what would Pakistan be without us?"[9]

Jinnah's dream had sewed frontier to lowlands like some ischiocopular freak, but democratic elections on December 7, 1970, promised to save the living half of the monstrosity. The results of the *general* elections, won by the Bangladeshi-dominated Awami League, are well known, but often forgotten are elections in Balochistan and the NWFP. Bhutto's Pakistan People's Party (PPP) secured majorities in Punjab and Sindh, but in Balochistan and NWFP, the National Awami Party (Wali) (NAP), a Leftist Pashtun nationalist party, formed coalition governments without the PPP.[10]

The fact, however, that the elections at the national level led to the dismembering of Pakistan changed everything. In April 1971, when Punjabi soldiers violently intervened in East Pakistan, Indian policy planner K. Subrahmanyam argued that Delhi possessed "an opportunity the like of which will never come

---

[6] Zulfikar Ali Bhutto, "The Islamic Heritage" (April 1, 1948), in *Z.A. Bhutto: Speeches-Interviews 1948–1966*, 19.

[7] Faisal Devji, *Muslim Zion: Pakistan as a Political Idea* (London: Hurst, 2013), 22.

[8] Rushdie, *Shame*, 91–2.

[9] *Baluch Qaum Ke Tārikh-Ke Chand Parishan Dafter Auraq (A Few Pages from the Official Records of the History of the Baloch Nation)*, ed. Malik Allah Bakhsh (Quetta: Islamiyyah Press, 1957), 43.

[10] Louis Dupree, "A Note on Afghanistan: 1974," *American Universities Fieldstaff Reports*, Asia Series, Vol. XVIII(8), 12.

again."[11] The signing of a major Soviet–Indian strategic agreement in August 1971 only added to tensions. In December, India invaded East Pakistan and forced 93,000 Pakistani soldiers to surrender in the largest capitulation since World War II. Indira Gandhi announced before the Indian Parliament that she had "avenged several centuries of Hindu humiliation at the hands of Muslim emperors and sultans."[12] Pakistan, in Bhutto's interpretation, was "confronted with an overwhelming military threat from India and Afghanistan, both armed and backed by the Soviet Union."[13]

Far from the triumph of Islam as "the incarnation of self-determination," Pakistan threatened to die as a piece of geographical clutter. The threat of destruction from without amplified the threat of dismemberment from within. After Bhutto's initial appointee for the Governor of Balochistan elicited disapproval among the NAP's coalition, in the spring of 1972, Bhutto nominated Baloch activists Mir Ghaus Bakhsh Bizenjo as Governor and Ataullah Mengal as the Chief Minister of the province. He emphasized that both served at the "pleasure of the President" in the "quest to achieve national unity."[14] Over the summer of 1972, however, Pakistani media reported of a meeting between Baloch and Pashtun separatists in London. That autumn, Bizenjo launched an ethno-administrative indigenization program that "repatriated" non-Baloch civil servants while Baloch replaced them. One Baluch Communist explained the context to East German diplomats: Pakistan was a Punjabi dictatorship that had occupied Baloch lands.[15] But "if equal rights could be secured for the Baloch and Pashtuns – like in Afghanistan – Punjabi dominance would be over, the raison d'être of the Punjabis in a state of Pakistan would become meaningless, and elements in the Punjabi Left would demand union with India."[16]

These policies threatened the "Punjabi and Pashtun military condominium" at the core of the Pakistani state.[17] As Gankovskiĭ had stressed, the Pakistan Army offered a vehicle for Punjabi and Pashtun janissaries to enter the landholding ranks and perpetuate caste privileges, privileges that NAP voters rejected.[18] Left-leaning Swedish author Jan Myrdal made the stakes clear, describing Army élites as convinced that "one can solve the problem [of Pashtunistan] with tanks and aircraft through a conquest of Afghanistan, through

[11] K. Subrahmanyam, quoted in Kux, *The United States and Pakistan, 1947–2000: Disenchanted Allies*, 206.
[12] V. Langer, *The Defence and Foreign Policy of India* (New Delhi: Sterling Publishers, 1998), 205.
[13] Zulfikar Ali Bhutto, Letter to Gerald Ford, June 13, 1975, Gerald R. Ford Presidential Library, National Security Advisor's Presidential Correspondence with Foreign Leaders Collection, Box 3, "Pakistan–Prime Minister Bhutto (1)" Folder.
[14] Cited in Farhan Hanif Siddiqi, *The Politics of Ethnic Difference: The Baloch, Sindhi, and Mohajir Ethnic Movements* (London: Routledge, 2012), 65.
[15] "Nationalitätenpolitik in Pakistan (Lage in Beluchistan," 2. MfAA ZR 3035/86, PA/AA Berlin.
[16] Ibid., 3.
[17] Michael Barry, *Massoud: De l'islamisme à la liberté* (Paris: Louis Audibert, 2002), 258.
[18] Ibid., *Kabul's Long Shadows: Historical Perspectives*, 65.

an annexation of Afghanistan and Pashtunistan and through a constant occupation of the country."[19]

Of course, Pakistan was no mere ethnic dictatorship, and the point of suppressing Pashtun nationalism was not to subdue Kabul, but to hold off Delhi. For Islamabad to win the long-term conflict with New Delhi, it would have to at least match, if not outstrip, India in military spending. But this was a problem of magnitude, not scale; only in 2013 did Pakistan's GDP match India's in 1980.[20] After the crushing defeat of 1971, moreover, it was clear that a two-front war against Soviet-aligned Afghanistan and India would end in disaster. Control of Pashtun and Baloch sovereignty was the only way to make up for military weakness. "In spite of all of its alliances with, for example, the United States," explained Soviet diplomat Vladimir Basov, Islamabad's fundamental interest was the security of this "Pakistani living space, to strengthen [itself], if necessary, against India – a dynamite detonator, so to speak."[21]

A February 1973 incident forced Islamabad to pursue this stance to its logical conclusion. On the evening of February 9, police in the capital stormed the Iraqi Embassy, where they discovered Soviet weapons and cash purportedly designated for Baloch rebels. Bhutto dismissed Bizenjo and Mengal, and the Pakistan Army invaded Balochistan with more than 80,000 soldiers.[22] But Baloch guerrillas melted into the landscape and kept Punjabi soldiers on the run. By the summer of 1974, the guerrillas cut off arterial roads and the rail line into the Punjab, halting coal exports, and kidnapped Punjabi oil workers in the Marri area. "We knew," reflected one former Army commander, "that we had to respond very forcefully or we would simply be unable to bring the situation under control." Soon, American-manufactured Chinook helicopters darkened the skies above the gorges and crags, allowing the Army to deposit troops deep into the field and snipe at Baloch militants.[23] The Shah of Iran supplied thirty U.S.-manufactured Huey Cobra helicopters manned by Iranian pilots and armed with cannons that spewed 750 rounds per minute.[24]

Yet if the core problem was the sovereignty of the formerly colonial frontier, strategic logic could not stop at the Durand Line. Afghan sovereignty, once a curious relict of an overburdened British Empire, now represented a

---

[19] "Dokumente über die Aufnahme diplomatischer Beziehungen der DDR mit anderen Staaten," 1 November 1963, Archiv des Auswärtigen Amtes MfAA C 1459/73. This excerpt comes from an edited edition of Myrdal's *Kulturers korsväg; en bok om Afghanistan* (Stockholm: 1960), which was then being translated into German for East German readers.

[20] IMF World Economic Outlook Database, updated April 2013, available online at: www.imf .org/external/pubs/ft/weo/2013/01/weodata/index.aspx.

[21] Vladimir Basov, Interview with Russian television, available online at: www.youtube.com/ watch?v=ab6bpIsUg_g&list=WLph1vvPu535MLrryLnpjA_xxiifFGlBog.

[22] Selig S. Harrison, *In Afghanistan's Shadow: Baluch Nationalism and Soviet Temptations* (New York: Canegie Endowment for International Peace, 1981), 36–7.

[23] Ibid., 7, 37.

[24] Mohammad Yunus, *Bhutto and the Breakup of Pakistan* (Karachi: Oxford University Press, 2011), 36.

fundamental threat to Pakistan. Pashtun yearnings for self-determination, over-whelmingly associated with the Left in the twentieth century, had to be channeled into forms other than the Third World nation-state. The Pakistan Army had historically done this as an assimilator and exterminator of Pashtun bodies inside of Pakistani territory, but the idiosyncratic investiture of postwar norms of sovereignty into a colonial border made Afghanistan a fully privileged object of international law. The Durand Line was "a mere line," but because "the possibility of actual (not only domestic) border zones and intermediary zones [was] excluded from this state-centric way of thinking about territory," Islamabad lacked a way to demobilize the Afghan state as a vehicle for Pashtun self-determination.[25] The irony was that the Afghan state was far from the Pashtun-dominated vehicle that the Musahibans presented it to be, and that Afghan Communists wanted it to become. But the aggressive vending of colonial tropes had fused with postwar expectations about nation-statehood and Pakistani strategic thinking and assumed a life of its own.

Bhutto needed a way to turn sovereignty from a limit on Pakistan to a brake on the Soviet Union. If Moscow's real aim were to expand to the Persian Gulf, "the shortest way," Pakistani diplomats were aware, "was through Pakistan."[26] And if war with Delhi and Moscow were inevitable, then Afghanistan and Pakistan were actually "in the same boat." Former Interior Minister Nasirullah Babar elaborated: "If it is the threat from the North (USSR), it is Afghanistan today and Pakistan tomorrow. If it is the threat from the South (India), it is Pakistan today and Afghanistan tomorrow.' You see, after 1971 Indian strategists had placed Pakistan and Afghanistan in the same category as the next target."[27] From this point of view, the war made more sense in alliance with Afghanistan than against it. Concretely, this meant two options: either replace Daoud with a quisling who would drop "Pashtunistan" altogether, or pressure him to confirm the Durand Line. While contemplating regime change, Pakistan still operated on the premise of state sovereignty as a structural anchor to policy choices. The point of a coup was not to destroy or annex Afghanistan, but rather to embed the accident of interwar Afghan decolonization into the much more restrictive privileges of the postcolonial nation-state.

---

[25] Carl Schmitt, *The Großraum Order of International Law with a Ban on Intervention for Spatially Foreign Powers: A Contribution to the Concept of Reich in International Law*, in *Writings on War*, trans. and ed. Timothy Nunan (Cambridge: Polity, 2011), 113.

[26] Memorandum of Conversation Between Henry Kissinger, Alfred L. Atherton (Assistant Secretary of State for Near Eastern and South Asian Affairs), Robert B. Oakley (NSC Staff), Aziz Ahmed (Pakistani Foreign Minister), Yaqub Khan (Pakistani Ambassador to USA), Iqbal Riza (Minister, Pakistani Embassy to USA), and Iqbal Akhund (Pakistani Permanent Representative to United Nations), September 30, 1975, Gerald R. Ford Presidential Library and Museum Digital Collections (Presidential Correspondence with Foreign Leaders), Pakistan-Prime Minister Bhutto (2), available online at: www.fordlibrarymuseum.gov/library/document/0351/1555842 .pdf.

[27] "Remembering Our Warriors: Babar 'The Great'" (Interview with Nasirullah Babar), *Defence Journal* (April 2001).

Yet domestic events continued to interrupt Bhutto's plans. On February 8, 1975, terrorists assassinated a top PPP lieutenant in NWFP. Two days after the killing, Bhutto banned the NAP from political activity and ordered the establishment of the so-called Hyderabad Tribunal to investigate the NAP for irredentist activity. The trial, however, galvanized a domestic anti-PPP opposition. Daoud, moreover, made negotiations on "Pashtunistan" conditional on the legalization of the NAP and release of its leadership.[28] Islamabad needed a new strategy. Responding, in the summer of 1975, the Pakistani intelligence agency (Inter-Services Intelligence, or ISI) armed Islamist rebels based out of the Panjshir Valley who attempted to overthrow the Afghan state. The attempt backfired, as the Afghan Army fought the rebels to a stalemate and Soviet diplomats ramped up pressure on *Pakistan* to cede territory to Afghanistan. When Islamabad refused, the Soviet Ambassador ominously responded: "Then God alone knows what will happen," arguing that no nation can "willingly agree to have its own people divided into two parts."[29]

But the Soviets were wrong. Shaken by the coup attempt, in the autumn of 1975, Kabul's diplomats "indicated a willingness to talk with [Pakistan] and said they had no designs on [Pakistani] territory – they only wanted the Pushtuns and Balochis protected."[30] As the then-Governor of the NWFP recalled, "Daoud was convinced by Mr. Bhutto in 1976...Daoud had accepted the Durand Line in 1976 and wanted peace with Pakistan."[31] In the summer of 1976, even in the wake of a guilty verdict at the Hyderabad Tribunal, Daoud initiated negotiations. Bhutto's strategy had worked. Islamabad had imposed a regime of limited sovereignty in its own frontier and was about to secure a final settlement that would eliminate the threat of Indo-Soviet meddling. Islamabad's motive and object may have been mad, but its means were sane, even brilliant: just as the Soviets had secured the European borders of wartime conquest in a system of maximalist territorial sovereignty, Pakistan could resolve its specific

---

[28] Aziz Ahmed (Pakistani Minister of Foreign Affairs), quoted in "Memorandum of Conversation, Washington, October 9, 1975, 11am," in *Foreign Relations of the United States, 1969–1976*, Vol. E-8 (Documents on South Asia, 1973–1976), Document 215, available online at: history .state.gov/historicaldocuments/frus1969-76ve08/d215.

[29] Zulfikar Ali Bhutto, Letter to Gerald Ford, August 17, 1975, Gerald R. Ford Presidential Library and Museum Digital Collections (Presidential Correspondence with Foreign Leaders), Pakistan-Prime Minister Bhutto (3), available online at: www.fordlibrarymuseum.gov/library/document/ 0351/1555843.pdf.

[30] Memorandum of Conversation Between Henry Kissinger, Alfred L. Atherton (Assistant Secretary of State for Near Eastern and South Asian Affairs), Robert B. Oakley (NSC Staff), and Aziz Ahmed (Pakistani Foreign Minister), Yaqub Khan (Pakistani Ambassador to USA), Iqbal Riza (Minister, Pakistani Embassy to USA), and Iqbal Akhund (Pakistani Permanent Representative to United Nations), September 30, 1975, Gerald R. Ford Presidential Library and Museum Digital Collections (Presidential Correspondence with Foreign Leaders), Pakistan-Prime Minister Bhutto (2), available online at: www.fordlibrarymuseum.gov/library/document/0351/1555842 .pdf.

[31] "Remembering Our Warriors: Babar 'The Great.'"

Cold War dilemmas by investing colonial cartography with the privileges of the postwar nation-state.

The question, however, remained whether Bhutto could keep ahead enough of domestic events to secure his foreign policy agenda. The anti-PPP opposition front that the Hyderabad Tribunal had united prepared for March 1977 general elections. Bhutto's PPP trounced the opposition, but allegations that Bhutto had rigged the elections and Bhutto's arrest of opposition leaders only multiplied street protests. In the background, Pakistani military élites, foremost among them Bhutto's protégé Muhammad Zia-ul-Haq, plotted a coup. On the evening of July 4, 1977, having sent loyalist officers to a "seminar" in a secure location, Zia ordered Army units to arrest the Prime Minister. The Punjabi general dissolved the National Assembly and all Provincial Assemblies, suspended the Constitution, and promised elections. Bhutto was soon freed, but on September 3, authorities arrested him on trumped-up murder charges. A kangaroo court sentenced him to death on March 18, 1978. After a lengthy appeals process failed, Bhutto was hanged at Rawalpindi's Central Jail on April 4, 1979.

Yet as Bhutto's corpse was taken to the grounds of the family's estate in Larkana, Pakistan, that postterritorial Muslim Zion, remained as territorially insecure as ever. Bhutto had sought to turn Balochistan and the NWFP into a space of permanent military rule where communists, socialists, and secularists were fair game. Yet Islamabad had failed to transform Afghanistan itself into a similar sacrifice zone. So long as Afghanistan remained a sovereign state, there was really no way to permanently disable the threat it represented. Using postwar sovereignty as a support, and forcing Kabul to accept the Durand Line was a good alternative, but the existential threat of the Hindu entity remained. Without a major crisis, Pakistan lacked for tools to achieve a fundamental transformation in Afghan state sovereignty. As pallbearers lowered Bhutto's remains into a grave inside the Gahri Khuda Baksh mausoleum, the territorial architecture of the planet seemed as unmovable as the mock Mughal tomb towering over the plains of Sindh.

An Afghan Spring?

None of the events in Pakistan left élites in Kabul secure. The Iranian and Pakistani intervention in Balochistan and the ban on the NAP had exposed Kabul's inability to pursue "Pashtunistan" as foreign policy beyond radio broadcasts. The Ministry of the Interior, run by PDPA Parchamists, had forestalled coup attempts by Mohammad Hāshim Maiwandwāl and, later, Lieutenant General Mir Ahmadshāh.[32] But the more challengers that Soviet-trained Army officers

---

[32] Snegirëv and Samunin, *Virus "A": Kak my zaboleli vtorzheniiem v Afganistan*, 35. Where this
       book is directly quoted, I am relying upon an official translation of the book, available online
       at: www2.gwu.edu/~nsarchiv/NSAEBB/NSAEBB396/FullTextVirusA.pdf.

decapitated, the more of a threat they represented themselves.[33] When Daoud ordered arms procurements from Western suppliers, the officers supervising these deals followed orders from Party leadership to sabotage talks.[34] Even had they not, Kabul could not barter Afghan gas (which flowed into the USSR) for American weapons; attempts toward having Iran or Gulf Arab states train officers went nowhere.[35]

Daoud's April 1977 visit to Moscow exposed a growing gulf between the two regimes. Alarmed by Daoud's suspicion of the PDPA, Moscow urged the fractious PDPA to unite.[36] Even if deep differences persisted between Parcham and Khalq, it was better to confront Daoud with a united front. But Moscow felt that had time on its side. "When Afghanistan was discussed in the Soviet Foreign Ministry offices," recalled one former spy, "the staff likened it to Finland as a similar neutral friendly state with predictable politics."

Events on the evening of April 17, 1978, shattered this illusion. That evening, PDPA notable Mir Ahmad Khyber hosted PDPA Central Committee member 'Abd al-Qadus Ghurbandi at his home in the *Mikrorayon*, the neighborhood of Soviet-built apartment blocks in eastern Kabul. Ghurbandi apparently convinced Khyber to join him for dinner at his own home on the western side of Kabul.[37] The next day, however, pedestrians discovered Khyber's body in a street between his and Ghurbandi's home.[38] Outraged PDPA leaders organized a large protest surrounding Khyber's funeral. Regime troops did not fire into the crowd but did have Parcham head Babrak Karmal arrested. The Left seemed scattered.

But on the afternoon of Thursday, April 27, shelling interrupted a Ministerial meeting at the Presidential Palace.[39] Soviet SU-7 fighters, MIG-21 jets, and helicopters strafed the building. The Afghan Air Force, following the orders of Khalq deputy Hafizullah Amin, had launched a coup.[40] By nightfall, tanks surrounded the Radio Kabul building. On the dawn of the 28th, troops sequestered Daoud in a reception room, pumped him and his family full of bullets, and dumped the bodies into a mass grave outside Kabul.[41]

The coup, dubbed the "April Revolution," unleashed a mafia of out-of-touch revolutionaries onto Afghanistan. Attempts at agrarian reform, antireligious

---

[33] US Embassy Kabul, "Why Baluchi Brothers?" (October 9, 1974), available online at Wikileaks: www.wikileaks.org/plusd/cables/1974KABUL06445_b.html.
[34] Snegirëv and Samunin, 34.
[35] Vladimir Basov, Interview with Russian television.
[36] Snegirëv and Samunin, 19.
[37] Kishtmand, *Yāddāshthā-yi siyāsi va ruydādhā-yi tārikhi: khāṭirāt-i shakhṣi bā burah'hā'i az tārikh-i siyāsi-yi mu'āṣir-i Afghānistān*, Vols. 1 & 2, 325.
[38] Snegirëv and Samunin, 59.
[39] Ibid., 63.
[40] Ibid., 27.
[41] Ibid., 68–70. "Body of Afghan Leader Identified," BBC News, December 4, 2008, available online at: http://news.bbc.co.uk/2/hi/south_asia/7764852.stm.

propaganda, and women's emancipation blighted the PDPA's reputation.[42] Tellingly, however, the PDPA took Pashtun state domination seriously. If, in April 1978, half of the Central Committee of the PDPA had been Pashtuns, by October three-quarters were.[43] General Secretary Nur Muhammad Taraki appointed Pashtun governors in the northern provinces, and reinstated a hated fifteen percent Pashto-language pay bonus.[44] Cubans poured into the halls of Kabul University; the university soon offered more courses in Spanish than in Uzbek or Turkmen.[45] As the PDPA refused to provide Uzbek- or Turkmen-language textbooks or instruction, many feared genocide.[46]

Such fears proved to be true, for the PDPA unleashed an orgy of violence on the old Afghan élite and society writ large. In less than a year-and-a-half in power, Khalq murdered tens of thousands, disproportionately targeting the bureaucracy, the intelligentsia, and minorities. Khalq started with several generals who had been close to Daoud as well as former Prime Ministers Musa Shafiq and Nur Ahmad Etemadi.[47] The Islamists jailed by Daoud came next. And following the Islamic Revolution in Iran, the PDPA killed 7,000 Hazara Shi'a in less than a year.[48] All the same, Amin reassured Soviet diplomats that "all plans and programs have to be strictly scientific and realistic."[49]

But when Taraki and Amin traveled to Moscow in December 1978 for the signing of a Soviet–Afghan Friendship Treaty, signs of a fundamental misunderstanding became clear. When the duumvirate descended upon the tarmac at Moscow's Vnukovo Airport, Brezhnev invited them to ride to central Moscow with himself and Stanislav Gavrilov, head adviser to the Foreign Ministry's Department of Afghan Affairs and a Persian speaker who volunteered to interpret. Gavrilov translated Brezhnev's Russian-language remarks into Dari, but Taraki feigned incomprehension.[50] The next day, minutes before negotiations

---

[42] Thomas Barfield, "Weak Links on a Rusty Chain: Structural Weaknesses in Afghanistan's Provincial Government," in *Revolutions and Rebellions in Afghanistan: Anthropological Perspectives*, eds. R. Canfield, and M. N. Shahrani (Berkeley: University of California Press, 1984).

[43] V.V. Basov, "Natsional'nyĭ vopros v usloviakh Afganskoĭ Revoliutsii" (January 1984), in Basov, *Natsional'noe i plemennoe v Afganistane. K ponimaniiu nevoennykh istokov afganskogo krizisa*, ed. V.B. Kravtsov (Moscow: NITs FSKN Rossii, 2011), 107.

[44] Author Interview, Abdulrakim Samodov, Dushanbe, Tajikistan, July 19, 2012; Ruben B. Nalbandiants, *Zapiski vostokoveda* (Moscow: Luch, 2002), 17–18.

[45] Author Interview, January 2014. The person interviewed on this subject has requested to remain anonymous.

[46] Basov, 108, 111.

[47] Gilles Dorronoso, *Revolution Unending: Afghanistan, 1979 to the Present* (London: Hurst and Company, 2000), 96.

[48] Ibid., 104.

[49] A.M. Puzanov, Diary Entry, July 11, 1978, "Record of Conversation with the Secretary of the PDPA Central Committee, Deputy Prime Minister and Minister of Foreign Affairs of the Democratic Republic of Afghanistan Hafizullah Amin," available online at National Security Archive: http://nsarchive.gwu.edu/NSAEBB/NSAEBB396/docs/1978-07-11%20Conversation%20with%20Amin.pdf.

[50] Snegirëv and Samunin, 205.

were about to begin, Taraki declared that "We members of the delegation that have arrived in the friendly Soviet Union, are Afghans. To be more precise, we are Pashtuns. This is why we would like Pashto to be used in this remarkable setting." After an Afghan military officer on hand, the only speaker of Russian and Pashto in the building, butchered the interpretation, the Soviet Foreign Ministry scrambled Vladimir Kozin, their only qualified Pashto speaker, to interpret. What was happening?

Taraki and Amin may have imagined themselves as true nationalists, but the act only reflected the intersection of three decades of "Pashtunistan," postwar self-determination, and the failure of development. Taraki and Amin had, thanks to the opportunities created by Kabul's engagement with the Cold War, entered not only Persianate Kabul but also the international Leftist bricolage governed from Moscow. They come of age as revolutionaries in an age when the nation-state, rather than federation or empire, offered the most attractive platform for self-determination. And they had been fed propaganda of how Afghanistan was, or should be, a Pashtun-dominated state. When Taraki and Amin spoke Pashto before non-Afghan audiences as representatives of the Afghan state, then, they announced not just their tone-deafness to how Kabul had actually historically secured international financing, but also the extent to which "isolated" Afghanistan was, and always had been, captive to global discourses beyond itself.

Not long after this bungle, Amin met Soviet Premier Kosygin. Pashtuns, Amin emphasized – so recalls the interpreter – had been wronged by the Durand Line.[51] But the chaos in Pakistan offered a historic opportunity for Taraki, the "Great Leader of All Pashtuns." Zia's regime was weak, Amin assured Kosygin, and Kabul could easily unite together Pakistani Pashtuns, Baloch, and the former Bhutto opposition to destroy Pakistan. All they needed was Soviet "financial support, arms, ammunition, and means of transportation and communication to do so." Here was a red flag if there ever was one. Surely Islamabad and Washington would assume that Moscow stood behind Kabul's adventures. But after thirty years of investment, could Moscow really abandon Kabul.

The situation was spiraling out of control. In February 1979, Maoist terrorists kidnapped and murdered the American Ambassador to Afghanistan. In March, insurgents overwhelmed the Afghan Army garrison in Herat. The PDPA urged Moscow to intervene, but the Politburo declined. "We must not allow the situation to seem as if you were not able to deal with your own problems and invited foreign troops to assist you," said Aleksei Kosygin.[52] He proved right: Afghan paratroopers and tanks recaptured the city, albeit with huge death tolls.

But as Kosygin's December meeting had underscored, the real problem was Khalq's line on "Pashtunistan." When the Pakistani Baloch activist

---

[51] Ibid., 207–8.
[52] Aleksei Kosygin, in "Zapis' besedy A.N. Kosygina, A.A. Gromyko, D.F. Ustinova, V.N. Ponomareva s N.M. Taraki" (March 20, 1979), National Security Archive.

H. Nizamani visited Kabul, Amin spoke openly of "the eventual incorporation of the adjacent Pushtun and Baloch areas of Pakistan into the 'homeland.'"[53] Amin dreamed in public speeches of a Pashtun-dominated ethnic state "from the Oxus to the Abasin," "from the mountains of the Pamir to the beaches of Gwadar."[54] When, on March 3, 1979, the PDPA Politburo released a decree exclusively in Pashto, fears of Pashtun state domination gained gravity. Amin declared that Pashtuns' genius made Leninist self-determination irrelevant; Khalq simply had to exterminate the feudal class, and national tensions would resolve themselves.[55]

Amin knew of what he spoke. Between April 12, 1979, and November 28, 1979, at least 4,784 Afghans were murdered at Kabul's Pul-i Charkhi prison for arbitrary reasons: most under charges of being an *ikhwāni* (a "brother," that is, members of Hekmatyar and Rabbani's Muslim Brotherhood), but also for carrying a flag stating "Allah Akbar," being homeless, or insulting the "Great Khalq Leader."[56] One former lecturer at Kabul University recalled being forced to watch a television broadcast of Taraki. When one of his colleagues threw his shoe at the television, political commissars accused him of treason and threatened to execute him. The lecturer froze: he had only thrown his shoe at an *image* of Taraki, he pleaded. The guards dragged the man into a courtyard; the lecturers heard shots crackle, then a thud.[57] All the same, the PDPA's spree of killing showed the limits that borders imposed: while some of the PDPA's victims *originated* from Iran, "Pashtunistan," or the "Free Frontier Area," most were Afghan citizens from provinces surrounding Kabul. Even as it drove many Afghans *out* of state territory, the PDPA presided over a weakly institutionalized Afghan state that barely penetrated the Kabuli hinterland, much less "Pashtunistan."

This, however, was what incoming Soviet advisers were out to remedy. Having learned its lessons from debacles like Guinea, Moscow knew that political control was what mattered.[58] And political control was what Kabul had, was what Kabul offered. Advisers surged into the ministries of the newly rechristened Democratic Republic of Afghanistan (DRA), rewrote the country's legal system, and built ever more infrastructure: gas pipelines from Charchuk and

53 Harrison, *In Afghanistan's Shadow*, 145.
54 "H. Amin's Address to Charmang and Bajaur People," *Kabul Times*, August 5, 1979; "This is a Revolution Which Handed Power from One State to the Other," *Kabul Times*, August 21, 1979.
55 Basov, "Natsional'nyï vopros v usloviakh Afganskoï Revoliutsii" (January 1984), 109.
56 Listing in "Afghan Death Lists" (Released KhAD execution records), available online at: www .om.nl/onderwerpen/internationale/death-lists/.
57 Author Interview, January 2014. The person interviewed on this subject has requested to remain anonymous.
58 For a full list of advisers present in Soviet ministries as of September 15, 1979, see "Shtatnaia rasstanovka gruppy sovetnikov v ministerstvakh i vedomstvakh DRA (po sostoianiiu na 15.09.79g.)," RGAE f. 365, op. 2, d. 2779, l. 59–82. The vast majority of advisers arrived in the summer of 1978.

Hoja-Gugerdag to the Soviet Union; copper-smelting plants; bridges; antiland-slide infrastructure along the Salang Pass; and hospitals.[59] Cargo exchange between the two countries grew to the point that the USSR accounted for forty percent of Afghanistan's total trade turnover, quadruple that of the nearest competitor, Japan.[60]

Amin exploited the aid to build his own personal dictatorship. When, in September 1979, Amin insisted that Taraki represent Afghanistan at a Non-Aligned Movement Summit in Havana, KGB officials tried and failed to talk "the Great Khalq Leader" out of flying.[61] En route back from Cuba, Taraki stopped in Moscow on September 10, where Brezhnev advised him to remove Amin. Upon his arrival in Kabul the next day, Taraki tried, but failed, to depose Amin at a Council of Ministers meeting. The day after that, September 12, Taraki invited Amin to the Presidential Palace for lunch, where bodyguards tried, but failed, too, to gun down Amin. A familiar script repeated itself as the Kabul garrison seized sites. Moscow activated an emergency plan to kidnap Amin, but Taraki had been smothered with a pillow and killed. On September 15, CPSU Party bosses received a telegram from Moscow informing them that Amin had replaced Taraki as leader of Afghanistan.[62]

Aware he was approaching a dead end, Amin sought a dramatic course change. The mass killings, he stressed, had been Taraki's fault. He sought détente with Pakistan, reaching out for a summit meeting with Zia in early December 1979. Fatally, however, Amin also contacted American *charge d'affaires* J. Bruce Amstutz. Having learned from the Guinean and Egyptian debacles, Moscow would not allow itself to be tricked again. In an October 29 memorandum, Politburo members noted that Washington was courting Kabul, and that "upon the availability of facts bearing witness to the beginning of a turn by H. Amin in an anti-Soviet direction, [the USSR should] introduce supplemental proposals about measures from our side."[63] The point, a later December 8 meeting stressed, was not just the opportunity cost of losing a long-time client, but rather that an American-allied Kabul would become a platform for Pershing missiles, a source of uranium for the Iraqi and Pakistani nuclear

---

[59] "Materialy po ekonomike i ekonomicheskim sviaziam Afganistana/proekty zakonov, zapisi besed, obzory, pis'ma," RGAE f. 365, op. 2, d. 2779; on infrastructure, see "Protokol 1-go zasedaniia Postoiannoǐ Mezhpravitel'stvennoǐ sovetsko-afganskoǐ komissii po ekonomich-eskomu i tekhnicheskomu sotrudnichestvu," Ibid., d. 2777.

[60] A.M. Boiarkin, "Tovarooborot vneshneǐ kommercheskoǐ torgovli DRA za 1 polugodiie 1358 goda," in "Kratkiǐ Obzor sostoianiia vneshneǐ torgovli Demokraticheskoǐ Respubliki Afgan-istan v 1 polugodii 1358g. (s 21 marta po 21 sentiabria 1979g.)," RGAE f. 365, op. 2, d. 2779, l. 86.

[61] The original plan was for Taraki to travel on an Afghan-owned Boeing jet recently acquired from America. Fearing sabotage, KGB officials managed to scramble a Soviet government plane piloted by a Soviet crew to carry Taraki to the Caribbean. In Snegirëv and Samunin, 384.

[62] Snegirëv and Samunin, 453.

[63] A. Gromyko, Iu. Andropov, D. Ustinov, B. Ponomarev, Memorandum, October 29, 1979, cited in Liakhovskiǐ, *Tragediia i doblest' Afgana*, 102.

bomb programs, and, implausibly, a wedge to integrate Soviet Central Asia and the Caucasus into a "new Great Ottoman Empire."[64] Amin had been a poor student of the optics of "Pashtunistan," but his course reversal endangered Afghanistan even more than his initial fanaticism had.

Nor had Amin's gestures toward détente impressed the generals in Rawalpindi, long convinced that Amin was a Soviet stooge and irremediable nationalist. Yet even as Taraki and Amin had failed to make any progress toward their obsession with an ethnic dictatorship, their brutality inside the Afghan state had reshaped the territories imagined as "Pashtunistan." By April 1979, 109,000 people had fled into Pakistan, a number that almost doubled to 193,000 by that September.[65] During Amin's rule, the number of refugees in Pakistan doubled again, to 386,916 people. Nearly half were children.

The outmigration furnished Pakistan with a perverse opportunity. The project of locking Afghanistan into territorial statehood had collapsed, but the PDPA ironically supplied Islamabad with the fragments it would need to achieve the much more radical project of subsuming Afghan state sovereignty altogether. Many of the *mujāhidin* were Afghan refugees, fragments of an Afghan population that Amin had forced into exile. The idea of arming Islamist guerrillas to overthrow a Pashtun nationalist state – the echo of the 1975 attempt to overthrow Daoud – was another fragment. The American and Chinese weapons that flowed into Pakistan were another fragment. Still another fragment was the ideology that lent this mix coherence, virulent Saudi-sponsored Sunni Islam easily spread among rootless youths. The insane attempt to build a Pashtun-dominated nation-state out of Afghanistan had turned the space at the core of "Pashtunistan" into a massive transnational workshop aimed at disabling Afghan sovereignty altogether. Yet there was one final fragment to this project, one whose appearance in Afghanistan revealed the global significance of the moment.

The Poverty of Politics

As millions of Afghans fled to neighboring Iran and Pakistan, the United Nations High Commissioner for Refugees (UNHCR) and humanitarian NGOs scrambled to respond to what was then the second-largest refugee crisis in history. To understand how they did so, however, requires delving into the origins of Cold-War-era humanitarianism, which date at least to the Biafra Crisis of 1967–70. Following a January 1966 coup carried out by ethnic Igbo officers

---

[64] Gromyko, quoted in "Zasedanie Politbiuro TsK KPSS," March 17, 1979, 3, available online at National Security Archive: http://nsarchive.gwu.edu/NSAEBB/NSAEBB396/docs/1979-03-17%20Politburo%20Session%20on%20Situation%20in%20Afghanistan.pdf; Liakhovskiĭ, *Tragediia i doblest' Afgana*, 109.

[65] Afghan Refugees Commissionerate, *Relief Work for Afghan Refugees* (Peshawar: Afghan Refugees Commissionerate, 1982), 2.

from southeastern Nigeria, interethnic killing, and a countercoup that ejected the Igbos from power, the Military Governor of Nigeria's Eastern Region declared a Republic of Biafra on May 30, 1967. Lagos attacked the region, leading to starvation and images of emaciated African children on television worldwide. Church groups and the constituent national groups of the International Committee of the Red Cross (ICRC) funneled aid from the islands in the Bight of Biafra to Port Harcourt, Biafra's seaport.

When Nigerian government armies captured Port Harcourt in May 1968, however, Biafran rebels lost access to the ocean. The ICRC was blocked from delivering aid. Lagos rejected humanitarian transit through combat lines; Biafran leadership similarly rejected any transit of aid through Nigerian territory. Negotiations over aerial transit rights proved inconclusive. The Nigerian government permitted only daytime deliveries of aid to rebel positions, which would expose Biafrans to fire and force aid organizations to halt clandestine aid flights from the islands of São Tomé (part of Portugal) and Fernando Po (a Spanish colony). When Fernando Po became independent Equatorial Guinea, the territorial crucible grew tighter. Neighboring Cameroon threw in its support for Nigeria, making overland deliveries to Biafra impossible. Yet when Gabon recognized the putative new country, ICRC leadership felt unable to work from there; Geneva's neutrality was too important.

Soon, Biafra collapsed, offering observers a grim lesson. "Images of children reduced to stick insects" and "the constant low wailing of dying babies" could bring postcolonial struggles to international attention, but territorial sovereignty offered dictators a license to kill.[66] Barring direct military intervention, postcolonial states could smother irredentism under the banner of sovereignty. Disgusted by the debacle, former employees of the French Red Cross reconsidered their principles. One doctor, Bernard Kouchner, had restrained from criticizing the ICRC, but after the catastrophe, Kouchner, a veteran of communist student politics, joined Biafra "veterans" Max Récamier and Pascal Grellety-Bosviel, as well as Jacques Bérès and Xavier Emmanuelli, to found an "expeditionary brigade for the Red Cross."[67] The group ran several ill-conceived missions in early 1970, but that November, freelance journalist Philippe Bernier published an article in the medical journal *Tonus* challenging young French doctors to spend their vacations volunteering for humanitarian missions.[68] "Are we mercenaries?" questioned the piece. Récamier responded,

[66] Michael Gould, *The Struggle for Modern Nigeria: The Biafran War* (London: I.B. Tauris, 2012), 15.

[67] Peter Redfield, *Life in Crisis: The Ethical Journey of Doctors Without Borders* (Berkeley: University of California Press, 2013), 54.

[68] Didier Fassin, "Subjectivity Without Subjects: Reinventing the Figure of the Witness," in *Humanitarian Reason: A Moral History of the Present*, trans. Rachel Gomme (Berkeley: University of California Press, 2012), 206. Many of the doctors associated with the group had studied in the late 1960s at the "red faculty" associated with the *Hôpital Cochin* in Paris.

and after several discussions, the editor of *Tonus*, Bernier, and Récamier formed an initiative, *Médecins sans Frontières*, or Doctors Without Borders (MSF). The project rested on a compromise: so long as MSF did not comment on the politics of internal conflicts, doctors ought to be able to operate in sovereign territory to save lives. Victims' plight demanded suspending politics for morality, working within, not against, postcolonial territoriality. Kouchner put it succinctly, explaining that "suffering children in the Third World are neither of the right or left."[69] But after a controversial trip to aid Iraqi Kurds, the *Tonus* faction left the group.[70] MSF started advocating for *témoignaige*, "witnessing," as a core part of its missions. A new generation of doctors joined the organization: men like Claude Malhuret, who worked for a year in Cambodian refugee camps in Thailand and grew disgusted with the Khmer Rouge, and Rony Brauman, the child of Polish Jews. Like Malhuret, Brauman had experience in the Cambodian refugee camps, where he became skeptical of political ideology if also cognizant of the organizational skill that even "mercenaries" had to possess.

The turn away from borders and ideology offered a curious symmetry to developments in the socialist world. Throughout the 1970s, socialist regimes faced economic stagnation and attacks on their Marxist credentials from both Maoists as well as reform Communist dissidents.[71] In response, regimes co-opted their opponents' terms and branded themselves as examples of "developed socialism" or "real socialism," in contrast to the utopianism of the European Left.[72] Any true humanitarian movement, scholars of Marx pointed out, had to embrace the proletariat – not the disillusioned Parisian medical student – as "representative of modern forces of production and who through its socio-political position will lend new qualities to social interaction."[73] Democratic centralism and the command economy may have been ugly compromises, but they were necessary in a brutal imperialist world. European Marxists who dreamed of democratic transition or a slow revolution through cultural hegemony, they could contend, were doomed to repeat the fate of an Allende or the decline of the "Eurocommunist" Italian Communist Party. Politics had to come at the expense of morality.

For MSF, the slogan was flipped. Revolution had never arrived, not from the shop floor, and not from Parisian students. Europeans' temporary infatuation

---

[69] *Bulletin Médecins sans Frontières* 6 (1977): 4–5.

[70] Redfield, 58.

[71] Rudolf Bahro, *Die Alternative: zur Kritik des real existierenden Sozialismus* (Cologne: Europäische Verlagsanstalt, 1977).

[72] The term *Realsozialismus* was apparently first used by Erich Honecker at the Ninth Conference of the Central Committee of the SED in May 1973. Peter Borowsky, *Die DDR in den siebziger Jahren*, Bundeszentrale für politische Bildung, available online at: www.bpb.de/izpb/10111/die-ddr-in-den-siebziger-jahren?p=all.

[73] Martina Thom, "Karl Marx und der reale Humanisimus," 6, Universitätsarchiv Leipzig R M50, Bd. 1.

with the orgiastic violence of Maoism only testified to a dying belief in the ability of the Left to achieve socialism through trade unions, parties, or politics *per se*. Faced with so many disappointments and the lack of a political critique of capitalism, the disillusioned turned to morality at the cost of politics. The real divide in the world was not between Washington and Moscow, but between Pinochet – or Pol Pot – and their victims. Revolution's failure in Italian factories and Guinean bauxite mines led Soviet and Eastern Bloc regimes to double down on the nation-state; European Leftists, however, saw in the revolution that never happened the need to abandon the scale of the nation-state altogether.

This disagreement over the virtue of the Third World nation-state did not obviously matter at first. Many of the theaters where humanitarian groups first intervened – East Pakistan, Nicaragua – centered around natural disasters where neither regimes' politics nor their incompetence upset contemporary views of the USSR as a necessary evil for the Left.[74] Humanitarianism offered an escape from the debates between "NATOpolis" and socialism.[75] But as organizations like MSF collected testimonies, a tension emerged.[76] More and more, brutality was carried out in the name of socialism, most visibly so in the case of the Vietnamese "boat people" who escaped Communism on dinghies. Yet few neighboring countries were willing to accept the refugees. The issue aroused especial outrage in postcolonial France, where a group of French intellectuals launched a campaign to run a floating refugee camp in international waters. The movement, "A Boat for Vietnam," crossed bitterly contested French political divides.[77]

But when Bernard Kouchner signed onto the movement, MSF was pulled into an unexpected schism.[78] MSF cofounder Xavier Emmanuelli (another former communist) and the Indochina veterans were skeptical of Kouchner's plan to run a floating refugee camp in a body of water the size of India. In an op-ed, Emmanuelli criticized "A Boat for Vietnam" as "A Boat for Saint-Germain-des-Prés," intimating that the unrealistic project was calculated more toward Parisian respectable opinion than refugees themselves.[79] "If this boat is a firebrand, an idea," he concluded, "then long live this imaginary boat that is to

---

74 Philippe Bernier, *Des médecins sans frontières* (Paris: Albin Michel, 1980).
75 E.P. Thompson, "Outside the Whale," in *The Poverty of Theory & Other Essays* (London: Merlin, 1978), 213.
76 MSF was not alone in collecting testimonies. The Jeri Laber Papers contain guidelines for "model testimonies" produced by Solidarités International, another French humanitarian group. See "Comment recueiller les témoignages des droits de l'homme en Afghanistan" and "Témoignage modèle" in Folder 15, Box 6, Jeri Laber Papers, Human Rights Watch Collection, Columbia University.
77 *Le Monde*, November 28, 1978; Anne Vallaeys, *Médecins sans Frontières. La biographie* (Paris: Fayard, 2004), 281.
78 Vallaeys, 282.
79 Xavier Emmanuelli, "Un bateau pour Saint-Germain-des-Prés," *Le Quotidien du Médecin*, December 4, 1978.

cross all the oceans of our culpability in order to receive the cries of the disinherited of all the countries where men are oppressed...But this does not make [the boat] functional or punctual. May it remain a symbol of our *fin de siècle*...of a derisively small boat that shall never arrive." At a subsequent board meeting, Kouchner pronounced MSF killed by "the bureaucrats of charity" and resigned.[80]

The Vietnamese debacle deflated MSF, but the schism between it and *Médecins du Monde* (MDM), Kouchner's new organization, affirmed an emergent antitotalitarian consensus. Rony Brauman described the Parisian debates over the "boat people" as "the culmination of the turn of the Leftist Marxists toward antitotalitarianism, the denunciation of the Marxism of the state."[81] But he explicitly noted that "human rights were not involved here; rather, the right to life of the Vietnamese." His remark underscores the extent to which events reflected a turn away from Marxism, not one toward "human rights." As Solzhenitsyn and "new philosophers" like André Glucksmann and Bernard-Henri Lévy joined Raymond Aron and Fracois Furet on Parisian bookstores, the Soviet romance had been decisively stamped out, albeit hardly replaced by programmatic alternatives.

Yet what we now call "humanitarianism" took on many forms, something that becomes clear if we examine Sweden, the other country, besides France, that produced the most active NGO to operate in Afghanistan. There, decades of Social Democrat rule had transformed a rural society into a model of social democracy. State interventions kept wages high, unemployment low, and workers happy. Because Swedish Social Democrats could imagine themselves as having mastered the politics of productivity at the scale of the nation-state, they did not need to position themselves in a transnational web of political alliances. Not that international engagement was lacking: Social Democratic Prime Minister Olof Palme positioned himself as a man of the Left by visiting Havana and comparing American bombing in Vietnam to Treblinka.

More significantly, however, Sweden boasted a terrifically organized grassroots anti-Vietnam War movement, the so-called *FLN-Grupperna* (National Liberation Front Groups). The movement unified Maoists dissatisfied with both Social Democracy and Soviet socialism with mainstream intellectuals who grouped around the newspaper *FiB/Kulturfront*. Stoked by Palme, who sought to outflank the Left, *FLN-Grupperna* activists romanticized "the heroic Vietcong fighting against white Americans" and supported Marxist regimes in Angola and Nicaragua.[82] When the Americans withdrew from Southeast Asia, however, and once Vietnam, and then China, began invading or occupying Third World countries themselves, the politics of antioccupation became muddled. Still, crucial lessons about sloganeering, organizational discipline, and a

[80] Vallaeys, 299.
[81] Brauman, *Mémoires*, quoted in Vallaeys, 290.
[82] Author Interview, Börje Almqvist, Stockholm, Sweden, June 22, 2014.

suspicion of bureaucracy had been learned. Received from the Maoist Left, too, was an appreciation of the role that the countryside and the peasantry had to play in national liberation movements.

More significantly, however, the days of self-satisfied spectatorship from the perspective of the European nation-state were over. When one veteran of the *FLN-Grupperna* started working at a newspaper in provincial Nyköping in the early 1970s, it was a front-page story if two workers were laid off at a factory.[83] Within a few years, though, not only were Swedish shoe companies outsourcing operations to Portugal; journalists themselves were being laid off. In 1976, Palme's Social Democrats lost elections, as businessmen rebelled against the wage bargaining consensus as "socialist." Interdependence in the form of European integration exploded the quest for economic justice through the nation-state. Faith in a progressive politics at the scale of the nation-state had withered, with little to replace it other than vague opposition to imperialism. "I was involved in party politics throughout the 1970s," explained one Swede, but by the end of the decade, he joked, "I entered my service for mankind or whatever."[84]

The April 1978 coup in Kabul thus presented both French and Swedish activists with an intellectual challenge. For many on the Swedish Left, revolution had not yet lost its appeal. One journalist recalled his initial excitement upon learning, over tea in Shimla, of a "real, live revolution" in Kabul, prompting him to race to the Hindu Kush via a trail of Pakistani and Afghan consulates.[85] French observers were more critical. After several years in Afghanistan and Pakistan, French physician Gérard Kohout was working in Paris, where, in April 1979, he received a phone call from MSF. Malhuret and MSF's leadership felt lost after *le clash Kouchner,* and were considering launching missions into Afghanistan.[86] Malhuret asked Kohout to conduct an initial survey for the organization, and soon the latter was on the ground. "The logical thing," he said, "would have been to connect with the officials there in Peshawar – the International Red Cross. I don't know why, but I kept my distance from them. In any event, I was taken to the French Embassy in Islamabad, where they proposed a meeting with the grand sachem of [UN] HCR [the United Nations High Commissioner for Refugees]. But I declined: the simple idea of submitting to an official structure was heresy to me. Instinctively, I didn't want to be a prisoner, to be controlled."[87] Kohout interviewed refugees: "They all said the same thing: massacres, destroyed, rebellions." Kohout considered entering Afghanistan, but hesitated: "that wasn't in my mandate," and the

---

[83] Ibid.
[84] Author Interview, Anders Fänge, conducted by telephone from Berlin, Germany, September 17, 2014.
[85] Author Interview, Börje Almqvist, Stockholm, Sweden, June 22, 2014.
[86] Vallaeys, 407
[87] Ibid., 408.

refugees' testimony made unambiguous the need for aid. Kohout reported back to Paris, but MSF's leadership remained skeptical. Plans for aid were tabled. As reports of horrors trickled out of Kabul, however, bureaucrats at SIDA (Swedish International Development Authority, the Swedish state development agency), grew concerned. Seeking expertise, Stockholm contacted Anders Forsberg, a young postgraduate who had visited Afghanistan twice during the 1970s. SIDA connected him with Carl Schönmeyr, a Swede and UNICEF's chief officer in New Delhi. Schönmeyr quickly found Forsberg a useful source, since his travels had acquainted him with intellectuals who became PDPA ministers.[88] Schönmeyr felt compelled to act. Afghanistan, he wrote to Forsberg, was a new Guernica, Lidice, or Oradour-sur-Glane – all sites of Nazi reprisals on civil populations, although none tied with Jewish suffering.[89] Events in Afghanistan may not have been a second Holocaust, but they did reflect a problem in global order. "Whereas similar man-made disasters in Biafra, Kampuchea, and Lebanon quickly forced the international community into concerted action," Schönmeyr wrote, "the lives and well-being of Afghans seem to leave the UN family of organizations untouched."[90] Neutral powers like Sweden, however, could influence UN agencies like UNICEF and UNDP, encourage their New York representations to work on "the Afghan social emergency" with said UN agencies, and form an international front of "Western European countries" and "Third World countries in general" to address the "social catastrophe *inside* Afghanistan."

Schönmeyr was only half right. The ICRC was permitted to provide medical services in Kabul in early 1980, but the PDPA "later reconsidered their position and asked delegates to interrupt operations after five months."[91] The group was let into the country in August 1982 to conduct interviews with prisoners (four-fifths of them with regime representatives present), but "ICRC staff had to leave the country in October."[92] When an earthquake devastated Kabul in January 1984, Kabul requested and accepted aid from the UNDP and the United Nations Disaster Relief Organization, but only in relation to the trembler.[93] When the UNICEF chief in Pakistan attempted to deliver medical supplies into Afghanistan, the Eastern Bloc members of UNICEF's Board threatened to unseat the organization's American head unless the trip was cancelled.[94]

---

[88] Author Interview, Anders Forsberg, Uppsala, Sweden, June 28, 2014.

[89] Carl Schönmeyr, Letter to Anders Forsberg, August 22, 1979, Personal Archive of Anders Forsberg, Sweden.

[90] Carl Schönmeyr, "The Silence of the United Nations–And How to Break It," Sveriges Riksarkivet SE/RA/730500/001/E 3:1, Peshawar 1984 (Rapporter, Korrespondens).

[91] *International Committee of the Red Cross Bulletin*, March 1987 (134), 2, in Folder 9, Box 3, Jeri Laber Papers, Human Rights Watch Collection, Columbia University.

[92] Ibid. For more on this episode, see Jeri Laber, Helskini Report Draft #1, Part Two ("Prisoners and Prisoners of War"), 1–3.

[93] M. Farid Zarif, Letter to Javier Pérez de Cuéllar (January 10, 1984), Folder 94, Box 9, Javier Pérez de Cuéllar Papers, Yale University.

[94] Author Interview, Anders Fänge, conducted by telephone from Berlin, Germany, September 17, 2014.

UNICEF was eventually authorized to vaccinate children in Kabul, but when it proposed that it conduct campaigns in rebel areas, the Afghans were crystal clear on their conditions: "discussion with dissident groups does not confer 'status' on these groups, e.g. UNICEF's past record in serving both areas of China in the 1940s, in Biafra, Vietnam in the 1970s and in Kampuchea and Beirut in the 1980s."[95] Nor were indigenous attempts at aid or rights monitoring more successful. Four faculty members at Kabul University founded a Committee for the Defense of Human Rights in 1982, but they were swiftly arrested and imprisoned.[96]

With the Swedes stalled, the French took a different approach. Following the Soviet invasion, Claude Malhuret contacted Juliette Fournot, a French oral surgeon who had lived in Afghanistan as a girl in the 1960s, to organize missions for Afghan refugees in UNHCR camps in Pakistan.[97] Yet Pakistani authorities refused MSF permission of continuing its work in the camps, leaving "only one possibility: to work in Afghanistan itself. This multiplied our obstacles, but it also brought our aid to the truly needy and where the assistance of official international organizations with diplomatic status could not penetrate."[98] Rony Brauman resisted the idea, but Kohout rebelled, saying he was going to work in Afghanistan no matter what.[99] Kohout launched a mission to Nuristan, but efforts to build a dispensary failed after squabbling between *mujāhidin* groups.

But a subsequent mission to the Hazarajat over the winter of 1981–2 was more successful. There, MSF established four dispensaries and a hospital in the Hazara highlands. And yet the region – hundreds of miles in Afghanistan's interior – was less than the tableau of misery, crisis, and emergency that MSF expected. "After two years," medics noted, "the Hazarajat, a natural fortress, is the seat of a liberation movement novel in its magnitude, its success, and, above all, its relative unity."[100] Prices had risen astronomically, but the region had avoided catastrophe through "a return to the old economic autarky of each valley." The organic relationship between Kabul and countryside actually benefited the Hazara. Every day, convoys of buses, trucks, and passenger taxis traveled from Bamiyan and Behsud to Kabul, guarded by *mujāhidin* and (outside the capital) Soviet troops. One *arbāb* (rural landlord) in Behsud explained: "They need our products (meat, wool, firewood) more than we need theirs (salt, sugar, tea, & petrol)." *Mujāhidin* commanders had even imposed export limits and taxes on outgoing firewood exports to the capital, causing prices in Kabul

95 James P. Grant (UNICEF Executive Director), Letter to Javier Pérez de Cuéllar (December 7, 1985), Folder 96, Box 9, Javier Pérez de Cuéllar Papers, Yale University.
96 Barnett Rubin, Letter to Robert Silvers (June 3, 1986), Folder 1, Box 6, Jeri Laber Papers, Human Rights Watch Collection, Columbia University.
97 Vallaeys, 414–15.
98 "La mission medicale de Médecins sans Frontières en Afghanistan (Situation en Mars 1982)," 1, Box "1982–1988," MSF Institutional Archives.
99 Vallaeys, 415.
100 "La situation dans le HAZARAJAT au printemps 1981," 1, Box "1981–84 Afghanistan. Rapports de Mission," MSF Institutional Archives.

to septuple and making "the inhabitants of Kabul colder than the Hazara this winter!"[101] PDPA rule had driven wealthy Kabuli Hazaras and their commercial networks back to the province, and some locals even saw the situation as a "small liberation" from Kabul.[102]

Yet in spite of these small victories, the medical situation in the Hazarajat remained dire. There was only one doctor to tend to three million inhabitants, making the Hazarajat "a medical desert."[103] But the first MSF team's report was vague in its diagnosis of what, exactly, this meant. The report's authors noted that their consultations "[have] led us to a definition of a rather individualized syndrome, 'bad-everywhere' syndrome" (a translation of *besyār dard* – "much pain"). Body pain and stomach pain constituted its main symptoms, but so, too, was a burning sensation in the eyes, the urethra, or the back.[104] "The absence of a statistical study," the report concluded, "forces us to abstain from definitive conclusions."[105]

The vagueness of "bad-everywhere syndrome" made the assumptions guiding MSF's mission clear. The contrast might be sharpest with Soviet advisers, who sought to mold healthy, trim, male bodies into guardians of the territorial state. For communist states, "it was the disappearance of the body that manifested the absolute and arbitrary nature of crude power, when even the physical trace of individuals or of entire peoples was erased. The body is political in the sense that in the last resort, it is what bears witness to power."[106] In contrast, rather than imprinting violence onto subjects' bodies, humanitarian reason was obsessed with somatic stigmata as a marker of truth. MSF's practice of *témoignage* (witnessing) documented signs of state-sponsored torture, using the body as a counter-site of truth against totalitarian power.

But cases of torture – jailers expertly applying pain to the human organism – were the ideal target of such somatic truth-telling. Clearly, one could not denounce hurricanes or earthquakes as having violated some sacred compact, even as they destroyed human bodies more comprehensively than a Pinochet or Suharto. Along these lines, it bears paying attention to the places where MSF operated. The Hazarajat, a mountainous internal frontier populated by ethno-confessional minorities, numbered among the regions least integrated into the Afghan state. But for humanitarian actors attuned to "catastrophic" conditions, such internal frontiers formed an ideal biotope. Reinterpreted as "catastrophe" or "emergency," their neglect meant that health conditions were appalling even

---

[101] Ibid., 17.
[102] "Rapport sur les Missions en Hazarajat (Afghanistan) de Juillet 82 a Mars 83," 2, Box "1981–84 Afghanistan. Rapports de Mission," MSF Institutional Archives.
[103] "La situation dans le HAZARAJAT au printemps 1981," 18, Box "1981–84 Afghanistan. Rapports de Mission," MSF Institutional Archives.
[104] Ibid., Annex: "Le syndrome du 'Mal partout' à propos d'un grand nombre d'observations," 1.
[105] Ibid., 3.
[106] Didier Fassin, "Truth Ordeal: Attesting Violence for Asylum Seekers," in *Humanitarian Reason: A Moral History of the Present*, trans. Rachel Gomme (Berkeley: University of California Press, 2012), 112.

in the absence of civil war. The French groups, one Swedish observer noted, had halted sending in specialized surgeons, since "the number of acute war injuries are not so numerous as to warrant a specialist surgeon." Still, he added, MSF's "medical reports clearly suggest a catastrophic situation in the Hazarajat regions," justifying a continued humanitarian presence.[107] If mountains, minorities, and margins were a problem for centralizing regimes, they formed the optimal human terrain where humanitarian actors could exploit the thin line between catastrophe and poverty, between medicine and politics, between the body of truth and the body of power.

Fortunately for MSF, however, the Soviet Army was more than capable of inscribing violence into Afghans' bodies. Early in the morning of October 31, 1981, Soviet gunships fired upon an MSF hospital in Jaghori (a village in the Hazarajat), razing it to the ground.[108] There were no staff or patients in the building: an unarmed helicopter had flown over the clinic three days earlier, prompting MSF to evacuate. But the attack confirmed the worst about the USSR, not least for a new Socialist government in France, which reiterated its support for MSF throughout the autumn and spring of 1981–2.[109]

That was all the better, since, by its own admissions, MSF's clinical work left much to be desired. As an internal report written from Jaghori explained, during their initial efforts, MSF doctors had handed out too many pills for treatments. The intensity of maladies like tuberculosis sometimes declined around MSF sites, but as medical supplies declined, the diseases returned.[110] "Bad-everywhere" syndrome, the report admitted, merely reflected MSF's malpractice. "Not all reasons for penetrating Afghanistan are good, and this role of the witness does not *ipso facto* justify any activity on the ground."[111] Yet the mission remained justified. "More and more," noted the report among calls for "an honest medicine," "the truly sick arrive to have themselves treated and hospitalized."[112] The report abandoned the maximalist position on *témoignage*, yet still remained essentially committed to the search for bodily truth beyond borders.

My Service for Mankind

This framing, however, was typical only for *French* humanitarianism. Back in Sweden, reflected journalist Börje Almqvist, "many of the people associated with the NLF groups saw [the Soviet invasion] as just another manifestation of

---

[107] Nils-Goran Sjöblom, Letter to J. Brohult, H. Isaksson, and H. Cedreus, April 12, 1982, Personal Archive of Anders Forsberg, Uppsala, Sweden.
[108] "Jaghori-81," 1–2, Box "1981–84 Afghanistan. Rapports de Mission," MSF Institutional Archives.
[109] Box "Afghanistan. 1982" at the MSF Institutional Archives contains dozens of such letters.
[110] "Rapport sur les Missions en Hazarajat (Afghanistan) de Juillet 82 a Mars 83," 10, Box "1981–84 Afghanistan. Rapports de Mission," MSF Institutional Archives.
[111] Ibid., 8.
[112] Ibid., 1, 17.

Soviet hegemony," but "we realized that being humanitarian meant money and not just words."[113] Meeting at an apartment in central Stockholm, Anders Forsberg and four others founded the Swedish Committee for Afghanistan (SCA), resolving "to have the affected civilian populations in Afghanistan as the target audience, not the Afghan refugees in Pakistan. Further, it would be a humanitarian effort with survival as the theme and primary goal."[114] Traces of Leftist inspiration were apparent, as the group's charter specified "support to the Afghan people's struggle for national independence."[115] Intellectuals like Jan Stolpe, a cofounder of *FiB/Kulturfront*, moderated the group, as did the fact that a board of directors included seats for representatives of Sweden's mainstream political parties.[116]

This mattered, because, as Carl Schönmeyr outlined in a letter to Forsberg, SCA had to influence not just opinion but also policy.[117] "The government and Parliament obviously stand at the center of this kind of action by the Committee," wrote Schönmeyr, but, he added, "a number of organizations and institutions may also be important recipients for this message: the Red Cross, Save the Children, [and] SIDA." Long-term funding, Schönmeyr thought, "would be sought through a national collection drive, 'Swedish Afghanistan Helper' ... A petition would be published in support of collection, and a public meeting would be held on Afghanistan to inform about the situation and collect donations."[118] In the short term, however – here was where the embedding in Parliament mattered – SCA would require state funding.

Obtaining state funding for a glorified guerrilla medical team? The idea was not as far-fetched as it may sound. Historically, Swedish aid to Third World countries had been parochial. Tunisia was a favored recipient in Africa, but the lack of a colonial history meant that Swedish administrators had little experience running projects in the field.[119] But the persistence of white rule in southern Africa made SIDA rethink its mission. In 1969, SIDA began supplying Rhodesian, South African, Namibian, and Angolan national liberation movements with free office space in Stockholm and scholarships at Swedish universities. If states had not yet experienced their national liberation from white rule, aid should go to the legitimate representatives of "the people" – black Africans, if not a specific ethnic group or tribe. Applying this logic, SIDA

[113] Author Interview, Börje Almqvist, Stockholm, Sweden, June 22, 2014.
[114] Carl Schönmeyr, "Afghanistans sakär vår. Del 1. Opinionsbildning i tysthetens tid," *Afghanistan-Nytt* 1 (2005), 8.
[115] Ändamål och Stadgar för Svenska Afghanistankommitén," Personal Archive of Anders Forsberg, Uppsala, Sweden.
[116] Author Interview, Jan Stolpe, Stockholm, Sweden, June 24, 2014.
[117] Carl Schönmeyr, Letter to SCA, April 3, 1980, Personal Archive of Anders Forsberg, Uppsala, Sweden.
[118] Schönmeyr, "Afghanistans sakär vår. Del 1. Opinionsbildning i tysthetens tid," 9.
[119] Ironically, Afghanistan was the exception here: SIDA provided funding to an agricultural cooperatives project in Baghlan Province in northern Afghanistan.

funded national liberation groups like the Zimbabwe African National Union and the Zimbabwe African People's Union in Rhodesia, and the South West African National Union and the South West African People's Organization in South-West Africa.[120] Soviet occupation and white rule were, from this perspective, essentially the same phenomenon; so SIDA should treat them the same. But there was considerable distance between Schönmeyr's vision and reality. SCA's financial reserves were barely a week's wages. Schönmeyr, ever perspicacious, suggested that SIDA finance SCA's inaugural November 22, 1981, advertisement in Sweden's largest newspaper. Without the funding diverted from SIDA's budget for "information on developing countries," the group could not have paid for the ad, which cost about $1,000 in present-day terms. It was, explained Schönmeyr years later, "not a bad creative interpretation of the rules . . ."[121] SCA collected enough money from private donors to organize operations and to apply for SIDA grants for "catastrophic aid" to developing countries. SIDA approved the application; a check was made out to Jan Stolpe. On a Friday afternoon, recalled Stolpe, he picked up the check – tens of thousands of dollars' worth – and kept it in his back pocket as he hiked around the Swedish countryside that weekend.[122] While waiting for a train at Stockholm's Central Station around that same time, Anders Forsberg saw a news ticker report on SIDA's decision. He nearly leapt off the platform in glee: "the days of us thinking in terms of hundreds of kronor were over."[123]

Money in pocket, SCA followed the "French doctors" more closely. In March 1982, Nils-Göran Sjöblom, a pharmaceutical logistics manager with private sector and UNICEF experience in Biafra, Jordan, Lebanon, Bangladesh, and India, visited Paris to speak with doctors from MSF, MDM, and *Aide Medical Internationale*, another splinter organization from the boat people crisis. Meeting with members of what he called "three ideal apolitical French organizations that have recently served in catastrophe work in Afghanistan," Sjöblom inquired after the possibility of SCA cooperating with them.[124] Agreement was reached for SCA to supply MSF with medicine while also supplying its own Afghan-run hospitals in the Hazarajat. (The Swedes, ever conscious of the ethics of Europeans breaching Third World sovereignty, themselves remained on Pakistani soil.)

The comparative valuation of European life – to enter a war zone or not? – underscored the degree to which the two groups reflected very different Leftist traditions. As Sjöblom returned to Stockholm, SCA organized a special session

---

[120] Author Interview, Pierre Schori, Stockholm, Sweden, June 24, 2014; Tor Sellström, Interview with Pierre Schori, June 28, 1996, available online at: www.liberationafrica.se/intervstories/interviews/schori/?by-name=1.

[121] Schönmeyr, "Afghanistans sakär vår. Del 1. Opinionsbildning i tysthetens tid," 8.

[122] Author Interview, Jan Stolpe, Stockholm, Sweden, June 24, 2014.

[123] Author Interview, Anders Forsberg, Uppsala, Sweden, June 28, 2014.

[124] Nils-Goran Sjöblom, Letter to J. Brohult, H. Isaksson, and H. Cedreus, April 12, 1982, Personal Archive of Anders Forsberg, Uppsala, Sweden.

of the Permanent International People's Tribunal to discuss not human rights but "serious and systematic violations of the rights of peoples."[125] The Tribunal, a loosely organized organization of European intellectuals, had evolved out of the 1967 Russell Tribunals against the Vietnam War and conducted investigation into causes like self-determination for Western Saharans, Filipino Muslims, and Eritreans, and state terror in Argentina and El Salvador. While the Stockholm Tribunal aimed at exposing Soviet crimes in Afghanistan, then, it drew more inspiration from Third World self-determinationism than from antitotalitarianism.[126] The two principles were not obviously harmonious, but the Soviet invasion had made the two one, testifying to a global moment.

SIDA funding in hand, Schönmeyr traveled to Peshawar in the summer of 1982 to interview potential *mujāhidin* partners. There, he wrestled with the challenges facing SCA: "Would it be possible, I thought, to run operations in Afghanistan from the neighboring country of Pakistan and without Afghan regulatory approval? And how would the government of Pakistan allow such a thing, given the eventual reaction from the Soviet Union, a superpower with destabilization of other countries as one of its well-proven specialties?"[127] Schönmeyr audited Afghan opposition groups and Afghan doctors' associations as potential partners. Those best qualified to practice medicine were third- and fourth-year Afghan medical students who had fled from Kabul to avoid the draft, but they had never graduated and lacked diplomas. Further, "in Afghanistan in the 1970s, 'doctor' could mean anything from someone with an M.D. to someone who had a first aid kit."[128] Schönmeyr tracked down former professors of medicine from Kabul University to interview the students and test their medical literacy.

This, however, was only the first step. Schönmeyr conducted interviews with *mujāhidin* leaders to confirm the political reliability of doctors and the advisability of sending, for example, a *Hezb-i Islāmi*-affiliated physician to territory controlled by another party. But finding honest Afghans was not always easy. Schönmeyr bungled, for example, by funding the Society of Afghan Doctors (SAD), a group that ran only one clinic inside of Afghanistan and discriminated among patients, favoring Pashtuns over non-Pashtuns. SCA cut off funding to SAD and developed its own intelligence arm that sent surveyors into the refugee camps to inquiry into the trustworthiness of applicants for SIDA

[125] "Tribunal Permanent des Peuples, "Session Afghanistan Stockholm 1–3 Mai 1981. Sentence," Thin Folder, SE/RA/730500/001/F 1:5; "Statute for the Permanent International People's Tribunal"; "Universal Declaration on the Rights of People–July 4, 1976," Thick Folder, SE/RA/730500/001/F 1:5.

[126] "What Is The Tribunal?" Thick Folder, SE/RA/730500/001/F 1:5.

[127] Carl Schönmeyr, "Afghanistans säkär vår. Del 2. Insatsplanering i Peshawar," *Afghanistan-Nytt* 2 (2005), 7.

[128] Author Interview, Anders Fänge, conducted via telephone from Berlin, Germany, September 17, 2014.

FIGURE 6. "Anders Fänge (to the left), the Swedish Committee for Afghanistan (SCA) representative in the SCA office in Peshawar in Pakistan. He is in a meeting with representatives (on the sofa) of a *mujahidin* front in Afghanistan in need of medical support." *Source:* Courtesy of Börje Almqvist.

aid. As a result of the stringent qualifications, SCA developed a reputation for being difficult to cheat and awarding aid on the basis of technical qualifications. Working with MSF (which made sure that Afghan-run clinics actually existed) and using its own fingerprinting system to guarantee delivery of medicine, SCA developed a thriving operation.[129] Following Schönmeyr's trip, SCA submitted a new request to SIDA for $130,000.[130]

The circumstances made for strange bedfellows. SCA had allied with *mujāhidin* groups since, as Börje Almqvist explained, "guerrillas had to swim like fish in the ocean of the people." "Mao had turned out to be an old fart," Almqvist explained. "All of the Confucianism, respecting your parents, and so on. But he did have some perceptive lessons about guerrilla warfare."[131] Development professionals like Schönmeyr and Sixten Heppling (a former Kabul UNDP program officer) joined forces with ex-journalists like Anders Fänge

---

[129] "Establishment of Health Units Inside Afghanistan," Folder "Peshawar 1982–1983 Korrespondens Rapporter," SE/RA/730500/001/E 1:5.

[130] Carl Schönmeyr, "Afghanistans sakär vår. Del 3. Genombrottet," *Afghanistan-Nytt* 3 (2005), 9.

[131] Author Interview, Börje Almqvist, Stockholm, Sweden, June 22, 2014.

(head of the Peshawar office for most of the 1980s) and the modernizing wing of *mujāhidin* parties. As Almqvist explained, even Gulbuddin Hekmatyar's *Hezb-i Islāmi* accommodated intellectuals for whom the group represented a "sleek" modern future.[132] United by a faith in the countryside and opposition to Soviet rule, the Swedes and the *mujāhidin* groups embarked on a decade-long partnership based in the territory formerly at the core of "Pashtunistan." Formerly, indeed: while Pakistani intelligence tolerated Ghilzai Islamist parties like Hekmatyar's, it crushed *Afghān Millat* ("Afghan Nation"), a pro-Pashtunistan nationalist party. Soon, it was more dangerous for *Afghān Millat* to be based in Pakistan than in Afghanistan. Pashtun self-determination would express itself on Pakistan's terms.

Meanwhile, however, the victory of the Social Democrats in September 1982 Swedish elections jeopardized SCA's plans. Olof Palme, whose support for SIDA's Afghan adventure could not be assured, retook power. Nonetheless, while waiting for news from SIDA, in the fall, SCA-equipped Afghan doctors embarked from the Pakistani FATA to deliver medical supplies to a clinic in Ghazni Province.[133] On January 11, 1983, SCA's Stockholm offices received a dispatch: "Sweden is the first country in the world to have used public funds to assist the war-affected Afghan people."[134] Parliamentary debates in the Swedish *Riksdag* a week later confirmed the legitimacy of the so-called "Swedish model." As one Moderate deputy argued, "Sure, Sweden has helped and continues to help [in Afghanistan], but modestly so in comparison with Swedish humanitarian actions in other parts of our world."

The emphasis on the "modesty" downplayed the use of state funding to promote transnational aid, but such were the contours of this project assembled in the conjuncture of a global moment. Pharmacists like Sjöblom had received training in earlier Third World disasters. Swedish money – first from SIDA grants, then from private citizens through the "globalization of conscience" – paid for medicine, pamphlets, and Afghans' salaries. It was those Afghan citizens who used Swedish-procured supplies to heal, and, later, educate their compatriots. Here was that final fragment in Pakistan's transnational project – humanitarianism. Humanitarianism conducted on Pakistani territory, indeed the territory formerly at the core of "Pashtunistan," was the final necessary fragment. A decade after war had transformed "that fantastic bird of a place, two Wings without a body, sundered by the land-mass of its greatest foe, joined by nothing but God," Pakistan had become host to an equally fantastic geography divided by cartography, but united by humanity.[135]

---

[132] Author Interview, Anders Fänge, conducted via telephone from Berlin, Germany, September 17, 2014.
[133] Carl Schönmeyr, "Afghanistans sakär vår. Del 4. Den svenska modellen," *Afghanistan-Nytt* 4 (2005), 10.
[134] Ibid., 13.
[135] Rushdie, 186.

Conclusion

American support for these humanitarian operations was surprisingly slow to form. True, the Soviet invasion of Afghanistan aroused immediate geopolitical concern in Washington, but moral outrage toward the intervention is surprisingly difficult to locate in the record. More common was talk of Afghanistan as "an unspeakable country filled with unspeakable people, sheepshaggers, and smugglers" or of the *mujāhidin* as "primitive fundamentalist Moslem tribesmen who make Khomeini look like a graduate student at M.I.T."[136] Initial American concern over the invasion focused on the threat to oil supplies from the Persian Gulf, not the egregious levels of violence dealt unto Afghans. Save for one article by journalist Michael Kaufman in the *New York Times*, the paper of record "apparently gave no credence to atrocity reports, at least until 1983."[137]

It made for a contrast with events in Paris. There, disillusioned socialists devoted a special summer issue of *Les Temps Modernes* to denouncing the Soviet invasion in nongeopolitical terms. "This must be the end to all of the 'even ifs' that weakly protected our dreams: that the USSR was socialist even if, that it was necessary to call this monster that devoured its own children 'socialism' even if...We find ourselves beside the lovable liberals, besides the wise professors attached to the values that we once could have readily qualified as formal."[138] Reporting from Peshawar, MSF coworker Michael Barry bore witness to the crimes of the PDPA and the Soviet Union at a Paris tribunal, itself an inversion of Sartrean public performances of justice like the International War Crimes Tribunal against the American war in Vietnam.[139] In 1981–2, a so-called *Bureau International Afghanistan* relied on Barry's reporting from inside of Afghanistan to pronounce Moscow guilty of "violation of the laws of war."[140]

Only thanks to these European efforts could a global conscience penetrate America. Rosanne Klass, Director of the Afghanistan Information Center at Freedom House, invited Barry and several Afghans to New York, where a press conference forced New York media to start covering the story. Soon, readers of the establishment periodical *Foreign Affairs* learned from MSF's Claude Malhuret of how Soviet clients exploited territorial sovereignty to slaughter their population.[141] Faced with rebels, Malhuret explained, "countries of socialist

---

[136] Fred Halliday, "Arc of Overreaction: Wrong Moves on Afghanistan," *The Nation*, January 26, 1980, 71–2; Alexander Cockburn, "Iowa and Afghanistan," *The Village Voice*, January 21, 1980.

[137] Rosanne Klass, "Genocide in Afghanistan," in *The Widening Circle of Genocide*, ed. Isabel W. Charney (New Brunswick: Transaction Publishers, 1988), 135.

[138] "Presentation," in *Les Temps Modernes* July-August 1980 (No. 408–409), 3.

[139] Barry, "Repression et guerre sovietiques," *Les temps modernes* July-August 1980 (No. 408–409), 171–232.

[140] Klass, "Genocide in Afghanistan," 136.

[141] Claude Malhuret, "Report From Afghanistan," *Foreign Affairs* 62(2) (1983/84), 426–35.

orientation" simply launched "massive reprisals against the population, sometimes including the extermination of a large part of that population."[142] Touring New York, Malhuret and other MSF staff met Helsinki Watch Chair Robert Bernstein, who connected them with colleague Jeri Laber and Yale political scientist Barnett Rubin.[143] Soon, Laber and Rubin traveled to Peshawar to collect testimonies of human rights abuses with the intention to compose an article for *The New York Review of Books*. American opinion had woken up.

But the new humanitarianism had obvious limits. Helsinki Watch had authored reports on human rights offenses in Eastern Europe and the USSR for years, but the KGB had crushed internal dissidents; the Moscow Helsinki Group closed in 1982 after nearly every member had been imprisoned or sent to psychiatric wards. Controversy dogged accusations of Soviet chemical warfare, and the Paris Tribunals carefully avoided accusations of weapons of mass destruction. Charges of genocide, too, were off the table, even if Afghan activists (unlike Schönmeyr) compared events to the Holocaust and Barry had used the word in the article for *Les Temps Modernes*.[144] Further, Rubin conceded, many European "democratic Left" audiences and "the Indian educated classes" remained blissfully disengaged from the war. Short of more coverage of PDPA crimes against Hindus and Sikhs, Rubin struggled to see how to engage a wider popular front.[145] Like it or not, the only partner humanitarians had in their struggle against real existing socialism was the Pakistani deep state.[146]

But Islamabad and the humanitarians faced a formidable challenge, namely an occupying force of 100,000 Soviet soldiers and tens of thousands of advisers. A race for time was on. On one side stood the Afghan communist state, the Soviet Union, and territorial sovereignty. Having learned, or so they thought, how to write not just the history of Afghanistan but also its future, Soviet advisers sought to raise a post-revolutionary generation of Afghans within the hermetic boundaries they imagined colonial draughtsmen to have left behind. On the other side was the humanitarian project of transnational morality, embedded into the *mujāhidin* groups based out of the territory once imagined as

---

[142] Ibid., 427.

[143] Author Interview, Jeri Laber, conducted via telephone from Cambridge, MA, May 7, 2014.

[144] The October 1986 issue of a newsletter produced by the Islamic Association of Afghan Students and Immigrants, a group based in Flushing, New York, featured a cover calling to "Stop the Holocaust in Afghanistan." Folder 12, Box 5, Jeri Laber Files, Human Rights Watch Collection, Columbia University.

[145] Barnett Rubin, Letter to Jeri Laber, Aryeh Neier, Eric Schwartz, and Arthur Helton (June 18, 1986), Folder 1, Box 6, Jeri Laber Papers, Human Rights Watch Collection, Columbia University.

[146] Anders Fänge confirmed that he was vaguely aware of Pakistan's interests in Afghanistan throughout the 1980s, but that "we were not as aware as we should have been that Pakistan really wanted to establish a friendly client." Fänge underscored that "our main focus at the time was on the national liberation of Afghanistan." Author Interview, Anders Fänge, conducted via telephone from Berlin, Germany, September 17, 2014.

"Pashtunistan." Faced with the human wreckage left to die by real existing socialism, they would disregard colonial cartography as part of a move away from the nation-state altogether. At the heart of it were the Afghan and Pakistani Pashtuns who, divided by empire, then engaged by development, were now caught between two new global projects. The days of mimetic isomorphism that animated the developmental moment had passed. Central Asia had become an arena for two new projects of world making. A terrifying experiment had begun.

4

From Pashtunwali to Communism?

> With the growth of the complexity of society, immediate experience with its events plays an increasingly smaller role as a source of information and basis of judgment in contrast to symbolically mediated information about these events.[1]

On the morning of August 19, 1981, Valeriĭ Sidorov, a Komsomol secretary from Leningrad, landed with his family at the Kabul Airport to commence a two-year tour in Afghanistan.[2] His first day in the country was delirious. His Soviet and Afghan fixers drove him and his family to the Hotel Kabul and handed him the keys to Room 104, just down the hallway from Room 117, where Maoists had assassinated the American Ambassador two years prior. Sidorov's family lay down to sleep and recover from the jet lag; for Sidorov, however, it was a workday. In spite of the heat, he changed into a black suit and rushed to the lobby, whence PDPA flunkies escorted him to a meeting with PDPA General Secretary Babrak Karmal. Karmal expressed his delight that Komsomol advisers like Sidorov had arrived to advise the PDPA's youth organization, the Democratic Organization of the Youth of Afghanistan (DOYA). Gratified, but also exhausted, Sidorov collapsed into the car and was driven back to the hotel.

Later that evening, Sidorov tucked his wife and children into bed and wished them goodnight. Exiting into the hallway, he knocked at the room of Nikolaĭ Zakharov, the head Komsomol adviser. Zakharov let his friend into the room, remarking on the oppressive heat, but noting that he had brought refreshments. He placed a melon onto the table and sliced into it. Halfway through the cutting action, however, the knife jarred against something. Zakharov pried the

---

[1] Albert D. Biderman, quoted in Sol Stein, "The Defense Intellectuals," *Ramparts* (February 1967), 32–7.
[2] *Mushavery* (Moscow: Mezdhunarodnye Otnosheniia, 2005), "Vsë bylo ne zria," 17.

melon open, revealing a bottle of *Stolichnaya* vodka somehow hidden inside of the fruit – "special melons and watermelons imported into Afghanistan by the advisers." The men sliced the melon into bite-size chunks, poured shots, raised their glasses, and toasted one another, anxious but excited, to the future of socialism in Afghanistan.

Sidorov and Zakharov were members of Komsomol-2, one of several teams of youth advisers dispatched to Afghanistan from 1979 to 1988 and Komsomol's most ambitious operation ever in the Third World. In 1967, two years after the founding of the PDPA, Party leaders formed a People's Youth Organization that agitated in the universities of Kabul and in Army barracks.[3] Yet such efforts were desultory: by 1978, the organization numbered only 5,000 members, most in Kabul. Nor was this a boutique problem. Marx, Engels, and Lenin had explicitly argued that youths were the future of any socialist state. Without a youth mobilization apparatus, the PDPA was doomed to lack a real social base. Komsomol, which had grown from zilch to a mass organization, represented what Afghan Communists wanted: an administrative system that could swell the ranks of the Party, engorge the police and Army, and provide a rationalized system of cadre management. For Third World Communist élites who had only a tenuous control over their state territory, the promise of a mobilizational, centralizing matrix of Party control held an obvious attraction. Shortly after the April Revolution, then, the PDPA requested such assistance from Moscow.[4]

The head of Komsomol's Cadre Sector, Natalia Ianina, dispatched a dozen top Komsomol *obkom* secretaries. Yet soon after "Komsomol-1" arrived in Kabul in the summer of 1979, the country descended into chaos. Parchamists had led DOYA, but following the April Revolution, Taraki and Amin remade the organization into a Khalqist machine.[5] Komsomol advisers in Kabul were disgusted, feeling that the PDPA had exploited Komsomol to abet the "establishment in Afghanistan of an Islamic Republic of nowhere near pro-Soviet character."[6] Later, while preparing an exhibition on Komsomol with 'Abd al-Rahmān Amin (Hafizullāh's son) in November 1979, Nikolaĭ Zakharov overheard 'Abd al-Rahmān boast that he was "prepared to walk over the corpses

3 "Information über die Demokratische Jugendorganisation Afghanistans (DJO)," Bundesarchiv SAPMO DY-24/22217.
4 "Die Beziehungen zwischen dem Komsomol und der Volksjugendorganisation Afghanistans," Bundesarchiv SAPMO DY-24/22217. Komsomol's operations in Afghanistan were the first and, to my knowledge, only major extended foreign intervention of Komsomol into a Third World theater. Sergeĭ Mazov observes that in 1961, Sergeĭ Pavlov, the head of Komsomol from 1959 to 1968, proposed training a competitor to the U.S. Peace Corps for deployment to Ghana, Guinea, and Mali. The Central Committee of the CPSU authorized the plan, but it was eventually nixed. Mazov, *A Distant Front in the Cold War: The USSR in West Africa and the Congo*, 225–6.
5 RGASPI f. M-3, op. 13, *Putevoditel'*.
6 N.I. Zakharov, "Kak eto nachinalos'," in S.L. Tkachenko and L.A. Koroleva (Eds.) *Mushavery. Assotsiatsia molodëzhnikh sovetnikov* (Moscow: Izdatel'skii Tsentr "Nauka, Tekhnika, Obrazovanie," 2005), 12–17.

of any internal dissenters" within the PDPA.[7] Was this the socialist revolution these men had risked their lives to support?

By December, Amin the elder had been liquidated, and Soviet troops, now occupying the country, had installed Parchamists like Karmal in Kabul. Yet the need for a youth organization remained pressing. In the spring of 1980, Ianina scoured her personnel archives and traveled around the Soviet Union to recruit rising stars. As Ivan Obratsov, an *obkom* secretary from Voronezh, recalled, "In the spring of 1981 they invited me to the Kiev Republican Komsomol School to share the experience of our Komsomol organization. Natalia Ianina turned up there. She began to ask me: education, whether I knew how to use technology or not, can I drive an automobile, and so on. They said that was it. But then later came the call from Moscow. 'There's a recommendation to send you to Afghanistan as an adviser of the Komsomol Central Committee.'"[8] Said Karimov, a graduate student who edited Russian-Dari dictionaries at the Lenin State University in Dushanbe, saw an announcement calling for Persian speakers to serve as translators in an undisclosed country.[9] After initial exams at Komsomol's offices in the Tajik capital, Karimov sat across a table from Ianina and a fellow native speaker of Tajik. The two grilled him for hours on the fine points of translation between Russian, Tajik, and Dari. The standards were high, but Karimov passed.

Like all of the other Komsomol advisers and translators, however, before departing for Kabul, Karimov attended courses in Moscow, Tashkent, and Chirchiq (the site of a military base near Tashkent) to learn about Afghan culture, receive paramilitary training, and absorb Ianina's ideas of Soviet manners. "Ianina was a strict, strict woman," Karimov recalled. Of the fourteen advisers and translators in Chirchiq one summer, five were dismissed: four for attempting to sneak out of the compound, the fifth because Ianina disapproved of how sloppily he had eaten his food in the mess hall. "That's not a Soviet person," she said. "We can't have any uncultured people here." The adviser pleaded his case: his wife in Leningrad threatened to divorce him if he didn't serve in Afghanistan and earn a big bonus.[10] Ianina placed him on the next flight out of Tashkent. "You're not a Tajik, you're not a Russian, you're a Soviet adviser," Ianina emphasized. "You're a citizen of the Soviet Union." For ambitious upstarts like Karimov, however, this was precisely the point: day after day of eating military-grade Uzbek gruel, throwing grenades, and having the sixty-three-year-old Ianina, dressed in fatigues, scream at them for 5:30 AM wakeup calls was a small price to pay for assimilation. By 1988, some 200 men passed

---

[7] Ibid., 13.

[8] "Iunost' zvaa vpered. Komsomol cherez gody i rasstoiania," *Kommuna: informatsionnyĭ portal Voronezha i voronezhskoĭ oblasti,* May 15, 2007, available online at: www.kommuna.ru/news/detail.php?ID=20879.

[9] Author Interview, Said Karimov, Dushanbe, Tajikistan, July 24, 2012.

[10] VLSKM advisers serving in Afghanistan received roughly three times their normal wage, a handsome sum by Soviet standards, but one they only learned of *after* signing up for the job.

under Ianina's watch, arriving, as Sidorov did one sultry August day, in Kabul to carry out their internationalist mission.

Once there, the Komsomol advisers had plenty of work. As Obratsov, deployed to Herat, recalled, "The youth were desperate for contact. And it was as if they had absorbed our ideological guidelines. I can remember the First Secretary of our Youth *obkom*, Kadyr Mantyk, an eighteen-year-old kid who could recite from memory Lenin's work *What Is to Be Done*. Or girls in *paranjas* (veils) would come by and join in the youth protests. For them, the revolution promised a new life, and they came to that new life through Komsomol."[11] The work was dangerous, but it also offered a chance to fulfill one's sense of idealism. One day, Obratsov escorted a caravan from the Soviet–Afghan border to Qandahar: "[We took] everything, *everything*, into a country with no [industrial] production whatsoever, no industrial objects. But we were trying to improve the economy of the country, to embed it within the framework of modern civilization. Now I understand the extent to which that was unrealistic. But then no such questions raised themselves. I knew that I was fulfilling a sacred responsibility: the defense of the frontiers of our Motherland." Some advisers worked in Kabul institutions like DOYA's Institute for Young Cadre.[12] Most, however, flew to provincial capitals within the nine administrative zones into which Komsomol divided Afghanistan. As Zaidullo Dzhunaĭdov, a Tajik Komsomol adviser, explained, this was no simple task. In the Soviet Union, Komsomol existed in an institutional ecosystem of collectivized agriculture, a command economy, urban settlement, and peace.[13] How to translate the Soviet system to a country with private agriculture, a market economy, and a rural, illiterate population? How to translate a territorial regime to a nonterritorial state? How to advance from *Pashtunwali* to Communism?

The Local Cold War

Before following the Komsomol advisers into the eastern borderlands, one must reconstruct those lands' prehistory at a moment when they became microtheaters in a global Cold War. As the German foresters' foibles in Paktia had shown, there were ways to understand eastern Afghanistan that went beyond the Durand Line. Indeed, the entire ribbon of land from Asadabad to Khost was a vast zone of exchange linking Afghanistan with Pakistan, China, and Tajikistan. Trade corridors, like those along the Kabul River, linked Kabul with Peshawar. Other routes went from southeastern Afghanistan into the Pakistani FATA and the passes further north; others, from the northern reaches of the Kunar Valley into the Karakorum Range and Xinjiang; others still, from the

---

[11] "Iunost' zvala vpered. Komsomol cherez gody i rasstoiania."

[12] Author Interview, Dushanbe, Tajikistan, July 18, 2012. The person interviewed for this information has requested to remain anonymous.

[13] Zaidullo Dzhunaĭdov, Author Interview, Dushanbe, Tajikistan, August 30, 2012.

same starting point to Badakhshan in the north to the Panjshir Valley to the southwest.[14]

Most Pashtuns in the east were Ghilzais, which (to risk repeating colonial stereotypes) adhered to the core traditions of *Pashtunwāli* – *badal* (blood revenge), *malmastiyah* (hospitality), and *nānāwātai* (asylum) – and retained the egalitarian, militaristic organization uncommon elsewhere. Tribes in this part of Afghanistan were known for forming *lashkars*, small tribal armies, and *badragahs*, armed escorts for guests and traveling merchants. Arguably, the difference between Ghilzai and Durrani Pashtuns of southern Afghanistan may be understood in terms of the tension between the cultures of *nang* ("honor") and *qalang* ("taxes").[15] Visions of the centralized, fiscally buoyant state may have enthralled urban Pashtuns like the founders of the PDPA as much as they did hierarchically organized Durrani Pashtun rulers and foreign experts. But to the more egalitarian Ghilzai Pashtun tribes that lived in proud poverty, centralization often came at their expense. Officials from Kabul came not to give things but to take them. Unimpressed by such so-called "progress," *nang*-oriented tribes sought to defend their own critical resources and interact with the state on their terms, not its.[16]

It was precisely for this reason that Afghanistan's east was hardly untouched by development. Provincial representatives from Paktia like Hajji Muhammad Iqbal, a logistics kingpin, lobbied for aid to "their" province.[17] Sensibly enough given his chosen industry, Iqbal lobbied for an international highway connecting Afghanistan's ring road with Pakistan via Paktia. Others dreamed bigger. In light of the impressive economic growth of Pakistan in the 1960s, the out-migration of Afghan Pashtuns into Pakistan, and what Afghan nationalists saw as a Punjabi dictatorship, some believed that applying a "Piedmont Principle" to Paktia made political sense.[18] If only Pakistani Pashtuns could see how good Afghan Pashtuns had it, they might support irredentism. As Sher Khan, a representative from Tani, argued, "the downtrodden Pashtun nation has not yet been able to realize its rights, and the population of our province can help them in many regards, even though their life [i.e. in Pakistan] is by no means easy."[19] The prospect of bringing the east under more centralized control, particularly with the help of foreigners upon whom blame could be shunted, also played a role.

---

[14] V.V. Basov, "Evoliutsiia sotsial'noĭ bor'by vostochnykh pushtunov Afganistana: eë osobennosti do i posle Aprel'skoĭ revoliutsii" (1985), in Basov, *Natsional'noe i plemennoe v Afganistane*, 189.

[15] Tribal Analysis Center, "Afghanistan's Development: An Instability Driver?" (August 2010), available online at: www.tribalanalysiscenter.com/PDF-TAC/Afghanistans%20Development .pdf.

[16] Author Interview, Vasiliĭ Kravtsov, Moscow, Russian Federation, October 23, 2012.

[17] Basov, 166.

[18] Martin, *The Affirmative Action Empire: Nations and Nationalism in the Soviet Union*, 274.

[19] Basov, 168.

Paktia was not the only eastern province to see social science interventions. The drainage basin of the Kabul River occupied a central place in Soviet developmental schemes. Soviet engineers built the Naghlu and Darunta Dams to control flooding and provide electricity to Kabul and Jalalabad, respectively.[20] In 1964, Soviet experts began investing in agriculture around Jalalabad.[21] Professors like Idris Akhundzadeh from the USSR's Central Institute for Sub-Tropical Cultures determined that Jalalabad's soil could foster citrus, dates, and olives. Bulldozers, excavators, and dump trucks soon removed boulders that centuries of river flow had deposited into the soil. Engineers built a 70-kilometer-long canal along which state enterprises could grow crops.[22] "With what hopes did the local inhabitants look upon us!" recalled Akhundzadeh. "The route of nomads went through the valley, but they understood what it would mean for the country, what it would mean for them, if these dead lands came to life. Already at the time of construction the nomads had settled around Jalalabad, and even helped us...you should have seen their eyes."[23] Azerbaijani olives, Akhundzadeh noted, grew to be five times as large in the Jalalabad soil as they did in Baku orchards. But efficiency was not the point. "Do you know what I dreamed about then?" reflected Akhundzadeh. "That the Jalalabad Irrigation Complex would be able to help smallholder peasants by providing them with sites where they could grow something."

Yet the developmental moment's promises rang hollow. "The development project for Paktia Province has not justified the expectations of the population," said one representative from the region in parliamentary debates.[24] "Enormous sums of West German *Deutschmarks* and *afghānis* are being spent on automobiles, the construction of cottages, the reception of any and all possible guests to the province, and fuel purchases, and yet the return from it all is miserable." The region, complained another deputy, "is in a very severe state, suffering from illiteracy, darkness, a lack of hospitals and medicines. The people do not even know what the word 'doctor' means." Accusations mounted. Kabul was not building enough schools, hospitals, or roads. It had failed to stop other tribes from felling *cedrus deodara*.[25] Historically, representatives from the tribal regions had revolted over too much state; now, over too little.

---

[20] Muhammad Azim Hashimi, "Osnovnye napravleniia po razvitiiu sistemy elektroznabzheniia Demokraticheskoĭ Respubliki Afganistan" (*Kandidat nauk* Dissertation, Moskovskiĭ Energeticheskiĭ Institut, 1984), 23.

[21] Sudzhan, "Olivkovaia vetv'," *Vokrug sveta* 8 (1987), 11.

[22] For more technical details on the canal, see I. Dzhurabekov, L. Vartazar'ian, and E. Zhilin, *Dzhelalabadskiĭ irrigatsionnyĭ kompleks v Afganistane* (Tashkent: "Uzbekistan," 1981).

[23] Sudzhan, "Olivkovaia vetv'," 11.

[24] The direct quotations in this paragraph are drawn from parliamentary session extracts in *Islāh*, October 18–20, 1969, November 8, 1969, and November 11–13, 1969; and *Kāruvān*, November 28–30, 1969, as quoted in Basov, "Evoliutsiia sotsialnoĭ borby vostochnykh pushtunov Afganistana: eë osobennosti do i posle aprel'skoĭ revoliutsii," 167–8.

[25] Basov, 169.

Socialism provided a language through which to articulate solutions to these problems. Kabul University started a branch campus in Jalalabad in 1963 that exposed students to a world of Leftist ideas, while secondary schools that Kabul built across the region provided employment for an upwardly mobile Leftist Ghilzai Pashtun intelligentsia.[26] These were men a generation younger than PDPA leaders like Taraki, keen himself to integrate a new generation of Ghilzai youth into transnational Pashtun Leftism. And given that the Pakistani state, dominated by military élites, industrialists, and latifundia grandees, was oppressing Pashtun socialists, their quest seemed righteous – and backed by muscle. Ghilzai Pashtuns served disproportionately in the Army's officer corps and received combat and ideological training in the Soviet Union before returning to serve on military bases in eastern Afghanistan, where most of Afghanistan's military bases were located. Khalqist cells infiltrated the officer corps.[27] By the mid 1970s, one-third of the PDPA's membership came from just seven provinces in the east and southeast.[28]

Yet powerful forces stood in the way of the Khalqist project, not least among them landowning élites and the Pakistani Establishment. Seeking to upstage Communists, on April 22, 1970 (the hundredth anniversary of Lenin's birth), mullahs protested against the central government, calling Kabul "apostates and agents of Communism."[29] One of the protests' ringleaders denounced Zahir Shah and the Mojaddedi family as traitors to Islam.[30] Government police forces arrested him, triggering a series of counterprotests in Jalalabad and Ghazni on May 27, 1970, in which thirteen mullahs were killed.[31] Granted, none of the protestors belonged to the religious élite in Nangarhar, which continued to support Zahir Shah. Nor were any armed with anything more than bricks or bats.[32] Yet signs of unrest grew. In November 1970, a mob attacked a PDPA protest in Mihtarlam, dismembering one PDPA activist. Rumors circulated that one of the instigators was a "Pakistani mullah."[33]

Daoud's 1973 coup d'état amplified the stakes in the borderlands. Mullahs who merely distrusted Zahir Shah now excoriated Daoud as a Soviet quisling. When Daoud undertook expanded road-building projects in the tribal zones,

---

[26] Ibid., 172.
[27] Ibid., 173. One Komsomol adviser in the 1980s worked as a military translator at an Afghan Army military base in Khost in the late 1970s that was increasingly staffed by Khalqist Ghilzai officers. Author Interview, Abduzahid Zakhirov, Dushanbe, Tajikistan, July 31, 2012.
[28] Ibid., 174. The provinces in question were Kunar, Nangarhar, Paktia, Paktika, Ghazni, Zabol, Laghman, and Logar (Khost only became a separate province from Paktia after 2001).
[29] Ibid., 180.
[30] The Mojadeddis were a family of prominent Muslim intellectuals in Afghanistan, said to be descended from the Third Caliph.
[31] For more on this episode, see M. Slinkin, "O politicheskoĭ deiatel'nosti konservativnykh krugov Afganistana v 60–70-x godakh," *Spetsbiulleten' IV AN SSSR* 2 (Moscow, 1980), 127–8.
[32] Basov, 181.
[33] *Karavan*, November 9, 1970; *Millat*, November 14, 1970.

tribal leaders suspected him as being less interested in empowerment than conquest. Daoud did little to ward off these rumors, as he attempted to levy more direct taxes on communities and exert Kabul's control over transborder trade.[34] Daoud's base of support in the provinces eroded, while his outspoken demands for "Pashtunistan" put Islamabad on high alert. Daoud burnished his image by granting Pakistani Baloch rebels' families asylum, but after the failed Pakistani-sponsored coup d'état of 1975, the triad of ISI-sponsored Islamists, the PDPA, and the tribes forced Daoud to reverse himself by calling for an "honorable solution" to the "Pashtunistan" issue. Daoud nearly reached a deal with Zia in a March 1978 visit to Islamabad. Yet having alienated Afghan religious élites and tribal leaders, Daoud became dependent on the PDPA officers who had delivered him unto power.

When those officers overthrew Daoud in April 1978, however, their policies catalyzed massive resistance. The Khalqists may have been radical in their position toward "Pashtunistan," but DOYA's slogans ("Every Afghan should be a Sovietist" and "Like the Soviet Union in every way") did little to assuage fears of Soviet domination.[35] In May 1978, mullahs attempted to incite rebellion on the grounds that the government was "anti-Islamic."[36] In Paktia and Kunar, rebels set the forests alight, and that autumn, PDPA offices in Zabol and Ghazni were torched, too. Cooler heads sought a political solution; in the summer of 1978, tribal elders from Jaji, Mangal, and Jarjan traveled to Rome to beg the exiled Zahir Shah to restore the monarchy. (The former King elected to remain in his Italian villa.) Attempts at moderation had failed. More common was language like that on the flyers spread on both sides of the border that accused Taraki and Amin of being Soviet spies.[37]

Afghanistan's east, once supposed to be a bridgehead into "Pashtunistan," was coming apart. From the point of view of Islamists and the Pakistani Establishment, Khalq was to blame. In the mind of the Pashtun Left, meanwhile, Punjabi imperialists were "de-Pashtunizing" ethnic kin through religious propaganda.[38] In early 1979, Taraki and Amin blinked. The two met with leaders of the Mangal, Ahmadzai, and Tota-Khel tribes and guaranteed the safe return of 'ulamā' from Pakistan. But the outreach consisted of "fundamentally parade-like events calculated for external effect. They provided no tangible result other than leading the Party into the delusion of a picture of superficial well-being."[39] Foolishly, moreover, Amin and Taraki then declared the April Revolution for all Pashtuns "from the Amu to the Indus" (i.e., both Afghan and Pakistani Pashtuns), predictably provoking Zia to butcher the Pakistani

---

34 Basov, 183–4.
35 Koshimsho Iskanderov, *Molodezhnoe dvizheniie v Afganistane* (1945–1990 gg.) (Dushanbe, 1992), 102.
36 Ibid., 187.
37 Ibid., 188.
38 Author Interview, Sakina Ziar, Oxford, United Kingdom, July 14, 2011.
39 Basov, 169.

Left.[40] By the autumn of 1979, when Amin murdered Taraki, the borderlands had become an arena for the battle between some 15,000 *mujāhidin* and the PDPA. In Asadabad, the one government-controlled city in Kunar Province, the Afghan Army slaughtered 800 civilians. In one sign of Amin's total delusion, he changed the name of Jalalabad to Tarunshahr ("Tarun City") in honor of a slain Army Colonel. Yet the arrival of Babrak Karmal did not alter the PDPA's basic challenges. Khalqist activists may have been hated, but they at least possessed local knowledge of the place that hated them. The Parchamists appointed to the east after 1979, however, had to contend with not only anti-PDPA elements, but also a Khalqist grass roots that viewed Parcham as a Soviet marionette.

Here, then, was the challenge facing Soviet advisers when they arrived in the Afghan countryside. Seeing the Soviet Union as "unavoidably involved in processes not specific to Russia," this chapter examines how Komsomol operatives faced problems in Afghanistan that derived primarily from the *territorial* premise of their developmental project.[41] In spite of the differences between Cold War ideologies motivating modernization projects, development remained enthralled with the possibilities presented by bordered political space.[42] This tension between gradient and polygon expressed itself most vividly when the Soviet Union's historical approach to development, which bound not only economics but also politics to territorial power, entered the transnational space of the borderlands. "Pashtunistan?" reflected former translator Abdulwahob Wahidov. "I was there. It's not on the map, but I was there!"[43] Only by the late 1980s did some advisers throw away their maps, give up on the dream of total PDPA coverage of the countryside, and devolve authority to local tribes. The shift, however, threw doubt onto the point of their presence: Soviet-style administration had not only proved irrelevant in Afghanistan, but was leaving mayhem in its wake. Nowhere near as straight as Nevskiĭ Prospect, the crooked road from *Pashtunwali* to Communism would reveal much about the limits of the Soviet project in a world increasingly as interdependent as the supposedly isolated borderlands that had become an unexpected theater in a global Cold War.

Toward a Politics of Territoriality

As advisers from Komsomol-2, the group that included Valeriĭ Sidorov, fanned out to provincial centers in summer 1981, their reports made clear that "the military-political situation in the 'East' Zone has not improved and remains extremely tense."[44] Jalalabad was the only city in the region that the PDPA

---

[40] Author Interview, Vasiliĭ Kravtsov, Moscow, Russian Federation, October 23, 2012.

[41] Stephen Kotkin, "Modern Times: The Soviet Union and the Interwar Conjuncture," *Kritika: Explorations in Russian and Eurasian History* 2(1), 113.

[42] Maier, "Consigning the Twentieth Century to History," 823.

[43] Author Interview, Abdulwahob Wahidov, Samarkand, Uzbekistan, July 22, 2013.

[44] B.V. Tivanov, "Otchët o prodelannoĭ rabote zonal'nogo sovetnika (Zona 'vostok') DOMA,'" August 1981, RGASPI, f. M-3, op. 13, d. 15, l. 116.

controlled, and *mujāhidin* had butchered pro-PDPA tribal elders. Desertions plagued the Army, and "90% of the border battalions had gone over to the enemy side, [including] more than 500 soldiers and Sarandoy officers, 320 of them with weapons." Years of writing reports for Komsomol superiors in the sticks had not prepared advisers for this. Jalalabad was a world apart from what one translator, Abdulwahob Wahidov, dubbed "our East" (by which he meant Uzbekistan).[45] In Jalalabad, recalled Wahidov, "people lived normally," but "people's power" ended outside the city walls. *Mujāhidin* bombed stalls in Jalalabad's bazaars, and once, when Wahidov visited Jalalabad's main market, he had to dive for shelter as a fully loaded camel with a bomb surgically implanted into its stomach exploded, leaving gore and mayhem behind. The citrus and olive orchards had become killing fields.

Not only that, but Komsomol advisers had few good "colonial handbooks" at their disposal.[46] Impressed with Vladimir Basov's initial work at the Embassy, Ambassador Fikryat Tabeev tasked him with writing "a handbook for the higher and middle-ranking leadership of the Soviet military and civilian institutions that had been actively recruited into the events in Afghanistan."[47] The resulting book, *Current Problems of the April Revolution*, offered an alternative framework to the class-driven official cant. Basov called events in Afghanistan a civil war, denounced Pakistan as a "Punjabi state," and criticized Islamabad's ambitions to establish a "Punjabi satellite." "Any shift of the eastern and southern Afghan Pashtuns to Pakistan or under their patronage," Basov argued, "would sharply weaken or would split the Afghan state and would, correspondingly, create difficulties in guaranteeing the security of the southern border of the USSR."[48]

Back in Moscow, however, Iurii Gankovskii struggled to impress his views on the political leadership.[49] The scholar had spent the winter of 1979–80 preparing a report for the Foreign Ministry calling for a reappraisal of Afghan policy. Andropov, Gankovskii later explained, "expressed his surprise and asked me whether the situation was really that bad. It was quite clear from several questions he raised that he was thinking in terms of some sort of settlement." Ignored, however, and disapproving of Basov's non-Marxist approach and insistence on viewing Pakistan as an ethnic dictatorship, Gankovskii lashed out. When Basov submitted *Current Problems* for consideration as a *doktor nauk* thesis, Gankovskii had students add their own "contributions" to Basov's book, transforming it into an "edited volume" ineligible for consideration and

45 Author Interview, Abdulwahob Wahidov, Samarkand, Uzbekistan, September 21, 2012.
46 M. Jamil Hanifi, "Vending Distorted Afghanistan," 258.
47 Basov, *Natsional'noe i plemennoe v Afganistane*, 11; Alan and Kläy, *Zwischen Bürokratie und Ideologie: Entscheidungsprozesse in Moskaus Afghanistankonflikt*, 60.
48 Kravtsov, Introduction to Basov, *Natsional'noe i plemennoe v Afganistane*, 13.
49 Quoted in Selig Harrison, "Making the Russians Bleed," in *Out of Afghanistan: The Inside Story of the Soviet Withdrawal*, eds. Diego Cordovez and Selig Harrison (New York: Oxford University Press, 1995), 96.

limited the book's eventual print run to 250 copies.[50] As a result, "it is no coincidence that over the course of the entire second half of the Soviet Afghan campaign, the majority of Soviet representatives in Afghanistan not only were unfamiliar with *Current Problems* but had never even heard of the availability of such a serious book."[51]

Hence, Komsomol advisers went to war with a severely blinkered conceptual apparatus. When Aleksandr Rebrik, one of the head Komsomol advisers in Kabul, prepared a text for the tenth anniversary of DOYA's founding, he used utterly conventional terms.[52] "Today," Rebrik's text began, "Afghanistan is a developing state that has selected for itself the noncapitalist path of development, orienting itself toward the ideals of socialism…However, on this path of progressive transformations, counterrevolution and imperialism have risen up."[53] Rebrik's explanation of who they were fighting against was also underwhelming. "It's not easy," wrote Rebrik, "to answer the question 'Who, precisely, are the enemy? How many of them are there? How long will this last? Why?' Namely they're those who were robbed of their looted wealth by the Revolution and those whose views are alien to the interests and needs of the nation and the goals of the April Revolution that have gone into counterrevolutionary formations."[54] The average level of knowledge was not high. As one adviser put it, "What Afghanistan was, and what was going on there, well, neither my wife or I knew anything."[55]

All the same, DOYA was hardly dead. As of August 1981, half of the organization's members in Nangarhar Province lived in the capital, Jalalabad, but there existed, at least on Komsomol's accounting sheets, dozens of members in districts outside of government or Party control.[56] DOYA had to establish "primary organizations" in schools and industrial enterprises in regions under government control, and underground DOYA cells in regions still controlled by *mujāhidin*. As the Afghan Army and the "limited contingent of Soviet forces" reclaimed territory, DOYA would fill this space with Party institutions, just as the CPSU and Komsomol interdigitated territory and enterprises in the USSR. This task was nothing new for the Komsomol advisers. When advisers described their Afghan assignment, they framed it as "youth work" or "Komsomol work" identical to their jobs back home. There was nothing interesting to describe. "Youth work – what can I tell you?" said one.[57] And they were right: there no

---

[50] Alan and Kläy, *Zwischen Bürokratie und Ideologie*, 59–60.

[51] Kravtsov, 12.

[52] Aleksandr Rebrik, "Strana, revoliutsiia, molodezh (k 10–letiiu Demokraticheskoĭ organizatsii molodëzhi Afganistana). Material v pomoshch' propagandistam, lektoram, dokladchikam," (Kabul, 1986), RGASPI M-3, op. 13, d. 213.

[53] Ibid., 1–7.

[54] Ibid., 9.

[55] Kireev, "Kandagarskiĭ dnevnik," Introduction.

[56] Tivanov, "Otchët o prodelannoĭ rabote zonal'nogo sovetnika (Zona 'Vostok') DOMA," l. 116.

[57] Author Interview, Abuzahid Zakirov, Dushanbe, Tajikistan, July 31, 2012.

formal difference between the work one would face in Pskov, Kaunas, Sakhalin, or Jalalabad.

This, however, was in many ways the problem. Komsomol work *was* formally identical in Kaliningrad and Qandahar, but Afghanistan was no greenfield for isomorphic development. The Soviet project was predicated on very specific assumptions about economies and political administration: "Unlike most noncommunist political parties," CPSU "members joined a party unit at their place of work. These party units were grouped together on a territorial basis – the so-called 'territorial-production principle.' This arrangement made it difficult to supervise life among nonworking groups such as pensioners and single mothers, and in residential areas in general, although territorial party organizations could be formed at the place of residence if desired. The historical origins of the territorial-production principle are obscure. It arose in the prerevolutionary period, out of the general Marxist belief that life in the modern world revolves around the factory, and out of the idea that the Communist Party was the party of the workers – who were to be found in factories."[58]

This principle went deep. In a 1986 documentary film on DOYA, for example, while the narrative begins with tiny rural DOYA committees, the viewer soon enters an orphanage, where the sons and daughters of killed Afghan Army soldiers perform woodwork, sew, and train as radio announcers.[59] Later, the film touts members of DOYA working in a camera factory. A short interview with a man introduced as Azizi Yahya presented the model Afghan socialist life. "I'm grateful for the opportunity provided to me to pursue my graduate study in Moscow," he says. "Having completed my study there," says the former machinist, "I'm becoming a teacher at the university." Today, when people often identify primarily through their gender, sexual orientation, or patterns of consumption, the idea that one's mode of production constituted identity may seem obscure. But the idea that political identity flowed as organically from one's position on the factory floor as did the sweat from one's brow was axiomatic for many until the onset of postindustrialism.

If, however, European trade unionists faced the *shuttering* of the old platforms for political confrontation at the scale of the nation-state – coal mines, steel plants, railway companies – in Afghanistan, none of these institutions existed in the first place. "Nonworking groups" constituted the overwhelming majority of the population, something even contemporary Afghan cartographers recognized in the DRA's first official atlas.[60] Outside of a small belt running from Kabul to Mazar-i Sharif, there were no enterprises in the country that employed workers on a mass scale.[61] Jalalabad (population:

---

[58] Peter Rutland, *The Politics of Economic Stagnation in the Soviet Union: The Role of Local Party Organs in Economic Management* (Cambridge: Cambridge University Press, 1993), 26–7.

[59] *Molodëzh Afganistana* (1986), directed by V. Shorokhov.

[60] *National Atlas of the Democratic Republic of Afghanistan* (Warsaw: GEOKART, 1985).

[61] Ibid., 24.

100,000) had 100 workers. The Afghan camera-makers captured an industrial, territorial imaginary that was literally just that.

Hence, as one incoming adviser in Jalalabad, Nodari Giorgadze, noted in 1982, DOYA faced an overwhelming task in the Afghan countryside. Even the Pakistani state across the Durand Line, wrote the Georgian, had never directly ruled its tribal territories.[62] But Akhundzadeh's legacy offered hope: the Jalal-abad Irrigation Complex could "transform Nangarhar – bordering Pakistan – into a blooming region and, in doing so, solve not only the economic challenges of the region but also the political and social problems of the region, turning the Pashtuns to sedentary life." If the PDPA rebuilt the state farms, more of the population would become settled, legible subjects of territorial politics.

Yet who would organize them? Giorgadze was just an adviser. DOYA had to take charge. Giorgadze attached detailed comments on the Jalalabad DOYA PC leadership to his 1982 report, a common practice meant to aid the DOYA Central Committee in Kabul. Giorgadze praised his colleague Maudzudin Khatak, the twenty-one-year-old Secretary of the Nangarhar DOYA PC. Khatak had strong revolutionary credentials: he "was a member of an underground PDPA PC and the Secretary of the Youth Organization. They threw him in prison when he was still a minor for his political activity, for his work with the masses, and his loud statements against the Daoud regime. He's from the Pashtun tribes, single, educated to a twelfth-grade level, a member of the PDPA since age twelve, from the intelligentsia, and born in Laghman Province."[63] Crucially, too, Khatak "was born in the same village as the PDPA Secretary for Nan-garhar, the Governor of the Province, the Commander of the *Sarandoy*, and the Director of People's Education for Nangarhar." Further, tribal elders and mullahs respected him. "He's modest, brave, and devoted to the cause of Saur and Soviet friendship (you can sense this sincerity in him with every footstep)." Khatak was an asset, someone who promised to bridge the Pashtun Left with the Soviet global project. Giorgadze recommended that he be promoted; the Nangarhar PDPA Central Committee, Giorgadze hinted, wanted to hire him as its Deputy Secretary to aid a Secretary who hailed, suspiciously, from the same village as Khatak.

But Khatak had faults, too. One had "to work punctually and precisely with him," but Giorgadze qualified that "to one extent or another, this is an eccentric-ity of character of practically all the Pashtun tribes."[64] Such armchair anthro-pology was common among advisers, particularly among Tajiks. Zaidullo Dzhunaĭdov searched for adjectives to describe Pashtuns: "disrespectful… uneducated…argumentative…what else?" Asked about a term that appears frequently in Komsomol reports, Dzhunaĭdov was direct. "Hot-tempered

---

[62] Nodari Giorgadze, "Spravka TsK VLKSM pri TsK DOMA v zone 'Vostok,'" RGASPI f. M-3, op. 13, d. 24, l. 87–8.

[63] Ibid., l. 109

[64] Ibid., l. 110.

[*vspyl'chivyĭ*]?" he said, referring to Pashtuns. "*Very* hot-tempered."[65] Mamadsho Davlatov, who taught at Kabul Polytechnic University, was more direct: "Pashtuns are barbarians."[66] Even if Pashtuns ran the state, Dzhunaĭdov underscored, only Tajiks and Persianized Pashtuns knew how to govern. Central Asian history, he argued, could be told in terms of the battle between progressive, settled, hierarchical Persian culture, and unruly, egalitarian Pashtun barbarism. These comments reflected a bittersweet postcolonial irony: both men, but especially Dzhunaĭdov, were assimilated citizens of a Soviet empire that had done much to generate knowledge about Central Asia. Rather than finding any solidarity with "fellow" Muslims, however, Dzhunaĭdov repeated the same colonial stereotypes about Pashtuns as state disruptors that had structured Ul'ianovskiĭ's May 1978 reaction to the April Revolution. Yet one should not make a straw man out of such views, however. Soviet Orientologists like Ul'ianovskiĭ were wise enough to explicitly discourage forced villagization, as Soviet-aligned Communists were doing in Ethiopia. Nor were Soviet actors unique in disparaging Afghans as backwards. Helsinki Watch's Jeri Laber recalled colleagues who slandered Afghans as women-mistreating barbarians ignorant of human rights.[67]

Komsomol would govern with the conceptual tools it had. Work began in earnest in March 1982, when Khatak and seven DOYA members visited Shinwar Province "to form any contacts with the local population."[68] Giorgadze stayed behind in Jalalabad but gave Khatak "help and presents from the Komsomol of Georgia." The trip to the Mamandi and Shinwari tribes established trust, leading to a second visit that June. The DOYA PC dispatched an "agitational automobile" outfitted with a radio, tapes of speeches by Babrak Karmal, and several Pioneer-themed souvenirs and children's toys. Two mullahs said to be "well-known and authoritative in Nangarhar" came along, too. The entourage visited the villages of Azoranu and Torkham before traveling through Nazyan, Lalpur, and Jani Khel Districts. "Practically everywhere," wrote Giorgadze, "the group was received warmly, people listened to the concert program, songs, poems, the speeches of the leaders of the Party and the government, they read newspapers and the leaflets, and they gladly attended and listened to our activists at popular meetings. Among the majority of the tribes, the members of the group were hosted overnight by the elders and leaders of the tribes."[69]

The Provincial Committee grew bolder. It enlisted more mullahs who saw youth organization as, "as they themselves said, 'a just, divine cause.'" After

[65] Author Interview, Zaidullo Dzhunaĭdov, Dushanbe, Tajikistan, August 30, 2012.
[66] Author Interview, Mamadsho Davlatov, Khujand, Tajikistan, September 6, 2012.
[67] Author Interview, Jeri Laber, conducted via telephone from Cambridge, MA, May 7, 2014.
[68] Rutland, 67–9.
[69] Giorgadze, "Spravka TsK VLKSM pri TsK DOMA v zone 'Vostok.' DOMA i natsional'no-demokraticheskaia revoliutsiia v DRA. G. Dzhelalabad, noiabr' 1982 goda," RGASPI f. M-3, op. 13, d. 24, l. 88.

obtaining the assent of tribal elders, DOYA founded primary organizations among the Mamandis and Shinwaris it had visited that May. And "in spite of the fact that these tribes had been fully relieved from military service by the state, a group of twenty-five men enlisted from local DOYA groups were sent by the tribal elders into active border patrols on the border with Pakistan," a measure designed to replace Afghan Border Guards who had defected to Pakistan. Giorgadze saw something novel: "The fact that this group of soldiers did not tire out led to, on November 1, 1982, a group of 300 young members of DOYA from the tribes of the Mamandi and Shinwaris gathering with weapons in hand in the role of border patrol soldiers to dependably guard the border of the republic."

All the same, Giorgadze's concern with the "border of the republic" revealed his enslavement to a territorial mentality, even as he worked in a profoundly pre-territorial theater. Similar analytic problems came up elsewhere. In just one calendar year, Giorgadze noted, DOYA's membership rolls had doubled. The Nangarhar DOYA had founded fifty-five primary organizations: "Housewives of the Localities of Keral," "Pathan Underground Organization," and a *lycée* in Narang. It all sounded impressive. Yet what did these numbers mean? Three years later, another Komsomol adviser, Georgiĭ Kireev, learned that there were only 10,000 PDPA members in all of Afghanistan, not including those in the Army or the Sarandoy.[70] DOYA members did not all go on to become PDPA members, granted, but Giorgadze would appear to be fudging his numbers in claiming 6,400 members in the Eastern Zone alone.[71]

Soviet administrative culture was taking its revenge. Komsomol advisers had to produce biannual typed reports roughly fifty single-spaced pages in length, including dozens of statistical tables. Reports hewed to the same format: military and political developments, ideological work, organizational work, and (optionally) subsections on work with Pioneers and female DOYA members. A section on cadre development closed out the report. Norms like these generated what advisers called *bumagotvorchestvo* ("paper-creation"), *kantseliarshchina* ("stationery-itis"), *otchëtnost* ("reportality"), or, most ubiquitously, *biurokratizm* ("bureaucratism"). In theory, the reports' final section offered space to suggest reforms, but the hypernormalized format hindered critiques of "exogenous" factors that were nonetheless crucial. Since the existence of socialism was built into the reports as an endogenous factor, however, reports could never raise "exogenous" factors of the "feudal" economy and "tribal" relations. The Soviet system, by so successfully linking together politics, economics, territory, and the Party within the USSR, became autistic when translated to contexts without.

To be sure, Brezhnev-era élites and administrators were not unaware of these problems. As Peter Rutland writes, "the Party pledged to put the USSR through

70 Ibid., l. 89.
71 Georgiĭ Kireev, Diary, January 29, 1986, available online at: http://kireev.info/w-4.html.

'accelerated socioeconomic development'" and "made great play of its 'scientific' approach to social problems." Local Party secretaries were encouraged to rethink administration, particular during the late 1970s, when "experiments" were in fashion.[72] And yet it was frequently difficult to determine what, exactly, such experiments did. "There were," writes Rutland, "cases such as the Rostov 'work without laggers' campaign, whose precise administrative and economic content is obscure, no matter how closely one scrutinizes the voluminous materials published extolling its merits." Experiments that feigned market mechanisms, like the so-called Shchekino method, questioned basic assumptions about the command economy. More broadly, without the later discursive separation of "socialism" from "stagnation," it was difficult to see the problems as specifically Soviet rather than inherent to bureaucracy.

"Unrealistic images persisted," in short, "because common sense, general knowledge, or field observation had lost the authority to discredit them."[73] *Formalizm* spoke to the territorial world of the Soviet Union, where actual factories occupied physical space where people actually worked and where Party cells actually existed. As one Komsomol secretary boasted, at its peak, "Komsomol was in every, [I repeat] in every branch of industry."[74] Viktor Struchkov, the head Komsomol adviser in Kabul from 1983 to 1985, described Komsomol as a "powerful system of discipline ... Whether we like it or not, the Soviet Union was a giant system for processing and training youth, without alternatives."[75] Translated to Afghanistan, however, this discursive world lost coherence. The terms on which one could criticize DOYA colleagues ("weak," "inert") bore within them the assumption that if only DOYA were "active," the situation would improve. But it did not, and neither did Komsomol's administrative style. One got the impression that the discourse was "of such utility, [was] needed so urgently and rendered so vital for the working of the system, that it [did] not even need to seek a theoretical justification for itself, or even simply a coherent framework."[76] "The organization," remarked one adviser, "is becoming an end unto itself."[77] As Abduzahir Zakhirov recalled, "Something about the relationship between the government and people wasn't clear. The government did its own thing, the people did their own thing."[78]

---

[72] For further confirmation of this pattern, see "Zapis' besedy s sekretarem pervichnoĭ partorganizatsii 10-go raĭona g. Kabula, sostoiavsheĭsia 28 sentiabria 1987g.," in Plastun and Andrianov, *Nadzhibulla. Afganistan v tiskakh geopolitiki*, 182.

[73] Lawrence M. Mead, "Scholasticism in Political Science," *Perspectives on Politics* 8(2) (June 2010), 454.

[74] Author Interview, Galina Tokareva, Moscow, Russian Federation, November 29, 2012.

[75] Author Interview, Viktor Struchkov, Moscow, Russian Federation, October 24, 2012.

[76] Michel Foucault, *Power/Knowledge: Selected Interviews and Other Writings 1972–1977*, ed. Colin Gordon (New York: Pantheon Books, 1980), 47.

[77] Kireev, Diary, February 20, 1986, available online at: http://kireev.info/w-4.html.

[78] Author Interview, Abduzahid Zakhirov, Dushanbe, Tajikistan, July 31, 2012.

Clever Afghans could exploit these contradictions. In 1983, for example, the Nangarhar PC founded a Primary Organization for the province's mullahs. Giorgadze filled out his tables and reported the statistics to Kabul and Moscow. A modus operandi emerged. Giorgadze offered patronage and support to the DOYA PC, the DOYA PC supplied Giorgadze with the numbers he needed for his reports, and local élites could exploit the PC to meet their own modest needs (cleaning a mosque, for example). Even as advisers slaved over their reports, there is little evidence in the archives or in the memories of the central Kabul-based advisers to suggest that the reports were ever actually read.[79] Advisers in the field were exchanging paperwork for patronage without being aware of it. They maintained the image, both in their "reportality," their paperwork, and their relations with DOYA, that the Party was one housewives' organization away from totality. And yet as so many complained in retrospect, both "action" and "content" were absent. The Komsomol–DOYA partnership, meant to create the foundations of a modern territorial state, unintentionally assumed the characteristics of postmodern discourse: advisers had only to "maintain [their] position in society by publicly performing a certain ritual, just like any other group of workers in the realm of discourse."[80]

This arrangement was obviously precarious. In Kunar Province, Giorgadze despaired over how to impose order on a long border with Pakistan, which, he noted, "groups of bandits cross...practically without any obstacles."[81] Again, Giorgadze did not lack for cadre. Daoud Māhmand, a twenty-year-old DOYA organizer in Asadabad, had studied in Tashkent and was "devoted to the cause of the PDPA and friendship with the USSR."[82] Yet managing a colonial frontier was not something that Māhmand was likely to have learned in Tashkent, for the administrative matrix that Komsomol was designed to implement was bound up with the idea of tightly controlled borders. Regimes like the Soviet Union "emphasized that national power and efficiency rested on the saturation of space inside the frontier."[83] No point within the frontier would be left untouched by the possibilities furnished by the printing press, fingerprinting, and steel. This emphasis on bordered space encouraged "spectacular border policing patterns designed to render a traditional territoriality legible for all," most visibly so in the form of the Berlin Wall.[84] Yet in Afghanistan, this

---

[79] Author Interview, Viktor Struchkov, Moscow, Russian Federation, October 24, 2012.

[80] David Lodge, *Small World: An Academic Romance* (London: Penguin Books, 1984), 28.

[81] Giorgadze, "Spravka TsK VLKSM pri TsK DOMA v zone 'Vostok.' DOMA i natsional'no-demokraticheskaia revoliutsiia v DRA. G. Dzhelalabad, noiabr' 1982 goda." RGASPI f. M-3, op. 13, d. 24, l. 91.

[82] Ibid., l. 112.

[83] Maier, "Consigning the Twentieth Century to History," 824.

[84] Jeffrey Kahn, "Islands of Sovereignty: Haitian Migration and the Borders of Empire" (PhD Dissertation: University of Chicago, 2013), 12; Rem Koolhaas, "Field Trip: A Memoir. The Berlin Wall as Architecture," in *S, M, L, XL*, eds. Rem Koolhaas and Bruce Mau (New York: Monacelli Press, 1995), 226–7.

mentality generated unrealistic expectations. The border meant nothing, and yet its very presence on maps tempted advisers to think in terms of the same strategies of enclosure available to transform invisible lines into sites of indexing and violence.

The Soviet administrative system had, it seemed, worked too well. It had linked Party and economy, and both of these with territory. But "by linking and integrating the products of so many ecosystems and communities," the Soviet system "obscured the very connections it helped create. Its tendency was to break free from space altogether, managing its activities with organizational charts that stressed function rather than geography."[85] The system's success made economics seem like intelligent design – irreducibly complex, rather than the result of manifold but traceable steps. But Afghanistan was the last place on earth where one could hope to find this administrative quilt. As a result, DOYA's membership consisted overwhelmingly of students and policemen, hardly the proletarians of socialist imaginaries. Try as it might to found primary organizations among remote mountain towns, without control of frontiers, without smokestacks and chimneys, a territorial Left was doomed. The Soviet achievement was formidable, but the connections it had obscured blinkered advisers to the passing of its moment in the history of sovereignty.

"If Not for Some Great Idea..."

Before moving the narrative into the latter half of the 1980s, it bears reflecting upon how, and on what terms, advisers understood their mission. Virtually all emphasized how the disciplinary role of the Party made it almost impossible to speak of a conscious decision to go to Afghanistan. "They decided, so you had to go," said Zaidullo Dzhunaïdov.[86] "We all lived under the reign of the word 'must' (*nado*)," explained Vyacheslav Nekrasov, "all of us heard at least once the phrase 'there's the opinion to refer you to...'"[87] Afghanistan often formed just one more stop on the great *komandirovka* (work trip) of life. Years of drudgery shaped Nekrasov: two years of Army service on the Chinese border; work on the BAM in the Far East; and, as dessert, Afghanistan. So ingrained were the patterns of Party assignments to a Eurasian "there" that when the Sverdlovsk *obkom* did call Nekrasov to say "there's the opinion to refer you" (to Afghanistan), Nekrasov grasped that "I had to come up with a legend for my family. I told them that I was planning to go to Mongolia. Just a year there, and then I can move us all somewhere else. I even unearthed a Russian–Mongol pocket dictionary somewhere for the sake of credibility." Like the unread Mongol–Russian dictionary gathering dust, Afghanistan was a vague

---

[85] William Cronon, *Nature's Metropolis: Chicago and the Great West* (New York: W.W. Norton, 1991), 257.

[86] Author Interview, Zaidullo Dzhunaïdov, Dushanbe, Tajikistan, August 31, 2012.

[87] *Mushavery*, 130.

"somewhere" (*gde-to*) in the minds of many: not hardship, not adventure, but just one more stop in a peripatetic Soviet life.

This attitude might seem cold to a liberal perspective that sees development work as an opportunity "to make a difference." But few Komsomol advisers saw Afghanistan as a field upon which they could project their personality. "I was," recalled Nekrasov, "a completely ordinary young man."[88] The endless cycling from post to post before a Party boss could "move us all somewhere else" made it difficult to identify with one's career, much less to view work as a transformational experience. Komsomol assignments were jobs into which one "turned up" or "fell into," not an opportunity for personal expansion; one adviser called a colleague "a decent person who turned up in this system."[89] A separate sphere of "human relationships" or "human values," not one's career, formed the proper realm for emotional investment – a place to recreate the intensity of common purpose that Komsomol did not. Nor should this surprise. The entire point of the institution was to turn emotional labor in "youth work" into a commodity interchangeable between Qandahar and Riga.

Yet the Soviet system unintentionally created possibilities for individual experimentation and ideas about international work as a means of doing so. Service in Afghanistan provided a way to escape, but also paradoxically to reinforce, a preoccupation with the idea of an ideal childhood. Viktor Struchkov emphasized that one could understand Soviet history as a struggle by a generation born in the wake of catastrophe to build a sane world for children.[90] "Whether we like it or not," recalled Struchkov, "the Soviet Union was a system for working with youth…Pioneers, Komsomol, the Party." Life alternated between disaster and an "uncanny enthusiasm" to create stability for the next generation. The result of this was "a relentless production of spaces designed for specific, predictable, and 'correct' forms of social intercourse…a soft-core gulag for the vulnerable" that declared childhood outside of Komsomol abnormal.[91] But once that goal was realized under developed socialism, this normalization of childhood, or at least the perception that because childhood had been normalized it could be scientifically managed, generated new anxieties. Normalcy had come at the cost of having to define success in terms of the Pioneers, Komsomol, and the Party. Compared to their fathers – men who had fought in the Great Patriotic War as a matter of course – what had they done? The first peacetime Soviet generation fulfilled a decades-long obsession with a tranquil childhood, yet, perversely, this achievement drove men to "test themselves" in "real life."

---

[88] Author Interview, Vyacheslav Nekrasov, Moscow, Russian Federation, October 17, 2012.
[89] Author Interview, Georgiï Kireev, Moscow, Russian Federation, November 10, 2012.
[90] Author Interview, Viktor Struchkov, Moscow, Russian Federation, October 27, 2012. For an exhaustive study of this theme, see Catriona Kelly, *Children's World: Growing Up in Russia, 1890–1991* (New Haven: Yale University Press, 2008).
[91] Rem Koolhaas, "Las Vegas of the Welfare State," in *S, M, L, XL*, 867.

Afghanistan constituted just that opportunity. Struchkov took the job with relish – "if not for some great idea, then to test what you're made of."[92] After a hyper-normalized childhood, "war was an interesting little bit of life" to test one's mettle. Ironically, of course, this journey to prove oneself "outside" of the system took place within it – within Komsomol. It was just one of many examples of how socialism not only imposed limits on, but also opened, avenues for the manufacture of the self.[93] Once in Afghanistan itself, advisers devoted themselves to nothing less than the professional management of Afghan childhoods. Nekrasov, remarking on his setting up a children's summer camp in northwestern Afghanistan, noted that it was the first time many of the Afghan children had their own bed, blanket, and pillow. "Someone was feeding them four times a day; for them, that was unbelievable."[94] Even as the professionalization of childhood had structured advisers' sense of ambition, the Soviet memory, and Afghan reality, of chaos during childhood undergirded a commitment to the therapeutic state as the proper outlet for one's emotional life. Hence why Komsomol represented not just "Party work" but also, for some, an "organization that inculcated a deep spirituality in its members." It speaks to the power of Komsomol that even as its remedial intervention into childhood had driven its members to seek out new forms of individuality outside those the organization prescribed, they remained deeply attached to the institution itself.[95]

Once again, there was a curious symmetry between the Soviet advisers and the European humanitarians on the other side of the Durand Line had defined for themselves. Both asserted the moral primacy of children, but for different reasons. For the Soviets, the point was that childhood constituted a crucible for the formation of political consciousness. When the Japanese ex-Communist documentary filmmaker Noriaki Tsuchimoto visited Kabul in 1985, for example, his minders included on his itinerary a field trip to the Vatan ("Fatherland") Orphanage located outside the capital.[96] Tsuchimoto was impressed. "The teachers were carefully selected and assigned here. This was because experimental, model education was the goal. I'm sure political education took place, but the priority was on practical skills." Visiting the cafeteria, the filmmaker noted, "these students would have a chance to attend colleges in the Eastern Bloc." Rather than mourning their lost families, "these children took their new lives as a matter of course, and were set to embark on their future."

In reality, children at the Orphanage were immediately drafted into the *Pishgāmān* ("Pioneers," and the equivalent of their Komsomol namesake), and many were forced into a ten-year program of mandatory education in the

[92] Author Interview, Viktor Struchkov, Moscow, Russian Federation, October 27, 2012.
[93] Kotkin, *Magnetic Mountain,* 22–3.
[94] Author Interview, Vyacheslav Nekrasov, Moscow, Russian Federation, October 17, 2012.
[95] Author Interview, Nikolaĭ Komissarov, Moscow, Russian Federation, October 16, 2012.
[96] Noriaki Tsuchimoto, *Another Afghanistan: Kabul Diary 1985* (2011).

FIGURE 7. Embedding Afghan children in the symbolic and material world of socialism. Note the toy bears – an animal with high cultural resonance in Russia but little
in Afghanistan – and the cranes and railroads, symbols of a promised material socialist
modernity. "Afghani pioneers receiving toys from the USSR. The Palace of Pioneers in
Kabul. The Democratic Republic of Afghanistan."
Source: Photographed by V. Sukhodolskiĭ, 1984. Courtesy of RIA Novosti.

Soviet Union.[97] Children were politics: "Those who were not members of the
Pishgāmān," recalled one survivor, "were subjected to attempts to recruit them
in the principal's office, where they were beaten up. If despite this they refused,
they were given threatening letters to their parents. In these it was stated that
the child wanted to go to the Soviet Union." Hence why orphans and father-
less children (the other main group at the Orphanage) were so valuable to the
PDPA. When the moral objections of parents were gone, the state could mold
the politics of the child. When Soviet citizens joked that their homeland "isn't a
country, it's a kindergarten," they unintentionally hit upon a darker truth about
the import the Soviet system ascribed to molding children.[98]

　　Yet this darker truth was also one that contrasted sharply with shifts in common sense about childhood outside of the Soviet Union. Only in the wake of

[97] "The Situation for Children and Youth in Kabul," *Eskilstuna-Kuriren med Strengnäs Tidning,*
　　19, Folder 5, Box 6, Jeri Laber Files, Human Rights Watch Collection, Columbia University.
　　The same report (drawn from an interview with an alumnus of the Watan Orphanage) noted
　　that it "was often shown to visiting Western journalists in Kabul."
[98] M. Zhvanetsky, "Detskiĭ sad," *God za godom* (Leningrad, 1991), 437.

the Second World War did children become "symbols of both wartime dislocation and postwar renewal."[99] Historians' contentions that childhood was a modern "invention" launched an entire scholarly field, childhood studies, that reaffirmed childhood, medieval and modern, as a distinct phase of life worthy of protection.[100] Buoyant, the politics of childhood "advanced progressively through the world after the Second World War, notably with the creation of UNICEF in 1946, the adoption by the United Nations of a Declaration on the Rights of the Child in 1959, and a Convention on the Rights of the Child held in 1989. This development paralleled a growing mobilization of nongovernmental organizations on the issues of child abuse from 1970 onward, then child labor during the 1980s, and finally pedophilia and incest in the 1990s."[101] Broadly, this move toward children as subjects of international monitoring marked a turn away from mid-century conceptions of children as "the biological and political future of national communities."[102] A shattered Europe demanded the mobilization of children to forge homogenous nation-states, but by the late twentieth century, such nationalist practices were framed as an invasion of children's prepolitical essence when adopted by Third World Communists. A turn away from the honor of the nation to the innocence of "the secularized Christ child" marked an ongoing shift whereby "humanitarianism, insofar as it distanced itself from the figure of the nation-state, abandoned the political field" in favor of interhuman solidarity.[103] And since Afghan "orphans' ranks were swelling," this clash between Soviet and humanitarian views of childhood would only assume greater prominence.[104]

With more orphans came the need for more youth advisers, particularly those with facility in the languages of Afghanistan. And yet the issues of identity discussed above expressed themselves differently for just such a group of Soviet citizens sent to die for "a great mistake," namely Tajik translators and advisers.[105] Afghanistan was just "across the creek" from Tajikistan, but it

99   Tara Zahra, *The Lost Children: Reconstructing Europe's Families After World War II* (Cambridge, MA: Harvard University Press, 2011), 8.
100 Phillipe Ariès, *L'enfant et la vie familiale sous l'Ancien Regime* (Paris: Plon, 1960). For the response to Ariès' work, see Nicholas Orme, *Medieval Children* (New Haven: Yale University Press, 2001).
101 Didier Fassin, "Massacre of the Innocents: Representing Childhood in the Age of AIDS," in *Humanitarian Reason: A Moral History of the Present*, trans. Rachel Gomme (Berkeley: University of California Press, 2012), 179.
102 Zahra, 20.
103 Stephen Hopgood, *The Endtimes of Human Rights* (Ithaca: Cornell University Press, 2014), 28; Didier Fassin, "Humanitarianism as a Politics of Life," *Public Culture* 19(3) (2007), 509; Zahra, 20.
104 Tsuchimoto, *Another Afghanistan.*
105 "Oģozi Bozsozī: Toǰikon dar čangī Afģoniston," in *Sad rangli sad sol: Toǰikon dar ķarni bistum*, ed. Salimi Ajubzod (Prague: Postscriptum Imprimatur, 2002), 230. The State Archives of Tajikistan tantalizingly contain a series of interviews with former Tajik soldiers, but as of the summer of 2013, the collection had been closed. The relevant collection is TsGART, f. 1048 (Voiny-internatsionalisty. Fond-kollektsii), op. 1 (1965–1990 gg.).

lacked the known world of the Soviet system.[106] As one Komsomol adviser from Badakhshan recalled his first impressions of Kabul, only after weeks could he shake the assumption that anyone wearing a turban or a *pakol* (the style of hat made famous by Ahmad Shah Mas'ud) was out to kill him.[107] He had much to learn: as his chauffeur explained to him, the mustachioed Soviet Tajik had to alter his facial hair: grow it out the shape of an "n," as Khalqists did, groom it up into the shape of a "u," as Parchamists did, or shave it off entirely. Flaccid mustaches would only confuse. He further recalled the bewildered reaction of Afghans when he described the names of Soviet Central Asian cities: "Dushanbe … Tashkent," he said smilingly, remarking that these names ("Monday" and "Place of Stone," respectively) were culturally intelligible to Afghans. But when he told them the name of the economic hub of his native republic, they were shocked: "*Leninabad* ?!?"

Stories like these aside, Afghans often received translators as "Muslims" or "Tajiks," not Soviets. One afternoon in 1982, Rakhmatullo Abdullaev, a Tajik translator, was traveling along the road from Jalalabad to Asadabad with Komsomol adviser Anatoliĭ Makushev to carry out a meeting with DOYA members. "All of a sudden," however, "there appeared several *dushman* (enemies)."[108] The *mujāhidin* carried automatic weapons and surrounded the Tajik and the Russian. But "then in between two of them there walked up to us a fellow without a uniform, without an automatic rifle, nothing, no weapons, and three or four people around him, his bodyguards. Who it was precisely, we didn't know. But it was obvious that he was someone respected."[109] Establishing that he could communicate through Abdullaev, the group's leader asked: "Where are you from?" Abdullaev recalls what followed:

I said, "From the Soviet Union."
"So," he said, "there are no Muslims there."
So I said, "Let's debate something [*davaĭte my posporim*]. If I can answer your questions about Islam as a representative of the Soviet Union, as a Muslim from the Soviet Union, [and you're not satisfied], then do what you want with us. But if I answer your questions, then you'll let us go."
So it was obvious that this was something really serious. And so there started … not so much a conversation as an argument, I want to say. He'd start asking questions, and I'd answer them.

The lead bandit asked "primitive questions" about Islam in the Soviet Union – whether mosques existed, what kind of prayers Soviet Muslims read – that Abdullaev dispatched with ease. Next came Abdullaev's turn to pose a question. The bandit leader gloated: there was no way a *kāfir* could stump him. Abdullaev

---

[106] Georgiĭ Kireev, "Kandagarskiĭ dnevnik," available online at: http://kireev.info/w-4.html.
[107] Author Interview, Dushanbe, Tajikistan, July 18, 2012. The person interviewed has requested to remain anonymous.
[108] Persian for "enemy," and a term used to describe *mujāhidin* by Soviets in Afghanistan.
[109] Author Interview, Rakhmatullo Abdullaev, Dushanbe, Tajikistan, July 25, 2012.

gathered his composure: "I said, 'You're a Muslim. Let's say you're sitting on a camel. You're going by a graveyard. You want to say a prayer for the deceased. But you don't want to stop. You're riding on the camel. Is it allowed to say that *surah* from the Quran out loud, or can you only say it to yourself?' [Laughter] He thought about it, thought about it." Beads of sweat gathered on Makushev's forehead.

And he said, "Yes, you can say it out loud."

I said, "No!" And suddenly everyone around me turned silent. Everyone who had been asking the questions turned to listen to me. And I said, "Look, I'll explain to you why not." Now remember, the leader had just said "Yes" in front of everyone. [I asked:] "Does the name of Allah appear in the [inaudible] *ayāt?*"

He said "Yes."

"Is it allowed to pronounce the name of Allah incorrectly?"

He said, "No, under no circumstances."

"So when you're riding on the camel, he's bucking you back and forth. Your voice is changing. So it's not all right to say the *surah* out loud."

And so that was an interesting incident. They said, "Fine," and let us go.

Abdullaev's recollection of the incident underscored how the Soviet system, while nominally opposed to autochthony, forged possibilities for "authenticity." "I had studied," explained Abdullaev, "with someone whose father had worked as a *qāzi* prior to Soviet power. Someone with an average level of education. And his son instructed us ... we didn't learn any [Arabic] grammar. There was no methodology whatsoever. Every mullah instructed his students with the same tools that he had studied himself. And there was a sort of a textbook we used ... *Haft-o-yak Sharif*, it's called. It's one-seventh of the Quran, but it's mostly short *surah*s – middle-length ones and short ones. We started with those, and in principle we studied not the Arabic language, but we knew how to read. We studied the rules of how to pronounce it. The mullah who taught us, I think he knew Arabic. But they just taught us how to read the *surah*." Abdullaev's education was privately arranged; so long as Abdullaev received good marks in school, he could continue the private tutorials. "After the *Haft-o-yak*," he explained, "we studied the Qurān, then Persian literature – for example, a collection of *ghazels* and Hāfez,[110] the *Kalilah wa Dimnah*,[111] and at the same time, all the other classics. Then there was a collection, *Chahār Kitāb*, the prose of the great theologians and poets who spoke about Islam, about the fundamental principles of Islam, [inaudible], religious rites, and so on, these kinds of books. In other words, they taught us the foundations of Islam, the foundations of belief, without a deep knowledge of Arabic."

---

[110] Hafez was a fourteenth-century Persian poet from Shiraz.

[111] The *Kalilah wa Dimnah* is a collection of animal-related fables originally produced in India and later (in its most famous version) translated into Persian by Nasrullah Munshi, a member of the Ghaznavid court.

Following his secondary education, Abdullaev studied at Lenin State University in Dushanbe, where he studied classical Persian literature. "We received a secular education," he said. "I studied in a university, studied the history of religion, not just the history of Islam, but also the history of Christianity, of Judaism, others...Buddhism, Confucianism, so we had a much higher level of information than a mullah who had also studied like us [in the village]." By the time Abdullaev held disputes with Afghans, then, he could sympathize with village mullahs' misunderstandings. "I knew their problems," Abdullaev said, "because I knew how they had studied. True, there were some [in Kabul] who had studied at the al-Azhar in Egypt...but there were few of them. [Whereas in the village, mullahs] fulfilled more the role of guides in the villages, sort of. They taught people about the truth...for example, they would help people memorize a few *surahs* in order to carry out the prayer properly, and, well, that was about it." One of the biggest problems in the Islamic World today, added Abdullaev, is that "there are very few well-educated mullahs." Yet what did "well-educated" really mean?

The Soviet experience had created possibilities for reinvention, and not only with respect to religion. In the summer of 1987, Komsomol deployed Said Karimov, the translator discussed earlier, to Khost, now considerably less forested than twenty years prior. Snipers lurked in the hills during the day, and landmines lay outside the city perimeter. Worse, Aleksandr Balan, the adviser for whom Karimov interpreted, had grown erratic.[112] By 1987, Karimov recalled, Balan's wife in Leningrad demanded a divorce, leaving Balan despondent; he ceased to take precautions in the field. Karimov, however, had no choice but to follow him. Worried, Karimov sought out Afghan colleagues, some of whom had clandestinely switched sides or kept their distance from the Soviets. One pulled him aside: he and several conspirators intended to murder Balan with a sniper shot to the head while the Russian drove his jeep outside the city. But, they made clear, they had no quarrel with a "fellow" Tajik. The Afghans recognized that Karimov had to travel with Balan, but they recommended that he sit diagonally across from Balan in the jeep's two-by-two seating configuration, lest a straight shot pierce straight through Balan and kill Karimov. Karimov never tested the proposition; Khost's Komsomol unit was airlifted out. Yet like Abdullaev's encounter with "fellow" Muslims, Karimov's encounter with "fellow" Tajiks underscored the ambiguity that Soviet Central Asians encountered "across the creek."

Again, however, it was the Soviet system that had enabled these ambiguities. Komsomol provided the framework for Soviet Tajiks to engage globally in the first place. As one Tajik *adviser* said, he regarded Natalia Ianina as his *mamochka* ("mommy"). She had to have taken a political risk in selecting a Tajik, as opposed to another Russian. "[For there to be] an adviser from such

---

a small republic – well, it was a sensation."[113] The Soviet system provided a similar boost to a Tajik native of Gorno-Badakhshan. Had he been born across the border in Afghanistan, the Tajik reflected, he would have been trapped in the idiocy of the village forever. Soviet Tajikistan, in contrast, offered him the chance to become a professional economist.[114] Indeed, Soviet higher education was a crucial link. Orientologists had strengthened the Tajik language through Cyrilicization, standardization of the written language, and support for Tajik as a language of administration and literature. As Abdullaev proudly recalled, when a Komsomol trainer in Dushanbe gave him a Russian-language technical document to translate from Russian into Dari, he translated 33 of 37 pages without error in the time allotted. Translators drawn from outside of academia, he boasted, managed one or two mistake-ridden pages.

Most fundamentally, the Soviet Union had created a Tajik state that, particularly in late 1970s, became a canvas onto which intellectuals projected visions of a "Tajik" Persianate World.[115] Travels to Afghanistan provided exposure to these "lost" moments of "Tajik" culture. "The translators," writes one Tajik scholar, "came back with suitcases and suitcases full of books, copies of the complete manuscripts of the *divan* of Maulana, the works of Hafez and Sa'adi and took them with them into Tajikistan. The first large quantity of translated *Qurāns* with commentary that came into Tajikistan were from Afghanistan."[116] Yet even though their travels as "Tajiks" in Afghanistan made translators aware of Persianate civilization, it was *Soviet* Tajikistan to which they returned. Recalled another Tajik who served in the Soviet Embassy in Mazar-i Sharif, "The customs officer at Termez took a look at me and asked, 'What's in those three boxes there? What do you have?' Each of the three chests was filled with books. 'Open one of them,' he said. So I did. He saw that it was books. He looked at the second box. I said that I'd open the third one for him, but he stopped me and asked me where I was from. 'From Tajikistan,' I said. He said, 'What are you doing? People spending their wealth, here you go and earn some money, and what do you do with it but buy books?' I said, 'This *is* wealth.'" The project of erasing the Emirate of Bukhara, of fusing the Ferghana Valley together with the Emirate's rump, had proven too successful for its own good. Trained to see a Soviet ethnographic construct in terms of autochthony, these men viewed the world in terms of a "lost" Tajik culture whose center was, implausibly, a city originally named Stalinabad – one more example of how the Soviet Union created no fewer possibilities for creative reinvention than it had obliterated.

---

[113] Author Interview, Abduzahir Zakhirov, Dushanbe, Tajikistan, July 31, 2012.
[114] Author Interview, Dushanbe, Tajikistan, July 18, 2012. The person interviewed has requested to remain anonymous.
[115] Mirzo Shakurzoda, *Točikon dar masiri ta'rikh*, quoted in "Oḡozi bozsozī: Toǰikon dar čangī Afḡoniston," 226.
[116] "Oḡozi bozsozī: Toǰikon dar čangī Afḡoniston," 230.

Conclusion

In May 1986, Babrak Karmal, the General Secretary of the PDPA since the assassination of Hafizullāh Amin, was replaced by Muhammad Najib, the former intelligence director who "had caught the eye of Soviet agents in Kabul as well as of leaders in Moscow even before the intervention."[117] Foreign delegations noted that Najib "exuded confidence, and facts and figures were at his fingertips. He conveyed the impression of being efficient, competent, assertive, and alert."[118] Among a field of contenders with much blood on their hands, Najib offered to reconcile the politics of "Pashtunistan" with Soviet desires for a pliant socialist neighbor. Afghan Council of Ministers Chairman Sultan 'Ali Kishtmand explained: "People said that the next leader of Afghanistan should be of Pashtun ancestry, since it was possible that the tribes beyond the Durand Line would rise up and fight against the interventions of Pakistan. There was also the possibility that the armed groups formed of great numbers of Pashtuns, and which received many weapons and much aid from foreigners, and which had become an object of trust for Pakistan, would consider negotiations and reconciliation with the leadership of Pashtuns in Kabul."[119] With Karmal soon handed the keys to an apartment in Moscow and a one-way plane ticket, Najib was ready to govern, buoyed by an aid package larger "than the USSR had ever given to any one country."[120]

The aid package was supposed to keep the PDPA afloat while Afghans learned how to rule themselves. By the middle of the decade, Soviet advisers dominated every level of the government. Najib described a typical meeting of the Council of Ministers: "We sit down at the table. Each minister comes with his own adviser. The meeting begins, the discussion becomes heated, and gradually the advisers come closer and closer to the table. So accordingly our people move away, and eventually only the advisers are left at the table."[121] Yuliĭ Vorontsov, a veteran diplomat and the Ambassador in Kabul from 1988 to 1989, agreed. "[Advisers] were everywhere," he said, "absolutely everywhere. It was the worst sort of colonial politics."[122] As new Soviet General Secretary Mikhaïl Gorbachëv and Foreign Minister Eduard Shevardnadze planned a Soviet military withdrawal, Kabul was supposed to prepare for the military vacuum so as not to collapse and delegitimize Moscow in the eyes of Third World clients.

[117] Kalinovsky, *A Long Goodbye: The Soviet Withdrawal from Afghanistan*, 96.
[118] J.N. Dixit, *An Afghan Diary: Zahir Shah to Taliban* (New Delhi: Konark Publishers, 2000), 97.
[119] Kishtmand, *Yāddāshthā-yi siyāsi va ruydadhā-yi tārikhi: khāṭirāt-i shakhṣi bā burahha-yi āz tārikh-i siyāsi mu`asir-i Āfghānistān*, Vol. II, 979.
[120] Kalinovsky, 101.
[121] B. Padishev, "Nadzhibulla, prezident Afganistana," *Mezhdunarodnye otnosheniia* (January 1990), 23.
[122] Artemy Kalinovsky, Interview with Iuliĭ Vorontsov, September 11, 2007, Moscow, Russian Federation.

This policy shift meant changes on the provincial level, changes we can see in advisers' parting reports from the east. Writing to Komsomol's Kabul office in November 1987, Komsomol adviser Oleg Maslov wrote "to share with you some of my reflections on the local activity of DOYA...What we're doing right now in Paktia, may, after some adjustments, be used by our boys in other provinces. Especially in Pashtunistan, where tribal relations are strong. Considering that the central advisers are planning to travel to the provinces before our arrival in Kabul, it's possible that the materials on Paktia might suit themselves to other provinces."[123] The fact that Maslov made suggestions at all spoke to the changed institutional atmosphere, as did both his direct, conversational tone and his report's lack of section formatting.

Maslov reflected that upon his arrival in Paktia, "tribal relations were strongly developed."[124] *Mujāhidin* ran amok. "Capitalism," he wrote, "penetrated our province and freakishly fused with the communal organization of society, with the tribal relations...The old 'friendly Pashtun spirit' has been replaced in a way gainful not to the tribes, but to certain people – as a rule, the tribal elders. They are the wealthiest among their tribesmen (as one might assume under a tribal primitive structure)." The inactivity of DOYA exacerbated problems. Despite a dynamic young secretary, "each department directed its work in a rather abstract (without concrete goals) way. In the collective one never felt that the coworkers were making the necessary contact to unite their affairs. Everyone acted by himself."[125] The Paktia DOYA PC claimed to coordinate the activity of primary organizations within its territory, but "many coworkers rarely visit the 'primaries,' while virtually no one goes to the villages." And even if Maslov had a plausible candidate for DOYA's Central Committee, Paktia's Deputy Secretary was lazy and spiteful. Because the Deputy was a Khalqist, however, Maslov could not sack him without triggering an internal Party revolt.

But Maslov found a solution in so-called "people's divisions." There was no point, he argued, in maintaining the fantasy that Party organizations did anything, or that they even existed in areas outside of Soviet military control. Why not, then, Maslov suggested, supply the tribes with weapons, halt conscription, and end land reform? Such was what Maslov and the DOYA PC agreed to at a November 10, 1987, meeting. He explained: "This year, the decision was made and recently effected to form national divisions of the tribes of Paktia. In my view, this is the crucial link in the system, and by pulling on it, we can reach the goal of National Reconciliation in the province. The essence of the idea is the following: their 'Boers' aside, the tribes could represent strong military

[123] Oleg Maslov, Letter to Dmitriĭ Ostroushko (November 13, 1987), RGASPI, f. M-3, op. 13, d. 151, l. 101.

[124] Ibid. "Nekotorye kharakternye osobennosti v provintsii Paktiia'" (November 13, 1987), RGASPI, f. M-3, op. 13, d. 151, l. 102.

[125] Ibid., l. 103.

organizations unto themselves, if provided with modern combat technology and trained cadres. All of this is something that people's power will give them. The leadership of the national divisions will be confirmed at the tribes' *jirgahs*. The core part of each division will be located in the tribe's place of residence and will concern itself with guarding the villages, escorting caravans full of food and materials for the tribes, the building of schools, irrigation systems, and so on."[126]

The DOYA PC intended to execute Maslov's scheme during the winter of 1987–8. Firstly, the PC would collect intelligence on the Mangal, Totakhel, Ahmadzai, Gardezi, Ladai, and Ahmadkhel tribes. Next, it would dispatch agitation caravans to recruit "tribal propagandists." These young men would be invited to Gardez for training (but also considered for scholarships to the USSR and East Germany). Next, the tribal propagandists would return to their villages to serve as liaisons between the PC and the tribes.[127] If everything went according to plan, DOYA activists based in Gardez could then visit the villages to conduct literacy courses and convince the locals to accept weapons and aid in exchange for being left alone. People's divisions, so Maslov thought, could transform DOYA from an institution of shambolic primary organizations to one that the tribes trusted, even if they were not really touched by it.

The policy testified to a shift in Soviet administrative thinking. The original rationale for DOYA's existence was to recruit Afghan youth into the police and the Army. Both of these policies reflected not just practical concerns but also, more broadly, a territorial moment in the global history of sovereignty. Conscription, especially into units that defended territorial borders, constituted "one of the key institutions by which the defense of identity space was built into the life cycle of male citizens."[128] In abandoning DOYA's claim to mobilize children into the belly of the Afghan state, Maslov was simply accepting reality. But the degree to which Maslov made this retreat explicit reflected how "the once-reassuring congruence between identity space and governance space" had weakened.[129] Advisers had gone from seeing in "ungoverned" tribes problems to finding in them solutions, "from imposing to yielding."[130] The material goods and services that Moscow provided the borderlands – weapons, scholarships to East Germany – remained the same, but once dissolved from their original mooring in a territorial Party, advisers allowed these instruments of violence and mobility to gravitate opportunistically toward alternative points

---

[126] Ibid., l. 103–4.
[127] "Plan raboty Paktiĭskogo provintsial'nogo komiteta DOMA po uchastiiu molodëzhi v sozdanii narodnoĭ divizii i nadboru rezerva kadrov DOMA na 2. polugodiie 1366 goda" (November 13, 1987), RGASPI, f. M-3, op. 13, d. 151, l. 109.
[128] Maier, "Consigning the Twentieth Century to History," 824.
[129] Ibid., 823.
[130] Rem Koolhaas, "Atlanta," in *S, M, L, XL*, 848.

of freedom, toward "diminished contextual nuisance."[131] The attraction of the territorial nation-state as the appropriate scale for political confrontation was dimming.

The end of Maslov's report most felicitously captured the shift in thinking. The adviser noted that he had convinced his DOYA colleagues to spend less time working in the "abstract," and more time practicing what he called *delovye igry* ("practice games").[132] "Since," he wrote, "Afghans love to sing, dance, and play [*popet', popliasat', i razygrat'*]," Maslov suggested that the Provincial Committee invite local peasants to engage DOYA members in a duel of questions about socialism. If the peasant felt he had won the duel, the remaining PC members in the room would have to defeat him. It bore an uncanny resemblance to the game that Rakhmatullo Abdullaev had proposed on the road to Asadabad. More substantively, it also spoke to how old structures of formalism and reportality were evaporating. Politics no longer had to do with the dispatch of loudspeakers and taped recordings of Babrak Karmal's speeches into the Afghan countryside, whereby centrally issued ideology, mechanically reproduced into sonic and electromagnetic waves, echoed into territorial space. Less still did politics have to do with the formation of primary organizations on sheets of paper. The idea of the centralized, coordinating, radiative territorial state had been replaced by a more informal, disputatious, and fluid politics of the kind that Maslov had identified and sought, desperately, to manage with the dwindling formal devices left to him.

Yet Komsomol had precious little time to test Maslov's proposals. In the spring of 1988, Moscow withdrew advisers from Khost and Paktia; other provinces evacuated in the summer. That August, Soviet newspaper correspondent Igor' Cherniak captured the mood among the advisers as they prepared to return home. "The advising apparatus had almost completely shut down," he wrote. "Our *mikroraĭon* emptied out: no more women, no more children."[133] Cherniak loitered in the Kabul Airport with the last Komsomol operatives, Aleksandr Gavriia and Iuriĭ Afanas'iev, and two Tajik translators. The team had completed its last project, a bathhouse in Kabul. "As of the next year, all social organizations in the country will have to become self-financing," wrote Gavriia. "That means tough times for DOYA. But a bathhouse – well, maybe it can be some source of revenue ... "

Gloom hovered over the capital. Gunshots crackled in the air. Gavriia had heard that a *mujāhidin* rocket attack had destroyed a Komsomol-built school. One Komsomol adviser, Aleksandr Pankratov, stepped on a land mine while abandoning his apartment and nearly bled to death before medics stabilized his condition. "There's rotten luck for you," Gavriia murmured. As the group sat

---

[131] Ibid., 843.
[132] Maslov, "Nekotorye kharakternye osobennosti," l. 106.
[133] I. Cherniak, "Internatsionalisty," *Sobesednik* 44 (October 1988), quoted in *Mushavery*, 50.

beside a table straining under a spread of grapes, watermelon, and tea, Gavriia insisted that they had to stay. "Let them know [in Moscow]," he said, "that they shouldn't hurry to call us back. We're still needed here." Cherniak paused: why? "What force is forcing [the Soviet advisers] to stay here? What's forcing them to risk their life on an hourly basis – every second? Don't get angry with me, boys. I won't pass on Gavriia's request. After all, how do we teach children to walk? At first we hold them by the arm, and then by the hand. But there then comes a time when we need to let go. Afghans can already do a lot themselves. They should take care of themselves."

Afghans were going to have to learn to "take care of themselves" quickly. By the autumn of 1988, all Komsomol advisers were evacuated. It marked a desultory ending to three decades of state-led developmental interventions in Afghanistan. Not even the Afghan borderlands of Nangarhar, Paktia, and Khost had been excluded from development. But whether it was Western assumptions about fiscality or the global economy, German ones about forestry, or Soviet ones about the primacy of production, none of these projects wanted to understand why territoriality, not Afghanistan itself, was the problem. None wanted to understand how the investiture of twentieth-century territoriality into a nineteenth-century colonial border was a doomed project. Komsomol advisers began to understand, but before long, they were replaced by postterritorial NGOs and *mujāhidin*.

But control over physical territory was not the only arena in which the Soviet and humanitarian projects would clash. The CPSU and the PDPA took seriously the idea that socialist revolution could resolve what they referred to as "the woman question," even in Afghanistan. It seemed like a brilliant marriage. The Soviet Union had "liberated" Central Asian women from the horsehair veil; and "medieval" though Afghanistan might have seemed, it actually boasted a vibrant indigenous women's movement. Encounters between Soviet feminists and their Afghan counterparts, however, revealed stresses in the Soviet project. By the end of the decade, the Soviet project would be plunged into crisis, challenged by a recrudescent women's movement centered around individual rights and "gender," neither traditional Leftist concepts. Territoriality seemed moribund. More than a million Afghans had been killed. Humanitarianism, however, now repackaged in a mobile, medical, and feminist guise, was about to be reborn.

5

Under a Red Veil

[We] never meant anything less by women's liberation than the creation of a society without domination; we never meant less than the making new of all relationships. The problem was that we did not know whom we meant when we said "we."[1]

On Wednesday, June 23, 1982, a group of Afghan women boarded a flight to Moscow to discuss their liberation. The war in Afghanistan may have posed challenges for organs like Komsomol, but it also presented opportunities for Soviet women's organizations. Just as advisers on the ground promoted women's education and membership in PDPA organizations like the Democratic Organization for the Women of Afghanistan (DOWA), Moscow-based organizations like the Committee of Soviet Women (CSW) engaged in international bridgebuilding with their Afghan counterparts. Having arrived in Moscow, the Afghan women, all members of DOWA, Kabul Soviets, or provincial cooperatives, spent three days at a joint DOWA–CSW seminar before departing for more meetings in with CSW colleagues in Uzbekistan.[2] The event presented itself as the apogee of socialist sororal unity. As CSW activists never tired of mentioning, socialism provided women with employment, education, abortion on demand, and childcare. Services like these meant that women in the Soviet Bloc, particularly its most developed corners, "had one of the

---

[1] Adrienne Rich, "Notes toward a Politics of Location," in *Blood, Bread, and Poetry: Selected Prose, 1979–1985* (New York: W.W. Norton and Company, 1986), 217.

[2] "Poriadok raboty dvustoronnego sovetsko-afganskogo seminara 'Puti i metody raboty sredi zhenshchin v pervye gody posle revoliutsii' (23–30 iiunia, 1982g., g.g. Moskva, Tashkent)," Gosudarstvennyi Arkhiv Rossiiskoĭ Federatsii (GARF), f. 7928 (Komitet Sovetskikh Zhenshchin), o. 3, d. 5583, l. 2–3.

FIGURE 8. Soviet–Afghan women's worlds. "A delegation of Afghan women led by
Aisha Dervash, the secretary of the Parwan Province' Council of the DOYA (Democratic
Youth Organization of Afghanistan), visiting the Soviet Women's Committee. Moscow.
1986."
Source: Photographed by V. Khromenko, 1986. Courtesy of RIA Novosti.

highest rates of paid female employment in the world."[3] In the countryside,
meanwhile, socialism had supposedly emancipated Central Asian women from
class oppression, a victory powerfully symbolized by the disappearance of the
paranja (horsehair veil). Internationally, the Soviet Union and its allies had
been the first to demand a convention banning discrimination against women;
indeed, it was in response to Eastern Bloc pressures that the International Year
of the Woman (1975) happened at all.[4] Supporting Afghan women engaged in
a struggle against capitalist exploitation seemed like a natural extension to this
tradition.

Given the apparent parallels with today's champions of "women's rights,"
one might be tempted to locate the Moscow seminar within a history that
begins with the UN's 1975 declaration of International Women's Year, continues on to the 1979 Convention on the Elimination of All Forms of

[3] Celia Donert, "Whose Utopia? Gender, Ideology, and Human Rights at the 1975 World Congress
of Women in East Berlin," in *The Breakthrough: Human Rights in the 1970s*, eds. Samuel Moyn
and Jan Eckel (Philadelphia: University of Pennsylvania Press, 2013), 77.
[4] Ibid., 73–4; Jocelyn Olcott, "Transnational Feminism: Event, Temporality, and Performance at
the 1975 International Women's Year Conference," in *Cultures in Motion*, eds. Daniel T. Rodgers,
Bhavani Raman, and Helmut Reinitz (Princeton: Princeton University Press, 2013), 248.

Discrimination Against Women (CEDAW), segues to the 1985 Nairobi Conference, and, finally, culminates in the 1994 Cairo Conference that recognized women's issues beyond family planning as essential to discussions about development. Such a narrative, however, would overlook how contingent this consensus really was. Even as they played a crucial role in launching the International Women's Decade, socialist activists argued for a specifically socialist and since-forgotten vision of women's issues. Only after the dramatic collapse of this vision, induced by *glasnost'*, could what we now inaccurately dub the global women's movement break through.

Far from an example of how Moscow opposed "Talibanization" *avant la lettre*, then, the Moscow seminar demonstrates the ironic role that the USSR played in the history of the women's movement. And yet the fact that Soviet activists – like their American counterparts three decades later – engaged so energetically for Afghan women should invite reflection on how interchangeable Afghan women themselves have been for radically different visions of women's advancement. Decades after one intervention proclaimed itself the defender of a vision of women's rights centered around class, Afghan women were inscribed with new subjectivities of human rights. The shift from a world in which class and the nation-state meant everything to one in which capital and obligations flow like quicksilver through the formerly buttressed walls of the nation-state has been powerful. Left open, however, is how much these repeated attempts to forge transnational feminist links reflect not a rich diversity of feminisms but rather Afghans' place within global hierarchies of inequality.

Afghan Feminism(s)

Before examining the 1982 seminar, one has to understand the multiple indigenous traditions of Afghan feminism of which the DOWA activists were only the newest exponents.[5] While actual women's *movements* date only from the postwar period in Afghanistan, under the Emirs Habibullah and Amanullah, Kabul saw inklings of liberalization.[6] Like in Egypt, Persia, and the Ottoman Empire, reforms referred to European norms of "civilization" and "included the admission of women and girls to educational institutions, their appearance in public, and certain legal questions" like inheritance and property ownership.[7] A 1921 Family Code curbed polygamy, forced marriage, and spousal abandonment; during the same decade, girls' schools opened in Kabul, and Afghan women studied abroad in Turkey.[8] Resistance to a sellout of "authentic" Islamic values

---

[5] Much of this section is derived from a dissertation written by Julia Bauer, a student in the *Asienwissenschaften* subfaculty of the Humboldt University of Berlin in 1985: "Zur Entwicklung einer Frauenbewegung in Afghanistan im Zeitraum von 1946 bis zur Gegenwart."

[6] For more on Habibullah's cultural reforms, see Gubar, *Afganistan na puti istorii*, 24–7.

[7] J.C. Griffith, *Afghanistan* (London: Pall Mall, 1967), 243ff.

[8] Wazhmah Osman, "Thinking Outside the Box: Television and the Afghan Culture Wars" (PhD Dissertation, New York University, 2012), 27.

was not far behind: during a major 1924 uprising in Khost, mullahs traveled through the region "brandishing in one hand the Qurān and in the other the *Nizāmnāmeh* (constitution), inviting true Muslims to choose between them."[9] Religious leaders rejected the pieties of Kabuli Afghan leaders whose marriages, often to foreigners, reflected minimal respect to Pashtun lineage.

The 1929 coup interrupted this reform trajectory. The legal reforms were annulled. Most Afghan women did not choose their husband; girls went uneducated, and men were separated from women in public. Some patterns continued, as Afghans with foreign wives – Zabuli and his Russian wife – sought glacial modernization. Americans, Europeans, and Japanese expatriates founded schools, anticipating the 1943 reopening of state women's schools. In 1946, Madame Asin, a French woman married to an Afghan, founded the first Afghan women's association, *Da Mirmaneh Tulaneh* (Pashto for "The Women's Society," DMT).[10] Zabuli lent patronage to the organization, and in 1947, the government seeded it with half of its annual budget.[11] Queen Humaira became its official patron; the wives of parliamentarians, its staffers.

DMT possessed modest aims. It conducted courses in stitching and obstetrics, employed women to produce clothing and supplies for soldiers and poor children, and ran a literacy program and educational programming course consisting "of the reading of the Koran, history, geography, writing, mathematics, and Pashto." A library with over 2,000 volumes and a rotating film program completed the cultural offerings. Soon, *Da Mirmaneh Tulaneh* became part of Zahir Shah's reformist politics of the 1950s, a time in which Kabul implemented WHO maternal health programs, employed women in libraries, banks, and airlines, and made de-veiling a condition for public employment.[12] But a trivially small percentage of Afghan women actually worked outside of the home; DMT was little more than a mouthpiece for the government. De-veiled, modern Afghan women demonstrated the country's progress to nodding foreign delegations and kept the foreign aid flowing.

Indeed, when Polish journalist Andrzej Bińkowski visited the capital in the late 1950s, DMT's offices painted an impressive picture.[13] Pulling up to DMT's offices, Bińkowski rang the doorbell. Let in, the journalist met yet another gate and a police officer; under normal circumstances, men and women spoke through the interior gate under supervision. Bińkowski's interpreter explained,

---

[9] Leon Poullada, *Reform and Rebellion in Afghanistan, 1919–1929: King Amanullah's Failure to Modernize a Tribal Society* (Ithaca: Cornell University Press, 1973), 85.

[10] Bauer, "Zur Entwicklung," 18.

[11] "Tarizda da mermeno zeirja tolana," *Mirman*, 1 (Kabul, 1953), 23.

[12] Bauer, "Zur Entwicklung," 15. For more on women's public health, see Parwin Ali Majrooh, "Afghan Women Between Marxism and Islamic Fundamentalism," *Central Asian Survey* 8(3) (1989), 95–6.

[13] For the original Polish, see Andrzej Bińkowski, *Podróż za rzeke Amu* (Warsaw: Wydawnictwo Ministerstwa Obrony Narodowei, 1960). For the German translation (used here), see *Von Taschkent nach Kabul* (Leipzig: VEB Brockhaus, 1961).

however, and the journalist was soon met by Zeynab Enayet Saraj, DMT's Deputy Director and "a cousin of Amanullah's who had long lived with her father and brother in the Afghan emigration in Tehran."[14] Bińkowski was entranced. "Whoever," he wrote, "like myself, had only seen Afghan women thickly veiled on the dusty streets pulsating with exotic life would find this black-haired woman sitting in an easy chair all rather unusual: the modern gray checkered skirt, the pink pullover, her petite black shoes with pencil heels, the discreetly applied eyebrows, and her fingernails painted in the same color as her pullover."[15]

As Saraj explained, "folding her long, slim fingers together," DMT prided itself on its girls' school.[16] She led Bińkowski to a classroom, where "the girls, all dressed in light blue outfits, got up from their seats and looked at us without any timidity, even though their faces were uncovered and their *chador*s hung on the coat hooks."[17] Bińkowski was impressed. "A true revolution was underway at *Da Mirmaneh Tulaneh* [...] Women, still not having separated themselves from the *chador*, were driving time forward by centuries in Afghanistan, here in the school." This was perhaps underrating the embedding of the institution among traditional élites. One member, Rokia Abubakir, was the sister of Sayed Rishtia, the Minister of Culture. Rishtia's daughter, meanwhile, edited the organization's magazine, *Lady* (*Khānum*), itself founded by Abubakir's husband, a dean at Kabul University. All the same, a Kabuli élite had built schools, theaters, restaurants, and workplaces where women worked unveiled. Based in Kabul, but with a new office opening in Qandahar that would employ 300 women, DMT sought emancipation in spite of segregation.

Such developments could not but interest Soviet observers. In 1958, the International Section of CSW began filing reports on Afghanistan.[18] Two years later, analysts at the organization and the Soviet Embassy in Kabul prepared detailed briefs on the history of women in Afghanistan, the history of DMT, and even women in rural Afghanistan.[19] In May 1961, CSW extended feelers to DMT.[20] Rona Mansuri, one of the leaders of DMT, invited two CSW representatives to Kabul, where they visited DMT's institute.[21] Soon, the Soviet Embassy and CSW provided Afghan women with scholarships to Soviet universities, activists with conference stipends, and DMT with a subscription to

---

[14] Bińkowski, *Von Taschkent nach Kabul*, 154.
[15] Ibid., 154–5.
[16] Ibid., 157.
[17] Ibid., 158.
[18] "Spravka o politicheskikh i ekonomicheskikh pravakh zhenshchin v Afganistane" (1958), GARF, f. 7928, op. 3, d. 67.
[19] "Spravochnye materialy" contains several such reports, each of which runs 20–30 pages in length. See GARF, f.7928, op. 3, d. 455.
[20] Letter from CSW to *Da Mirmaneh Tulaneh*, May 13, 1961. GARF f.7928, op. 3, d. 656, l. 4.
[21] Letter from Nina Voronina to Rona Mansuri, September 27, 1961, GARF f. 7928, op. 3, d. 656, l. 10.

Soviet Woman, the official Soviet women's magazine. Soviet ideas about "the woman question" found fertile soil in Kabul. The more women attended Kabul University and the Soviet-sponsored Kabul Polytechnic University, the wider their worlds grew. One alumna saw a team of five Soviet engineers – four men, one woman – moving into an apartment in the Mikrorayon neighborhood. Reared on stories about the evils of Communism, she assumed that the woman was the men's shared property. Only later did she discover that the woman was their *supervisor*.[22]

Soon, Afghan Communists assembled the institutions of a feminist Left. DOWA was founded in 1965; its first political program demanded equal rights for men and women regardless of their social position or ethnic background, and described the organization as consisting of working women, working peasant women, female members of the intelligentsia, housewives, and others.[23] Granted, like the PDPA itself, DOWA was no mass organization: it had seven members at the time of its founding. But it soon challenged the assumptions of polite society. Illegal, DOWA recruited among DMT members, encouraging them to discuss "the real reasons for the oppression of women."[24] Members of DMT had contented themselves with a long march toward emancipation; DOWA saw emancipation as just part of the struggle against capitalist domination. By 1978, DOWA claimed 2,000 members and 2,500 sympathizers. Its leader boasted that "in the middle of the seventies there was almost no city, no village, in which DOWA did not have an influence."[25]

The woman who said these words was Anahita Ratebzad, who embodied the aspirations of the Afghan female intelligentsia. Ratebzad was born in the village of Gulnara in Kabul Province in 1931, then attended the Francophone Malalaï Lycée, trained as a nurse at the Chicago School of Nursing, received her MD from Kabul University, and, finally became one of four women elected to Afghanistan's Parliament in 1965. If in different ways from Amanullah and Zabuli before them, female Afghan intellectuals were running against the grain of rural norms. Rather than looking abroad for "progressive" wives, male intellectuals with sympathies on the Left, like Babrak Karmal (Ratebzad's husband) could now build lives with empowered, urban Afghan women.

Kabul feminism was changing. Earlier, it had mimicked the aspirations of European expatriates and contented itself to be mentored by aristocratic Kabul élites. But the expansion of higher education and the Cold War arena changed that. DMT had once hidden itself in Shahr-i Nau; now, groups held regular meetings at Zarnegār Park in the city center. "One corner," said an alumna

---

[22] Author Interview, Sakina Ziar, July 14, 2011, Oxford, United Kingdom.
[23] *Asāsnāmeh-yi sāzmān-i damukrātik-i zanān-i Afghānistān*, Manuscript 1969, 2, cited in Bauer, "Zur Entwicklung," 29.
[24] Interview with Ms. Najiba, Member of the Central Committee of DOMA, Kabul, January 1984, cited in Bauer, 54.
[25] *Matn-i asnād-i awalin konferāns-e sartāsari-ye zanān-e Afghānistān* (Kabul, 1980), 25.

of Kabul University, "was dominated by the Russian orientation, one by the Muslim Brothers, one by the Maoists, and one by the royalists." When the government encouraged women to work as bus drivers, flight attendants, and telephone operators, professors at the Faculty of Islamic Studies at Kabul University launched a protest movement that catalyzed into a proposed constitutional amendment to bar Afghan women from studying abroad.[26] In the same year, DMT launched a birth control campaign, but it fizzled out. An Afghan woman on the Left might one day attend PDPA protests or solidarity meetings for woman tortured in Pinochet's prisons. The next day, she might be dodging acid attacks from Islamists in the halls of Kabul University. Lecture halls, public parks, constitutions; bodies, wombs, unveiled faces: never before had the meaning of Afghan women's bodies been so public, so electric.

In 1975, Daoud re-christened DMT as the "Organization of the Women of Afghanistan" (OWA), devoted to "campaigns against illiteracy among women, forced marriage, and superstition."[27] It celebrated International Women's Year, developed statistics on women's welfare, and founded provincial committees to promote OWA's goals. None of this, however, satisfied the Left. DOWA members insisted that "the [International Women's Year] actions were done for the sake of appearance and that the weekly meetings of the members of the commission occurred more as a tea-drinking circle and to exchange gossip about the latest events in the city than as work toward the 'year of the woman.'"[28] In DOWA's official newspaper *Women of Afghanistan*, activists promoted proletarian internationalist organizations like the Women's International Democratic Federation (WIDF).

Ratebzad and DOWA, however, were not the only oppositional voices in this debate. One Meena Keshwar Kamal, the daughter of educated Kabuli Pashtuns, had grown politically conscious during her studies at Kabul University.[29] Many of her classmates from the same Malalaï Lycée that had educated Ratebzad married, then disappeared, from her social world of women. But if Ratebzad had found liberation in American higher education and, later, Soviet socialism, Meena's generation distrusted real existing socialism. Meena married Faiz Ahmad, a Maoist intellectual; at their marriage, men and women were served the wedding feast together, rather than in segregated fashion. In 1976, Keshwar Kamal founded the Revolutionary Association of the Women of Afghanistan (RAWA), an underground group that promoted literacy among young women and printed political literature against the Daoud regime.[30] The nation-state,

---

[26] Osman, "Thinking Outside the Box: Television and the Afghan Culture Wars," 34.

[27] Bauer, 25; Erika Knabe, *Frauenemanzipation in Afghanistan* (Hain: Meisenheim am Glan, 1977), 171.

[28] Interview with Adela Naba and Mrs. Najiba, Kabul, Afghanistan, February 1984, cited in Bauer, 27.

[29] Melody Ermachild Chavis, *Meena, Heroine of Afghanistan* (New York: St. Martin's Press, 2003), 4.

[30] Ibid., 65.

they argued, did *not* have a monopoly on women's issues. Afghan women had to protect themselves – but not through imitation of Europeans, not through Leninist capture of the nation-state, and certainly not with the support of Leonid Brezhnev.

These Kabuli debates about the proper scale for the women's struggle coincided with those at the United Nations. On the banks of the East River, however, women's rights became subordinated to self-determination. When the General Assembly debated proposals for CEDAW, both Soviet and Third World leaders eagerly signed on. For Moscow, signing CEDAW re-affirmed its progressive image, especially compared to Washington, where a Republican-controlled Senate blocked adoption of CEDAW. For Third World despots, meanwhile, CEDAW reinforced the primacy of the nation-state as the optimal scale for women's political confrontation. Countries' CEDAW-mandated reports on the situation of women were written exclusively by domestic observers and certified only by a committee of self-anointed "experts" from Third World states. One could argue that CEDAW was worthless not out of misogyny, but precisely because it legitimized oppression under the aegis of "culture."[31]

Back in Kabul, the April Revolution complicated the politics of women's issues. The bloodshed that followed the Revolution exiled Ratebzad and other Parchamists to Ambassadorships in the Eastern Bloc. Ratebzad found refuge in Belgrade, a short flight away from Prague, where her husband Babrak Karmal also became an Ambassador.[32] From 1978 to 1979, a Khalqist group, "The Women's Organization of the People," claimed a monopoly on women's issues. DOWA members only later noted that "the organization had worked in illegality, fought against the efforts of the Amin Group, and finally actively took part in the struggle toward the overthrow of Amin."[33] In any event, after 1978 any gradualist approach to "the woman question" was gone, even as the structural commitment to solve the "question" through the (Communist) nation-state remained untouched.

The Soviet intervention delivered the Parchamist diaspora unto power. Ratebzad followed Karmal, now General Secretary of the PDPA, back to Kabul as the Minister of Education; in November 1980, DOWA hosted its inaugural national conference, which included over 2,000 Afghan women and 21 foreign delegations.[34] The conference spoke in the language of class, promoting "productive work" as "the first and most important condition for equality between men and women [and] the only road to the removal of the economic dependence

[31] Betty Friedan, "Scary Doings in Mexico City," in *"It Changed My Life": Writings on the Women's Movement* (Cambridge, MA: 1988), 454; Jocelyn Olcott, "Globalizing Sisterhood: International Women's Year and the Politics of Representation," in *The Shock of the Global: The 1970s in Perspective*, eds. Niall Ferguson, Charles S. Maier, Erez Manela, and Daniel J. Sargent (Cambridge, MA: The Belknap Press of Harvard University Press, 2010), 281–93.
[32] "Moscow's New Stand-In," *Time*, January 7, 1980.
[33] Bauer, 36–7.
[34] *DRA Annual* (Kabul, 1980), 1000.

of women and toward the development of her abilities and talents."[35] In 1981, it opened its first women's club, resumed publication of *Women of Afghanistan* in Dari, Pashto, and English, and launched a daily 30-minute radio program and a weekly hour-long television show. In November 1982, DOWA hosted the international conference of the Soviet Afro-Asian Solidarity Committee, where Ratebzad gave the keynote speech; conversely, DOWA participated in international antifascist and socialist women's conferences throughout the early 1980s.[36] And because the UN had delegated women's issues to the state, DOWA members could attend the UN's World Conference on Women in Copenhagen in 1980.

DOWA boasted unprecedented prestige, but conditions in the countryside left room to doubt the chances for its project. Some DOYA propaganda events in Takhar reportedly attracted 500 girls and young women.[37] And when Nodari Giorgadze arrived in Jalalabad, he praised the work of five girls from the lycée in Sorkhrud who participated in raids of hiding places in local houses, noting that the girls, "not fearing the bandits, disarmed them and delivered them to a filtration point."[38] In another operation, four girls "captured two *dushman* who had changed into women's clothing and were trying to flee into the mountains." And yet if PDPA "raids" of women's schools in Laghman Province indicated attendance rates of close to 100% for the first grades, the more advanced the class, the more the rates of attendance dropped; at one women's lycée, only 68% of registered students attended at all.[39] In many provinces, DOYA's Sections for Women's Outreach remained unoccupied for months, hindering everything.[40] Elsewhere, as in Faryab Province, because DOWA did not have a direct institutional link to DOYA, it "stood apart and withdrew" from the youth organization.[41]

And yet the Soviet Union was not the only possible partner for international cooperation. In autumn 1981, the French Socialist Party (PS) invited RAWA's Meena to speak at their Party Congress. François Mitterand had recently been elected President, delivering the PS unto power. Just before Meena's visit, Mitterand, speaking at a conference on trade in Cancun, declared France's

---

35 Bauer, 38.
36 Ibid., 43.
37 "Spravka sovetnika TsK VLKSM po zone Severo-Vostok za period s dekabria 1981g. po noiabr' 1982g.," RGASPI f. M-3, op. 13, d. 26, l. 96.
38 "Spravka TsK VLKSM pri TsK DOMA v zone 'Vostok.' DOMA i natsional'no-demokraticheskaia revoliutsiia v DRA. G. Dzhelalabad. Noiabr' 1982 goda," RGASPI f. M-3, op. 13, d. 24, l. 113–4.
39 Ibid., ll. 48–9.
40 "Otchët sovetnika DOMA zony 'Iug' po itogam raboty za III. kv. 1360 g. (s sentiabria po 22 dekabria 1981 goda)–G. Semchenko," RGASPI f. M-3, op. 13, d. 16, ll. 72–3.
41 "Godovoĭ otchët o rabote PK DOMA provintsii Far'iab v period s 1 akraba 1361g. po 1 akraba 1362 / 2 noiabria 1982–2 noiabria 1983g.," RGASPI f. M-3, op. 13, d. 36, l. 147–8.

solidarity with "the trade unionists who have been imprisoned, the unemployed who sell their blood to survive, the Indians hunted down in their forests, the workers without rights, [and] the peasants without land."[42]

Meena spoke to a European Left that was then at a turning point – Social Democrats and Socialists opposed to Soviet and American hegemony, who prioritized employment over inflation, and wore their sympathy for Leftist rebels on their sleeves. At the PS Congress, Meena appeared on stage with Salvadorean, Guatemalan, and Namibian resistance fighters, but she "was given the most clamorous applause of the day." As Socialist leaders prepared to govern for the first time ever and make contentious economic policy – "it is the bankers or us," declared one – they found a potent humanist mascot.[43] Soviet guest and chief of the CPSU Central Committee's International Department Boris Ponomarëv was less amused; he stormed out of the hall in boycott. While still in France, Keshwar Kamal held talks with French Prime Minister Pierre Mauroy and PS General Secretary Lionel Jospin. She traveled to Belgium, Germany, and Norway, where audiences received her as a symbol of justice untainted by American or Soviet imperialism. In West Germany, for example, she met with Foreign Minister Hans-Dietrich Genscher's staff, explaining that Afghans "don't want Soviet or American hegemony. We're fighting for world peace."[44]

Yet the reception of Third World interlocutors like Meena was about to change. Older visions of justice met resistance. Once the PS nationalized French industry, speculators "adventured their wealth" and attacked the *franc*.[45] The truth that "the resources in the hands of some twenty banks can render nugatory the efforts of national monetary authorities" revealed itself quickly.[46] Arguably, France could have defended the *franc* if Mitterand had asserted the primacy of politics and decided it was better to live in a *Deutschmark* zone than a European monetary zone. But rather than forging economic justice within the socialist nation-state against the "corsairs of economic interdependence," the PS reconciled international finance capital with social democracy.[47] Mitterand embarked on a *tournant de la rigeur* toward austerity. "Capital," summarizes one historian, "had won in the battle of wills and ideologies. The socialist experiment had failed. Mitterand had succeeded only in destroying redistribution as

[42] "Discours de M. François Mitterrand, Président de la République, devant le monument de la Révolution à Mexico, mardi 20 octobre 1981 (Discours dit de Cancun)," available online at: http://discours.vie-publique.fr/notices/817144500.html.

[43] Richard Eder, "A French Socialist Puzzle: After Winning, What?" *New York Times*, October 27, 1981.

[44] Franz Waushkuhn, "Eine Frau kämpft für die Freiheit ihrer Heimat," *Hamburger Abend-Blatt*, January 19, 1982.

[45] John Maynard Keynes, *The Economic Consequences of the Peace* (New York: Harcourt, Brace, and Howe, 1920), 11.

[46] Joseph S. Nye and Robert O. Keohane, "Transnational Relations and World Politics: An Introduction," *International Organization* 25(3) (Summer 1971), 341.

[47] *El Universal* (Mexico City), June 19, 1975, quoted in Olcott, 256.

a legitimate alternative once and for all."[48] As Régis Debray, the author of Mitterand's Cancun speech, reflected, "we passed from a period of utopian revolution to one of practical pessimism."[49]

For French Socialists, in short, social democracy in Europe was more important than socialism in the nation-state.[50] And rather than seeking an unpredictable path between NATO and Moscow, Mitterand would urge upon European colleagues the need to agree to the deployment of "Euromissiles."[51] Yet the more the Left justified itself in a web of Atlanticist alliances, the more its politics shifted from redistribution to recognition. At MSF, for example, Rony Brauman sought to shake up "the 'bad conscience' of the white man." Too many Europeans, he said, held the West was responsible for the misery of the Third World. However, he continued, "in confining the inhabitants of the South, Africans, Asians, and Latin Americans in the unequivocal posture of victims of the egoism and the cynicism of the moneyed classes of the north, this dolorism exonerated people of all responsibility for their own history."[52] In 1982, MSF ran a colloquium on "the question of the rights of peoples faced with totalitarianism," while in 1985, the duo founded an NGO that aimed "to analyze development problems and human rights without referring to the concept of the Third World, whose unity does not in fact exist."[53] The French Senate later hosted a conference exposing the "ready-to-wear" ideology of Third-Worldism.[54]

The terms on which Europeans allowed victims of injustice to testify were changing. MSF had already taken a step in this direction with its diagnoses of *mal partout* among the residents of the Hazarajat. There, rather than championing the *mujāhidin* guerrillas – exponents of "the ultimate possible mode of subjectification in the political realm" – MSF doctors had medicalized political subjectivity. The appearance of nonpartisanship had demanded the translation of injustice into clinical diagnosis. Gradually, however, the medicalization of politics as a "victim subjectivity to which social agents much make reference" became a principled rather than a practical stance.[55] Rather than demanding

---

[48] Rawi Abdelal, *Capital Rules: The Construction of Global Finance* (Cambridge, MA: Harvard University Press, 2007), 59.

[49] Quoted in Rone Tempest, "Socialists' Fall from Grace Imperils Mitterand," *Los Angeles Times*, March 10, 1992.

[50] Tony Judt, *Postwar: A History of Europe Since 1945* (New York: Penguin, 2006), 553.

[51] Ibid., 591.

[52] Vallaeys, *Médecins sans Frontières. La biographie*, 470–471.

[53] Vallaeys, 475; "The Liberte Sans Frontieres Foundation-Goals," 1–2, Box "Afghanist 1984," MSF Institutional Archives.

[54] "Deroulement du Colloque 'Le Tiers-Mondise en Question," Box "Afghanist 1984," MSF Institutional Archives. The conference included figures like Jean-François Revel, Alain Besançon, Jean-Claude Casanova, François Fejtö, Branko Lazitch, Carlos Franqui, and Emmanuel Le Roy Ladurie.

[55] Didier Fassin, "Subjectivities Without Subjects: Reinventing the Figure of the Witness," in *Humanitarian Reason*, trans. Rachel Gomme (Berkeley: University of California Press, 2012), 222.

economic redistribution, the wretched of the earth were to express themselves through suffering. Where guerrillas had conducted themselves in the language of historical justice, now emaciated children and traumatized women did so through "the exhibition of pain."[56]

This phenomenon was not confined to the French scene. Whereas the first editions of SCA's *Afghanistan-Nytt* newsletter consisted of crude mimeographed news reports, the organization appreciated the power of photography in spreading its message. SCA's Anders Forsberg shared photographs of an Afghan girl with a large chunk of her right shoulder taken out by shrapnel or enemy fire, and a boy without a leg sitting in a hospital.[57] "Afghanistan angers us," reads the caption above the wounded girl; below were SCA's bank details. These appeals to donor audiences, however, reframed Afghans not as heroes, but as victims whose primary mode of subjectivity was victimhood.[58] In linking bodily stigmata to donations, such advertisements marked a shift away from a politics of Leftist solidarity to a skeptic's search for truth in the bodies of victims, like some humanitarian Thomas. Meena's sojourn coincided, in short, with a turn from the rebel to the victim as the dominant political subjectivity expected from subaltern interlocutors.[59]

For her part, Meena remained wedded to traditional discourses of telluric resistance. During an interview on Belgian television, for example, she noted that "the movement that has developed in Afghanistan is a national movement, a movement of students," that controlled "more than eighty percent of the territory of the country."[60] This vision of a war in the countryside and the universities was consonant with the Maoist registers that had been the key of SCA's or MSF's founders in the 1970s – but not with the new registers these reformed revolutionaries were inventing in the 1980s. Likewise, one Afghan comic book found in MSF's archives glorifies a young Afghan boy as a fully fledged fighter who avenges the destruction of his village by gratuitously murdering Soviet officers. Yet the comic concludes by depicting the boy as a virtuous *mujāhid* alongside his father, not a traumatized waif.[61] These Afghan texts illustrated the broader problem of establishing "a normative foundation for settling the question of what ought properly to be included in the description of women," or children, for that matter.[62] Humanitarian propaganda marshaled women

[56] Ibid., 219.

[57] The photograph of the young woman is reproduced in *Afghanistan-Nytt* 3(4) (1991), 40.

[58] Fassin, 210.

[59] Fassin, "Truth Ordeal: Attesting Violence for Asylum Seekers," 109–29.

[60] Interview with Meena Keshwar Kamal (1981), available online at: www.youtube.com/watch?v=ztadMrtImaY.

[61] *Shirkhān-i dalir va hamrāzām-i javānash*, Box "Afghanistan. 1982–1986. Rapports. Infos génerales," MSF Institutional Archives.

[62] Judith Butler, "Contingent Foundations: Feminism and the Question of the 'Postmodern,'" in *Feminists Theorize the Political*, eds. Judith Butler and Joan Scott (New York: Routledge, 1992), 16.

and children as authentic, innocent victims of "totalitarianism" (in France) or "occupation" (in Sweden), but these inscriptions of a subjectivity of victimhood erased Afghans' radical visions of justice from the global public sphere.

For the moment, however, incipient global shifts in the politics of the "woman question" seemed distant from occupied Afghanistan. Not only had DOWA driven opponents like Meena to Pakistan. More than that, economic dislocations and the PDPA's policies had ironically created one of the best job markets for women in Kabul in Afghanistan's history. With the PDPA presiding over a violent state apparatus ready to implement *their* program of social change, the prospects had never seemed brighter for women like Ratebzad. On the international stage, moreover, DOWA had inherited the UN framework for women's issues that ceded to them the monopoly on the representation of all Afghan women. The women, then, who traveled to Moscow, may have still looked to the Soviet Union for inspiration, but they could speak with their CSW colleagues no longer as pupils, but as equals. Territoriality, sovereignty, and real existing socialism had proven fearsome sisters.

What We Talk About When We Talk About Feminism

The Moscow seminar had begun. Yet the speeches of the CSW activists to their DOWA colleagues raise several methodological issues. Memories of developed socialism frequently highlight how a regime of "authoritative discourse" dominated all public speech.[63] Aleksei Yurchak argues that late Stalinist policy shifts froze the "Soviet discursive regime."[64] Prior to this period, one could curate "meta-discourses" that challenged core features of real or ideal socialism. In the mid 1930s, for example, newspapers featured public discussion on the new Soviet Constitution.[65] Reader contributions may have been manipulated, but the staging itself reflected the assumption that citizens could enrich the terms of "socialism." Not everything was up for debate, of course. "Only the discursive 'master' – Stalin – could challenge key tropes, like Lenin, or assumptions like the leading role of the Party."[66]

Following Stalin's death, however, authoritative discourse unmoored itself from the anchor of the "publicly circulating subjective knowledge of a 'master' outside discourse."[67] A predictable register of tropes replaced the extradiscursive "master," but the source of this register's authority remained unclear. Ideological debates continued, but no one possessed the last word on dogma, as had Stalin. Nor could one draw "objective" answers from monastic study of classic texts. But this formalization of authoritative discourse "demagnetized"

---

[63] Yurchak, *Everything Was Forever Until it Was No More*, 36–37.
[64] Ibid., 37.
[65] Ibid., 42.
[66] Ibid., 43.
[67] Ibid., 46.

socialism.[68] Compared to the Stalinist participatory democracy of the 1936 Constitution, the formulation of the 1977 Constitution involved little public input. "Master signifiers," like Lenin, the Party, or Communism, had colonized the possibilities for talking about everyday subjects.[69] "We simply did not speak with each other about work or studies or politics," said one person. "Everyone understood everything, so why speak about that. It was not interesting."[70]

Hence, one cannot analyze the remarks of official activists as if their speech were the product of autonomous, independent liberal subjects. Most of the CSW activists drew from a well-established stock of tropes while glorifying the liberation of Central Asian women in the 1930s as *the* central experience that could inform their Afghan colleagues. The conditions of Uzbek women in the 1930s obviously differed from those of Afghan women in the 1980s, but the *hujum*[71] had become so entrenched in authoritative discourse that activists struggled to view events in Afghanistan in any other light. The conference began with opening remarks by Nalia Bekmakhanova, a Kazakh historian who discussed the situation of "Oriental women" in the former Russian Empire. Russian women had suffered under the Romanovs, she explained, but their suffering was that of subjects of advanced capitalism.[72] Russia's Caucasian and Central Asian subjects were, in contrast, stuck in a backward, premodern "natural economy."[73] Tsarist Eurasia and Afghanistan were the same place – economies in a state of objective backwardness according to the *piatichlennaia* scheme.

But the Revolution, Bekhmakhanova explained, had changed everything. More specifically, de-veiling had emancipated Central Asian women. After Uzbek women gained land and water rights, she argued, they "started to work in a system of cooperation. But working under the *paranja* or veil was difficult. And in the families of workers, poor peasants, communists, and Komsomol workers, and among the studying youth, women with the agreement of their family were the first to take off the veil. The *baĭs*[74] waged a cruel struggle against this. In 1927, in Uzbekistan alone, 203 women activists died."[75] (This

---

[68] Benjamin Nathans and Kevin Platt, "Socialist in Form, Indeterminate in Content: The Ins and Outs of Late Soviet Culture," *Ab Imperio* 2 (2011), 313.

[69] Yurchak, 73–4.

[70] Ibid., 129.

[71] "Hujum" is a word that was used in Turkic languages to describe the de-veiling and women's emancipation strategies introduced in Stalinist Central Asia in the late 1920s.

[72] N.E. Bekmakhanova, "Razvitie obshchestvenno-politicheskoĭ aktivnosti zhenshchin," GARF f. 7928, o. 3, d. 5583, ll. 54–5.

[73] See, in particular, Karl Marx, *Capital*, Vol. 2, Chapter 4: "The Three Formulas of the Circuit," available online at: www.marxists.org/archive/marx/works/1885-c2/cho4.htm.

[74] *Baĭ* was a social category that became ubiquitous in Soviet critiques of prerevolutionary conditions in Central Asia. Perhaps coming from the Turkic *boy* for "a wealthy person," it came to symbolize a rich, feudal, landowner or wealthy shepherd who symbolized what *kulaks* did in European Russia.

[75] Bekmakhanova, "Razvitie obschcestvenno-politicheskoĭ aktivnosti zhenshchin," l.64.

message, it bears stressing, was not intended only for Afghans. At a seminar for Mongolian women's activists in 1977, CSW representatives spoke in terms almost identical to those they would use for DOWA five years later.[76])

Granted, perhaps Afghanistan was not fundamentally different from the Uzbek countryside of the 1920s. Komsomol field operatives despaired "that there is no possibility for working in far-flung villages due to the great backwardness and fanaticism of women there. In the city of Khost, there are only 10–12 women – the wives of offices from different provinces and Kabul – who don't wear the *paranja*. Among the local population, no one takes such a liberty, since all women's work takes place in the home and in the women's lycée."[77] The point, however, is that in both cases, resistance to de-veiling was less of a class than a religious or social phenomenon. Insisting that not just the Uzbek but also the Afghan story were best explained through the lens of class, however, Bekhmakhanova drained the Soviet history of the relevance it could have to DOWA activists.

These Soviet obsessions made for an odd contrast to contemporary international trends in the imagining of women's history. Recalling her early education, one American historian saw women's history as isolated from "a world of significant knowledge."[78] "My commitment to women's history came out of my life, not out of my head," she reflected. This may well have been equally true for many of the Soviet women like Bekmakhanova, or her Uzbek counterpart Meli Akhunova, both part of the first generation of female academics in Soviet Central Asia. But the study of women in the Soviet Union remained captive to the binds of nation and class. Soviet studies of women celebrated the "solution of the woman question" in the past, rather than turning to injustices that might still persist under socialism. "Patriarchy," so popular a concept in the West, was a myth, orthodox Marxists could argue. People who claimed that gender was "a social category imposed on a sexed body," or that gender, like capital, produced "people who claim to choose what they are supposed to want, and claim to want what they have" had it all wrong.[79] False consciousness, not gender, was the snake that seduced humans away from their true nature.

Obviously, this was a gendered vision of feminism if ever there was one. The idea that only sooty, gendered, physically exhausting, and historically male-dominated professions could liberate bodies and minds from exploitation

---

[76] Meli Akhunovna, Untitled Speech, GARF f. 7928, op. 3 d. 4215, l. 134.

[77] "Otchët sovetnika TsK VLKSM V.P.–za 6 mesiatsev 1985/85," RGASPI f. M-3, op. 13, d. 121, l. 80

[78] Gerda Lerner, "Women Among the Professors of History: The Story of a Process of Transformation," in *Voices of Women Historians: The Personal, the Political, the Professional*, eds. Eileen Boris and Nupur Chaudhuri (Bloomington: Indiana University Press, 1999), 1.

[79] Joan W. Scott, "Gender: A Useful Category of Social Analysis," *American Historical Review* 91(5) (December 1986), 1056; Kathy E. Ferguson, *The Feminist Case Against Bureaucracy* (Philadelphia: Temple University Press, 1984), 177.

glorified gendered masculine workers as the *telos* of humanity. Female bodies, it seemed, existed neither to bear children, nor to make love, but to be subjected to the Chaplinesque indignities that the assembly line of modern times had long inflicted on fathers, sons, and husbands. Disabled bodies, "deviant" sexualities, or queer distinctions of sex, gender, and body that those bodies' owners bestowed upon them had no place in this order. No wonder that this vision of every (wo)man a factory worker felt limiting. "For many women I knew," wrote one feminist, "the need to begin with the female body – our own – was understood not as applying a Marxist principle *to* women, but as locating the grounds from which to speak with authority *as* women."[80] Even taking Marxism on its own terms, it was never quite clear how this vision of "awakening and formation of social consciousness," of speaking not from a, but *the*, worker's perspective was supposed to be realized in a country where, as one PDPA member admitted, "there's absolutely no working class in the sense of a mature and politically conscious class. We have workers, but no working class."[81]

And yet let us listen to what the CSW activists had to say themselves. Another speaker, S. Turchaninova, underscored how Soviet modernization had transformed a generation of Central Asian women. Moscow had invested mightily into "socialist enterprises for the cotton and silk industries in Central Asia," she noted, but "women of the East" still had to be "recruited into production."[82] In the 1920s, Turchaninova explained, work exchange schemes sent "local women" from Central Asia to textile-producing centers in Russia and Ukraine. "Here," she added, "were created all the necessary conditions for the raising of the cultural level, for the successful mastery of modern technology, and for the achievement of professional mastership for the female workers and trainees."[83]

Like her colleague, Turchaninova drew on the citational phrases of authoritative discourse ("enormous socialist enterprises," "rich revolutionary and life experience," "active participation," etc.). Many of these phrasings constituted "displaced agency," where it is never clear who is doing what, "contributing to the general circularity of the constative dimension of discourse."[84] But the message was clear. Production and work, not bourgeois musings on "gender," awaken us to our alienation. True progressives did not pause to gloat in the fatuous superiority of "national culture," much less that of a mythical global sisterhood of *women*. They recognized their economic alienation and reclaimed their agency as producers in an industrial economy, thanks to the democratization of the means of production.

[80] Rich, "Notes Toward a Politics of Location," 213.
[81] "Zapis' besedy s sekretarem pervichnoĭ partorganizatsii 10–go raĭona g. Kabula, sostoiavsheĭsia 28 sentiabria 1987g.," in Plastun and Andrianov, 182; Turchaninova, 37.
[82] S. Ia. Turchaninova, "Vovlechenie zhenshchin v obshchestvennoe proizvodstvo," GARF f. 7928, o. 3, d. 5583, l. 46.
[83] Ibid.
[84] Yurchak, 71.

Once again, one could note a curious and disquieting symmetry between the Soviet and Western position on "the woman question." Soviet women's activists were clear that "power" had to do with economics and "liberation" with the democratization of the means of production. Women could emancipate themselves through technical education and work. Such a view of women's justice, however, remained enthralled with the national economy as the proper scale for liberation. This was why the obvious objection that the factories in which Afghan women were supposed to work were not competitive missed the point – it dismissed the primacy of politics. On the other side of the Iron Curtain, however, "woman" and "gender" had become categories strong enough to stand independently of "worker" and "class." There was, as the French thought, no apparent contradiction between denouncing Soviet crimes against women while also pursuing socialism in one country; gender and economics were separate issues.

Nonetheless, with Meena a marginal refugee and the treacherous French under siege from financial speculators, activists in Moscow could rest assured in the truth of their convictions. It was, however, now the Afghans' turn to speak. What would they bring to this socialist conversation?

Let Me Speak!

One must approach the DOWA activists' speeches with a few methodological points in mind. Most Afghans were illiterate; the women at the seminar were not; all of the attendees came from northern Afghanistan or Kabul.[85] The archives are mute on the women's ethnicities, and all of the Afghan women at the conference spoke in Russian.[86] Further, one must be mindful of how actors who encountered the Soviet state adjusted their language to meet audiences' expectations.[87] That said, what we find here is unusual: the DOWA activists could ably deploy the citational discourse of Sovietese. But when encouraged to speak extemporaneously, they described their world on their own terms.

Several of the DOWA activists' prepared remarks were indistinguishable from those of their hosts. Jamilia Nahid, the head of the delegation, introduced the group as devoted to "the actualization, realization, and preservation of the rights of Afghan women that were envisioned by the revolutionary order of the country. The People's Democratic Party of Afghanistan is a party of the working class, a party of all the laborers of the country." The PDPA, she continued, was the champion of these collective rights; the Party, she explained, "proceeds

---

[85] GARF f. 7928, o.3, d. 5583, l. 5.

[86] All of the documents in the stenogram for the seminar are in Russian, save for one press release in Dari prepared by DOWA.

[87] Alexander Morrison, Review of Robert Crews, *For Prophet and Tsar*, *The Slavonic and East European Review* 86(3) (July 2008), 553–7; Jeff Sahadeo, Review of Sahadeo, *For Prophet and Tsar*, *Central Asian Survey* 27(1) (March 2008), 105–6.

toward the resolution of the woman question in Afghanistan and exerts all of its energies toward the further engagement of women into the national life of the country. To the women of Afghanistan has fallen the enormous honor of, with the entire nation, and with a resolute step, going along the road that has opened up before them and solving the questions standing before the country, and, along with that country, overcoming all difficulties."[88]

Nahid had mastered her mentors' tortuous phraseology: verbs transmogrified into noun phrases ("actualization, realization, and preservation of the rights of Afghan women"), citational complex modifiers ("enormous honor," "with great interest"), and "noun phrases" – nouns modified by participles themselves drawn from authoritative discourse, like "the road that has opened up before them" (*po shirikoĭ otkrivsheĭsia pered nimi doroge*).[89] Other DOWA members interpreted the Afghan past in terms amenable to Soviet historiography, noting that before the Revolution women lived under the "oppression of feudal and prefeudal conditions" and "economic backwardness." "The life of an Afghan woman was bound by the four walls of her home," and "the husband sat at home, or in the garden, and had no work other than relaxation" while women carried out back-breaking work: gathering brushwood, raising children, carrying potable water "for dozens of kilometers," and growing crops.[90] Here, again, was the difference between Soviet discourse and emergent Western concept of "patriarchy." Communists agreed that men dominated women, but they laid the blame at the feet of economic bases rather than ideological superstructures.

This canned rhetoric was not unique to the seminar. Throughout the Second World, Afghan women were learning to apply paint-by-numbers Marxism to their own conditions. Near East Berlin, for example, an Afghan woman was busy researching Afghan women's history, contending that "Everyone who knows anything of history also knows that great social revolutions are impossible without the feminine ferment. Social progress may be measured precisely by the social position of the fair sex (plain ones included)."[91] The "prefeudal" state of Afghanistan paradoxically demanded that trade unions agitate for women to enter the shop floor. Only then could "the woman take up the same social position as the man"; only then could women begin the "long-term and complicated process in which centuries-old traditions must be surmounted." The student was merely crystallizing the conventional wisdom of the Old Left: rather telling crusty male trade unionists that "no one was going to listen to

---

[88] GARF f. 7928, op.3, d. 5583, l. 129.
[89] Patrick Seriot, *Analyse du discours politique soviétique* (Paris: Institut d'études slaves, 1985).
[90] Sultana Omid, "Razvitie obshchestvenno-politicheskoĭ aktivnosti zhenshchin," GARF f. 7928, o.3, d. 5583, l. 130.
[91] Amina Wahab Zada, "Die Notwendigkeit der Gleichberechtigung der Frau unter den Bedingungen der national-demokratischen Revolution in Afghanistan und Aufgaben der Gewerkschaften um Kampf um ihre Verwirklichung," (Dissertation, Gewerkschaftshochschule "Fritz Heckert," May–June 1987).

him," women had to ally with them as the most primal institution of political struggle at the scale of the nation-state.[92]

Back at the meeting in Moscow, following the DOWA activists' prepared remarks, Valentina E. Vavilina, the head of the Soviet delegation, turned to her guests. "We were," she said, "very touched by your gratitude in your address to Soviet warriors, thank you. But you didn't say anything about yourself. How did you become an activist? It would be very interesting for us to find out. Perhaps someone will say something about themselves in the next presentations?"[93] They did. Aziza Dodmanesh, the Jowzjan DOWA Provincial Committee Secretary, began telling her Soviet colleagues about her life. "In the name of the women of the province located in the north of our country – Afghans, Turkmen, Uzbeks, female peasants and those engaged in the production of hides," she began, "allow me to pass on to Soviet women our very best wishes. I'd like to tell you a bit about the life of women living at home, about the life of women who go around in the chador, about the conditions of their lives."

She proceeded to paint a picture of her world. "The Provincial Soviet in the province of Jowzjan," she explained, "was able to organize work among women who are employed in housework, in other words, among the most backwards parts of the female population." DOWA members went deep into the countryside, she explained, to tell women "about the events that are going on in Afghanistan, about the real course of all of the events, about what the enemies of the April Revolution are up to. We tell them about the activity of Soviet women." Afghan women had learned from the experience of their Soviet counterparts, she explained, and were now ready to "consciously take an active part in those events that the DOWA is carrying out. They consciously fight for the foundation of a new social order in the country." She continued, describing her work with Afghan Uzbek women:

Among our women there are also representatives of the Uzbek nationality, Uzbek women who wear the veil (*pokryvalo*), who cover their face with the *chador*. Together with other women, with representatives of other nationalities, united in the ranks of the provincial section of our organization, they, too, give all of their strengths toward the defense of the gains of the April Revolution. They say, 'We'll never fall under the influence of the enemy propaganda, since we've already listened for thousands of years to what they say—we know the essence of their propaganda perfectly well.'

And they really understand the role and the meaning that the enormous contact with Soviet comrades had, the help of Soviet warriors in warding off the aggressors, in putting pressure on all of the hearths of the counterrevolution in the country, and in part in the province of Jowzjan. Afghan women meet with Soviet warriors, and they are grateful for the help that they have provided to the ancient land of Afghanistan.

[92] Rosalind Delmar, quoted in Ann Coote and Beatrix Campbell, *Sweet Freedom: The Struggle for Women's Liberation* (Oxford: Blackwell, 1982), 7.
[93] GARF f. 7928, o.3, d. 5583, l. 4, 269.

In our province the women, the majority of whom are peasants, support the policy that our party and government is carrying out. Carrying their weapons with them, they defend the gains of the April Revolution, [and] they are grateful to the women whose sons arrived in Afghanistan in order to defend the Afghans against the aggression of imperialism.[94]

Dodmanesh had hardly abandoned the terms of authoritative discourse; several complex modifiers dot her remarks ("consciously fight," "consciously take an active part"). She described her struggle as one in alliance with Soviet soldiers against "imperialism," and spoke of "counterrevolution." But she framed her project primarily as a provincial struggle. The fight in Jowzjan, she explains, is against not *class* foes, but "enemies" active for thousands of years. Hence, only Afghans – veiled Uzbek Afghans, at that – possess the historical experience (not class consciousness) to fight back, since they have "already listened for thousands of years" to their foes. Dodmanesh, in short, had exposed the myth of women's automatic solidarity with the working class for what it was. Common sense might have lost the authority to discredit Soviet authoritative discourse, but one could hardly dismiss a real, live, talking Afghan woman.

Soon, another DOWA member stood up to speak. "I myself," explained the twenty-one-year-old Narsi Hussein, "am from Laghman Province." Hussein went on to explain her work in eastern Afghanistan. "Fortunately," she said, since the "second stage of the Saur Revolution [...] we could organize, and now in Laghman Province 210 women belong to our organization, 143 of whom are illiterate. They participate in literacy courses that were formed for them, they participate in special clubs." Not only that, women had left their families and gone to the border to defend, along with Afghan Army forces, the border with Pakistan. Hussein then turned her attention to the women of neighboring Kunar Province, where "even in a chador, a woman does not have the right to go out far from her own home." In spite of this, ninety-five women living in Kunar Province are members of the PDPA.[95]

Hussein's unrehearsed remarks were full of tropes of authoritative discourse, such as the euphemistic "second stage of the Saur Revolution" (i.e., the Soviet occupation). Nor would her cataloging of the numbers of illiterate women have not been out of place in a Soviet history tract. Citational phrases like "actively participate" populated the horizon of her lexical landscape. And yet Hussein, too, went beyond established discourse in her remarks. Instead of thanking CSW women, she explicitly thanked their sons, fighting on the front lines with Afghans. She recalled how, after the "second stage of the Revolution," Afghan women "went out toward the Soviet forces and brought them everything that they had at home. They did this according to the tradition of hospitality – one always has to give one's best items to the guest, one has to offer the finest

94 Ibid., l. 263–5.
95 Ibid., l. 266–8.

delicacies to him – Afghan walnuts, walnut cookies which resemble cedar cones. The warmest reception that I ever saw given to Soviet soldiers was given to these Soviet forces."

Rather than reaffirming the CSW seminar as an occasion devoted to "women-to-women things," Hussein unintentionally highlighted the aggressive, militaristic heteronationalism that had enabled the CSW–DOWA encounter in the first place.[96] As generous as CSW had been, it was the violent penetration of Afghanistan by tens of thousands of Soviet troops that ensured DOWA's survival in the short term. Hussein highlighted this fact, unsaid during the rest of the seminar, but rather than presenting herself as an equal to the Soviet soldiers, she depicted her engagement with Soviet Army in terms of unpaid domestic work. Whereas most of the CSW speeches stressed the necessity precisely of women getting *out* of the home, Hussein emphasized their participation in the domestic economy. Marshaled by élite Soviet women to personify unmediated Afghan authenticity – "to make the subaltern speak" – Hussein had shown the distance of CSW from Afghan women.[97]

Like their Komsomol counterparts in the cedar-poor borderlands, the CSW activists struggled to realize "the dream of a common language" with Afghans. Class promised forms of "primary intensity" with Afghan interlocutors, yet all too often these comrades were poor members of a class-motivated global sisterhood.[98] The DOWA activists who spoke at the seminar failed to see the veil as a primordial issue for women's activists. They had, much like the male Nangarhari mullahs with whom Giorgadze worked, their own provincial struggles for which they seemed glad to appropriate Soviet support. But few saw *economic* exploitation and the *nation-state* as the key tropes and arenas for political confrontation. They appropriated the material, moral, and, to some extent, rhetorical arsenal that the Soviet Union had furnished, but they remained distant from internalizing the subjectivity of Soviet authoritative discourse. DOWA activists' re-appropriation of this discourse spoke, then, not only to their creativity, but also to the impotence of the Soviet global project to fashion a world according to its own rhetorical and institutional grammar.

It marked the beginning of a decline in discursive confidence, a fracturing, in the project of a specifically Soviet approach to "the woman question." The Soviet project had dramatically reshaped the former colonies of the Russian Empire, and outside of its borders, it had charged women's lives with new possibilities. Seeing the female Soviet engineer in the Kabul Mikrorayon, of receiving *Soviet Women* with illustrations of professional women – this had not been

[96] Friedan, "Scary Doings in Mexico City," 454.
[97] Gayatri Spivak, "Can the Subaltern Speak?" in *Marxism and the Interpretation of Culture*, eds. Cary Nelson and Lawrence Grossberg (Urbana: University of Illinois Press, 1988), 271–316.
[98] Adrienne Rich, quoted in Daniel Rodgers, *Age of Fracture* (Cambridge, MA: Belknap Press of Harvard University Press, 2013), 149; Ibid., "Compulsory Heterosexuality and Lesbian Existence," in *Blood, Bread and Poetry* (New York: Norton, 1986), 51.

a fantasy. Yet Soviet women seemed to be speaking past Afghans. "Much of what is narrowly termed 'politics' seems to rest on a longing for certainty even at the cost of honesty, for an analysis which, once given, need not be reexamined," shrewdly wrote an observer of Marxist feminism.[99] How long could old terms of commonality – "we," "woman" – persist?

From "The Woman Question" to Human Rights

Just as CSW's and DOWA's vision for Afghan women seemed theoretically muddled, on the ground, Afghan women faced terrifying conditions on the ground. Komsomol advisers attested to *mujāhidin* attacks on women's schools, and the PDPA's bloody history hindered recruitment.[100] In Helmand, reported one adviser, girls feared joining DOYA because of death threats. Internal Party disputes added to others' hesitation. When one adviser asked girls in Lashkar Gah why they did not join DOYA, one girl asked: "What kind of organization are we joining – a Khalqist one or a Parchamist one? You should sort out your differences first, then agitate among us."[101] But DOWA's real problem went deeper. The overwhelming majority of Afghan women remained outside of the formal economy and, hence, DOWA's reach. DOWA sought to counter this by forming "housewives' committees," but reports frequently noted "the weak activism of housewives, the majority of whom completely lose their ties with the committees of DOYA after they get married. This is conditioned by national traditions and Sharia laws."[102]

Perhaps Meena had a point? One Komsomol adviser in Helmand pleaded to Kabul that there was "no point in talking about the meaning and the importance of work in the country and the villages. [...] If the leadership of the Provincial Committee won't understand that the country is 90% peasants, then nothing will help."[103] In northern Afghanistan, one adviser reported that parades had attracted large numbers of DOWA activists, many of whom were workers at the textile factory in Pul-i Khumri.[104] But, they added, DOYA's beachheads were a women's hairdressing salon and a seamstresses' shop – far cries from utopia, sooty utopia. And outside of the provincial capital, DOYA's outreach to women had "a purely episodic character" due to "interdepartmental division and misunderstanding of the meaning and urgency

[99] Rich, "Notes toward a Politics of Location," 217.
[100] "Otchët o rabote provintsial'nogo komiteta DOMA provintsii Gazni noiabria 1982. po noiabr' 1983g.," RGASPI f. M-3, op. 13, d. 39, l. 132.
[101] "Otchët sovetnika TsK VLKSM v provintsii Gil'mend o prodelannoĭ rabote s noiabria 1982g. po noiabr' 1983g.," RGASPI f. M-3, op. 13, d.38, l. 72.
[102] "Itogovyĭ otchët sovetnika TsK VLKSM pri DOMA Kutsenko V. Za period s oktiabria 1986 goda po sentiabr' 1987 goda pr. Lagman," RGASPI f. M-3, op. 13, d. 148, l. 81.
[103] "Itogovyĭ otchët o rabote Gil'mendskogo PK DOMA za period 1 mizona 1365 goda po 1366 goda," RGASPI f. M-3, op. 13, d. 150, l. 50.
[104] "Itogovyĭ otchët sovetnika TsK VLKSM pri PK DOMA provintsii Baglan oktiabr' 1986g.- sentiabr' 1987g.," RGASPI f.M-3, op. 13, d. 151, l. 51.

of joint activity as a result of an absence of mutual respect and mutual understanding."[105]

Indeed, perhaps not just Meena but also Narsi Hussein had a point. Had not solving the "woman question" under the aegis of the 40th Army been an illusion from the start? One American working in a refugee camp near the Afghan–Pakistani border recalled how "a group of black-clad women, their faces marked with weariness yet full of dignity faced me one hot day in May 1984." They had been raped, they explained, by Soviet soldiers, and dozens of their family members had been killed. They had fled their homes "one hundred miles away, walking for days with so little access to water that they were reduced to eating mud to obtain what moisture they could."[106] Hundreds of miles away in the other direction, Czechoslovak intelligence agents based in the Islamic Republic of Iran established that Afghan women refugees were being recruited to carry out suicide attacks in Lebanon. Their families, reported one agent, were compensated with jobs, housing, and Iranian passports.[107] Some Afghan women fought back. Meena Keshwar Kamal's group, RAWA, built hospitals, schools, and orphanages in Afghanistan and Pakistani refugee camps. But Kamal was assassinated in February 1987 in an apparent (if improbable) joint operation between the Afghan KhAD (the Afghan secret police and equivalent of the Soviet KGB) and *Hezb-i Islami*. In any event, Afghan women had too many enemies and too few friends.

Yet events in the Afghan arena were also captive to global shifts in the possibilities for women's political confrontation. Between the 1975 Mexico City Conference and the 1985 Nairobi Conference, the number of NGOs and independent activists participating alongside state delegations quadrupled.[108] Even as the USSR and DRA terrorized such organizations within their own borders, the idea that the state was not the sole legitimate representative of all women within its borders gained traction. If a bewildered Betty Friedan had been taken aback by the tone at Mexico City, in Nairobi, the U.S. delegation (Alan Keyes and Maureen Reagan) withered a paragraph in the Nairobi Conference's final report that singled out the needs of Palestinian and South African women, the only two such national groups isolated for such special attention.[109] They may have been making a political point, but one that was consonant with wider shifts. Indeed, partly because the Reagan Administration ended U.S.

---

[105] Ibid., 52.

[106] Kathleen Howard-Merriam, "Afghan Refugee Women and the Struggle for Liberation," Paper for MESA Conference, San Francisco, California, November 28–December 2, 1984, Arthur Paul Collection, University of Nebraska-Omaha.

[107] "Podgotovka terroristov na territorii Irana i ikh deĭstviia" (1986), 49–50, MfS HA X 1948, BStU.

[108] "1975 World Conference on Women," available online at: www.5wwc.org/conference_background/1975_WCW.html.

[109] "Report of the World Conference to Review and Appraise the Achievements of the United Nations Decade for Women: Equality, Development and Peace" (1986), available online at: www.5wwc.org/downloads/Report_of_WCW-1985.pdf.

funding for organizations that performed or promoted abortion as a means of population control, traditional institutions of "women's policy" like the International Planned Parenthood Federation were left sucking for air. This left a void that smaller actors interested in education as part of a population control platform could fill. Groups like the Women's Global Network for Reproductive Rights and Development Alternatives with Women for a New Era redeemed women's needs from an instrumental tool of anti-Zionist or anti-apartheid activists to a meaningful concept in a revitalized feminist international.[110]

Mikhaïl Gorbachëv accelerated this shift as *glasnost'* encouraged the return of a Soviet "meta-discourse."[111] Reflecting on the need to talk differently about the socialist project had once been illegal, but after 1986, Party secretaries were encouraged to engage in "real self-criticism," to admit "real problems," and to propose a "creative approach" in ways beyond the "experiments" of the 1970s. Urges to rediscover "the pure word of Lenin" became ubiquitous.[112] Yet the belief that key discursive anchors could be democratized so quickly proved folly. "The tight narrative structure of authoritative discourse meant that with the undermining of one master signifier, the whole system was undermined, and quite soon the discursive field began crumbling."

This collapse is easy to see in the speeches of CSW delegations to Third World audiences. Stories of liberated Central Asian women still featured prominently, but authoritative discourse had dissolved. Speaking to delegates to a 1988 conference of Indian women's activists, Z.E. Timofeeva, an editor at *Soviet Woman*, informally "quoted" Lenin when she explained the relevance of the 1920s: "At that time Lenin instructed the Party: 'We need Communist work among the female masses. But political work includes a meaningful piece of educational work among men. We should remove the old, slaveholding point of view, down to its very last piece, from both the Party as well as the masses.'"[113] Central Asian women remained, but the authoritative discourse structuring their past disappeared. Soon, the preoccupation disappeared altogether. By 1990, CSW was sending female activists to conferences in Geneva to discuss Kazakhstan – but in the context of the hazardous effects of nuclear testing on pregnant women.[114]

Yet the shifts inaugurated by Gorbachëv were not only discursive. Under Gorbachëv's foreign policy of "new thinking," Soviet patience toward Third World delegations declined. Central Asian cities were repurposed as conference sites not just for "countries of socialist orientation," but also for joint Soviet–UNESCO seminars on child literacy.[115] The fixation with the nation-state as the

---

[110] Matthew Connelly, *Fatal Misconception: The Struggle to Control the World's Population* (Cambridge, MA: Harvard University Press, 2008), 327–69.
[111] Yurchak, 292–6.
[112] Ibid., 294.
[113] Z.E. Timofeeva, Untitled Talk, GARF f. 7928, o. 3, d. 7033, l. 28.
[114] O. Romashko, Untitled Speech, March 1990, f. 7928, o. 3, d. 7665, l. 22–6.
[115] GARF, f. 7928, o. 3, d. 7471, l. 110.

premier arena for political conflict was ebbing, a trend that the Soviet Union's October 1990 Law on Public Organizations accelerated. Even as the Law regulated every aspect of NGOs' existence, it recognized them for the first time in Soviet history: a recognition that "human beings exist not only as citizens of sovereign nation-states and as members of other separate groupings, but also as individuals."[116] Moscow had reversed its position on whether the Soviet state, or its Third World counterparts, really had a monopoly over society. Women's issues had been freed from the crucible of the regulating, sterilizing, aborting state.

But if there was no such thing as society, what was the role of the Communist Party, much less government-organized organizations like CSW? If Soviet citizens were sovereign individuals whose diversity eluded monolithic representation, it was difficult to justify constitutional protection for the CPSU. In March 1990, Gorbachëv abolished the article in the Soviet Constitution that granted the CPSU a "leading and guiding force in Soviet society." Gorbachëv appears to have thought that organizations like CSW would coexist with non-Communist NGOs, which Union Republics would then regulate in a reformed Union of Sovereign Republics. In the fall of 1990, CSW officials met with the United Nations Development Fund for Women to plan a two-week training course where UNDP labor economists would "assist [CSW] in developing a training programme for the Training of Trainers for Women Entrepreneurs. These women would, thereafter, modify the training programme to suit the needs of the different Republics and other regions in the USSR, and themselves train female entrepreneurs."[117]

Geopolitics, however, rendered such possible futures history. The Soviet collapse financially devastated women, gutted CSW, and bequeathed Soviet successor states with the illiberal "oversight" bureaucracy of the Law on Public Organizations. The winner of these unexpected events was the push to relocate women's rights away from the nation-state to the sovereign individual. Yet processes outside of Western control – the explosion in NGOs, Gorbachëv's abandonment of the Third World, and the Soviet collapse – had played a significant role in leaving this vision unchallenged. With self-determination and proletarian internationalism dead, the United Nations became a forum where Western leaders could present themselves as part of a women rights vanguard. It was a striking sign of how much had changed when, at the Fourth UN Conference on Women in Beijing, delegates applauded Hilary Clinton when she declared that "human rights are women's rights and women's rights are human rights once and for all."[118]

---

[116] International Network for a UN Second Assembly, "Proposal for a United Nations Second Assembly," GARF f. 7928, o. 3, d.7471, l. 162.

[117] GARF, f. 7928, o. 3, d. 7662, l. 10.

[118] Hilary Clinton, "Remarks to the U.N. 4th World Conference on Women Plenary Session," September 5, 1995.

Conclusion

Once and for all indeed: the Soviet women's movement had become a footnote to an ironic transformation of sororal internationalism. Soviet activists took pride in their past achievements, but they became rhetorically and intellectually inarticulate in a world where the revolution and the nation-state had lost their roles as vanguards of a workers' – or women's – movement. More broadly, however, the CSW activists' wish to take Afghan women as a symbol – the most oppressed element in a class imaginary – was not just a Soviet phenomenon. The European Left celebrated RAWA in the 1980s as a symbol of "freedom" and "democracy," but inquired little into their actual politics. RAWA's newspaper declared the organization in favor of not only for "freedom, democracy, and women's rights in Afghanistan" but also against "the disgraceful stain" of foreign troops in Saudi Arabia, itself "an explicit sign of intervention and gunboat policy." Singled out for RAWA's support were the "just struggles of the peoples of Palestine, South Africa, Eritrea, Iran, Kashmir, Latin America, and others against the fascist regimes in their lands."[119] Afghan women had a vision of global justice, just not one foreigner cared to listen to.

Once Afghanistan lost its geopolitical relevance, the plight of Afghan women aroused limited attention. European socialists and American human rights crusaders no longer needed to "discover" the Afghan woman as a symbol of their humanist credentials. At Human Rights Watch, the shift of Afghanistan from the Helsinki Watch Division to a new Middle East Division meant a loss of country-specific institutional expertise.[120] Reduced to tokens of humanity, then ignored, Afghan women occupied a tragic place in the humanitarian global project's vision of justice. The insistence on politics at the cost of morality turned the Afghan woman into a male factory worker; the insistence on morality at the cost of politics turned her into a victim. For them, it may not be too much to quote the bitter reflections of the KGB's former chief analyst: "'Human rights' as a concept disappeared from the arsenal of foreign policy picklocks once its political goal had been achieved: the extermination of its primary opponent, the USSR."[121]

Only later did Taliban atrocities re-energize a once-limp global conscience. Most famously, in 1996, the U.S.-based Feminist Majority Foundation (FMF) launched a "Campaign to Stop Gender Apartheid." Shrewdly navigating Capitol Hill and the American grassroots, the Foundation prevented Washington from recognizing the Taliban regime and played a role in halting UNOCAL's plans to build a gas and oil pipeline across Afghanistan.[122] In an

[119] "Let's Unite and Foil the Treacherous Plot of Installing Gulbuddin in Kabul" (Declaration dated December 27, 1990), in *Payām-i Zan* (March 1991), np.

[120] Author Correspondence with Jeri Laber, May 8, 2014.

[121] Nikolaĭ Leonov, *Likholet'e* (Moscow: Mezhdunarodnye Otnosheniia, 1995), 165.

[122] Ann Russo, "The Feminist Majority Foundation's Campaign to Stop Gender Apartheid: The Intersections of Feminism and Imperialism in the United States," *International Feminist Journal of Politics* 8(4) (December 2006), 565.

eerily commodified recapitulation of Soviet gender discourses, in February 2001, the group "promoted the purchase, in remembrance of Afghan women, of a 'burqa swatch,' meant to be worn on one's lapel to demonstrate solidarity with Afghan women through the appropriation of a 'Muslim' garment."[123] Adding to the phantasmagoria was a public reading of a monologue about life as a woman in Afghanistan in front of a sold-out crowd at Madison Square Garden – headlined by Oprah Winfrey. The culmination of the event came when a burqa-clad RAWA activist herself joined Oprah on stage, "moving like a silent, anonymous hill of cloth toward the stage. When the cloth was lifted, a young woman emerged, dressed in the casual jacket-and-pants outfit that would blend in on any university campus in the world."[124]

Call it "sexual exceptionalism."[125] What is clear is that the politics of feminist opposition to the Taliban became much more fraught after 9/11. FMF did not openly support the invasion, but its advocacy was marked by "a consistent resort to the cultural, as if knowing something about women and Islam [...] was more urgent than exploring the history of the development of repressive regimes in the region and the US role in this history."[126] Images of oppressed Afghan women flooded American media, and both President Bush and First Lady Laura Bush repeatedly turned to the liberation of Afghan women as a justification for the overthrow of the Taliban regime. When, in the spring of 2002, the American women's magazine *Ms.* highlighted the work of FMF in contributing to the liberation of Afghanistan, RAWA vituperated the magazine as "the mere mouthpiece of hegemonic, US-centric, ego driven, corporate feminism." Not only that, it lambasted FMF for turning a blind eye to the numerous warlords brought into the Karzai regime. The whole affair, RAWA's American champions concluded, was "a sorry indication of the future of hegemonic feminism in the US."[127]

As of writing, however, campaigns to promote Afghan and Pakistani schoolgirls as paladins of humanity have reached new highs. Whereas women's lives were once marshaled against occupation of Afghanistan, today the precarious educational status of Afghan and Pakistani women is marketed as the only indefensible accomplishment of American–Afghan "partnership." Is it? As the United States positions itself "as the site of authoritative condemnation" of the mistreatment of women, it reaffirms "terrorist corporealities" that delegitimize men in "Af-Pak" as objects of military extermination at worst and feminist condemnation at best.[128] Meanwhile, discourses that champion the

---

[123] Jasbir Puar, *Terrorist Assemblages: Homonationalism in Queer Times* (Durham: Duke University Press, 2007), 6.

[124] Margaret Spillane, "The V-Word Is Heard," *The Nation*, February 15, 2001.

[125] Puar, 3.

[126] Janet Abu-Lughod, "Do Muslim Women Really Need Saving? Anthropological Reflections on Cultural Relativism and Its Others," *American Anthropologist* 104(3) (2002), 784.

[127] Elizabeth Miller, "An Open Letter to the Editors of Ms. Magazine," April 21, 2002, available online at: www.rawa.org/tours/elizabeth_miller_letter.htm.

[128] Puar, 4.

heroism of activists like Nobel Laureate Malala Yousafzai (who lives in exile in the UK) "allude to the unsalvageable nature of Muslim women even by their own feminists, positioning the American feminist as the feminist subject par excellence."[129] Whether the challenge is "culture," the peripheral position of Afghanistan and the NWFP in a globalized capitalist economy, or the extreme levels of violence visited on these territories, the gap between dream and reality in the region remains great. It is unclear how many "reactionaries" – no longer defined as frustrated peasants but rather enemies of humanity – will have to be exterminated for this project to take root.

Such are the entangled histories of the Soviet Union, women's rights, and Afghan women's history. Soviet Bloc regimes played a crucial role in making women's issues international, even as later discursive moves to "privilege recognition over redistribution" have obscured this prehistory.[130] Organizations like the Women's World Bank and UNIFEM – born in the dawn of the Decade for Women – "planted the seeds of what has become the microfinance orientation of development programs," and it is unlikely that Yousafzai or fellow Nobel Laureate Kailash Satyarthi could have found such traction without these precedents.[131] Still more silent in our accounts of today's activists, however, is the ironic, tragic, and violent story of the Soviet Union's outreach to Afghan women – a vision whose human wreckage and, to a lesser extent, rhetoric of redemption, overlap with those of contemporary Western projects. However impressive the rhetorical shifts and institutional achievements of the international feminist movement has been since the time of the Moscow seminar, one must hope that today's descendants of Soviet activists remain mindful of the contingent – some would say precarious – ideological journey they have taken to reach their current commanding heights.

---

[129] Ibid., 5.
[130] Nancy Fraser, "Feminism, Capitalism, and the Cunning of History," *New Left Review* 56 (March–April 2009), 113.
[131] Olcott, "Transnational Feminism," 254.

6

Borderscapes of Denial

Borders die and they arise; they move, disappear, and reappear unexpectedly. They impose their mark upon the experience, the language, and the space they inhabit; upon the body, with its health, and with its disease; upon the psyche, with its divisions; on politics, with its absurd fissions; upon me.[1]

It is tempting to see the confrontation of the Soviet Union and humanitarian NGOs as a clash of territorial empire with postterritorial "nongovernmentality," in which power manifests itself either through bordered space or its disintegration.[2] SCA's propaganda materials painted the Soviet occupation of Afghanistan as following the logic of Tsarist annexations of Khiva and Bukhara, while Soviet actors mooted partitioning Afghanistan so as to ensure a "sphere of influence" over the country's north.[3] Internally, SCA and MSF possessed maps that captured the more complicated truth of a vertebrate of Soviet power nonetheless challenged by cells of "liberated areas."[4] All of these maps invited different interpretations, but the concept of space throughout remained that of a surface or container worth controlling in contiguous bits.[5]

But seeing the clash of global projects in this way risks reading out the manifold hidden ways in which Soviet power and its challengers processed territory. As geographers remind us, neither people nor armies always process space in terms of contiguous territory.[6] Far from an empty dimension, space

---

[1] Claudio Magris, "Come i pesci il mare," *Frontiere, Novi Argumenti* 38, 12.

[2] Mann, *From Empires to NGOs in the West African Sahel: The Road to Nongovernmentality.*

[3] Undated Map, File "Diverse document från 80–talet," SCA Institutional Archives; Nikolaï Leonov, *Likolet'e,* 206.

[4] Map, Afghanistan Information Centre (January 1989), File "Diverse document från 80–talet," SCA Institutional Archives.

[5] Friedman, *Covert Capital: Landscapes of Denial and the Making of U.S. Empire in the Suburbs of Northern Virginia,* 123.

[6] Kevin Lynch, *The Image of the City* (Cambridge: MIT Press, 1960), 20

is "the product of interrelations," the medium through which "we conceive of a meeting-up of histories."[7] These "meeting-ups," however, do not occur because "everything is connected to everything" or "because all places are connected."[8] Rather, the connection of "local" spaces into co-constituted landscapes, in which one place *is* the other, takes place through an exchange in which goods and ideas imbricate not just metropole in colony, but vice-versa – even in seemingly postcolonial contexts, as well.[9] Space is thus "a simultaneity of stories-so-far," involving as it does the agency of lives engaged by transnational assemblages and narratives.[10]

Nowhere testifies to this phenomenon more clearly than the dual borderscapes constructed along Afghanistan's northern and eastern edges during the 1980s. From 1981 to 1988, 62,000 Soviet Border Guards normally stationed on Soviet soil occupied northern Afghanistan down to the ring road that Eastern Bloc engineers had built years earlier. Paradoxically, the need to protect "the security of the southern border of the USSR" demanded extending the border *into* Afghanistan itself. Officially, the Border Forces had never left Soviet territory – a fiction all the more astonishing as they notched up 41,216 Afghans killed and lost nearly 3,000 of their own comrades.[11] Having migrated out of the border spaces that gave juridical violence spatial expression, these standard-bearers of Soviet territorial integrity became a walking death strip that exerted power not by annexing space but by redefining it as a zone of exception and legal aporia. The static border had morphed into "a situation, a permanent, slow-motion evolution, some of it abrupt and clearly planned, some of it improvised"; the colonial draftsmen's line had morphed into a violence curtain.[12]

Humanitarian actors challenged the Soviet borderscape by transforming the Durand Line and Afghanistan's internal frontiers into a moral and institutional geography no less spectacular than its Soviet counterpart. If the Soviets used the security of the USSR's southern border to justify their secret invasion of northern Afghanistan, groups like MSF and SCA justified their transgression of the Durand Line through recourse to the nutritional and medical emergency inside Afghanistan. If Soviet youth advisers shuttled orphans and other children outside of occupied Afghanistan to co-constituted points of intimacy inside the Soviet Union, humanitarian actors countered with their own transnational

---

[7] Doreen Massey, *For Space* (London: Sage, 2005), 4, 9.

[8] Friedman, 124.

[9] Catherine Hall, *Civilising Subjects: Metropole and Colony in the English Imagination* (Cambridge: Polity, 2002).

[10] Massey, 9; Susan Bibler Coutin, *Legalizing Mores: Salvadoran Immigrants' Struggle for U.S. Residency* (Ann Arbor: University of Michigan Press, 2000); Mimi Thi Nguyen, *The Gift of Freedom: War, Debt, and Other Refugee Passages* (Durham: Duke University Press, 2012).

[11] "Pogranichnye voĭska SSSR v voĭne v Afganistane," *Veteran Afganistana* 2(151) (2009), available online at: www.rsva-ural.ru/library/mbook.php?id=891.

[12] Rem Koolhaas, "Field Trip," 220.

project of nationalist education and medicalized networks of imperial intimacy. And if the Soviet Union sought to exploit the informational sovereignty
offered by the Third World nation-state, humanitarians would seek to invert
the moral and administrative geography of the United Nations to delegitimize
these very privileges. Afghanistan's borders had to be breached, its internal
frontiers sutured, its sovereignty suspended – all of this, however, not in the
service of telluric annexation but rather to network points of suffering into a
transnational bricolage that eschewed "epistemes of separation" for an ethics
of interdependence.[13]

The banks of the Amu-Darya and the East River had, together, become part
of two competing co-constituted borderscapes of denial – denial in two senses,
for neither party was fully comfortable with admitting the tenuous logic of
its humanitarian invasion. The extension of the southern border of the Soviet
Union into Afghanistan in order to protect it was never officially acknowledged,
even if participants in the Border Forces' intervention received medals for their
service.[14] Thousands of Border Guards entered Afghanistan, but thousands
stayed behind to perform the official border as a coherent dividing line, mask-
ing how "foreign" and "domestic" space had invaginated one another.[15] Conversely, humanitarians originally stressed the violation of Afghan sovereignty,
or the destruction of Afghanistan as a nation. But as the Soviet occupation continued, humanitarian actors found themselves constructing institutional expres-
sions of Afghan sovereignty and nationhood rather different from traditional
norms of the Third World nation-state or the nation purportedly identified with
it. Both Soviet and humanitarian actors had invested heavily into the alibi of the
nation-state as the alibi for their interventions, but the hyphen connecting the
two concepts had come to be just one in an ark of "stories-thus-far" involving
Afghan state and nation alike.

"Live Work"

Securing northern Afghanistan mattered to Moscow for several reasons. It was
only via northern roads that Soviet military transports could deliver supplies to
Herat, Qandahar, or Kabul. The north's mineral resources financed one-third
of Kabul's state budget, and provinces like Balkh and Baghlan "constituted the
decisive part of the agrarian sector of the national economy of the country."[16]

---

[13] Maier, "Consigning the Twentieth Century to History," 819.
[14] Mary L. Dudziak, *War-Time: An Idea, Its History, Its Consequences* (Oxford: Oxford University Press, 2012), 28.
[15] Friedman, 20.
[16] Robinson and Dixon, *Aiding Afghanistan*, 75, 108–109; "Soglashenie mezhdu pravitel'stvom soiuza sovetskikh sotsialisticheskikh respublik i pravitel'stvom demokraticheskoĭ respubliki Afganistan ob ekonomicheskom i tekhnicheskom sotrudnichestve," in Ministerstvo Innostran-nykh Del SSSR, *Deistvuiushchie dogovory, soglasheniia i konventsii, vstupivshie v silu s 1 ian-varia po 31 dekabria 1985 goda*, Vol. XLI (Moscow: Mezhdunarodnye Otnosheniia, 1987),

A socialist authoritarian north would buffer Uzbekistan and Tajikistan from a world now full of Khomeinis and Zias; more tactically, too, it would prevent *mujāhidin* forces from staging direct attacks on Soviet territory. The men guarding the Soviet side of the border had long internalized their mission to stop such incursions. Indeed, many knew no other world than the border. Pavel Polianskiĭ was carrying on his father's service in the Takhta-Bazar battalion and saw the Turkmen border as the family's "sign of fate."[17] Pavel had decided to enter the Border Forces when in fourth grade, married another veteran's daughter, and instilled "love and respect toward the [Border Forces'] green cap" in his son. Igor' Muchler's family history went back even further. His father began his service in Belarus in 1924, but was transferred to Central Asia, where Igor' grew up.[18] "In my youth," Muchler recalled, "I imbibed in everything that was connected with the border." He mastered the Turkmen and Tajik languages and "never thought a destiny other than that [of the border]." Asked why he joined the Guards, his response was direct: "For an idea." Masculine figures had invested heavily into the border and its defense.

But it was not at first obvious that the Border Forces would have a role in Afghanistan itself. When Komsomol advisers first arrived in the northern Afghan lowlands in 1980, they observed "relatively sustainable people's power and support for it in several districts, sub-districts, and villages."[19] Indeed, DOYA's northern Provincial Committees numbered among the country's largest.[20] To the east, however, in northern Badakhshan, clandestine Soviet operations aimed at the "cleansing" of a "village zone" to a depth of 150 kilometers into Afghan territory began as early as January.[21] In the spring of 1980, Border Forces clandestinely invaded the area surrounding Gulkhan, a village in Afghan Badakhshan. Commanders met with elders to explain "that the Soviet unit had arrived for the extension of aid to the local dwellers; hence, should the inhabitants experience a shortage of some staple (salt, flour, kerosene), they should come to the Border Guards."[22] The Border Forces denied any official policy, but PDPA secretaries "organized border trade between Tajikistan and Afghanistan." DOYA and PDPA officials felt secure enough to move into the mountains, especially after a May 1980 operation stationed Soviet Border Forces on the Afghan–Pakistani and Afghan–Chinese borders in Badakhshan.[23] Yet a policy designed to keep Afghans inside bordered space had the opposite

134–6; Petr Ivanchishin, "Zona osoboĭ otvetstvennosti," in *Po obe storone granitsy* (*Afganistan: 1979–1989*), ed. V.I. Gribanov (Moscow: Granitsa, 1999).

[17] Pavel Polianskiĭ, "Povtoril by vse snachala," in *Po obe storone granitsy*, 227–8.

[18] Igor' Muchler, "Proval inzhenera Bashira," in *Po obe storone granitsy*, 277.

[19] Iu. M. Alekseev, "SPRAVKA o deiatel'nosti DOMA zony 'Sever' za period s 20 noiabria 1980g. do 20 noiabria 1981g.," RGASPI M-3, op. 13, d. 15, l. 27.

[20] Iskanderov, *Molodëzhnoe dvizheniie v Afganistane (1945–1990 gg.)*, 103, 107.

[21] Iu. I. Zavadskiĭ, "Pogranichniki v afganskoĭ voĭne," in *Po obe storone granitsy*, Vol. 2.

[22] Gennadiĭ Zgerskiĭ, *Po obe storone granitsy*, 11.

[23] Iu. I. Zavadskiĭ, "Pogranichniki v afganskoĭ voĭne."

of its intended effect, as hundreds of Afghan refugees streamed into Soviet territory.[24]

The dilemma grew more complex as *mujāhidin* massacred entire Afghan villages bordering the Amu-Darya. "All of this," explained Border Forces commander Gennadiĭ Zgerskiĭ, "was done deliberately with the goal of provocation, toward the inhabitants of the border area and, of course, the border units themselves. Hence a clear, direct threat to the inviolability of our border had arisen." Such events demanded a strong reaction, particularly as more and more of the Soviet Army's regular units rotated to central and southern Afghanistan.[25] Hence, in early 1981, Kabul officially requested "the introduction of irregular divisions from the Central Asian District [...] into several points that would aid the security of the border and defense of the local population."[26]

A vast operation at once criminal and clandestine had begun. One spring day, a camouflaged helicopter touched down at the regional base of the Soviet Border Forces near Pyandzh, a town on the northern banks of the Amu-Darya River. Out disembarked some dozen Border Guards, among them Iuriĭ Dagdanov, a unit commander based in Dushanbe. Having moved closer and closer to the Afghan border in the course of his assignments, he sensed that he was destined for Afghanistan. He tried to be brave – brave, he added, like the Native Americans portrayed in the East German cowboy films he loved.[27] He was anxious, but felt proud to wear the handsome uniform of a Border Guard – the green hat, the green epaulets – and awaited orders.

But his superiors' order surprised him: they *collected* the green gear of the Border Forces and handed out red epaulets – Soviet Army epaulets – for the young men to don. "Don't write anything," they ordered. "No one was supposed to know that Soviet Border Guards were serving in 'Afghan.'" The helicopter transported them across the river; lights in Soviet villages were still visible that evening. Dagdanov described his Afghan tour as a period when "we killed without documentation and without insignia," nor was he the only veteran to mention the strict secrecy of the entire operation. "In letters and scribblings home," wrote Dmitriĭ Mantsev, "under no circumstances were we to mention any military actions. All of our Border Guards were officially continuing to carry out their service on native soil."[28]

The distinction between the domestic and the foreign had been dissolved, with disastrous consequences for Afghans. In March 1981, Anvar Khalikov, a Tajik Border Officer stationed in southern Turkmenistan, learned that two

---

24 Ibid., "Ot Kushki do Pamira," in *Po obe storone granitsy*, Vol. 2.
25 "Pogranichnye voĭska SSSR v voĭne v Afganistane."
26 Zgerskiĭ, 10.
27 Iuriĭ Dagdanov, "Na voĭne kak na voĭne," in *Po obe storone granitsy*.
28 Dmitriĭ Mantsev, "ChP afganskogo masshtaba," in *Po obe storone granitsy (Afganistan 1979–1989)*, Vol. 2, ed. V.I. Gribanov (Voronezh, 1999).

colleagues had not returned from their border patrol.[29] Khalikov dispatched helicopters to search for the men, worried that Afghan bandits led by one Madkarim might have kidnapped his officers. "We conducted intelligence on Madkarim and established that several years ago he had been arrested for violating the [Soviet] border, sentenced on suspicion on espionage, and made to serve his punishment in a special settlement in Irkutsk *oblast'*, where he had a concubine and a daughter and learned Russian. Upon his 'repatriation,' they turned him over to the Afghan authorities. But knowing the Russian language, he often turned up along the border under the pretext of grazing his herd, which the leader of his band had exploited to kidnap the Border Guards."[30] Employing an ad hoc militia of sixty armed Afghan Turkmen shepherds, Khalikov found Madkarim and his two wives (one Russian, one Afghan) in a safe house. "He denied the murder of our soldiers and hid his knowledge of Russian," wrote Khalikov. The Guards transported Madkarim to the airport at Meymaneh, where the provincial KhAD officer executed him on the tarmac.[31]

The incident illustrated how the redefinition of the borderscape forged new spatiotemporal landscapes in which Afghans could be arbitrarily murdered.[32] Emergency had allowed for a temporary suspension of Soviet border restrictions facing *inward*, allowing Afghan refugees to enter Soviet nation-space. The same state of emergency, however, turned Madkarim into the subject of an extended manhunt conducted by "domestic" Afghan and "foreign" Soviet forces, even though he had never left Afghan territory himself. The fact that "the" border was a fissiparous thing, composed of Turkmen tribes, Soviet border officials, and Afghan intelligence agencies mattered little. The redefinition of the north as a space of transnational emergency meant that Afghans could effectively become legally inside the USSR – or at least its border space – even as they remained physically outside of the country. Tellingly, while in the "domestic" Soviet Union, Madkarim had been allowed not only to live, but also to conceive of a future beyond himself. Once ejected into the aporic space at once "foreign" (Afghanistan) and "domestic" (a border zone), he lost even the guarantees present in even the GULaG. Practices of extreme violence had escaped the border spaces "that provided the governing logic of inside and out on which they depended."[33]

Yet security conditions in the north worsened.[34] Of the twenty-four districts in the entire Northern Zone, Kabul controlled seven. In Balkh, PDPA officials could enter only ten of the province's 455 villages "without escort from

---

[29] Anvar Khalikov, "Tak deĭstvuiet razvedka," in *Po obe storone granitsy*, 83.

[30] Ibid., 86.

[31] Ibid., 88.

[32] Nancy D. Munn, *The Fame of Gawa: A Symbolic Study of Value Transformation in a Massim (Papua New Guinea) Society* (Durham: Duke University Press, 1986).

[33] Ibid., 297.

[34] Iu. M. Alekseev, "SPRAVKA o deiatel'nosti DOMA zony 'Sever' za period s 20 noiabria 1980g. do 20 noiabria 1981g.," RGASPI M-3, op. 13, d. 15, l. 27.

armored vehicles and military units." In less than a year, *mujāhidin* butchered over 100 DOYA members. In Deh Kazi, "two paralyzed peasants who had received the land of a feudal lord were chopped to pieces"; in Meymaneh, bandits "brutally tortured and killed the three sisters of a female schoolteacher for the fact that she had continued to teach and not wear the *paranja* in spite of multiple threats from the bandits."[35] The training of engineers continued at the gas institute in Mazar-i Sharif, but its students hailed almost exclusively from the city itself, as students from the provinces felt it too dangerous to travel to classes. Militants threatened to murder those who stayed in school, and many of those who remained behind harbored anti-Soviet attitudes.[36]

Nor were *mujāhidin* merely sniping at Soviet and PDPA forces. As we saw in Chapter 2, revolutionaries in northern Afghanistan had long entertained ties with Beijing, a relationship that the Soviet invasion only intensified. East German intelligence agencies reported Chinese military trainers present in Pakistani refugee camps, while Beijing supplied Maoists in Badakhshan with weapons and – ironically – Chinese border guard uniforms to prepare for the announcement of an independent republic.[37] Nor were such groups lacking for cash: one Komsomol adviser noted that *mujāhidin* had taken over the lapis lazuli mines at Sar-i Sang, using the exports to buy supplies from their Chinese and Pakistani patrons. Soviet Army Forces were more than capable of striking back – 5,000 were reported killed after a November 1981 bombing raid on the mines.[38] But with ever more regular Army units needed for combat further south, the Border Forces would have to assume more responsibility.

Hence, recalled Zgerskiĭ, "the leadership of our country took the decision to introduce the Border Forces into the northern provinces of Afghanistan." Directive P32/81, issued on December 22, 1981 by the Central Committee of the CPSU, assigned 8,000 Border Guards to "a belt of responsibility with an average depth of 100–120 kilometers, the so-called *Zelënka*, up until the radial road that connects the centers of the northern provinces. The order was given to liquidate organized banditry in this belt as well as the bases for the storage of weapons, ammunition depots, and other material goods located within it and around it."[39] Working closely with the 40th Army forces that remained

---

[35] Ibid., 29.

[36] GARF, f. 9606 (Mininsterstvo vysshego i srednego obrazovaniia), op. 11, d. 282, "Otchët o rabote kollektiva sovetskykh spetsialistov Gorno-neftianogo tekhnikuma g. Mazari Sharif za 1982–1983 uchebnyĭ god," l. 8, 13.

[37] "Ausbildungs- und Versorgungszentren afghanischer Konterrevolutionäre auf pakistanischem Territorium," Docs. 208–17, Folder JHR 21985, Abt. X, BSTU; "Über die Entwicklung und Rolle politisch unterschiedlich motivierter afghanischer Rebellengruppen, die gegen die Regierung der DRA als konterrevolutionäre Gruppen in Erscheinung treten," Docs. 9–16, Folder 27384, Abt. X, BSTU.

[38] Nikolaĭ Poliakov, "Spravka sovetnika TsK VLKSM po zone Severo-Vostok za period s dekabria 1981g. po noiabr' 1982g.," RGASPI M-3, op. 13, d. 26, l. 117–118.

[39] Zgerskiĭ, *Po obe storone granitsy*, 10; "Pogranichnye voĭska SSSR v voĭne v Afganistane."

stationed in the north, the Border Forces were tasked with "creating an idiosyncratic buffer zone, one that would firmly separate warring Afghanistan from
Soviet soil."[40] In addition to occupying Afghanistan to a depth of 100 kilometers, P32/81 subjected a band of territory 10 kilometers south of the border to special protection, creating two tiers of space that were physically in
Afghanistan but administratively redefined as relevant to Soviet security.

General Zgerskiĭ's name for the extended border zone – "*Zelënka*" – was
telling; the word means "brilliant green," but it also refers to a topical anti-
septic. In February 1982, the "systematic cleansing" of the north began. After
inaugural operations in Kunduz Province, Border Forces moved on to Tashkur-
gan and Andkhoy as their next targets. "Whoever was there in the 'Afghan,'"
reflected one Border Guard, "knows what a 'cleansing' of villages means. Block
off the village from all sides and then…that's why at first they got armed formations of Afghans who were loyal to the government installed in Kabul to
do it."[41] Freed of bureaucratic checks, Border Guards felt liberated. "No more
scribbling, no more unnecessary paperwork, no more pestering paperwork,"
reflected Viktor Shevelev. "Only live work!" Another Border Guard agreed.
"It's fashionable today to criticize 'the Party machine' and 'the totalitarian
regime,'" wrote Dmitriĭ Mantsev. "But I'd note that in many senses it was precisely thanks to this arrangement of Party and political work that our forces
succeeded in completed the tasks laid out before them."[42] The frequency with
which the Border Guards compared their operation to the "Road of Life" that
had supplied besieged wartime Leningrad was as awful as it was candid.[43]

And yet the use of domestic metaphors to describe a foreign space was apt.
While the Border Forces enforced the penetration of Afghan geographic space
by Soviet juridical space, Komsomol advisers oversaw the co-constitution of
Soviet and Afghan space through youth exchanges. Virtually since arriving in
Afghan territory, soldiers and advisers alike saw children as both a threat and
opportunity. Homeless children were often recruited by *mujāhidin* to lay land
mines near Border Forces' posts while begging for bread.[44] During the summer,
Afghan students headed to "fed internships" in Pakistan, "from which students
returned as not poorly trained fighters ready for terrorist activity."

DOYA countered with several schemes. In some provinces, it launched
Student Labor Divisions as a "peaceful alternative to the Pakistani vacation
voyages," training "more than 1,000 fighters" ready to be assimilated into
organizations of Party and state.[45] In others, such as Baghlan, it ran summer

---

[40] Dmitriĭ Mantsev, "ChP afganskogo masshtaba," in *Po obe storone granitsy*, Vol. 2.

[41] Sergeĭ Bogdanov, "Dvazhdy rozdennyĭ," in *Po obe storone granitsy*, 199.

[42] Mantsev, "ChP afganskogo masshtaba."

[43] Iuriĭ Spiridonov, "Most druzhby," in *Po obe storone granitsy*, Vol. 2; Iuriĭ Miliukov, "Razvedka–
glaza i ushi komandira," in Ibid.

[44] Vladimir Pankratov, "'Vatan'–oznachaet rodina," in *Po obe storone granitsy.*

[45] Pankratov was describing a program in the north, but a similar scheme was also tested in Helmand Province. See "Otchët sovetnika TsK VLKSM v provintsii Gil'mend o prodelannoĭ rabote
s noiabria 1982g. po noiabria 1983g.," RGASPI f. M-3, op. 13, d. 38, l. 82.

camps, transferring children to a Pioneer Camp in Kyrgyzstan.[46] In others, like Helmand or Nangarhar, children of particularly troublesome Pashtun or Baloch tribes were targeted for recruitment for long-term studies in the Soviet Union; in one case, students were recruited for summer vacations when they visited a Komsomol–DOYA ethnographic exhibit titled "Tribes and Peoples in the DRA" held in Lashkar Gah, the former American logistics center.[47] The programs developed and expanded over the course of the decade, primarily targeted at orphans and homeless children, but soon seen as a means to move the "offspring of tribes, especially the children of tribal leaders and other influential personalities" as a long-term military tactic in "tribal zones."[48]

The fact that these Afghan children arrived in Soviet spaces normally used for "domestic" Soviet children underscored how Moscow had imploded distinctions between a "foreign" Afghanistan and a "domestic" Soviet Union in a way that went beyond annexation or territorial expansion. No longer a "foreign" space, PDPA-controlled Afghanistan, like socialist Angola, Ethiopia, and Mozambique, became a supplier in a global socialist traffic in children that saw their "best interests" in moving them from "indigenous" national contexts to socialist contexts.[49] Falling under the aegis of DOYA and the Border Forces, Afghan children entered an imperial space that linked Afghan landscapes with orphanages and institutes of higher education from Ukraine to Tajikistan; in at least one case, an Afghan boy was taken as a "guest" to a Soviet host family.[50] Many were linked with the Soviet Union temporally, too, as many entered the country as part of a ten-year educational exchange program while still only in their teenage years.[51] Young as they were, it is not an exaggeration to say that the some 11,000 Afghan children sent to the Soviet Union had a far more intimate knowledge of the actual lived spatiality of the USSR than most Soviet citizens. Arguably, they had been under Soviet jurisdiction from the moment that the Soviet border extended over them.

---

[46] "Spravka o rabote PK DOMA Baglana s noiabria 1983g. po maĭ 1984 g.," RGASPI f. M-3, op. 13, d. 64, ll. 61–62.

[47] "Otchët o rabote provintsial'nogo komiteta DOMA provintsii Gel'mend za period s noiabria 1983g. po noiabr' 1984g.," RGASPI f. M-3, op. 13, d. 63, l. 31, 60.

[48] "Informatsiia o rabote Nangarkharskogo provintisal'nogo komiteta v noiabre 1984–oktiabre 1985g.," RGASPI f. M-3, op. 13, d. 86, l. 80.

[49] According to the Raoul Wallenberg International Committee, as of 1985, 65,000 children had been taken from Third World countries to socialist countries. Afghans sent to the Soviet Union (11,0000) constituted the second-largest group, after Ethiopians sent to Cuba (12,000). Human Rights Watch Archives, Jeri Laber Papers, Box 6, Folder 5, "The First Estimates of Abducted Children."

[50] "Deti Afganistana v SSSR. Afganskiĭ mal'chik Zabnullo v gostiakh u sem'i Aleksandra Posmashina. Gorod Slaviansk-na-Kubani," Photographed by Petshakovskiĭ (January 1, 1985), RIA Novosti Online Archive Item No. 830999.

[51] "Otchët sovetnika TsK VLKSM pri DOMA okruga Khost – Obratsova V.A. (noiabr' 1984–maĭ 1985)," RGASPI f. M-3, op.13, d. 87, l. 17.

FIGURE 9. Performing the imaginary of the border as dividing line between domestic and foreign space – the one safe for children, the other only for adults – at a rally in Kushka, Turkmen SSR. "Children of Kushka presenting flowers to Soviet troops during a rally marking the return of the Guards armor regiment from Afghanistan."
Source: Photographed by Iuriĭ Somov, 1986. Courtesy of RIA Novosti.

What made this co-constituted landscape difficult to see from inside of the USSR itself was a borderscape of denial that demarcated the "foreign" from the "domestic." Already in Tsarist times, colonial administrators erected a monument in Kushka designating it as the southern of four compass points determining the Empire's orientation to the world. A century later, Kushka hosted elaborate ceremonies for Soviet soldiers returning to the "homeland." But by positing the border as a concrete material space, rather than a conceptual space of maximum arbitrary violence that could become mobile, the festivities masked how the border had reproduced "fractal sets of hierarchy" into Afghan domestic space.[52] By demarcating Soviet space for children and Afghanistan as a space for adults, they masked Soviet regimes of international child trafficking. And by stressing the military role of returning Soviet citizens, they masked how civilian and Party institutions had drifted into Afghanistan, too.

The Soviet borderscape of denial found expression not only in material form. One of the most interesting figures that repeatedly figures in the memoirs of Border Guards is the "Chekist wife" – that is, the wife of the Border

---

[52] Maier, *Among Empires*, 60–1.

Guard.[53] And while not always recognized, their labor constituted a key aspect of Soviet imperialism. Such women not only bore the children that motivated their husband's protection of homeland as a familial duty; more than that, given the long absences associated with Border Guards' service and the official non-existence of the Afghan mission, they bore a considerable emotional load. One Border Guard recalled his deployment from Irkutsk to Afghanistan on April 18, when his wife was nine months pregnant; his son was born two days after he left for Afghanistan, "so both dates are tied together for him."[54] Another was called up for service only a few weeks after his daughter's birth, but his wife assured him "not to worry about me and the kids – everything will be alright."[55] Though distant from the border itself, these women managed the emotional fallout of imperialism, whether by uprooting themselves and their families constantly, managing unpredictable schedules, or rebuilding domestic spheres that demanded defending.[56] Given the explicit ban on photography or correspondence from Afghanistan, marriage assumed added burdens as a space either of truth telling, or of lying about service anywhere but Afghanistan to an amiably gullible spouse.[57] "It's hard to imagine what my wife experienced, what she felt during those years," recalled one Border Guard. "But," he added, "she chose her fate herself."[58]

Invisible as the borderscape of denial may have made certain Soviet–Afghan intimacies, it was generating several potentially disastrous outcomes for Afghans. Medical tests were run on the Afghan children before they were allowed into the Soviet Union, but due to the general lack of birth registration or passportization in Afghanistan, even under the PDPA, many children entered the USSR without effective paperwork proving their legal status or nationality, rendering them "effectively stateless."[59] Not only that, in the absence of any international legal regime for children's rights, champions of international law did not have any instrument via which they could in theory, if not in practice, bring Moscow to justice. Documented only by number and quantity – the Komsomol archives mention such trafficked children frequently but only rarely by name – Afghan children had been displaced into a precarious legal situation.[60] However much they were positioned physically and temporally in the Soviet

---

53 Andrew Friedman, Interview with *Against the Grain* (July 16, 2014), available online at: www .againstthegrain.org/program/978/wed-71614-imperial-suburbs; Igor' Orekhov, "My ny byli zhestokimi…" in *Po obe storone granitsy*.
54 Oleg Neĭ, "Doroga k domu," in Ibid.
55 Valeriĭ Parkhomenko, "Nebo v tot den' bylo goluboe," in Ibid.
56 Sergeĭ Bogdanov, "Dvazhdvy rozhdennyĭ," in Ibid.
57 Igor' Orekhov, "My ny byli zhestokimi…" in Ibid.
58 Aleskandr Koliberdin, "Ne prosto poloska zemli," in Ibid.
59 "Otchët sovetnika TsK VLKSM pri DOMA Provintsii Balkh–Siroshtan V. XI.1984–V.1985," RGASPI f. M-3, op. 13, d. 85, l. 7; *Children Without a State: A Global Human Rights Challenge*, ed. Jacqueline Bhabha (Cambridge, MA: MIT Press, 2011), xii.
60 From what the files allow to reconstruct, Komsomol was primarily engaged with the movement of Afghan orphans to the Soviet Union; a parallel program existed for the sons and daughters

Union, they were, in a sense, nowhere, lacking as they did the means to establish citizenship in Afghanistan or the USSR.[61]

Afghans were not unaware of the risks involved for their children in such schemes. On the ground in Kunar Province, the Komsomol adviser noted resistance to the sending away of the children of influential locals on vacation trips to the Soviet Union, prompting "significant changes to the preliminary lists" of children to be sent away.[62] Advisers near Mazar-i Sharif understood the opposite dynamic, noting that Afghan Army officials at a Soviet military base and gas workers "actively patronized" their children's home with their offspring, leading to 140 children being sent from Balkh and Samangan Province in 1984–5.[63] But most Afghans harbored "suspicion" toward DOYA-run orphanages and children's centers. It was not hard to see why. Thrust into DOYA youth centers, children were socialized to think of themselves as part of an international, translocal community of children, conducting correspondence with school classes from Sverdlovsk, in the Soviet Union, to Bulgaria (where one student's father had received his technical education).[64] In light of this aggressive transnationalization of childhood, families had to limit their children's intimacies.

Over time, Soviet advisers grew concerned about the scheme, too, albeit for another set of reasons. Jalalabad-based Komsomol adviser Oleg Mordasov noted that while DOYA had overfulfilled its quota of seventy-five children to be sent to Kabul for preparation for study in the USSR, only twenty-five of the ninety children sent there actually ended up traveling to the Soviet Union.[65] The main reason, stressed Mordasov, for the "dropout" of so many children was their "family situation" – namely, the fact that they had one. At the same time, however, Mordasov openly questioned the purpose of sending so many orphans to the Soviet Union. "Can our country receive all of these unsupervised children?" he asked. Even if more restrictive health screening measures were imposed on Afghan orphans before their entry into Soviet territory – which he favored – "will a child who has lived for almost 10 years in the USSR and detached from a country be able to return to live there normally without relatives or the material basis for living?" There was, in short, a "certain

---

of the PDPA *nomenklatura*, but it appears to have been subordinated to KhAD, the Afghan equivalent of the KGB.

[61] Susan Bibler Coutin, *Nation of Emigrants: Shifting Boundaries of Citizenship in El Salvador and the United States* (Ithaca: Cornell University Press, 2007), 116–17.

[62] "Otchët o rabote sovetnika TsK VLKSM pro DOMA provintsii Kunar noiabr' 1983g.–sentiabr' 1984g.," RGASPI f. M-3, op. 13, d. 61, l. 47.

[63] "Otchët sovetnika TsK VLKSM pri DOMA Provintsii Balkh–Siroshtan V. XI.1984–V.1985," RGASPI f. M-3, op. 13, d. 85, l. 7.

[64] "Otchët o rabote provintsial'nogo komiteta DOMA provintsii Gel'mend za period s noiabria 1983g. po noiabr' 1984g.," RGASPI f. M-3, op. 13, d. 63, l. 31; "Otchët sovetnika TsK VLKSM v Paktii za 6 mesiatsev 1985/86," RGASPI f. M-3, op. 13, d. 121, l. 74.

[65] "Informatsiia o rabote Nangarkharskogo provintsal'nogo komiteta v noiabre 1984–oktiabre 1985g.," RGASPI f. M-3, op. 13, d. 86, l. 89–90.

iconicity" between the sick Afghan orphan screened in Kabul and the Afghan orphan too decontextualized from its "home" environment to be politically useful, both of which occupied the role of potentially invisible enemies threatening to penetrate the Soviet homeland and burden it with illness or social claims.[66]

In light of these concerns, Mordasov favored scaling back the orphan transfer program and instead "seeking more attention to the problem of homelessness from our Afghan comrades." To compensate, he also encouraged deepening youth exchanges for the offspring of PDPA *nomenklatura* and tribal élites. After being sent to the USSR or drafted into paramilitary "sons' divisions" as early as age ten, such youth had a far better chance of "influencing the mass of people" and "applying their knowledge" than did denationalized orphans. As advisers acknowledged, they, as much as the *mujāhidin* groups that recruited from Pakistani refugee camps, were engaged in a paradoxical struggle to determine the proper nationalist content that transnational assemblages would impart unto Afghan youth. Which diaspora, in short, was the "real" Afghanistan? Which co-constituted landscape – the one stretching across the Amu-Darya, or across the Durand Line – could forge the diasporic intimacies that would authentically embody the Afghan nation?

The Humanitarian Cloud

Spectacular as the Soviet borderscape may have been, shrewd observers recognized it only as the physical and military manifestation of a deeper structural problem in world order, namely the informational wall that Moscow had erected around the Third World nation-state. In light of such a "national catastrophe," wrote SCA's Carl Schönmeyr, "one would have expected that one of the UN's specialized programs – UNICEF, the WHO, the World Food Programme (WFP) – would have broken this silence regarding the fate of millions." But none had. "Does an Afghan child have no value until it reaches the border and is registered as a refugee in Pakistan?" asked Schönmeyr.[67] The answer was obvious. Just as the Soviet–Third World alliance had sought maximum informational penetration of human rights violations inside of South Africa or Israel, it had built a firewall around the borders of the Third World nation-state.

The refusal of neutral international bodies like the FAO, UNDP, or WFP to act meant that humanitarian guerrillas had to create their own counter-archive of medical emergency that would justify their presence. A logic of what would later be called "mobile sovereignty" or "humanitarian geopolitics"

---

[66] Kahn, 283. See also Jean Comaroff, "Beyond Bare Life: AIDS, (Bio)politics, and the Neoliberal Order," *Public Culture* 19(1) (Winter 2007), 198.

[67] Carl Schönmeyr, Letter to Carl Tham (State Secretary, Swedish Foreign Ministry), August 13, 1982, 3, Folder "Peshawar 1984 (Rapporter, Korrespondens)," SE/RA/730500/001/E 3:1.

had been broached.[68] If moral entrepreneurs could assert an emergency inside of sovereign territory and promote the urgency of resolving it in a global media landscape, traditional sovereign privileges and the long timelines associated with UN agencies' actions could be subverted. Emergency time demanded immediate action. Afghanistan offered the ideal biotope to test out this new model: even as the Third World nation-state remained administratively firewalled by the United Nations, Afghanistan's literal border and its internal frontiers were wide open.

It sounded simple – except for the fact that the frontier, in many cases, consisted of the Hindu Kush. Since the spring of 1982, MSF conducted medical interventions into villages in Badakhshan, arriving via mountain passes from Chitral, Pakistan.[69] "Since no one was providing medical supplies, MSF went to Badakhshan," explained one report.[70] But the process was incredibly consuming – the initial mission lost a third of its supplies en route – and MSF's initial scout, Gérard Kohout, returned to Paris, admitting that "I had lost my vital energy." Command of the Badakhshan missions fell to Juliette Fournot, operating largely independently from Peshawar and entrusted with MSF's project of moral entrepreneurship. Badakhshan, stressed the initial report, "was not 'covered' by any medical organization, which, for Afghanistan, means no medical care other than those provided by the Soviets to the inhabitants of Faiẓābād." Having established that the Soviet medical supplies were "mediocre" and that denizens outside of Faiẓābād barely received care, MSF was left in an awkward position when initial examinations of 11,000 adults and 3,000 children registered just thirty Afghans with war wounds.[71]

Data was similarly spotty on the issue of hunger. In the late 1970s, Afghanistan was still recovering from a drought that had caused a multi-year famine that killed tens of thousands.[72] Then, international organizations invested "more than $69 million in development projects and emergency operations" and delivered 100,000 metric tons of food to all twenty-nine provinces.[73] The Soviet invasion, however, brought operations "to an abrupt close," while

---

[68] Mariella Pandolfi, "'Moral entrepreneurs,' souverainetés mouvantes et barbelés: le bio-politique dans les Balkans postcommunistes," Anthropologie et Sociétés 26(1) (2002), 29–51.

[69] One such expedition is richly photographed and described in Emmanuel Guibert, Le photographe (Marcinelle: Dupuis, 2010).

[70] "Mission été 83," 1, Folder "Badakhshan," MSF Institutional Archives.

[71] Ibid., 2. The Afghanistan archives of MSF include two registers of patient records (each containing several thousand records), one from the Anguri Clinic in Ghazni, the other from the Yaftal Clinic in Badakhshan. Both documents are located in the box "Afghanistan 1980–1981 Relevés medicaux +++ Trésors historiques."

[72] Michael Barry, Personal Account of Famine Conditions in Northwestern Afghanistan (Kabul: USAID Afghanistan, 1972). For its history, see Mari Michener Oye, "Government Legitimacy, Local Politics and the 1971–2 Famine in Afghanistan" (M.Phil. Thesis, University of Cambridge, 2013).

[73] Office of the United Nations Co-Ordinator for Humanitarian and Economic Assistance Programmes Relating to Afghanistan, First Consolidated Report (September 1988) (Geneva: 1988), 76.

occupation halved per-capita grain production.[74] Moscow shipped 250,000 tons of grain to the country, but this failed to compensate for the shortfall.[75] When MSF sent medics to Badakhshan to research nutrition levels, however, there, as in the Hazarajat, "food production was found to be of generally acceptable levels."[76] Infant mortality rates were "more or less typical of less developed countries." MSF's French and Belgian wings teamed up with *Médecins du Monde* and Norwegian and British doctors to survey Badakhshan, Nuristan, and the Hazarajat.[77] Other areas could not be surveyed, but that was all right – the very logic of mobile sovereignty assumed the incompleteness of data. Unlike a census, which aimed at slow, but total, informational saturation of bounded national space then fed to a centralized capital, humanitarian informational gathering depended on swift, fragmented, and necessarily incomplete picture and dispatching it around the world.

MSF's Juliette Fournot was not aware of the contradictions involved in her mission. "At the time," she explained, "MSF was motivated by the desire to provide the means to effect a measurable medical action that would demonstrate the justice of our ambitions and not only satisfy the nobility of our aspirations."[78] As she knew from operations outside of Soviet-controlled Faizābād, where a clinic had saved hundreds of mothers through caesarean sections, MSF was practicing a "good medicine." But MSF's Paris leadership, Claude Malhuret excepted, dismissed the operations as not "medically respectable" and denied Fournot funding for transportation on the grounds that Peshawar's rickshaws could handle her needs. "I dreamed of carrying out true medical work in Afghanistan," said Fournot, but Paris continued to interfere, refusing, for example, the disbursing of vaccines on the grounds that it did not trust Fournot to disburse them in a war zone.

Malhuret adopted a different tack: the real issue was not the *efficacy* of MSF's medical interventions *per se*. Indeed, as internal reports noted, this was a losing argument. On September 25, 1984, Malhuret published an article in *Le Monde*, titled "The Right to Rescue and Witness." Claude Malhuret defended MSF's missions in Afghanistan, writing that "we cannot blame anyone in favor of the moral imperative [to save lives] evoked against customary policy

---

[74] UNOCA, "Afghanistan: Operation Salam Programme for 1992" (November 1991), Preface (authored by Benon Sevan), United Nations Archives. See also Thomas H. Eighmy, *Afghanistan's Population Inside and Out: Demographic Data for Reconstruction and Planning* (Islamabad, 1990).

[75] Igor' Muchler, "Proval inzhenera Bashira," in *Po obe storone granitsy*, 278. According to an issue of the *Afghan Medical Mujahideen Journal* (a publication produced by Afghan doctors based in Australia), following the Chernobyl disaster, residents of Kabul noted increases in rates of leukemia and birth defects, sparking rumors that Moscow had diverted irradiated grain to Kabul. Jeri Laber Papers, Box 3, Folder 23, Human Rights Watch Papers, Columbia University.

[76] "Nutrition and Health of Afghan Children of Teshkan in Badakhshan," 28, Folder "1982–1988," MSF Institutional Archives.

[77] Ibid., 32.

[78] Vallaeys, *Médecins sans Frontières. La biographie*, 439–41.

rules."[79] More than that, he reframed MSF in Afghanistan as "pioneers of a new international law in perpetual evolution." Just as the Geneva Conventions had granted protection to prisoners of war, the world needed new rules guaranteeing "the protection of humanitarian teams that provide assistance and journalists trying to inform." The problem, Malhuret stressed, was not epidemiological but epistemological. If the Soviet Union and its Third World allies had altered international regimes of sovereignty to favor sovereign maximalism, MSF had to understand that the local (Badakhshan) and the global (international law) were one and the same front. Only by bringing more information gleaned from the Afghan body to the global public could one change international norms undergirding the right to witness, the right to heal.

And yet as Fournot was about to discover, the embedding of MSF's information in a global humanitarian cloud could have mixed consequences. Seeing an opportunity in early 1985, Freedom House's Afghanistan Information Center invited Malhuret back to the United States, where he enjoyed an audience with Vice President George H.W. Bush. Soon, thanks to the intervention of New Hampshire Senator Gordon J. Humphrey, Fournot herself was invited to testify before Congress, which she did on March 4, 1985.[80] Precisely as Fournot had feared, however, the media intervention among the Americans was a success. Taken to various Washington think tanks, Fournot discovered that officialdom seemed more interested in Soviet tactics than Afghan lives. The day after her testimony, USAID officials offered her a million dollars in funding, which she refused – "there was no question about receiving even a dollar from the American administration." All the same, French information had opened the gates for American cash to flood the frontier; Congress soon passed a package of $60 million in humanitarian aid for Afghanistan, and by year's end, Peshawar was the base for sixty-six NGOs, the largest concentration in any single place in the world.

Yet the surge of American funding involved unsavory partners. American Cold Warriors like Charlie Wilson were perfectly happy to direct not just humanitarian but also military aid to the frontier through radical anti-Soviet intermediaries like Gulbuddin Hekmatyar's *Hezb-i Islāmi*. The Pakistani military élite was delighted, for "they had discovered the means of continuing their 'great game': eventually establishing a friendly regime or extending their protectorate over Afghanistan."[81] At the same time, recalled Fournot, "our MSF teams remarked upon the presence of combatants who were clearly not Afghans. Indeed, without yet knowing it, we witnessed the arrival of Wahhabi fundamentalists from the Middle East. Algerians, Saudis, and Syrians, deported

---

[79] Claude Malhuret, "Le droit de secourir et de témoigner," *Le Monde*, September 25, 1984.
[80] "Statement of Dr. Juliette E. Fournot, Director of the Afghanistan Mission of Medecins sans Frontieres, Before the Congressional Task Force on Afghanistan" (March 4, 1985), Folder "Afghanistan. 1982–1986. Rapports. Infos génerales," MSF Institutional Archives.
[81] Vallaeys, 448.

from their country for extremist activity, had landed here, financed by Riyadh." More and more of the *Jam'iat-i Islāmi* flyers that Komsomol advisers captured featured text not only in Persian and English, but also in Arabic.[82] Eastern Bloc security agencies were aware of the shift, too, noting in 1985 the arrival of one Osama bin Laden, "who is seen as the head (Emir) of all of the Arabs fighting in Afghanistan."[83]

SCA was not unaware of the ambiguities involved in embedding aid with the *mujāhidin* and the company they kept. When a representative from the Swedish Foreign Ministry visited Peshawar, SCA representatives noted "we discussed Sweden's support for liberation movements earlier in history – groups like the [Vietnamese] PRG [Provisional Revolutionary Government] or in South Africa. In those cases, we provided support once the liberation movement was representative of the population and had geographical influence and domination." The problem, conceded the diplomat, was that "the resistance movement in Afghanistan has not yet fit into this template." SCA pushed back: "I pointed out [that] there parts of the resistance that met these criteria were beginning to crystallize, which [the diplomat] could not deny. He thought that Sweden had previously been at the forefront when it comes to such contacts, and that we should do it, even now."[84] Convinced, SIDA never supplied less than eighty-seven percent of SCA's total income for years to come.[85]

A thriving operation developed. By 1984, SCA was delivering thousands of kilograms of medicine monthly to Afghan-run hospitals all across the countryside – far-flung Herat and Farah Provinces received almost as much assistance as did more accessible Kunar or Badakhshan Provinces.[86] Three parties in particular – Burhanuddin Rabbāni's *Jam'iat-i Islāmi*, Gulbuddin Hekmatyar's *Hezb-i Islāmi*, and Mohammad Nabi Mohammadi's *Harakat-i Inqalābi* – received the bulk of Swedish medical shipments, receiving, respectively, 41%, 23%, and 12% of the 51,000 kilograms of supplies delivered in 1985.[87] SCA

---

[82] Jami'at-I Islāmi, "Mushāvar-i balandpā-yeh kubā-yi beh lebās-i mahali-yi āfghāni," archived as "Kserokopiia stat'i iz zhurnala Islamskogo obshchestva Afganistana o bor'be 'zashchitnikov Islama' s inostranoĭ razvedkoĭ," RGASPI op. M-3, op. 13, d. 100.

[83] "Information" (May 18, 1985), Doc. 000031, Folder HA XXII, Abt. X, BSTU.

[84] Untitled Report, 2, Folder "Peshawar 1984 (Rapporter, Korrespondens)," Folder "Confidential," SE/RA/730500/001/E 3:1.

[85] "Budget 1/11/1985–31/10 1986, Svenska Afghanistankommittén, Peshawar," np, Folder "Peshawar 1985–87"; "Budget 1987–Katastrofbistånd till Afghanistan Svenska Afghanistankommittén," "Sammanfattning–Kostnader och Inkomster, 1987," Folder "Peshawar 1985–87,"; "The Swedish Committee for Afghanistan – Annual Report 1988," 44, Folder "Peshawar 1988"; "Budjet 1989 – Hjälpverksamheten," 2, Folder "Peshawar 1988"; "Budget 1990 – Svenska Afghanistankommittens Hjälpverksamhet," 2, Folder "Peshawar 1988." All folders in SE/RA/730500/001/E 3:3.

[86] "Verksamhetsberättelse/Afghanistankommittén i Peshawar 1989," Table 3 ("Provinsiell Medicinfördelning 1984, kg.,") in Folder "Peshawar 1985–1987," SE/RA/730500/001/E 3:3.

[87] "Årsberättelse för 1985, Svenska Afghanistankommitteen Peshawar," 12, Folder "Peshawar 1985–87," SE/RA/730500/001/E 3:3.

soon carried out so many deliveries that the group's Peshawar office drafted a standard contract stipulating SCA's terms of engagement. "Representing the people of Sweden in this contract," it noted, "is the Swedish Committee for Afghanistan," and "representing the people of Afghanistan in this contract is the Emirate of the territory that bears the name of that Emirate and which is administered by the Emir or the General Commander."[88]

In both its negotiations with SIDA diplomats as well as the *mujāhidin*, SCA had embraced a highly flexible concept of sovereignty to be applied toward authoritarian regimes. As Schönmeyr had stressed, a crisis like the one in Afghanistan could have been optimally been dealt with like crises in Biafra, Cambodia, or Lebanon – recognized internationally as such, if not resolved.[89] But not only had the Soviet Union and the Third World put up an informational wall around Afghanistan at the UN; more than that, noted the diplomat, this strategy contrasted shamefully with the enthusiasm with which "the Palestinian issue has been pushed on the agenda of each and every UN organization for years." Rather than acquiescing to Moscow's championing of the nation-state – an aspiration for Palestinians but a garrote wire for Afghans – Stockholm had to champion an alternative position. Anti-apartheid, anti-Zionism, and a flag did not make a state legitimate. A true concept of postcolonial freedom did not express itself merely in a black or Palestinian nation-state, but rather in the *trans*national liberation movement that spoke the language of human rights and had claims, however modest, to territory.[90]

This made *mujāhidin* commanders ideal interlocutors. In their correspondence with SCA, *Jam'iat-i Islāmi* commanders stressed that "we hope that in addition to your humanitarian assistance (*komak-hā-yi insān dustānehshān*), you can take the grievances and barbarous actions that have been committed by this enemy of humanity that subjugates the human rights of those nations that it has colonized and that you can bring them to attention and the enlightenment of world public consciousness."[91] Ahmad Shah Mas'ud thanked SCA for the "humanitarian aid (*komak-i bashar-i dustāni*)" and gold mining equipment that helped him finance his operations from the Panjshir Valley.[92] The language in these statements was probably targeted for its readership; *Hezb-i Islāmi* issued decrees to Afghans speaking of a "just divine government" and

[88] "Mavāfaqatnāmeh," 1, Folder "Peshawar 1985–1987," SE/RA/730500/001/E 3:1.

[89] Carl Schönmeyr, "The Silence of the United Nations – and How to Break It," Folder "Peshawar 1984 (Rapporter, Korrespondens)," SE/RA/730500/001/E 3:1.

[90] Arjun Appadurai, *Fear of Small Numbers: An Essay on the Geography of Anger* (Durham: Duke University Press, 2006), 25.

[91] *Jam'iat-i Islāmi* (Balkh Committee) Letter to SCA, January 27, 1985, Folder "Peshawar 1985–1987," SE/RA/730500/001/E 3:3.

[92] Ahmad Shah Mas'ud, Letter to SCA, May 14, 1985, Folder "Peshawar 1985–1987," SE/RA/730500/001/E 3:3.

FIGURE 10. "The present Chief Executive of Afghanistan, Dr. Abdullah Abdullah, when it all started. The young Dr. Abdullah began working as a practicing doctor for the Swedish Committee for Afghanistan (SCA). Here checking a patient outside the first main SCA hospital in Panjshir. It was November 1985. Soon after he joined the inner circle of the legendary commander Ahmad Shah Massoud."
Source: Courtesy of Börje Almqvist.

made no mention of human rights.[93] But the registers of humanitarianism and the idea of the global media space that it relied upon had traveled far.[94]

And yet when Helsinki Watch's Jeri Laber visited Peshawar, she discovered several disturbing trends. Having gone to Pakistan to write about the *Soviet* indoctrination of Afghan youth, Laber published a piece in *The New York Review of Books* on how Saudi-sponsored *madraseh*s had "totally brainwashed" Afghan youth for deployment against the Soviet Army and the PDPA.[95] Laber was making an important point: however much humanitarians had distanced themselves from earlier affinities for guerrilla war, their liberal projects were impracticable without being embedded among

93 RGASPI f. M-3, op. 13, d, 176, l. 44.
94 Fassin, "Subjectivity Without Subjects: Reinventing the Figure of the Witness," in *Humanitarian Reason*, 206; Pandolfi, "'Moral entrepreneurs', souverainetés mouvantes et barbelés: le bio-politique dans les Balkans postcommunistes," 42.
95 Jeri Laber, "Afghanistan's Other War," *New York Review of Books*, December 18, 1986; Author Interview, Jeri Laber, conducted via telephone from Cambridge, MA, May 7, 2014.

Pakistani-sponsored militias. More fundamentally, whatever parallels with South Vietnam or apartheid humanitarian actors made for themselves, Pakistan was interested in intervention primarily insofar as it offered the chance to direct the project of Pashtun self-determination away from the Third World nation-state entirely.

And yet the project to delegitimize a socialist Afghan nation-state had taken on a life of its own, for another unlikely processor in the humanitarian cloud was about to translate the iconicity of Soviet occupation with apartheid to meaningful international institutions. The crucial party was Freedom House's Rosanne Klass, who, in 1983, persuaded Norwegian activists to launch a tribunal similar to those in Stockholm and Paris.[96] Its reception prompted the Norwegian Foreign Ministry to press the United Nations Commission on Human Rights (UNCHR) to appoint a Special Rapporteur to investigate human rights in Afghanistan.[97] It was a novel move: until the early 1980s, Special Rapporteurs had been assigned to South Africa, Israel, and, later, U.S.-backed dictatorships in Latin America.[98] The Norwegians proposed as their candidate Felix Ermacora, a respected Austrian jurist who had reported on apartheid and Pinochet. On March 15, 1984, the UNCHR approved a mission "to examine the human rights situation in Afghanistan with a view to formulating proposals which would contribute to ensuring the full protection of the human rights of all residents of the country before, during, and after the withdrawal of all foreign forces." Ermacora, the first Special Rapporteur for a socialist country, was promptly refused a visa.[99] All the same, interviews in Pakistan and research in the Switzerland-based *Bibliotheca Afghanica* allowed him to complete a damning report – so damning that Moscow prevented its translation from English into other official UN languages.[100]

---

[96] This episode is documented in much more exhaustive detail in the Rosanne Klass Papers at the Johns Hopkins University.

[97] Paul Bucherer-Dietschi, "Bibliotheca Afghanica," *British Society for Middle Eastern Studies* 11(1) (1984), 65–6.

[98] Marc Limon and Hilary Power, *History of the United Nations Special Procedures Mechanism: Origins, Evolution, and Reform* (Washington: Brookings Institution, 2014).

[99] The UNCHR had requested the Secretary-General to task someone with "a study of the human rights situation in Poland" following the one-year anniversary (1982) of the declaration of martial law. However, "as the expert was appointed essentially to assist the Secretary-General with the preparation of a report and was not given an independent mandate," the mission of the expert (Argentine diplomat Hugo Gobbi) was not technically a Special Rapporteurship. Like Ermacora, Gobbi was refused a visa and had to rely on interviews with exiles. Limon and Power, 27; Bernhard D. Nossiter, "U.N. Chief to Hold Inquiry on Rights in Poland," *New York Times*, December 21, 1982.

[100] Felix Ermacora, *Report on the Situation of Human Rights in Afghanistan, Prepared by the Special Rapporteur, Mr. Felix Ermacora, in Accordance with Commission on Human Rights Resolution 1985/88*. UN Document E/CN4/1985/21, February 21, 1985. Author Interview, Börje Almqvist, Stockholm, Sweden, June 22, 2014; "Writer Faults U.N. on Afghan Report," *New York Times*, November 19, 1986, Jeri Laber Files, Box 6, Folder 22.

The episode demonstrated a number of important trends in the battle for the future of Afghanistan. Even without direct access to a country itself, the episode showed, one could construct an oppositional archive of humanitarian knowledge that recast the emergency time justifying intervention. But Moscow was aware of this strategy, and it tried – however lamely – to degrade the Report into an event of import only to the Anglophone world. On a more fundamental level, however, the use of the Special Rapporteur position bespoke a disturbing change in the administrative territory controlled by the Third World. The institution was of very recent provenance, dating to a 1967 United Nations Economic and Social Council (ECOSOC) resolution that authorized investigations into racial discrimination and apartheid, but also left open "the question of the violation of human rights in every country."[101] In a world where alternative legal landscapes sealed themselves off to Third World justice – notably so the International Court of Justice, which failed to condemn apartheid in 1967 – the Human Rights Commission allowed Third World delegations to claim moral territory.[102] Yet once the Commission began investigating rights abuses in Latin America in 1975, it indirectly reclassified the situation in South Africa or the Palestinian Territories from *sui generis* problems that blighted the entire planet to examples of a phenomenon that could occur anywhere in the world – even in Third World or socialist states.[103] As soon as "human rights" became something expressed not in the sovereignty of a Palestinian state, but in an anonymous, tortured body, states like Afghanistan – at once part of the Third World and the socialist world – could be placed in the docket and judged by Europeans. A hard-won administrative and juridical landscape had been inverted.

Parallel to these efforts at the United Nations, humanitarians fought over the status of Afghan children. At the same time that the Soviet Union mobilized Afghan youth into a socialist diaspora, educationalists and humanitarians in Pakistan challenged this project of transnational nation-building. In 1983, SCA's Peshawar team began working with Batinshah Safi, an exiled Afghan who ran 250 schools for Afghan refugee children in Pakistan and eastern Afghanistan, to expand his educational network deeper into Afghanistan. Over the next year, Safi completed curriculum development and began dispatching materials and salaries to schools in Afghanistan, part of an initiative dubbed the Afghanistan Educational Committee (AEC).[104] Action was needed urgently, and not just because the refugee crisis threatened to create a "generation of illiterates."[105] Worse, as Ingemar Andersson reported from a

101 ECOSOC Resolution 1235 (XLII) (August 1967).
102 Ryan Irwin, *Gordian Knot: Apartheid and the Unmaking of the Liberal World Order* (Oxford: Oxford University Press, 2012).
103 Limon and Power, 6.
104 "Afghanistan Educational Committee Annual Report 1985," SE/RA/730500/001/E4/1.
105 Batinshah Safi, Ingemar Andersson, and Anders Fänge, *A Generation of Illiterates? Information From and About the Afghanistan Education Committee* (Peshawar, 1985).

conversation with Norwegian activists, "the Russian occupiers are making great efforts to 'Russify' Afghanistan, not least through major educational initiatives."[106] If Afghanistan were not to simply disappear as a nation, then it needed urgent educational aid through the humanitarian-enabled diaspora.

Emboldened, SCA and Norwegian NGOs provided seed money – several hundred thousand dollars – to help AEC expand operations. Combined with donations collected from French Catholic NGOs during a trip to Europe, Safi could educate Afghans from the Indus to Herat. A curriculum department in Peshawar composed Dari- and Pashto-language textbooks. The books were then printed in Lahore and delivered to Peshawar. There, *mujāhidin* groups' educational representatives received the books and cash to pay for teachers' salaries. They were, however, obligated to return with sheets of teachers' signatures, photographs, and films of classes to receive further funding. The system was not perfect – only a third of textbooks actually reached schools – but by 1985, AEC supported 193 teachers at 82 schools that educated 8,417 students as far west as the Afghan–Iranian border.[107]

Like their Soviet counterparts, however, initiatives like AEC rested on a number of ambiguous assumptions about what, precisely, legitimized intervention into young Afghans' lives. To experienced observers of the nationalist mobilization of children, claims of Soviet brainwashing played pitch-perfect to an established tradition of viewing "collectivist" education as one of the defining features of totalitarianism, whether in its Nazi past or its Soviet present.[108] Such views implicitly played up the family as a virtuous counterpoint to state mobilization, even as nonstate actors – like Safi, one might add – had a long history of claiming the right to educate and nationalize children despite parents' wishes. The significance of the Soviet invasion was, then, not that it had generated a generation of illiterates – Zahir Shah and Daoud had managed that without international protest– or that it produced a highly mobilized generation of Afghan youth – DOYA rarely enrolled more than three percent of the population in its administrative zones – but that it gave nationalist educationalists like Safi the emergency time they needed to launch unprecedented campaigns of their own scarcely possible on the dismal budgets of the Musahiban era.

Nor was this ambiguity over children's rights limited to Europeans. Thanks to Helsinki Watch's lobbying, in October 1985, *Reader's Digest* published a piece on Soviet "kidnapping" of Afghan youth.[109] In February 1986, the U.S. Department of State produced a Special Report on "Soviet Influence on Afghan

---

[106] Ingemar Andersson, Letter to Afghanistan-Hjelpen i Norge (April 4, 1985), SE/RA 7305000/001/E3–3, Folder "Peshawar 1985–1987."

[107] "Afghanistan Educational Committee Annual Report 1985," SE/RA 730500/001/E4/1.

[108] Tara Zahra, *Kidnapped Souls: National Indifference and the Battle for Children in the Bohemian Lands, 1900–1948* (Ithaca: Cornell University Press, 2008), 264–73.

[109] John Barron, "Trained as a Terrorist – At Age Nine," *Reader's Digest* (August 1985), 69–73.

Youth."[110] And in September 1986, American Jewish activists announced a protest march to coincide with Mikhail Gorbachëv's visit to New York. The education of Afghan children in the USSR, the group explained, appeared "on the surface to be innocent and humanitarian and in the traditions of the Judeo-Christian West."[111] But, protestors asserted, because of the length of the program (ten years), the children's young age, their isolation from "national mores," and the use of "brainwashing," Moscow's transformation of "these children into future Soviet agents, provocateurs, terrorists, traitors to Afghanistan, and enemies of their own families is a crime beyond any heretofore known to civilized man." The dizzying swing in the group's announcement – what appeared to be "Judeo-Christian" do-gooding turned out to be a world-historical crime – neatly captured the ambiguity that Cold Warriors attached to nationalist education. Setting aside the question of whether Afghan "national mores" belonged to said "Judeo-Christian traditions," the group merely repeated Cold War stereotypes about totalitarianism when, in reality, the two largest groups of children transferred – orphans and children of élites – represented much more ambiguous cases where there was either no conflict or even an identity of interest between state and familial interests.

More than that, if unbeknownst to said American Jewish groups, the Soviet Union was not the only empire to move Afghan souls across national borders. In nearby Suffolk County, Democratic Congressman Robert Mrazek and several constituents sponsored medical treatment for multiple Afghan children in hospitals on Long Island's North Shore.[112] Earlier that summer, Congressman Charlie Wilson, famous for securing hundreds of millions of dollars' worth of defense appropriations for the *mujāhidin*, sponsored the travel of nine young Afghans to Houston, Texas, where they received privately funded reconstructive surgery.[113] After the surgery, they spent six months at a Victoria, Texas, facility operated by Devereaux, a private nonprofit organization specializing in treatment centers for "mentally disturbed and developmentally disabled children." There, reported the local press, the nine boys "spent their first full day of residence playing soccer, throwing a disk, and watching *Raiders of the Lost Ark*." Coca-Cola, J.C. Penney, and Wal-Mart all donated goods to the group, and a visit to a cattle ranch was planned.[114]

---

[110] Paul Trottier (US Department of State, Bureau of Public Affairs), "Soviet Influence on Afghan Youth," (February 1986), Jeri Laber Papers, Box 6, Folder 5 (Children / General), Human Rights Watch Papers.

[111] "Let the Children Go. Free the Kidnapped Children of Afghanistan" (September 21, 1986), Jeri Laber Papers, Box 6, Folder 5 (Children / General), Human Rights Watch Papers.

[112] "Afghan Children Receiving Medical Treatment on Long Island," (September 2, 1986), Jeri Laber Papers, Box 6, Folder 5 (Children / General), Human Rights Watch Papers.

[113] Devereaux Foundation, "Special Project: Children from Afghanistan," Jeri Laber Papers, Box 6, Folder 5 (Children / General), Human Rights Watch Papers.

[114] Marsha Moulder, "Afghan Boys Take Life Easy in the U.S.A.," *Victoria Advocate*, Jeri Laber Papers, Box 6, Folder 5 (Children / General), Human Rights Watch Papers.

Treated as a curiosity, this group of Afghan boys nonetheless possessed a more intimate knowledge of humanitarian spatiality than perhaps anyone. Given their background, the boys would have almost certainly been *de facto* stateless and lacked proper travel documentation, but they had been let into the American nation-space without issue (their parents had stayed in Pakistan). Devereaux's "facility" was actually a formerly unoccupied building that had been renovated and licensed as a Personal Care Facility on an *ad hoc* basis by the Texas Department of Health specifically for their visit.[115] Nor was it really clear, who, exactly, the boys were. Interviewed, Wilson said that "some of the boys were Afghan fighters who were wounded while battling the Soviet-backed regime in their country. Others were innocent victims of the war."[116] But maybe ambiguity was the point. Unpassportized and administratively invisible Afghan children could easily be articulated through the spaces protecting the American homeland thanks to medicalized subjectivities that justified their expedited movement to privatized points of care. Similarly to the Soviet borderscape, journeys to imperial homelands – rest homes in Ukraine or a Texan suburb – reaffirmed the "domestic" landscape as a destination of freedom and health that was fundamentally other and foreign to the Third World war zones perpetuated by suburban Cold Warriors like Wilson.[117]

What distinguished such Western landscapes from their Soviet counterparts were "the figures used to describe individuals, and with which they are identified, whether or not they recognize themselves through them."[118] From the Hazarajat to Texas, actors endorsed a medicalized vocabulary to position the Afghans they had implicated in transnational assemblages. The focus was on trauma, not violence; on resilience, not resistance; on victims, not heroes.[119] This discursive shift overlapped with older framings of national liberation, whether as part of an "ideological sedimentation," as with the French and the Swedes, or as part of a strategy of deliberate obfuscation, as with Charlie Wilson's statement on the Afghan boys. Internationally, moreover, Afghanistan had to be reclassified not only as a medical catastrophe but also possessed of moral iconicity with South Africa or Israel. Throughout, however, new categories of medical knowledge – some of them very recently rehabilitated, in the case of trauma – legitimized Afghans' insertion into co-constituted humanitarian landscapes. Whereas the number of sick or dying orphans in the country had prompted Komsomol to reconsider its own transnational children's worlds, it was precisely the growing number of such medicalizable human subjectivities that motivated further humanitarian intervention.

---

[115] Deveneaux Foundation, "Special Project: Children from Afghanistan."
[116] Janet Elliot, "9 youths find someone cares after all," *Houston Post*, Jeri Laber Papers, Box 6, Folder 5 (Children / General), Human Rights Watch Papers.
[117] Friedman, 287.
[118] Fassin, 202.
[119] Didier Fassin and Richard Rechtman, *The Empire of Trauma: An Inquiry Into the Condition of Victimhood*, trans. Rachel Gomme (Berkeley: University of California Press, 2009), 160.

Here, then, was the real "doctrinal abyss dividing mankind" – one that
divided not the socialist world from the capitalist West, but rather an ethics
of bordered political space from a morality of precarious lives.[120] New humanitarian forms of subjectivity – centered on the victim, the child, and the traumatized – had been mobilized to capture global public opinion. Administrative and
juridical spaces at the United Nations had been inverted. Accused of interference, humanitarians had followed dissidents' calls: "Interfere more and more.
Interfere as much as you can. We beg you to come and interfere."[121] And yet
try as they might to storm the combination of real existing socialism and Third
World sovereignty, SCA and MSF remained confined to Afghanistan's internal
frontiers and the diaspora. Parallel one another as the landscapes of humanitarianism and socialism did, it was unclear which would triumph among an Afghan
people whose aspirations remained national in content, but whose future had
become inescapably transnational in form.

Borderscape of Neglect

As the Soviet occupation continued, concerns mounted over the possibility
of a general famine. The chaos of the April Revolution and the Soviet invasion had taken place against the background of stable weather patterns, but in
1984, drought struck. The crisis threatened to destabilize the political ecology
that undergirded MSF–*mujāhidin* strongholds like the Panjshir Valley, the Hazarajat, and Badakhshan.[122] Such regions had survived occupation, thanks to
subsistence economies, but, feared French and Swedish operators, added ecological stress could force them into dependence on grain markets in Soviet-
controlled territories. In Soviet-controlled Taloqan, for example, whose grain
market served populations in western Badakhshan, Komsomol advisers noted
that prices for basic goods had more than doubled since the early 1980s.[123] The
PDPA governor had decreed price controls to stabilize the situation, but since
trade was "conducted 100% by the private sector," a black market in wheat,
rice, chickpeas, and potatoes thrived. The Soviets lacked the means to squeeze
Afghan merchants – so far, at least – but the rising prices applied pressure on
rebel-held internal frontiers.

What to do? MSF's Claude Malhuret signed off on a new initiative: since
transporting food from Peshawar to Afghanistan could devastate the livelihood of local farmers, MSF's doctors would provide direct financial aid to

---

[120] Zbigniew Brzezinski, quoted in Sargent, *A Superpower Transformed*, 65.
[121] Aleksandr Solzhenitsyn, Speech (June 30, 1975), printed in *Solzhenitsyn, the Voice of Freedom.
    Two Addresses by Aleksandr I. Solzhenitsyn* (Washington: AFL-CIO, 1975), 23.
[122] "Food Situation in Afghanistan Winter 1984/85 Proposals (Meeting Held at Médicins Sans
    Frontières Headquarters on October 24, 1984," Folder "Famine Afgh," MSF Institutional
    Archives.
[123] Aleksandr Egorov, "Otchët sovetnika TsK VLKSM po provintsii TAKHOR za 12.83–12.84,"
    RGASPI f. M-3, op. 13, d. 64., l. 115.

families and "leaders known for their concern of the welfare of civilians in their areas."[124] MSF agreed, along with fellow French NGOs AFRANE and *Guilde du Raid*, to disburse a total of $700,000 to commanders; SCA was already funneling around $150,000 in private contributions to the same areas and had an application outstanding with SIDA for $200,000.[125] Later, MSF teams ran a combination of food-for-work programs and cash handouts among villagers across Badakhshan. The private traders that Komsomol advisers had observed delivered wheat to Keshem, a district center on the road to Badakhshan's capital, Faizābād, whence it flowed into the valleys and mountains held by *mujāhidin* and MSF.[126] A precarious archipelago of money, wheat, and consciousness connected markets in northwestern Afghanistan with French checkbooks and the Swedish fiscal state.

Two rival landscapes of intimacy and hunger now overlaid one another. MSF observed that PDPA officials checked trucks heading in and out of Faizābād for grain shipments, seeking to starve the countryside, even if the market there remained perpetually low on grain.[127] But the Soviets' ability to translate one geography of power – roads, capitals, armies – into strategic gains remained limited. Supposed affinities of identity, much less ideology, were fraying. As Zaidullo Dzhunaïdov, a Tajik Komsomol adviser deployed to Faizābād, explained, Soviets and Afghans were two peoples divided by a common language.[128] When Dzhunaïdov arrived in the autumn of 1985, he ordered locals to complete the Palace of Culture: winter was coming. "How much?" asked one man. Dzhunaïdov felt outraged: "I was raised in a climate of patriotism, and there was the sense that there are things you should do for free...that you're happy to give two years of your life for your country." He finally convinced the locals to volunteer, but "reorienting brains" was nigh impossible. Managing such cultural divides was not a problem unique to the Soviets – MSF representatives had to convince *mujāhidin* commanders to allow the medical education of women.[129] But there was a huge difference between coercing labor and paying for it with grain, between building an autarkic socialist borderscape and a humanitarian one that flushed Afghan markets with Western donations and tax revenues.

And yet both groups were increasingly questioning the ideological landscape they had helped to build. In July 1986, an MSF convoy en route to Badakhshan

[124] "Food Situation in Afghanistan Winter 1984/85 Proposals."
[125] Anders Fänge, Letter to Juliette Fournot (January 23, 1985), Folder "Juliette," MSF Institutional Archives.
[126] Bernhard Chomilier, "Starvation in Badakhshan–Interim Report 19.05.89," 4; "Food Assistance Program in Badakhshan–Interim Report" (1989), both items in Folder "Badakhshan," MSF Institutional Archives.
[127] Chomilier, 4.
[128] Author Interview, Zaidullo Dzhunaïdov, Dushanbe, Tajikistan, August 31, 2012.
[129] Abdul Malek, Letter to Najmuddin Khan (Emir of Jurm and Baharak) (June 22, 1989), Folder "Badakhshan," MSF Institutional Archives.

was kidnapped by *Hezb-i Islāmi* fighters who apparently intended to swap the French for Soviet weapons that they could then use to crush *Jam'iat-i Islāmi* in Nuristan.[130] Juliette Fournot demanded an audience with Gulbuddin Hekmatyar in Peshawar – she was refused, as Hekmatyar was meeting with important Arab guests – but learned from Hekmatyar's wife that Saudi Wahhabis, not Afghans, exerted real control over his Hekmatyar's forces in the northeast. Later, Fournot would recall being joined in a discussion with Hekmatyar and *mujāhidin* foot soldiers by a "rich Saudi" – whom she later recognized as Bin Laden – famed for his munificence in financing schools, orphanages, and hospitals. Fournot went to the lead USAID officer in Islamabad, Larry Crandal, criticizing Washington's unconditional funding of Hekmatyar as "demented," and noting that what the Americans viewed as an anti-Soviet resistance group was instead transmitting Wahhabism into the "Afghan social and political tissue." Crandal dismissed Fournot as naïve, telling her to stick with medicine. MSF had brought Afghanistan to the attention of a global public, but what began as a campaign against totalitarianism had enabled a quest to obliterate Afghan statehood.

Fatefully, at precisely the same time, Soviet advisers had begun to doubt the suitability of the Third World nation-state as a vehicle for socialism. As the colleague of one adviser reflected, "I kept on bugging him with 'naïve' and 'philistine' questions pointing to the fact that Afghanistan was a multinational society, that it was impossible to establish peace there through force, and that there was no point in us having yet another Soviet Central Asian republic like Turkmenia or Tajikistan. Even without them, we already had enough freeloaders in Russia."[131] Economics had to assume the primacy once assigned to politics. Hence, even as technical advisers continued to construct familiar *ob"ekty* like tractor plants and dams, Mikhaïl Gorbachëv was blunt, telling Afghan leaders to "forget about socialism" and to allow more private enterprise.[132] Afghanistan's 1987 Constitution "guaranteed the security of private investment," which Najib called "a driving force of National Reconciliation.

As part of the campaign to sell the policy shift, a team of Soviet journalists interviewed Afghan businessman Rasul Barat, a Pashtun from Mazar-i Sharif who had inherited his father's Soviet trading contacts.[133] When not running his factories, he imported and sold foreign automobiles. But Barat's life was also tragic. "I lost my father and my brother in the fire of the civil war," he said. "If one of my cars breaks down, I can buy another one, or a third one

[130] Vallaeys, 450–2.
[131] Ivan Ukhanov, "Ubit po zakazu," in *Victor Polianichko–chelovek i grazhdanin. Ocherki vospominaniĭ* (Moscow: Izdatel'stvo "Kliuch", 1994), 38.
[132] Robinson and Dixon, 137; Anatoliĭ Cherniaev, "The Afghanistan Problem," *Russian Politics and Law*, 42(5) (September–October 2004), 32–3; "Record of a Conversation of M.S. Gorbachev with President of Afghanistan, General Secretary of the CC PDPA Najibullah, Tashkent, 7 April 1988," in *Cold War International History Project Bulletin*, Issue 14/15, 175.
[133] Aleksandr Gorianov, "Torgovliia–sestra mira," *Novoe Vremia* 15 (1988), 14–15.

for that matter. But I won't be able to ever find a new father or brother."
Barat's eyes swelled up as his son wandered into the room. "There's my hope,"
he said. "He'll have to continue our family business, our contacts of business
and friendship with the USSR."[134] New direct commercial ties between Cen-
tral Asian *oblast*'s and Afghanistan had allowed Barat to establish businesses in
Tashkent, part of "a joint enterprise between my firm, Barat, and the Soviet side.
The Director will be Soviet, but I'll appoint the Afghan who will be the Deputy
Director."

Yet there was more to Barat's family history than met the eye. Sixty years
earlier, Indian informants had notified British agents in Kabul that "the most
active Soviet trader propagandist in Kabul is one Barat, or Baratoff, who spends
much of his time in the bazaars."[135] Indian merchants, the British reported,
despised Barat for selling wine at massive discounts and offering "to supply
petrol to be sold at whatever price the shopkeeper wishes." Given his ability
to undercut competitors' prices by more than 50 percent, "all of his proposed
transactions are obviously subsidized." Barat the younger, in short, was merely
duplicating his father's exploitation of a Soviet–Afghan transnational community founded on imperial friendships and a melting of borders. Indeed, such
border-bending had turned Barat into the owner of a large estate with two
swimming pools, multiple Mercedes-Benzes, and a stable of exotic horses, some
of which "cost more than the Mercedes."[136] Barat had enriched himself through
intimacies that dissolved "inside" and "outside," but given that such friendships
were founded on violent occupation and the exclusion of less well-connected
merchants from the Soviet command economy, it was little wonder that some
resorted to murder as an appropriate means of "redistribution."

The shift from ideology to economics also presented DOYA with challenges.
Few of Balkh's enterprises wanted to hire young workers, or would only do so
on an at-will basis. Factories, once temples of an industrial order that seemed
prepared to turn Afghan men into socialist laborers, now constituted revolving
doors of adjunct employment. "As long as this continues," wrote one adviser,
"the question of the increase of a layer in the youth organization will remain
open."[137] As the market told young Afghan men that their labor was worthless, only DOYA remained – a refuge of permanent childhood for male bodies.
In Balkh, the PC organized visits to the families of those killed defending the
revolution, whom DOYA members provided with "material aid" and whose
land they tilled at a discount rate. Advisers founded a "youth cooperative,"

[134] Ibid., 15.
[135] "Diary of the Military Attaché, British Legation, Kabul for the Week Ending June 30, 1928,"
NA FCO 402/9, quoted in *Afghanistan Strategic Intelligence*, Vol. 1, 896.
[136] Rone Tempest, "Northern Area Seen As Fallback Position for Afghan Regime," *Los Angeles
Times*, May 20, 1988.
[137] "Otchët sovetnika TsK VLKSM pri PK DOMA Balkh Osviannikova V.I. za period oktiabr'
1987 po maĭ 1988 goda," RGASPI f. M-3, op. 13, d. 173, l. 10.

where, on fifteen acres of land confiscated from landowners, DOYA members grew produce.[138] But what was to do be done with all of this unemployed male labor, absent the mobilizing apparatus of the Party?

Not only DOYA was contending with surplus Afghan bodies, for the Border Forces had shifted their strategy since Najib's arrival. "There was nothing close to resembling a peaceful situation at that time," recalled Gennadiĭ Zgerskiĭ, but the Border Forces "stopped planning attacks on bandits and acted only in response to active sorties."[139] And by the summer of 1988, the Border Forces had a new task: covering the retreat of the 40th Army. Officers guarded the highways from to Kushka and Termez as the withdrawal proceeded. One officer recalled "a not entirely ordinary operation" in September and October 1988.[140] "We had to evacuate an entire settlement of the families of activists who supported the new regime. They moved them from the north of the country to near the Soviet border. On a modest square, there gathered some 600 people in lingering expectation: men, women, old people, children. [...] Four helicopters, flight after flight, carried groups of refugees to a temporary camp specially constructed for them in the district of Bala Murghab." Many PDPA members would not be considered for asylum until the final collapse of the regime in 1992.

The precarious fate of these would-be political emigrants demonstrated how the "contorted spatiality" of a borderscape granted Soviet authorities maximum flexibility in its controlled disintegration.[141] The covert extension of the border into northern Afghanistan had marked only the most vivid expression of the internalization of the country, a process visible through Afghan children, merchants like Barat, or the Afghan–Soviet dual nationals who staffed bureaucracies on both ends of the relationship.[142] Yet the always-present performance of the border as an ontologically meaningful barrier also meant that partial members of the community could be left "outside" if need arose.[143] Even Afghan PDPA members with "limitless belief" in their Soviet allies could be left to "expire with impunity" when their fates became irrelevant to the "security of the southern border of the USSR."[144] Just as the mutually constitutive weave of the "domestic" and the "foreign" had enabled the "making live" of youth mobilization, so, too, now it permitted the "letting die" of hundreds who had expected "that you won't leave them in trouble, that you'll extend your hand to help them." Old borderscapes of intimacy had closed; new cartographies of neglect had opened.

[138] Ibid., ll. 1, 14–15.
[139] Zgerskiĭ, "Kak eto bylo," in *Po obe storone granitsy*, 15.
[140] Roman Bezrukov, "Ne ogrubeli ikh serdtsa," in *Po obe storone granitsy*, 261–2.
[141] Kahn, 317–18.
[142] Ibid., 318.
[143] Left open is the question of how this case of refugees and asylum-seekers compares with other Soviet-Third World cases, such as Iran, Greece, Chile, or (for postsocialist Russia) Syria.
[144] Jean Comaroff, quoted in Shipley, Comaroff and Mbembe "Africa in Theory", 669.

Conclusion

The Soviet border had been shut – against humanitarian meddling, and against Afghan barbarism. One KGB officer who returned to Kushka felt a wave of relief as he strolled among Turkmen pastors, who welcomed him "home." "In the *kazans* (large stewpots) there stewed the soup and *plov* prepared by the denizens of the Turkmen villages, hot tea, too. This war had finished."[145] A few days later, a senior dentist for the Border Forces departed Kushka for Ashgabat. While loading his belongings onto a plane, he "noticed the Border Guards who were unloading their helicopters, taking off their machine guns, and storing away their ammunition. It was the first time we had seen soldiers removing military equipment. For the course of several years they had done the opposite. The war in Afghanistan had ended."[146]

The responsibility to protect the security of the southern border of the USSR, however, had not. In 1989–90, Border Forces based in Gorno-Badakhshan launched several amphibious rescue missions across the Amu-Darya when Sunni *mujāhidin* groups threatened Ismaili Shi'a villages.[147] And when Tajikistan declared independence on September 9, 1991, the 12,000 strong "Group of Russian Border Guards in Tajikistan" stayed put to defend what officially remained a Russian state border from *mujāhidin* incursions.[148] Yet a mere decade after the "southern border of the Soviet Union" had been extended to protect Soviet soil, the border now produced hierarchies of difference between Moscow and Dushanbe. The "Russian" officers ran an unusual recruiting scheme whereby Tajik citizens could serve with the Border Guards and earn more, as a private, than did the Commander-in-Chief of the Tajik Border Guards. And whereas Tajik recruits were ineligible for Russian citizenship, status of forces agreements allowed Russian officers to obtain Tajikistani citizenship for their service.[149] By 1997, most of the 20,000 "Russian" officers guarding the border were ethnic Tajiks; only in 2005 did the border become sovereign property of Dushanbe.[150] In Turkmenistan, Russian officers guarded the border until December 1999. Since then, however, Turkmen "sovereignty" gives lie to the fact that UN-manned health stations pockmark the border to

---

[145] Viktor Pastukhov, "Kaĭsar," in *Po obe storone granitsy*, 127.

[146] Georgiĭ Mogil'nitskiĭ, "Moĭ pervyĭ patsient–Anatoliĭ Reka," in *Po obe storone granitsy*, 360.

[147] Vyacheslav Aboimov, "Kishlak Zangirë," in *Po obe storone granitsy*, 110–2.

[148] Michael Orr, "The Russian Army and the War in Tajikistan," in *Tajikistan: The Trials of Independence*, eds. Mohammad-Reza Djalili, Frederic Grare, and Shirin Akiner (Richmond: Curzon Press, 1998), 156.

[149] V. Strugovets, "The Southern Borders of the CIS: Who Is Protecting Them and How," *Krasnaia Zvezda*, August 4, 1994.

[150] Stephen Kotkin, "Trashcanistan," *The New Republic*, April 15, 2002, 29; John Heathershaw, "The Global Performance State: A Reconsideration of the Central Asian 'Weak State,'" in *Performing Politics in Central Asia: Ethnographies of the State*, eds. Madeleine Reeves, Johan Rasanayagam, and Judith Beyer (Bloomington: Indiana University Press, 2013), 39–61.

serve the "thousands of Afghans who cross into the country looking for hospitals or clinics."[151]

The frontier's transformation from an external Soviet border to a postcolonial one has not always been a happy one for the men who served it. For decades, Soviet Central Asians' deep embedding within empire left them confident that "the Soviet Union stood behind me."[152] With independence, however, has come consignment to economically marginal states coveted less as subjects of territorial incorporation than as suppliers of cheap, disposable labor. Since 1991, more Tajiks and Uzbeks have migrated to Russia than any other group – not, however, as co-equals or potential residents, but as "guest workers."[153] Today in Moscow, reflects one former Soviet Tajik adviser, "a Tajik is at the bottom of the food chain."[154] It marked a colossal loss. Soviet Central Asians had once traversed the border embedded in "narratives of likeness, camaraderie and friendship." Yet as the imaginary "inside" of empire retreated, "race could arise as an instant resource to biologize, essentialize, and give an aura of solidity to imperial logics of difference."[155]

For the Afghans who did make it across the Amu-Darya, diaspora is full of painful reminders of former intimacies. After the collapse of the Najibullah regime, many PDPA élites "came to Russia in the hope of finding refuge, but unfortunately their hopes were not realized and even former senior politicians were left to fend for themselves."[156] And yet the move to "the place where the death of one's most deeply held political projects, believes, or country itself were orchestrated" infused old socialist intimacies with new guarantees, for Moscow offered "the reserve cadre of the PDPA" a safe house that few Western capitals offered to a diaspora of complicity.[157] When, for example, one former KhAD officer applied for asylum in the Netherlands, he openly divulged his past, reasoning "that if he disclosed it, he could not be returned to Afghanistan, where his life would be in danger."[158] The Dutch police investigated his past, but finally denied his application after obtaining evidence that he had approved the murder of thousands of people from 1978 to 1979. Tellingly, the crucial piece of evidence in the case were 154 pages of so-called "Death Lists" obtained from

---

[151] "Turkmenistan: Providing Health Services on the Afghan Border," *IRIN News*, July 17, 2003, available online at: www.irinnews.org/report/20498/turkmenistan-providing-health-services-on-the-afghan-border.

[152] Author Interview, Mamadsho Davlatov, Khujand, Tajikistan, September 6, 2012.

[153] Sergeï Sobianin, Interview, May 30, 2013, available online at: www.youtube.com/watch?v=J7Zo6lIg2Jo.

[154] Author Interview, Mamadsho Davlatov, Khujand, Tajikistan, September 6, 2012.

[155] Friedman, 217.

[156] Omar Nessar, Interview, in "Moscow's Afghan War," BBC News, December 17, 2004, available online at: http://news.bbc.co.uk/2/hi/south_asia/4090557.stm.

[157] Friedman, 280; Homayun Qadiri, "Afganskaia diaspora v Rossii," April 24, 2011, available online at: http://afghanistan.ru/doc/19990.html.

[158] David Loyn, "The Death List That Names 5,000 Victims," August 25, 2014, BBC News, available online at: www.bbc.com/news/magazine-28645671.

an Afghan woman living in Hamburg – originally obtained, incredibly, by none less than former Special Rapporteur Felix Ermacora.[159] The part of the diaspora, however, for whom the ghosts of the borderscape remains most haunting are the some 700 Afghan orphans who live in the Russian Federation today. Following the collapse of the Soviet Union, many of them hoped to return to living relatives in Afghanistan, but, explains one Russian activist, "there was no money in [Russia], so no one was going to deport anyone." Having spent their entire childhood and adolescence in Russia, these men are now caught in legal aporia. When one Mohammad Naim applied for a permanent residency visa, "the formulation of the rejection sounded especially absurd: 'He's not in the archives.' It turned out that after so many years of living in Russia, studying in an *internat* and a technical college Mohammad Naim simply did not exist on the necessary sheets of paper."[160] The only way out for such Afghans – many of whose wives and children were Russian citizens – was to travel, undocumented, to Kabul, where they could then formally apply for a visa at the Russian Embassy.[161] Naim did so, but his application was rejected, leaving him the choice of either taking his chances as an undocumented migrant in Pakistan or to "repatriate" himself to Russia and apply for refugee status there, in spite of explicit insistence that this will "not represent an argument to the Russian Migration Services."[162]

Stories like Naim's, like Osman's, remind us that "Afghanistan is interactive, not isolated; dynamic, not stable; diverse, not homogenous, and dependent on, rather than autonomous from its surroundings."[163] And yet this transnational interaction took place beyond the media of imperial expansion or humanitarian internal frontiers. Afghanistan's engagement with the global was mediated through a web of co-constituted landscapes that could assume – or shirk – responsibility as they rearranged space. Such engagements, such debts, arose from politically meaningful spatial arrangements not readily acknowledged by the states whose territorial imaginaries they nonetheless buttress. Sometimes these arrangements only appear, ephemerally, as the rejection stamp on a Russian visa application, or a UN report available only in English. Other times, they take on material shape as a health facility in Texas, or a Komsomol *internat* in Ukraine. Such manifestations of the ideological career of the Third

---

[159] "Afghanistan Death Lists of 5,000 People Executed to End Uncertainty of Relatives," September 18, 2013, RAWA News, available online at: www.rawa.org/temp/runews/2013/09/18/afghanistan-death-lists-of-5000-people-to-end-uncertainty-of-relatives.html.

[160] "Bez rodiny" (2008), *Upolnomochen zashchishchat'* (Journal of Plenipotentary for Human Rights in Rostov Oblast), available online at: http://ombudsman.donland.ru/Default.aspx?pageid=51406.

[161] Elena Sleptsova, "Vygnat', chtoby potom – priniat'" (March 6, 2007), KM.RU, available online at: www.km.ru/v-rossii/2007/03/06/sotsialnye-problemy-v-rossii/vygnat-chtoby-potom-prinyat.

[162] "Bez rodiny."

[163] Hanifi, "Quandaries of the Afghan Nation," 101.

World nation-state may be less visible than the phantasm of the "national economy," but these spatial formations and the "exercises in lofty denial" that accompany them define Afghanistan's relationship with the world no less than the dams and sawmills, the gas plants and cotton fields, the brick factories and salt pits, of days past.[164]

[164] Maier, *Among Empires*, 60–1.

7

The Little Platoons of Humanity

The Afghanistan-Pakistan borderlands of the late 1980s constitute a microcosm of change in the global concept of sovereignty. If the borderlands of Turkestan had still constituted a surface on which the fantasies of bordered power could be enacted, then the deserts of southern Afghanistan, located over a thousand miles south of the Amu-Darya, demanded different strategies of control. There, in a turn from the democratization of the means of production to the democratization of the production of violence, Soviet advisers entrusted control of the border to nonstate auxiliaries. Secure in the privileges of territorial sovereignty – guaranteed, paradoxically, by transnational armies – real existing socialism could replicate itself within the Third World nation-state and "contaminate the whole world with the antidemocratic particularities of Soviet society."[1]

There were two ways to vaccinate the planet against this risk, however, and Afghanistan became the index case for both. The first, inaugurated by none less than CPSU General Secretary Mikhaïl Gorbachëv, was to disenchant Third World sovereignty, as the *GenSek* did when he agreed to the Geneva Accords and, in doing so, abolished a traditional Soviet veto on UN Peacekeeping Missions. Postcolonial states, once a platform whose belated decolonization in an era of territorial sovereignty made them ideal hosts for Leninist infection, became neutralized arenas for something called "the political process." Quarantined under the adult supervision of international élites – not Soviet advisers – atavistic postcolonies could reenter the society of nations. The second inoculation against real existing socialism was more straightforward: team up with guerrillas and "turn ideology into facts on the ground."[2] But as the Soviet Union withdrew from Afghanistan, humanitarian NGOs were forced to embrace this

---

[1] Andreï Sakharov, *Memoirs*, trans. Richard Lourie (London: Hutchinson, 1990), 385–6.
[2] Hopgood, *The Endtimes of Human Rights*, 6.

strategy sooner than they might have preferred. Used to conducting informational war from mountainous internal frontiers, the little platoons of humanity found themselves owning governance in lowlands and cities.

Caught between these two models – UN aid administered through the nation-state and transnational humanitarian aid administered through NGOs – Afghanistan once again improbably captured a symmetry of global projects. Three decades ago, it had been American modernization *contra* Soviet nation-building; a decade prior, real existing socialism versus European humanitarianism. Now, however, as the Security Council no longer blocked UN interventionism, two new possible futures suggested themselves. Could the United Nations, freed from subaltern internationalism, turn Afghanistan into a new kind of international protectorate? Or was the future one in which states "increasingly disengaged from the project of governing national territories" and succumbed to warlordism and "government by NGO"?[3] The UN types in besieged Kabul were resolute, declaring that "there should be a Sir Robert Jackson type."[4] Yet the zeitgeist and institutions that sustained such men were as extinct as some prehistoric monster. As the Afghan state was revealed to be a fiction in all but its attachment to a radically transformed United Nations, left behind was not only Najibullah in the UN compound, but also "the ubiquitous concept of the 'failed state' itself as implicit acknowledgement that states really were rather important."[5]

"Through the Prism of a Stereotype"

In 1985, Komsomol adviser Georgiĭ Kireev and Iuriĭ Sal'nikov, a senior CPSU Central Committee adviser, performed the familiar ritual: the stay in Hotel Rossiia on Red Square, the early-morning flight to Tashkent, the sour, acrid airport coffee, the meager buffet at the Tashkent airport canteen.[6] But when advisers like them finally disembarked from their Antonov-25 planes onto the tarmac of the Qandahar Airport, it was clear that they faced challenges. The minder who fetched one new arrival advised him to stay down during the jeep ride to the advisers' compound – *mujāhidin* shot at vehicles on the airport road with grenade launchers and rifles.[7] Soon, however, both Kireev and Salnikov sped through the "dusty sidewalks of an Oriental city" and met their Afghan

---

[3] James Ferguson, "Seeing Like an Oil Company: Space, Security, and Global Capital in Neoliberal Africa," *American Anthropologist* 107(3) (September 2005), 380.

[4] "Meeting with Undersecretary of State Armacost" (February 4, 1988), 1, Folder 99, Box 9, Javier Pérez de Cuéllar Papers, Yale University.

[5] Mark Mazower, *Governing the World: The History of an Idea* (New York: The Penguin Press, 2012), 423.

[6] Author Interview, Iuriĭ Sal'nikov, Volgograd, Russian Federation, November 4, 2012. Author Interview, Georgiĭ Kireev, Moscow, Russian Federation, November 10, 2012; Kireev, "Kandagarskiĭ dnevnik," October 16, 1985, available online at: http://kireev.info/w-4.html. All subsequent references to Kireev's diaries refer to this source.

[7] Kireev, Diary Entry, October 16, 1985.

colleagues, "men with slim chances not only of survival but also of an easy death."[8]

The two men sent to Qandahar embodied very different Soviet lives. The Soviet project had furnished an entire career for Sal'nikov: a bachelor's degree in engineering in Leningrad, then years of factory and Party work in Volgograd. The Persian-language refrain that so commonly described advisers' experience – "from *Parchamist* to *Komunist* to *Parvā nist*" (Parchamist, Communist, "I don't care") – never entered his mind.[9] Kireev, in contrast, saw himself as a misfit. As a young man, he had joined the Komsomol out of a vague desire to "change the world for the better." Yet "the system was not only tough but cruel. I had to somehow find a new way in life." But Kireev had few options, for "a few naïve and vehement presentations at the plenums of the Komsomol *obkom* and the CPSU had turned me into a local dissident in the eyes of the Party leadership, and my friends from the *obkom* made clear to me that my career was going nowhere."

Hence, whereas most advisers feared assignment to a country many disparaged as "Assghanistan," Kireev leapt at the chance to take "a trip across the creek."[10] While first terrified of certain death, Kireev realized that "if [*mujāhidin*] actually wanted to kill me, they could do it." Embracing the insignificance and futility of his mission, Kireev accepted his stay in Qandahar as an opportunity to understand the illegitimacy of Soviet socialism. "I don't divide the world into good guys and bad guys," Kireev said, "only good and bad institutions." All the same, Kireev added, he considered Sal'nikov a "coward" for his collaboration with the Soviet system.

Coward or not, Sal'nikov was the Party's point man in the city. The economy assumed top priority. Qandahar boasted twenty-nine enterprises: paper combines, three factories, a brickworks, mills that produced napkins and blankets, and a jam factory.[11] But few were online; few had any heating; fewer, electricity. Many business owners had fled to Pakistan. Afghan socialists had to refurbish the factories, connect them to heating systems, and generate the working class that Afghan capitalists had not. If, one colleague insisted, the PDPA could connect farmers in the Helmand River watershed with processing plants in Qandahar, the region could feed an implausible fifty million souls.[12]

Yet the situation in Qandahar was rather mixed. True, twenty-seven of the twenty-nine enterprises in the city were working. The textile combine, the jam

---

[8] Iuriĭ Sal'nikov, Diary Entries, January 6, 1985 and January 16, 1985, in *600 dneĭ v Kandagare. Dnevniki 1984–1986* (Volgograd: Izdatel', 2010), 20, 36.

[9] Author Interview. Many advisers repeated this same refrain to me. Kireev's diaries record a slightly different version, with advisers going from "internationalism" to "Chekism" (a pun on collecting checks and scrip chits from Vneshtorg, the organization that paid advisers) to "Parvanism" (not caring). Kireev, Diary Entry, October 19, 1985.

[10] Leonov, *Likholet'e* (Moscow: Mezhdunarodnye Otnosheniia, 1995), 26.

[11] Author Interview, Iuriĭ Sal'nikov, Volgograd, Russian Federation, November 4, 2012.

[12] Iuriĭ Sal'nikov, Diary Entry, Friday, February 8, 1985, 73.

factory, and a wool factory fulfilled production targets at 100 percent, and a new KamAZ truck factory had recently started operation.[13] Customs income had increased five percent from the preceding year, while PDPA-mandated *subbotniki* (mandatory days of "volunteer" work) earned the PC 456,000 *afghānis* annually.[14] Sixteen *ob"ekty* were under construction. When a reporter from *L'Humanité*, the paper of the French Communist Party, turned up in Qandahar, Sal'nikov showed off the city's factories, bragging that even the Frenchman "he acted as if people in France wouldn't believe him if he wrote that government institutions were working."[15] And yet fifteen of Qandahar's twenty-nine industrial enterprises had no Party members among their ranks. Six employed only nonunionized workers. Repeated power outages meant that even model enterprises operated at far under capacity.[16] Enterprises paid workers sporadically. The local statistics office lacked cadre. All of the dry goods in the bazaars came from Pakistan.[17] Some of this could be fixed through deliveries from the USSR, but, as Sal'nikov pithily captured, "You can deliver cement to a country, but you can't deliver an Afghan working class."[18]

Not only transnational terrorism but also transnational economic forces, in short, threatened the ideal of the socialist national economy. A mere stroll through the lobby of an advisers' meeting at the Ariana Hotel in Kabul – which Kireev visited in October 1985 – was enough to demonstrate this. While there, he wrote of a "cult of thing-ism" (*kul't veshchizma*) among advisers wearing Montana blue jeans. "In several stores around town," he noted, "there are Russian-language signs hanging: 'Coats for order. Ready-made.' You can see this best-seller among us. Indeed, all of us advisers are in leather jackets."[19] Likewise, when Afghanistan expert Viktor Korgun traveled to Kabul, his seminars for officers soon descended into boisterous debates over black market exchange rates between Polish and American cigarettes.[20] When one brigade drunkenly raised the Soviet flag over Kabul's Bala Hissar fortress, Korgun lambasted them: the Soviets, he declared, were *not* a colonial power. And he was right in one sense: Moscow was far from turning Afghanistan into a dumping ground for Soviet manufactures.

More than that, however, humanitarian missions challenged Soviet hegemony over the population itself. Sal'nikov was not unaware of such missions. It was, he explained, common knowledge that MSF doctors worked along the border, but "the USSR had no interest in harming them." As the earlier incident in Jaghori showed, blowing the French to smithereens would have caused more

---

[13] Sal'nikov, Diary Entry, April 23, 1985, 147.
[14] Ibid., 148.
[15] Author Interview, Iuriĭ Sal'nikov, Volgograd, Russian Federation, November 4, 2012.
[16] Sal'nikov, Diary Entry, April 23, 1985, 149.
[17] Author Interview, Iuriĭ Sal'nikov, Volgograd, Russian Federation, November 4, 2012.
[18] Sal'nikov, Diary Entry, Wednesday, February 1985, 95.
[19] Georgiĭ Kireev, Diary Entry, October 20, 1985.
[20] Author Interview, Viktor Korgun, Moscow, Russian Federation, October 15, 2012.

nuisance than it eliminated. Further, the territories that constituted such groups' strongholds were either borderlands or internal frontiers – territories where the Afghan state had been weakly institutionalized in the first place. Increasingly, there were two "Afghanistans" – the humanitarian landscape of frontiers and mountains, and the Soviet landscape of Kabul and the cities.

More daunting for the moment were by now long-familiar problems of Soviet administration. Articulating problems, much less solutions, felt impossible. After a dinner with PDPA and KhAD officials to celebrate the anniversary of the October Revolution, Kireev described proceedings as "a gathering in our traditional style: a speech rewritten year to year, an opportunity for the guests to speak.... You see something immutable here, like a vigil."[21] Soviet life, reflected Kireev, consisted of "real life" and "fantasy life" – "the ideological picture that was constantly drawing itself...the parades, Victory, everything." Even Sal'nikov recognized something too "formalistic, too ossified about the way [Afghans] were going about their work." "Arguably," he reflected, "one could say that we often see the Afghan situation through the prism of a stereotype that has emerged through the forms and methods of our own Party and state apparatus."[22]

Ideologically blinded, Sal'nikov and Kireev still had to contend with very real threats. In theory, Qandahar City sat inside a "Green Zone" that extended ten miles outside of the city. More accurate, however, was its informal reputation as a "special zone" (*osobyĭ raĭon*) of violence.[23] When one Tajik translator worked in the city from 1986 to 1987, he woke up at 5:00 AM, worked in the city until noon as Soviet convoys cleared mines, then returned to his compound, an abandoned fruit factory at the heart of the city, to bunker himself in against grenade attacks.[24] Nor were advisers the only targets. In spring 1985, the Qandahar PDPA PC convened a *loya jirgah* to propose economic reforms.[25] *Mujāhidin* groups warned that all who attended would be killed. "The *jirgah* lasted for two hours," wrote Sal'nikov. "Afterwards there was a lunch for the delegates. Mutton stew with potatoes and a traditional *plov*. On the tables oranges and bananas. For dessert – tea. The forks and spoons we had didn't suffice, however. People ate *plov* with their hands." But Sal'nikov's Orientalist musings soon gave way to reality. The next evening, thugs gunned down the Director of the Local House of Pioneers in central Qandahar. Pedestrians tried to approach the dying man, but snipers fired warning shots. "No one else decided to approach," wrote Sal'nikov, "and the man died, his corpse laying there in the road until the morning."

[21] Author Interview, Georgiĭ Kireev, November 10, 2012, Moscow, Russian Federation.
[22] Sal'nikov, Diary Entry, July 29, 1985, 241.
[23] Author Interview, Georgiĭ Kireev, Moscow, Russian Federation, November 10, 2012.
[24] Author Interview, Haydar Kurbanov, Dushanbe, Tajikistan, July 26, 2012; Kireev, Diary Entry, February 11, 1986. During the ISAF occupation of Afghanistan, this compound was renamed Camp Nathan Smith.
[25] Sal'nikov, Diary Entry, April 14, 1985, 144–5.

Morale had reached a low point in Qandahar. Kireev counseled the First Secretary of the DOYA PC, calming him. "I said to him, with the examples of our revolution and the war, that one had to be an optimist; we had had it hard, too, but we still built a superpower. They could have that, too [I said]. They just had to believe. I recited Maiakovskiĭ's poem 'In Four Years There Will Be a City' and said that Qandahar, too, could be a flowering city."[26] But could it? Kireev's citation of a poem from an age when government possessed boundless ambition to transform citizenries could not but feel anachronistic. Qandahar remained distant from smokestacks and state monopolies. As Sal'nikov admitted, there was not one government-owned store in Qandahar, while independent truckers transported forty times more cargo than the KamAZ fleet.[27] Developments bespoke not the triumph of the territorial nation-state, but instead its transnational de-institutionalization – a process, however, that the Soviets could try out for themselves.[28]

Soviet Transnationalism and the New Tribe

Global projects, projects like the Soviet union of ideology and territoriality, always have and always will demand translation to the local scale, and Qandahar was no exception. Even though the PDPA had overthrown a Mohammadzai regime in Kabul, in Qandahar, Mohammadzai Communists still ruled.[29] Both the province's military boss, General Hakim, and the police commander were Mohammadzais – people who "can go to any district in Qandahar and return alive. Their authority among the people serves as their armor." Yet as elsewhere, the PDPA struggled with mobilizations. "Conscription into the Army," recalled Kireev, "fundamentally took place in the form of raids. The Army and the *Sarandoy* would surround the city or the village, capture all of the men above the age of service, and then would sort out whether they had served or not, whether they were healthy or not, and so on."[30] Little wonder that so many recruits were keen to escape.

This made policing Qandahar Province's 410-kilometer-long border with Pakistan impossible.[31] The crucial link, explained General Hakim to Sal'nikov in February 1985, was the border crossing of Spinboldak, "a sheer rock mountain rising from the flat desert."[32] But as late as 1985, the PDPA had not even

---

[26] Kireev, Diary Entry, October 17, 1985.

[27] Sal'nikov, Diary Entry, April 23, 1985, 147, 149.

[28] Mark Mazower, "Governing the World: The Rise and Fall of an Idea," Public Lecture at Columbia University, November 28, 2011, available online at: www.youtube.com/watch?v=imY8H3TUh88.

[29] Sal'nikov, Diary Entry, January 18, 1985, 43.

[30] Kireev, Diary Entry, November 25, 1985.

[31] Sal'nikov, Diary Entry, February 4, 1985, 70.

[32] Robert Kaplan, *Soldiers of God: With Islamic Warriors in Afghanistan and Pakistan* (New York: Vintage Departures, 2001), 203.

introduced passports to the country.[33] The Party also lacked the men to police the border, but there was "the possibility of forming a youth border patrol brigade of 1,000 men. [The] KhAD and the Tribal Administration is working on this problem."[34] When this plan failed, however, the KhAD proposed outfitting local tribes with Soviet weapons.

The advisers were skeptical. "The tribes don't mind getting money," objected Kireev, "but they don't particularly want to fight."[35] Retorted Sal'nikov: "As long as the tribes don't provide help to the [Afghan] army, nothing will come of our work here. The tribes don't want to work with Pakistan–they're carrying out a war themselves against Zia ul-Haq's regime." But Sal'nikov saw the contradiction. "But then who are we making a revolution with? Feudal lords, merchants, mullahs – these are the people we're making revolution with. They're at the head of the Party and the government! We have to take weapons away from the tribes, not give them to them."[36] Yet if not tribes, who was Sal'nikov proposing to arm?

Enter Ismatullah Muslim, an Achakzai Pashtun whose tribe's homelands straddled the border. Muslim had begun the war fighting the PDPA and the Soviet Army, "conducting both military and smuggling activities in the area between Qandahar and Quetta."[37] Yet Zia ul-Haq had tired of Muslim's unwillingness to join one of the Peshawari Islamic parties – Achakzais like the hard-drinking, secular Muslim had little interest in cooperating with religious extremists.[38] A 1984 falling-out between Muslim and Zia prompted Muslim to defect to the DRA, where he was named a General in the Afghan Army. Days after Muslim had crossed into Afghanistan alone, in mid-May 1985, Zia announced a bounty of a million rupees to anyone who could capture Muslim within three days – dead or alive. For a Party that struggled with developing a "social base," the Achakzai bandit and his army of thousands of tribesmen represented a welcome partner.

But there was a more subtle dimension to recruiting Muslim. Why, one may ask, did the Pakistani intelligence services not court southern Durrani Pashtun tribes more aggressively? There was, after all, no shortage of antiregime sentiment among tribes in Qandahar or Helmand Province, but Islamabad included no such groups into the Peshawar-based Alliance of Seven. The reason why, as Michael Barry explains, has to do with Islamabad's mission to transform the possibilities for Pashtun self-determination. Since the mid 1970s, Pakistan had entered into partnership with lower caste Afghan Pashtun Islamists who,

---

[33] Author Interview, Iurii Sal'nikov, Volgograd, Russian Federation, November 4, 2012.

[34] Sal'nikov, Diary Entry, February 4, 1985, 70.

[35] Kireev, Diary Entry, November 16, 1985.

[36] Sal'nikov, Diary Entry, June 29, 1985, 193.

[37] Rubin, *The Fragmentation of Afghanistan: State Formation and Collapse in the International System*, 159.

[38] Tribal Analysis Center, "Pashtun Tribal Dynamics" (October 2009), available online at: www.tribalanalysiscenter.com/PDF-TAC/PashtunTribalDynamics.pdf.

even if never integrated into the Pakistani Establishment the way high-caste Pakistani "Pathans" were lusted after the possibility of power in Kabul. The arrangement between such Barakzai upstarts and the ISI was simple: "if Afghan Pashtun Islamists like [themselves] were to be lastingly empowered in Kabul, they would cap and replace Afghan secular nationalism (including its notorious Marxist variant) with an "Islamic" identity closely allied to Pakistani interests which should permanently recognize the Durand Line and the primacy of Pakistani diplomacy, and forever deny any possibility of Indian political influence in Kabul."[39] According to such logic, Tajik Islamists like Ahmad Shah Mas'ud were instrumental allies; Marxists, secularists, and Pashtun nationalists, the enemy. Just as Punjabi generals had successfully orchestrated a junior role for high-caste Pashtuns in their domination of the Pakistani state, now, too, Afghan *Ghilzai* Pashtuns would take on a secondary junior role in an inverted Durrani Empire: ruled from the Punjab, not Qandahar; by Punjabis and Ghilzai Islamists, not Durrani nationalists.

Yet by recruiting Muslim, the PDPA PC could construct precisely the broad alliance of Durrani Marxists and secularists needed to push back against the Pakistani–Ghilzai assault. In a divergence from historical patterns, an Ahmadzai Pashtun (Najibullah) could push back against Pakistan while supported by Mohammadzai Pashtuns from Qandahar.[40] Exploiting Zia's Pashtun policy to bring the Achakzais, a historic competitor to the Mohammadzais, over to the side of the PDPA – to turn a tribal alliance into a bordered state – made perfect sense. And even as thugs like Muslim may have had little interest in cooperating with the Soviets' project of state-building, the allure of uniforms, roads, and a customs post was too much for an entrepreneurial warlord to resist.

But the strategy bore risks for precisely these reasons. Sal'nikov observed that "to the southwest of Qandahar, near the road, there lives a tribe of Alizais. They don't make contact with people's power. Often, they conduct attacks on the road and engage in skirmishes with the Sarandoy and army posts. All attempts by the provincial leadership to negotiate with this tribe have not led to any results."[41] Other tribes had been assimilated and even supplied the PDPA with "some of the finest Soviet-era Afghan Army generals."[42] Yet the tapestry of tribes and allegiances created a devilish problem. One week after Sarandoy forces clashed with Alizais to the southwest of the city, two Achakzai elders

---

[39] Barry, *Kabul's Long Shadows: Historical Perspectives*, 66.

[40] The pattern reversed itself again back to the norm after the American invasion of Afghanistan in 2001 when Hamid Karzai, a Popolzai Pashtun from Qandahar, surrounded himself with Ahmadzai Pashtun allies. During the 2014 presidential elections, two of the leading candidates were either Ahmadzais (former Finance Minister Ashraf Ghani) or Persianized Kabuli Mohammadzais (Zalmai Rasul).

[41] Sal'nikov, Diary Entry, February 4, 1985, 66.

[42] Tribal Analysis Center, "Achakzai Tribe" (October 2009), available online at: www.tribal analysiscenter.com/PDF-TAC/Achakzai Tribe.pdf.

marched into the Governor's office: "Aerial bombing strikes had been conducted on the positions of Achakzai posts. The leaders reckon that this was
done as an instigation: someone doesn't like the fact that the Achakzais want
to reach a nonaggression agreement with people's power. They warned us: if
this happens one more time, war is on."[43] Nurzai tribes who held longstanding
disputes with Muslim's Achakzai tribe, meanwhile, considered the Qandahar–
Spinboldak road *their* property.[44] What to do? The PC needed bodies, but giving Muslim the imprimatur of state power threatened to intensify a Pashtun
civil war that Kabul desperately needed to internationalize against Pakistan.

Predictably, tensions erupted the day Muslim's 2,000 soldiers entered Afghan
territory. As the Achakzais marched through Spinboldak, they refused to be registered by state Border Guards.[45] Upon crossing into their "homeland," several
fired their weapons in the air in spontaneous celebration. Outraged, the head
border officer arrested Muslim's top lieutenant and locked him in an outhouse.
When Muslim learned of the incident, he bolted to the border. There, he pum-
meled the officer, ripped his uniform apart, and had him hog-tied and tossed
him in the trunk of a car. Arriving back at the Qandahar Governor's office, he
dragged the bound border officer into the room with him and flung him onto
the Governor's desk. "Here," he shouted, "are the scoundrels, here are these
political idiots who tried to hinder my people from returning to their homeland, they stood up between revolutionary power and the people, they allowed
misconduct that should have been washed away with their blood. But I'm not
going to judge them – I'm handing both of these devils to the KhAD."

With allies like these, who needed enemies? In control of the border, Muslim
began charging rival Nurzais to use the crossing. Nadir Khan, the head of the
local Nurzai tribe, threatened to murder the local *Hezb-i Islāmi* commander
Yunus Khalis (his future son-in-law) if he did not supply him with weapons.[46]
When Sal'nikov traveled to Spinboldak in November 1985, the Nurzais had
left Afghanistan altogether.[47] And in early 1986, anti-PDPA Mohammadzai
armies stormed Spinboldak, where "the Ismatists fought to the death, but even
their superiority in weapons didn't give them the chance for an unconditional
victory."[48] In response, Muslim issued an ultimatum: supply him with Soviet
tanks or he would leave for Pakistan.[49] Soviet leadership declined, instead offering nightly bombing raids along the border. Sal'nikov explained: "[Muslim]
forgot (or didn't know) that in a revolution or war everyone has their place.
His place was the border, his task to reliably guard the border with his bands
of Achakzais."

[43] Sal'nikov, Diary Entry, February 10, 1985, 75.
[44] Rubin, 159.
[45] Iuriĭ Sal'nikov, Diary Entry, May 10, 1985, 174.
[46] Kaplan, 203.
[47] Sal'nikov, Diary Entry, November 16, 1985, 324.
[48] Ibid., Diary Entry, January 5, 1986, 381.
[49] Ibid., Diary Entry, January 13, 1986, 395.

Sal'nikov's phrasing reflected a larger transformation. Both Zahir Shah's Kingdom of Afghanistan and Daoud's Republic conceived of "the" government as a unitary entity.[50] This was always truer in international norms than in reality; frontiers and borders projected a unified front that masked vacuums in domestic administration. State border guards represented the "edge" of Afghan territorial state space that behaved like a unitary object in its encounters with other states. "The foundational premise of state sovereignty," in other words, "traditionally assumed that members of the international system have no right to pierce the veil of statehood." Yet not only had Pakistani-based *mujāhidin* and Western NGOs pierced that veil; now, *Soviet* advisers like Sal'nikov were casualizing government into such horizontal networks. Muslim's ritual humiliation of the Afghan Border Forces – professional guardians of Afghan statehood – underscored the point. The inverse of the Soviet Border Forces' invagination of Soviet "inside" and Afghan "outside," Muslim showed how nonstate actors could collapse internal Afghan state functions if tolerated by the Soviets. It raised a dark question: what would happen if nonstate actors like Muslim, or indeed the likes of Hekmatyar, descended from the mountains to conquer Kabul, Afghanistan's link to the international scale itself?

Kireev's and Sal'nikov's assignments to Qandahar were coming to an end. Kireev felt discouraged: "I left Qandahar with a desire to destroy that system." Yet signs of change were becoming visible. There were solicitations to Soviet citizens for suggestions on how to reform socialism. "I was very naïve at the time, so I wrote in with several radical suggestions: getting rid of Article Six of the Constitution, on the leading role of the Communist Party. Of course, there was no response."[51] Not only that, the promises that Kireev's Party bosses had made him turned out to be lies. He was dispatched to Kostomukhsho, a company town near the Soviet–Finnish border built around one of the largest iron mines in the world. "After my assignment," wrote Kireev, "I didn't stick around in the Party organs for long. I worked for a bit as an instructor in the CPSU *gorkom*, then I went to the teachers' school, left the Party, and organized the city's first informal political organization, 'Democratic Initiative.'" In general, I dipped my head in the direction of *perestroĭka*.[52] Dispatched to expand Sovietism abroad, Kireev devoted himself to dismantling it at home.

And yet as Sal'nikov's return showed, the power of the Soviet global project to replicate itself, to connect economies and institutions, remained formidable. Having completed his assignment in Qandahar, Sal'nikov left Qandahar on a Friday, flew back to Volgograd over the weekend, and was at his desk writing reports on the city's central heating system on Monday morning.[53] No offer

---

[50] Anne-Marie Slaughter, *A New World Order* (Princeton: Princeton University Press, 2004), 12–13.

[51] Author Interview, Georgiĭ Kireev, Moscow, Russian Federation, November 10, 2012.

[52] Kireev, "Kandagarskiĭ Dnevnik," Afterword.

[53] Author Interview, Iuriĭ Sal'nikov, Volgograd, Russian Federation, November 4, 2012.

for PTSD treatment was forthcoming, Sal'nikov noted with regret. It may have been a personal tragedy, but it was only the logic of the Soviet global project: imposing a new institutional order on vastly different geographies, redefining the meaning of politics "through the prism of a stereotype," and turning operators like Sal'nikov into bureaucratic commodities interchangeable across a world transnational in form and socialist in content.

Authoritarianism at Large

As Sal'nikov and Kireev returned home, the Soviet global project's initial attempt to forge an Afghan state seemed to be fading. Afghanistan, like Angola and Ethiopia, was supposed to be the place on the planet's surface where Revolution remained possible. The transformation of postcolonies into nation-states fit, moreover, into the prevailing view of international order. For far from becoming a handmaiden to Anglo-American designs, the United Nations (especially its General Assembly) had become a soteriological destination for former colonies. Since tributaries, empires, trusteeship zones, protectorates, and their ilk had all become historic relics, the proliferation of the nation-state was the only conceivable outcome to decolonization.

Ironically for a power whose founder had proclaimed the *transitory* nature of nations and the state, Moscow supported this program. Aided by the Soviet Union since the mid 1970s, the General Assembly had granted the Palestine Liberation Organization (PLO) observer status, effectively expelled South Africa, and denounced Zionism as a form of racism. The only conceivable future for the postcolonial nation, it seemed, was the nation-state – the Jews, the constituent nations of the USSR, and national causes with leaders less entrepreneurial than Yasser Arafat excepted. Soviet-backed organizations like the Afro-Asian People's Solidarity Organization, whose Congress Kabul hosted in 1981, gave despots a platform to defend the nation-state and claim vast swaths of the planet into "peace zones" barred from American interference.[54] As late as the mid 1980s, such visions appeared as a permanent "structural conflict" destined to be "an enduring characteristic of the international system" for which "there are no solutions." "The triumph of sovereignty" had created "major incongruities between underlying power capabilities and transnational principles and norms."[55]

And yet this obsession masked over several fundamental global shifts that could not but affect the nation-state's role in the international arena. Between the mid 1960s and the 1980s, world trade tripled; the value of offshore

---

54 "Address of Comrade Babrak Karmal, General Secretary of the CC of the PDPA and President of the Revolutionary Council of the DRA," in *Proceedings of the 10th Session of AAPSO*, (November 18–21, 1981, Kabul, Afghanistan), 23. Bibliothek des Bundesarchivs, Berlin, Germany.

55 Krasner, *Structural Conflict: The Third World Against Global Liberalism*, 313–4.

holdings rose from one to sixteen percent of world GDP.[56] While the world of real existing socialism presented, for a time, a countermodel, the debt crises of the mid 1980s eroded this fiction, too, leaving only the supposed identity between nation and territory as "the main one in which fantasies of purity, authenticity, borders, and security [could] be enacted."[57] But as defenders of Third World nation-states were reticent to admit, the idea of the territorial nation formed, "as the ideological alibi of the territorial state, the last refuge of ethnic totalitarianism."[58] And even as after Arafat proclaimed a Palestinian "Declaration of Independence" in the fall of 1988 (recognized by the General Assembly as a proclamation of a Palestinian statehood), such posturing in the language of the nation-state often merely represented an alibi "to escape the specific state regime that is seen as threatening their own survival."[59] In short, globalization and the experience of forced migration generated myriad "post-national formations" that questioned the nation-state's role as a shorthand for the postcolonial future.

CPSU and Soviet area studies specialists grappled only dimly with these global shifts in the possible forms of sovereignty. Following the breakdown of early 1987 direct negotiations with Pakistan, Gorbachëv sought the input of time-tested area studies specialists like Iuriĭ Gankovskiĭ.[60] In May 1987, Gankovskiĭ recommended to Anatoliĭ Cherniaev that "a non-partisan [emphasis Gankovskiĭ's] figure should occupy the post of the head of the Afghan government, one who enjoys authority not only within the country and beyond, but also, above all, in the Muslim countries of the Near and Middle East."[61] Soon, "key decision makers in the Politburo began thinking along the lines proposed in Gankovskiĭ's memorandum."[62]

Yet other advisers saw such suggestions as a waste of time. One line of criticism came from Gorbachëv's own foreign policy advisers, who argued that the romance of the Third World nation-state had to end. Moscow's own attempt to master forces beyond the nation-state – the international Communist movement – had run out of steam. But the Brezhnev-era turn toward countries

---

56 Sargent, *A Superpower Transformed*, 5.
57 Stephen Kotkin, "Kiss of Debt: The East Bloc Goes Borrowing," in *The Shock of the Global: The 1970s in Global Perspective*, eds. Niall Ferguson, Charles S. Maier, Erez Manela, and Daniel J. Sargent (Cambridge, MA: Harvard University Press, 2010), 80–93; Appadurai, *Fear of Small Numbers: An Essay on the Geography of Anger*, 23.
58 Appadurai, *Fear of Small Numbers*, 159.
59 Appadurai, *Modernity At Large: Cultural Dimensions of Globalization* (Minneapolis: University of Minnesota Press, 1996), 164–5.
60 Kalinovsky, *A Long Goodbye: The Soviet Withdrawal from Afghanistan*, 110.
61 Iu. V. Gankovskiĭ, "Dokladnaia zapiska Iu. V. Gankovskogo (Institut vostokovedeniia AN SSSR) A.S. Cherniaevu o meropriatiakh po razresheniiu konflikta v Afganistane," May 22, 1987, Gorbachëv Foundation Archives, f. 2 (Materialy A.S. Cherniaeva, op. 1 (Lichnye materialy A.S. Cherniaevu)), d. 2, *kartochka* 729, l. 1.
62 Kalinovsky, 116.

of socialist orientation had been even more disastrous, leaving corpses, unrepayable debts, and questionable strategic benefits in its wake. Merely encouraging allies like Najib to de-stress Communist ideology was insufficient. In a diary entry, for example, Anatoliĭ Cherniaev defined "Karmalism" (in reference to the former Afghan General Secretary) as "the dogmatism of Marxism-Leninism plus parasitism in relation to the USSR. In general we have a shitload of Marxists in Africa, too."[63] The problem, in short, was not so much Afghanistan *per se* as the tendency to inscribe a politics of the future in the Third World nation-state itself.[64]

Another line of criticism came from proponents of a more radical transnationalization of the conflict – intelligence operatives like Vasiliĭ Kravtsov and diplomats like Vladimir Basov who saw the Afghan adventure through the lens of Pashtun self-determination. Propitiously, then, claims Kravtsov, in early 1987, KGB operatives confirmed that Gankovskiĭ had been leaking the logistics of a putative Soviet withdrawal to Pakistani informants.[65] Because of Gankovskiĭ's patrons in the International Department, prosecuting him for treason was not feasible. Still, the KGB secured Gankovskiĭ's demotion to the title of IV AN SSSR's "Head Consultant." The way was now open for a generation of Soviet scholars of Afghanistan to apply their vision to the building of an Afghan state. In June 1987, Basov collaborated with Soviet Afghanistan expert Roman T. Akhramovich and Eduard Bagramov, a specialist on the psychological origins of nationalism, to author policy recommendations for the PDPA.[66] Najib, they argued, had to recognize the depth of the emotional and irrational roots of nationalism, encouraging non-Pashtun cadre, especially in the Army.

And yet it was not so clear if these struggles among specialists still represented an intellectual victory for Gankovskiĭ. In his work, after all, Gankovskiĭ had emphasized the durability of the Pakistani state precisely because of the way that it had coopted Pashtuns into the military and economic élite. Only by accepting that Pakistan was more complicated than a "Punjabi dictatorship" dominated by industrialists and feudal lords could one understand that calls to "Pashtunize" Afghan foreign policy would disintegrate the precarious connection between Afghan nation and state. Geopolitics aside, any legitimate Pashtun identity politics would demand transnational expression in both Afghanistan and Pakistan – not through the totalitarian culturalism of the PDPA.[67] Basov, Akhramovich, and Bagramov, in contrast, remained prisoners to a vision of state legitimacy "in which national self-rule must rest on some sort of tradition

---

[63] Anatoliĭ Cherniaev, Diary Entry, August 28, 1987, National Security Archive.
[64] For a later judgment along these lines, see Georgiĭ Shakhnazarov, "Dokladnaia zapiska M.S. Gorbachëvu o probleme otnosheniĭ s 'tret'im mirom,'" October 10, 1989, Gorbachev Foundation f. 5, op. 2, d. o.
[65] Author Interview, Vasiliĭ Kravtsov, Moscow, Russian Federation, November 15, 2012.
[66] V.V. Basov, "O natsional'nom voprose v Afganistane" (June 1987), in Basov, *Natsional'noe i plemennoe v Afganistane*, 233–59.
[67] Appadurai, *Modernity at Large*, 147.

of natural affinity."[68] Yet as Kabul manifestly failed to live up to this principle, the Soviet scholars were encouraging sub-national groups "to use the logic of the nation to capture some or all of the state."

Regardless of its inner character, however, the Afghan state still had to interface with the outside world. And for the moment, this meant the illiberal internationalist order of the Soviet Union and the Third World. But as we saw earlier through the intimacies of the Barat family, genuine economic interdependence was hard to fake. In August 1986 and September 1987, the CPSU Central Committee and the Council of Ministers signed two decrees that allowed Soviet Union Republics to conduct economic policy with foreign states.[69] The decrees enabled several partnerships between Soviet *oblast's* and Afghan provinces. This was a distinctively Soviet way of institutionalizing *horizontal* links across states in a way that reinforced, rather than challenged, authoritarian power verticals. The Afghan state's constituent parts now possessed increased freedom to interact with their equivalents across national borders, but the units that were interacting remained anchored in the territorial Party apparatus and an illiberal authoritarian state.

Under the new policy, the Kazakh Republican Komsomol sought to improve ties. On September 12, 1987, Qandahar PDPA bigwigs arrived in Alma-Ata to observe Party and state institutions.[70] A month later, planes shipped goods to Qandahar; the first Kazakh delegation visited Qandahar in January 1988. As Kazakh officials soon learned, however, economic interdependence demanded a flexibility that the command economy seldom encouraged. Since few factories in Alma-Ata produced export goods, packaging was only available in Cyrillic script. Designing packaging with labeling in Pashto (which uses the Arabic script) or with symbols understandable to an illiterate exceeded the abilities of managers. The result – deliveries of Kazakh grain in old USAID bags marked "Gift of the United States of America to the Afghan People" – probably achieved the opposite of its intended goal.

But marketing issues were ephemeral to the core problem. Locals had a choice beyond just Soviet goods. "When sending goods to Qandahar," read one guide for new advisers,

One should never let the thought arise – "Well, Afghanistan isn't an economically developed country, its provinces will take goods of whatever quality." But goods of any quality *won't* do it. The issue is that in the stores of Afghanistan, including in Qandahar, they sell calculators, fabrics, Japanese watches, fashionable blue jeans and skirts from Thailand, Hong Kong, shoes and women's clothing from Great Britain, and so on. Of course, the prices for these goods are very high, but an Afghan has the ability of juxtaposing one

[68] Ibid., 157.
[69] *Kandagar–pobratim Alma-Atinskoĭ oblasti (v pomoshch lektoru–propagandistu po internatsional'nomu vospitaniiu)* (Alma-Ata: Kabinet komsomol'skoĭ raboty Alma-Atinskoĭ Obkom LKSM Kazakhstana, 1988), 14.
[70] Ibid., 17–20.

to the other, comparing them, analyzing them, of personally seeing Soviet-made goods, goods from the other socialist countries, and analogous capitalist-made goods. It's not hard to come to a conclusion about the fact that questions about the improvement of the quality of goods lie in the realm of great practical policy and are, as we can see, an issue of not only domestic but also foreign policy.[71]

Soviet internationalism found itself contending with economic globalism on terms not of its own choosing once again. Much earlier, when Soviet advisers operated in settings like China, they had to worry little about "the intrusions of international economic integration on national economic policy."[72] But Afghanistan was different. As we saw in the case of the West German foresters and *cedrus deodara*, colonial cartography made a mockery of imagining the Afghan national economy as a closed entity. Now, Soviet advisers were repeating the same mistake, but with the added burden of making control of the economy a central political expectation. Competing with transnational economic flows meant that the Soviet global project had to come to terms with lessons that observers of international affairs had long internalized: "World peace may not, as the IBM slogan has it, come through world trade, but buying a Toyota or a Fiat may very well influence one's attitudes toward Japanese or Italians."[73]

Shifts in international capitalism burdened the Soviet mission, then, but Soviet leadership was about to make the structural challenge exponentially more difficult through interventions at the United Nations. When Gorbachëv signed the Geneva Accords in April 1988, guaranteeing the withdraw of Soviet forces from Afghanistan by early 1989, he unintentionally anchored Afghanistan in a United Nations system different from the one Moscow and Third World despots had built over two decades. 1988 was the watershed year: the year of the declaration of Palestinian "statehood," but also of a Nobel Prize for the United Nations' Peacekeeping Forces. It was an odd choice: the missions had never been envisaged by the UN's founders, and Soviet obstructionism had limited deployments since 20,000 blue helmets deployed to the Congo from 1960 to 1964. The 1970s saw only three missions, all in response to Arab-Israeli wars, and then none at all until 1988.

The reason for such missions' absence, however, had been precisely the illiberal internationalism that had constituted a joint Soviet–Third World project. Since the Congo Crisis, "the high point of the anti-colonial U.N.-U.S. Symbiosis," the Soviet Union and Third World states had deployed a Soviet veto in the Security Council and a numerical majority in the General Assembly to prevent meddling into internal affairs.[74] Just as the United Nations provided a forum to

---

[71] Ibid., 20.

[72] Richard N. Cooper, *The Economics of Interdependence: Economic Policy in the Atlantic Community* (New York: McGraw-Hill Books, 1968), 151.

[73] Keohane and Nye, "Transnational Relations and World Politics: An Introduction," 341.

[74] Mazower, *Governing the World*, 261; Sergey Mazov, *A Distant Front in the Cold War: The USSR in West Africa and the Congo, 1956–1964*, 164.

conduct endless inquiries *inside* Israel and South Africa, it could be exploited to keep such inquires outside of the Third World nation-state – until Ermacora's intervention, at least. Yet as Gorbachëv abandoned the Soviet veto on peace-keeping missions, all of the places where Leftist confrontation at the scale of the nation-state seemed promising – Afghanistan, Angola, Nicaragua – played host to peacekeepers. Without the Soviet veto at the Security Council, Western critics of the Third World no longer had to confine themselves to internal frontiers like the Hazarajat to report on misdemeanors. Guarded, ironically, by peacekeep-ers who hailed overwhelmingly from the Third World, experts arrived to watch Vietnamese officers, Cuban internationalists, and Soviet advisers go home.

And yet this move toward peacekeeping and "the political process" itself failed to grapple fully with the realities of transnational political movements. The three main tenets of the Afghan peacekeeping mission, UNGOMAP – mon-itoring the Soviet withdrawal, monitoring the Pakistan–Afghanistan border, and overseeing the return of refugees – all revolved around the idea that the nation-state, rather than the transnational diaspora Afghans had become, rep-resented the *telos* of Third World statehood. If the 1980s had shown anything, it was that Afghans – like Sikhs, Kurds, or, soon, former Yugoslav citizens – might prefer an ethno-nationalism reliant on diasporic links to the exclusion-ary prison of the nation-state.[75] All the same, as SCA member Börje Almqvist recalled, UNOCA (United Nations Office for the Coordination of Humani-tarian and Economic Assistance Programmes Relating to Afghanistan) "began declaring random areas inside of Afghanistan 'zones of peace' and trying to con-vince refugees to move to areas where it was certain they would be killed."[76] Those Afghans without the means to apply for asylum in Europe were thus left with the choice of remaining in legal aporia in Pakistan or facing grim odds of survival in a "homeland" some of them hardly remembered.

As if to emphasis the divergence in visions of the future as a political ques-tion, near-simultaneous with Gorbachëv's acceptance of peacekeeping missions was a new, distinct emphasis on the Soviet Union as a *European* power. Part of the impetus owed to some of the changes discussed earlier in Chapter 5. As French Socialists ditched their dreams of socialism in one country, PS élites like Jacques Delors devoted themselves to reinventing the European Economic Community as something meatier than just a free-trade area.[77] The overthrow of dictatorships in Portugal, Greece, and Spain, likewise, expanded the project to the Mediterranean, making the European project "less abstract and, there-fore, among other things, more interesting to young people."[78] For Communists no longer able to rail against the abstraction of "capitalism," Europe *qua* insti-tutional project represented both an alternative and a challenge. Gorbachëv,

[75] Appadurai, *Modernity at Large*, 163.
[76] Author Interview, Börje Almqvist, Stockholm, Sweden, June 22, 2014.
[77] Abdelal, *Capital Rules: The Construction of Global Finance*, 64.
[78] Judt, *Postwar: A History of Europe Since 1945*, 630.

who viewed the Spanish Social Democratic Prime Minister Felipe Gonzalez as his ideological soulmate, traveled repeatedly to Western European capitals, speaking of a "Common European Home" extending from the Atlantic to the Urals. As if to distance himself from the old program of real existing socialism, the General Secretary spoke – in front of the Council of Europe in Strasbourg – of the need to create a "European legal space" through the collaboration of humanitarian law experts from the Soviet Union and Western and Eastern Europe.[79]

Yet this return to Europe brought rather murky consequences. Born out of solidarity with Biafrans and Vietnamese, movements like MSF and the SCA had forced European attention toward a Global South that had always been imbricated in, if not always visible in, postcolonial metropoles. According to one summer 1968 public opinion poll, French citizens had ranked the Biafra crisis as the single most important world issue.[80] Yet by the mid 1980s, MSF itself began to argue explicitly against the Third World as an ideological project. More prosaically, nationalist imaginaries gained traction as economies sputtered, guest workers did not return home, and the number of asylum seekers increased thirtyfold.[81] Twenty years after the butchery in Biafra engaged French public opinion, it was debates over the permissibility of headscarves in state schools that occupied domestic attention. True, "Europe" as an alternative narrative to socialism or decolonization did not *necessarily* tack in a xenophobic direction. But the fact that both Soviet and Europeans élites so rapidly divested their hopes from a "concept of freedom expressed in the sovereignty of a black state" at the same time that the United Nations dismissed novel transnational formations would have grave consequences for Afghanistan.[82]

The Shock of the Transnational

Following the signing of the Geneva Accords in April 1988, UN Secretary-General Javier Peréz de Cuéllar designated Prince Sadruddin Aga Khan, the former head of the UNHCR, as the coordinator of the UNOCA.[83] The credentialed, elegant Prince Sadruddin turned to fund-raising, some of it from unlikely sources. At an October 1988 donor conference for "Operation Salam," the complex of developmental projects coordinated by UNOCA, Moscow pledged

---

[79] Mikhaïl Gorbachëv, "Europe as a Common Home" (Speech), July 6, 1989.

[80] John J. Stremlau, *The International Politics of the Nigerian Civil War, 1967–1970* (Princeton: Princeton University Press, 1977), 227.

[81] Fassin, "Truth Ordeal: Attesting Violence for Asylum Seekers," 116.

[82] Connor Cruise O'Brien, *Murderous Angels: A Political Tragedy and Comedy in Black and White* (Boston: Little, Brown, 1968), 57.

[83] Antonio Donini, Eric Dudley, and Ron Ockwell, "Afghanistan Report: Coordination in a Fragmented State" (December 1996), available online at: http://web.cas.suffolk.edu/faculty/druke/UN/UN%20OCHA%20FIELD%20GUIDELINE/documents/145.pdf.

$600 million, most "in the form of commodities."[84] It marked a notable shift. The *goods* that Moscow was transporting to Afghanistan remained the same, but the institutional tracks they took had changed. Ties between states remained, but they now floated in a thick transnational aether epitomized by NGOs, the United Nations, and scales other than the state.

Yet as former SCA operatives explained, the interaction between UNOCA and established NGOs was complex. MSF's Juliette Fournot recalled bristling at how "a slew of NGOs that had never worked with Afghans or even in any refugee camp in the world flooded Peshawar."[85] Bolstered by far larger sums of cash than MSF could muster, such groups swarmed *mujāhidin* offices to discuss how to disburse millions of dollars. SCA's Anders Fänge, meanwhile, bristled at Prince Sadruddin's dismissive approach to them and their experience. UNOCA engaged almost exclusively Geneva-based NGOs in the postwithdrawal Afghan theater, which prompted established organizations to found an Agency Coordinating Body for Afghan Relief and Development (ACBAR) as an umbrella organization for the groups that actually had experience in Afghanistan.[86] Conversely, however, while UNOCA and UN agencies had limited room for action in those territories under *mujāhidin* control – like Panjshir – UNOCA also cooperated with *Peshawar*-based NGOs to coordinate aid activity to, for example, rebel-held Kunar and Paktika Provinces.[87]

Moscow and Kabul now had to walk the tightrope between the illiberal internationalism they had long embraced and the transnational actors that challenged them. Operating around the primacy of the Third World nation-state, Moscow and its partners had historically sought to "upgrade" or "downgrade" actors to or from precisely that scale. For the Palestinian cause to become fully legitimate, the PLO had to be defined as its sole legitimate representative, then become an observer to the General Assembly, then finally, be recognized as a nation-state, the *telos* of national life. Likewise, Moscow and the Third World's strategy toward Israel and South Africa hinged upon promoting the PLO and the African National Congress (ANC) as the only possible legitimate representatives of those territories, since Zionism and apartheid were seen as not only unjust but *incompatible* with a legitimate international order. Friends had to be redefined as states; enemies, as "nonstate nothings."[88]

Now, however, the tables were now turned on Moscow. *Mujāhidin* actors and men like Schönmeyr had chosen the transnational scale precisely because

---

[84] Office of the Co-ordinator for United Nations Humanitarian and Economic Assistance Programmes Relating to Afghanistan, "Operation Salam: First Coordinated Report" (February 1989), 5, 13.

[85] Vallaeys, 453.

[86] Author Interview, Anders Fänge, conducted via telephone from Berlin, Germany, September 17, 2014.

[87] "Operation Salam: First Coordinated Report," 25–8.

[88] Schmitt, *The Großraum Order of International Law with a Ban on Intervention for Spatially Foreign Powers*, 113.

of the way it allowed them to obviate the frozen global order the USSR and the UN had sought to enforce through the Durand Line. Asymmetry of scale, once a challenge, had become a strategy. Even if agencies like UNICEF now very much treated the *mujāhidin* groups as functionally equivalent to the Kabul government, such guerrillas' lack of international recognition provided maximum flexibility to ignore the DRA's borders and extract international resources to provide services inside the DRA's territory.[89] The good news was that, for the moment, few states were prepared to treat *mujāhidin* groups the way they did the PLO. Jordanian diplomats explained that while Riyadh had extended diplomatic recognition to the *mujāhidin* because of its relationship with 'Abd al-Rāb Rasul Sayyāf, "the Arafat of the Afghans," Amman "felt that recognition was premature since matters on the ground were still unclear."[90] But the Jordanians' position left an opportunity open: what if the *mujāhidin* and their sponsors captured Kabul itself? And how would such a transnational capture of the nation-state square with the UN framework now in place to regulate the conflict?

The question was about to be posed in less academic ways. Since arriving, UN-sanctioned UNOCA teams had undertaken fact-finding missions "to assess the real needs of the population and to start planning for rehabilitation and reconstruction."[91] In December 1988, UN officials entered Herat Province from Iran to conduct the first UN visits there in nine years.[92] They found chaos: half of the city was simply leveled, most of the trees and buildings around Herat had been destroyed, and more than half of the villages in the province were. In light of DOYA and Komsomol's mission to protect Afghan children, the UNOCA team's findings at the Provincial Hospital were grim. "During the last five years," they wrote, "the Provincial Hospital has conducted 373 amputations mainly due to anti-personnel mines. The great majority of amputees were children below 15 years.... No artificial limb facilities are available in Herat." Likewise, in Kunar, UNOCA team met almost no women or children. Roads were heavily mined, and "large areas of pine forest have been stripped."[93]

Yet in coordinating aid to these regions, UNOCA encountered a problem. If, in Pakistan, the United Nations provided assistance through NGOs and UNHCR refugee camps, west of the Durand Line, UNOCA had only a mandate to provide "development assistance to areas under the control of the Kabul

[89] James P. Grant, "Child Immunization Throughout Afghanistan" (December 7, 1985), Folder 96, Box 9, Javier Pérez de Cuéllar Papers, Yale University.

[90] "Note to File" (March 14, 1989), Folder 104, Box 10, Javier Peréz de Cuéllar Papers, Yale University.

[91] Office of the Co-ordinator for United Nations Humanitarian and Economic Assistance Programmes Relating to Afghanistan, "Operation Salam: First Coordinated Report" (February 1989), 18.

[92] The Salam-1 mission took place slightly later, in December 1988; it consisted of seven officials who traveled around Herat Province for seven days. For more on the operation, see "Operation Salam: First Consolidated Report," 18.

[93] Ibid., 25.

government." UNOCA and the UN were international bodies that liaised with *states*, not with mobile sovereignties. But there was only one Afghan state, namely the dictatorship that Moscow had built. The question thus arose: what would happen if Kabul lost control of their countryside entirely? After the Salam-3 team discovered dire conditions in the Panjshir Valley, Prince Sadruddin and UN agencies launched an aid mission from Kabul, all "with the concurrence of the Kabul authorities and of the receiving authorities in the Panjshir."[94] UNHCR officials purchased fertilizer, UNICEF medicine shipments, but everything was diverted by *mujāhidin* before reaching the Panjshir.

The episode raised an uncomfortable question. Hitherto, most NGO activity had been concentrated in internal frontiers like the Hazarajat, Badakhshan, or border areas whose centers were still occupied by Soviet troops. Humanitarians could concentrate on providing aid to the population, collecting testimony, and, in doing both, generating the emergency time that justified their continued presence in Afghan territory. Former UNICEF diplomats like Carl Schönmeyr had regarded the transnational scale as a detour precisely because of the irresponsibility of UNICEF and UNDP a mere decade earlier. Now, however, with those organizations increasingly civilized but still embedded into an international system that recognized the Kabuli state, Afghan state collapse would leave NGOs entirely in charge of governance over massive swaths of territory. Performing state triage was not what either MSF or SCA had signed up for when they initially engaged in the Afghan crisis, but they had been taken hostage by the intersection of their commitments, problems of scale, and Pakistani foreign policy. For the moment, the only thing holding up the byzantine structure was the assumption that Najib would continue to control enough territory in which UNOCA could operate and that the *mujāhidin* would not conquer Kabul itself.[95]

Was this right? Barring major changes in strategy, cabled Soviet diplomat Vladimir Basov in August 1988, "the war in Afghanistan will continue and, assuming current tendencies continue, it will end in victory for the opposition."[96] The only hope was to transform Afghanistan into an international protectorate. Moscow had to insist on "the halting of all weapons imports into Afghanistan, ultimately working toward the demilitarized status of the [Afghan] state." Fanciful though Basov's suggestion might sound, he was merely reiterating one of the mandates of the UN peacekeeping team in Afghanistan – monitor the withdrawal, encourage refugee return, guard borders. Indeed, a United Nations Good Offices Mission in Afghanistan and Pakistan

---

94 Ibid., 24.
95 "US, Soviets agree to Halt Arms to Combatants in Afghanistan," *Washington Post*, September 14, 1991, 1. This fact led to many of the contradictions in UNOCA's mission.
96 V.V. Basov, "Soobrazheniia ob uglublenii politiki natsional'nogo primireniia i novom etape razblokirovaniia afganskogo konflikta" (August 31–September 1, 1988), in Basov, *Natsional'-noe i plemennoe v Afganistane*, 266.

(UNGOMAP) had been set up for this very purpose. Yet as the official UN account explains, "A number of difficulties unavoidably hampered the effectiveness of the work of UNGOMAP's inspection teams. These included the rough nature of the terrain, the time which lapsed before many of the alleged incidents were reported, and the security conditions prevailing in the area of operation."[97] In response to Pakistani and Afghan charges of border violations, UNGOMAP had established five additional checkpoints on the Pakistani side of the border, but to little effect.[98] But with no indefinite mandate to protect the Durand Line, once UNGOMAP had certified the withdrawal of Soviet forces in February 1989, it left, turning the border into no-state's-land.

One might ridicule UNGOMAP for its lack of resources – $14 million and fifty military observers, or about one man for every thirty-three miles of border. A Congo-style intervention it was not. Yet the more fundamental problem with UNGOMAP was the lack of political appetite left for the Third World nation-state qua political project. In 1978–9, after all, activists like Carl Schönmeyr had linked humanitarian activity with transnational *mujāhidin* groups precisely because the Soviet Union had blocked assistance through UN organs like the UNDP, UNCIEF, or the WHO. Colonial cartography made transnational humanitarian action feasible, but Moscow's backing of Third World sovereignty made it necessary. Now, however, with Moscow pulling back from its Third World commitments, UNGOMAP administrators found themselves scrambling "to provide reliable protection so that the lives of its representatives were not jeopardized."[99] But with no such guardian forthcoming, UNGOMAP dissolved completely in March 1990.

As Soviet troops completed their withdrawal, could Kabul protect itself? On March 6, 1989, Pakistani Prime Minister Benazir Bhutto met with senior ISI officials and U.S. Ambassador to Pakistan Robert Oakley to discuss their next move.[100] ISI Chief Hamid Gul went bullish, arguing for an attack on Jalalabad. The shift toward conventional military warfare against an Afghan National Army equipped with Soviet arms presented risks, but if *mujāhidin* took the city, the road to Kabul would be wide open. It was a mistake. Afghan pilots flying Soviet planes and a detachment of Soviet SCUD missile operators bested Gulbuddin Hekmatyar and 'Abd al-Rāb Rasul Sayyāf.

Nor were Pakistani-support *mujāhidin* successful further south. In Qandahar, KGB officers like Kravtsov (deployed in 1989) went beyond Sal'nikov's old

---

[97] "Afghanistan/Pakistan–UNGOMAP–Background," available online at: www.un.org/en/peace keeping/missions/past/ungomap/background.html.

[98] "Report of the Secretary-General" (October 20, 1989) 2, Folder 109, Box 10, Javier Pérez de Cuéllar Papers, Yale University.

[99] "The Future of UNGOMAP After 15 February 1989" (January 19, 1989), 6, Folder 111, Box 11, Javier Pérez de Cuéllar Papers, Yale University.

[100] Kalinovsky, 180.

halfway role to become ersatz tribal agents. Lieutenant General Nur ul-Haq Ulumi, a Barakzai Pashtun and Afghan Army official who had distinguished himself at Jalalabad, was appointed as the Governor of Qandahar Province. Kravtsov got to work with Ulumi and Popolzai élites like Azizullah Karzai (Hamid Karzai's uncle). The KGB man declared that it was official Soviet policy to establish Qandahar as a "Durrani city" and that Pakistani Punjabis wanted to ethnically cleanse the city. Soon, he began negotiating Soviet arms and cash deliveries to local Durrani tribes in order to push back against the Saudi- and ISI-backed *Hezb-i Islāmi* militias of Gulbuddin Hekmatyar. After several days of *jirgahs*, a deal was struck. Local Popolzai élites guaranteed the safety of a 300-truck convoy dispatched from Turkmenistan, through Herat, and down to Qandahar. Not one shot was fired along the entire route. Thanks to the Soviet weapons, tribal militias and the DRA Army defended the city from Hekmatyar's militias. Two transnational invasions of Afghanistan had been stymied.

Often forgotten, however, it was precisely this postwithdrawal window that posed painful questions for humanitarian entrepreneurs. SCA's longtime slogan had been "Soviets Out of Afghanistan!" – pithy, but also possible.[101] One of SCA's founding members, Gösta Hultén, resigned in 1988 – "it wasn't Sweden's role to occupy the country or transform it," he said, "only to donate money to help Afghans."[102] Other SCA members were more pragmatic. But with SCA still highly dependent on SIDA funding (81.6% of all funding for the 1990 fiscal year), the organization remained dependent on political will in Stockholm.[103] SIDA scrutinized its funding terms more carefully and noted that its original contract had specified "catastrophic aid." As a result, SIDA backed away from its original formula of granting five times the sum of SCA's domestic collections.[104] The idea of Afghanistan as a zone of catastrophe had initially offered Schönmeyr a way to stage an intervention, but the Soviet withdrawal revealed the ideological anchors of SIDA's policy. The emergency of occupation was one thing; mis-governance by a Mugabe or "indigenous" civil war, another.

Likewise, events in Jurm, Badakhshan, showed the limits of MSF's politics of precarious lives. The MSF medical teams rotating through Badakhshan had long enjoyed good relations with local authorities, but by the late 1980s, a local lieutenant of Ahmad Shah Mas'ud began to resent the French. He proceeded to disrespect MSF hospital staff, bringing loaded Kalashnikovs into the hospital

[101] Author Interview, Jan Stolpe, Stockholm, Sweden, June 24, 2014.
[102] Author Interview, Gösta Hultén, conducted via telephone from Arninge, Sweden, June 27, 2014.
[103] "Budget 1990, Svenska Afghanistankommitténs Hjälpverksamhet," Folder "Peshawar 1988," Sveriges Riksarkivet SE/RA/730500/001/E 3–1.
[104] Author Interview, Anders Forsberg, Uppsala, Sweden, June 28, 2014.

grounds and demanding that his soldiers be treated before civilians.[105] On the night of April 27, 1990, twenty-eight-year-old French doctor Frédéric Galland was murdered by *mujāhidin*. MSF responded by withdrawing all doctors from Afghanistan.[106] It would return only in the summer of 1992.

The decision exposed the politics of life that had underwritten MSF's missions in Afghanistan. Faced with totalitarian inhumanity or foreign occupation, humanitarian actors had called for "a politics of life that reestablishes solidarity between human beings and gives equal value to lives."[107] So strong was this belief that even when Soviet forces destroyed MSF installations, the question of withdrawing from Afghanistan was never really debated.[108] But once the Soviet Union withdrew, even MSF, which had gone beyond SCA in sending Europeans into the field, rethought its stance. Rather than advocating for a general right to asylum for all residents of Jurm, Brauman explained the decision as follows: "A million deaths, almost five million refugees, almost as many displaced in the interior of the country. And thousands of people, young but seasoned combatants for the most part, who do not know how to live other than at arms. How to intervene in this country under such conditions?"[109] A radical politics of the present had given way to a temporally distended sobriety that referred to future risks and present costs.

The postwithdrawal window had revealed a brutal truth. Humanitarianism had originally called upon the equality of European and Afghan lives, but throughout the engagement, "hierarchies of humanity were passively established, though rarely identified for what they were – a politics of life that, at moments of crisis, resulted in the constitution of two groups of individuals."[110] Without the Soviet alternative to motivate visions of emergency, humanitarian actors fell back upon an ever-present distinction that the ethic of equal life could not disguise, namely that between political subjects with the freedom to escape the nation-state and Afghans left to fate. Many justified their own withdrawal from Afghanistan in terms that affirmed their own political agency while alluding to the multigenerational nature of the Afghan conflict: "I told myself that I had to leave before everything tipped over there, otherwise I would have

---

[105] Éric Mouzin, *Approche de l'Afghanistan à travers six mois de mission humanitaire avec MSF* (Doctoral Thesis, Université René-Descartes, Paris, 1990), np.

[106] Vallaeys, 458.

[107] Fassin, "Hierarchies of Humanity: Intervening in International Conflicts," in *Humanitarian Reason*, 241.

[108] It is worth noting that during its decade-long operation, Komsomol saw two advisers killed in action and one kidnapped and presumably murdered, yet only withdrew once the Soviet Army itself withdrew from the country. In other words, Komsomol cynically linked the politicization of childhood with the violence and power of occupation, but it also denied advisers of their own political subjectivity in going to Afghanistan and excluded any thoughts of pulling out because of "risk."

[109] Brauman, quoted in Vallaeys, 458.

[110] Fassin, "Hierarchies of Humanity," 240–2.

stayed there all my life."[111] The Afghan child who had symbolized humanity had grown up to become a permanent dependent at best and a murderer at worst.

Yet with the Soviet Union itself now approaching catastrophe itself, both the moral and the political landscapes of the frontier were rapidly changing. In 1990, Kabul received only ten percent of contracted fuel deliveries.[112] The Afghan Army began to disintegrate, and after years of unsuccessful attempts, *mujāhidin* forces captured Khost in April 1991. The victory opened up new frontiers for Peshawar-based NGOs to operate inside Afghanistan under the umbrella of sovereign power. A September 23, 1991, joint meeting between UN representatives and ACBAR created a joint NGO planning organization, the Eastern Paktia Coordination Group.[113] Geographies of intimacy thought lost reemerged. As Danish humanitarian workers marched by the cedar stumps, they discovered that "although most physical inputs of the Germans now lie in ruins," the Afghans they had trained were still there.[114] As if to demonstrate the shift in zeitgeist, the Danes located an archive of German-produced data on Khost's forests and agriculture and ferreted it to an umbrella NGO archive in Peshawar.[115]

Once a showcase for the national economy, the Khost basin had become a hive of transnational humanitarianism. De-mining was the first priority: the 40th Army and the Afghan Army had left a death strip of 300,000 antipersonnel mines around Khost City, while locals estimated another 200,000 mines scattered throughout the province.[116] Peshawar-based UNOCA teams conducted de-mining operations, while the UN authorized two Peshawar-based Afghan NGOs to run de-mining operations of their own.[117] Soon, a startlingly diverse range of institutions moved in to run schools, hospitals, and job centers. Yet more astounding than the range of activities *per se* was the diversity of organizations. European state agencies were there, as were the UNDP and UNICEF. Joining them, however, were sixty independent NGOs funded by the donations of Norwegians, Swedes, French, Germans, Britons, and British *Muslims*, in the case of the British group Muslim Aid.[118] No longer a frontline in the struggle for the national economy or the imagined nation-state, Khost had become a swap meet for transnational institutions and identities.

---

[111] Juliette Fournot, quoted in Vallaeys, 458.

[112] Rubin, 171.

[113] Marion Couldrey (ACBAR), "Eastern Paktia Coordination Status Report" (June 24, 1992), 1.

[114] Asgar Christensen and Bernt Glatzer (Danish Committee for Aid to Afghan Refugees / DACAAR), *Coordinated Rehabilitation in the Khost Region: A Brief Profile of Khost and a Proposal for a Joint Approach* (Peshawar: DACAAR, 1991).

[115] Marion Couldrey (ACBAR), "Eastern Paktia Coordination Status Report" (June 24, 1992), 2.

[116] Ibid., 13.

[117] The two Afghan NGOs were the Mine Clearance Planning Agency and Afghan Technical Consultants.

[118] For the full list, see Couldrey, 59–60.

Using the same trails and roads as Pashtun loggers of a generation ago, development now flourished not in the nation-state but in its absence. Yet NGOs were hardly immune to the challenges that had bedeviled the West Germans. The state was nowhere; culturally alien Afghans, everywhere. New, however, was an awareness that locals had to be the subjects, not the objects, of development. "In the absence of anything like a state power which could provide peace and justice," wrote one aid coordinator, "tribes should be invented if they did not already exist."[119] And the new humanitarians were also self-aware enough to see the interlocutor problem for what it was, recognizing their native informants as "the man who spoke a Western language most fluently, but by no means [he] with a leading or decisive role." Echoing Häselbärth's old gripes, the coordinator noted that "NGOs have complained that every time they come to an area they meet another *shurā*." And yet, she continued: "So what? Do we want to aid *shurā*s, khans, and commanders? It is important to find out whom these representatives represent and whom they do not represent. It may neither be possible nor desirable to avoid all these representatives, but at the same time it is irresponsible to avoid close contacts with the whole population."[120]

Doing business in Khost, however, depended on goodwill not only with local tribes but also with the likes of Jallaludin Haqqani.[121] When the Afghan Army garrison surrendered, the conquering *mujāhidin* groups established a "Security Council" that claimed a monopoly on provincial security and military affairs but devolved most other business to the tribal *shurā*s. The humanitarian greenfield was fleeting, as the Security Council quickly sprouted a "Technical Committee" that oversaw humanitarian activity. Humanitarians had to register with the Council before consulting with local tribes on projects, were required to submit copies of technical documents to the Council, and were subject to opaque regulations and penalties if tribes registered complaints. In early 1992, the Security Council began overriding tribal *shurā*s' choices over developmental projects.[122] NGOs could do nothing but "encourage tribal *shurā*s to defend their own decisions and to ask their representatives to speak out on their behalf." Without the paladin of the state, humanitarian actors turned out to be precariously dependent on the illiberal *mujāhidin* groups.

Such naïveté belonged to the zeitgeist. Throughout the 1980s, Western observers had seen in groups like Poland's Solidarity a nascent "civil society" capable of deliberating on its shared interests and future without the "leading

---

[119] Ibid., 7.

[120] Ibid., 8.

[121] Asgar Christensen and Bernt Glatzer (Danish Committee for Aid to Afghan Refugees/DACAAR), *Coordinated Rehabilitation in the Khost Region: A Brief Profile of Khost and a Proposal for a Joint Approach* (Peshawar: DACAAR, 1991).

[122] Marion Couldrey (ACBAR), "Eastern Paktia Coordination Status Report" (June 24, 1992), 11.

role" of the Communist Party.[123] Where such institutions were not rooted in authoritarian societies' past, the thought went, money could implant them in their future. SCA's Anders Fänge explained that UNOCA authorized roughly a million dollars to fund Afghan NGOs and "created a system where you, as an Afghan, if you had a Board of Trustees and a few scraps of paper, could get a grant of $10,000 with very little supervision over how you could spend it."[124] Thirty-five indigenous NGOs had registered with UNOCA by the end of 1990; another forty by the end of 1991.[125] Predictably, however, "the vast majority of the NGOs that were founded in this period were fraudulent."[126] Complaints mounted, too, as UNOCA sought to administer both Kabul charities and the alphabet soup of Peshawar-based NGOs.[127]

But the new faith – not the national economy, not socialism, but civil society – was a growing church. In 1991, UNICEF and the Afghan Women's Council (the successor to DOWA) polled Kabuli women on their needs, and by the end of the year, UNICEF and the Women's Council ran workshops in knitting, embroidery, raising chickens, and other home-based revenue-generating skills.[128] Some 500 women received training in "leadership" and "community-building." In 1992, one report foresaw, UNIFEM could commence work with the Afghan bureaucracy "to ensure that, in planning and executing their projects, the agencies concerned should take the needs of women into account." In a set piece dating back to at least the 1960s but updated for the new internationalist zeitgeist, a UN service, UNIDATA, trawled the country, generating statistics on "human welfare indicators."[129] Stripped of their embarrassing associations with Sovietism, UN agencies could prove useful political handmaidens of politically neutralized development. States, no longer the enemy, could be educated to uphold their responsibility to protect.

Yet as the troubles in Khost had shown, civil society initiatives depended on control of territory. In the context of Kabul, this meant, for better or for worse, that without Soviet-trained officers and SCUD missiles guarding the capital, there would be no Afghan bureaucracy to enlighten. Not only the

---

[123] Andrew Arato, "Civil Society Against the State: Poland 1980–81," *Telos* (Spring 1981), 34–6. Tellingly, the scholarly study of civil society exploded nearly simultaneously with the collapse of the Soviet Union and the Republic of Afghanistan. The key work here was Arato and Cohen, *Civil Society and Political Theory.*

[124] Author Interview, Anders Fänge, conducted via telephone from Berlin, Germany, September 17, 2014.

[125] UNOCA, "Afghanistan. Operation Salam Report for 1991," 2.

[126] Author Interview, Anders Fänge, conducted via telephone from Berlin, Germany, September 17, 2014.

[127] UNOCA, "Operation Salam Programme for 1991. Progress Report January-June 1991. Humanitarian and Economic Assistance Programmes Relating to Afghanistan," 9.

[128] "Afghanistan. Operation Salam Report for 1991," 35.

[129] "Ghazni Health Facilities Map" (UNIDATA, 1989); "Province of Paktyka: Tribal Territories" (UNIDATA, 1990); for one example of several provincial socioeconomic surveys, see "Afghanistan, Wardak Province: a Socio-economic Profile" (Peshawar: UNIDATA, 1991).

complaints of humanitarian groups under Haqqani and Hekmatyar, but also the disappearance of the earlier UNOCA mission to the Panjshir had suggested as much. If *mujāhidin* groups could collapse the pocket of Kabuli power altogether, UNOCA activities in the capital would have to halt. Granted, since the UN also funneled aid to NGOs through Peshawar, its influence in the frontier would not disappear. But as NGOs pondered their willingness to feed, heal, and educate tens of tens of millions of people from the Indus to the Amu, it was unclear who, exactly, would take over state functions in the space shattered by the PDPA's irredentist fantasies.

When, then, the Soviet Union collapsed in December 1991, leaving the Afghan Army unpaid and unfed, civil war devoured dreams of civil society. In early 1992, Qandahar fell to the *mujāhidin* commander Gul Agha Sherzai, a powerful rival of the Karzais. In April 1992, Kabul was surrounded from the north by Ahmad Shah Mas'ud's and 'Abd al-Rashid Dostum's northern militias, the south by Hekmatyar's *Hezb-i Islāmi*, and from the east by a separatist wing of *Hezb-i Islāmi*. The rising transnational waters had reached the peak of the nation-state and its link to the international order. Najibullah was surrounded.

Najib's final actions as President of the Republic of Afghanistan bore unintended irony. Firstly, he personally oversaw the departure of all remaining Soviet (now Russian) advisers, the last witnesses to a multidecade Soviet attempt to forge socialism at the scale of the nation-state. Najib later tried himself to fly to India, but Dostum's militias had captured the airport. The transnational armies once conceived as a project to get around the territorial state had consumed it entirely. Bodyguards escorted Najib to the UN compound, where he took refuge. On April 24, 1992, Najib's Republic was formally replaced by an Islamic State of Afghanistan, which was swiftly recognized at the UN. The UN had recognized the transnational seizure of power as legitimate, while Najib, effectively stateless, clung to the one neutral piece of territory in the country.[130]

Conclusion

By the spring of 1992, Afghanistan was a wreck. Warlords battled with one another for control of territory, roads, and cash crops like opium. Formerly a marginal producer of poppies, Afghanistan had become the world's leading origin of opium by an enormous margin; today, it produces over ninety percent of world supply.[131] The visions of Iurii Sal'nikov and colleagues – connect grain in the Helmand with processing plants in Qandahar and feed a nation – had

---

[130] Kalinovsky, 208. See also Phillip Corwin, *Doomed in Afghanistan: A UN Officer's Memoir of the Fall of Kabul and Najibullah's Failed Escape, 1992* (New Brunswick: Rutgers University Press, 2003).

[131] United Nations Office on Drugs and Crime, "UNODC 2010 World Drug Report," 43.

given way to darker transformations in the place of the Afghan economy and state in the world.

Still, the magnitude of the human tragedy should not distract, analytically if not emotionally, from the ways in which that country – not in spite of but in many ways *because* of the Soviet occupation – had been drawn into fundamentally global processes. Sal'nikov and Communists had thought in terms of national markets, but the violence they engendered embedded Afghanistan into a global industry that generates hundreds of billions of dollars. Humanitarians crossed state borders to help "the Afghan people," but ended up reifying transnational visions of Afghan nationalism. Gorbachëv sought to buttress the staying power and legitimacy of a sovereign Afghan state through his endorsement of the Geneva Accords and acceptance of peacekeeping missions, but ended up delegitimizing Third World state sovereignty in the process.

Together, however, these ironies forged the prerequisites of post-Cold War humanitarianism and internationalism. The pitiful staffing of UNGOMAP actually made it the exception in a new generation of peacekeeping operations. Operations in Mozambique, El Salvador, and Cambodia eased the transition from war to peace, and between 1987 and 1994, "the number of peacekeepers in blue helmets rose from ten thousand to seventy thousand, and the peacekeeping budget swelled from $230 million to $3.6 billion, dwarfing the regular operating budget of the U.N."[132] Yet as the UN intervened in theaters like Somalia, Haiti, and Rwanda not to promote "the political process" but – to quote a 1992 Security Council Resolution – because of "the magnitude of the human tragedy," the limitations of UN deployments became painfully clear.[133] In Srebrenica and Rwanda as in UNOCA-administered Afghanistan, UN peacekeeping forces stood by passively as transnational armies murdered civilians and overthrew governments. As refugees from these conflicts fled, often to seek asylum in European countries, humanitarians faced a moral "problem from hell."[134] The "failed state," not the totalitarian socialist state, represented the new paradigm for Third World crises, but it was nigh impossible to do good in such arenas without superpower intervention. Was it legitimate for intellectuals who had originally sought to *escape* politics to endorse NATO-led military interventions into postcolonial states?

For the moment, however, Afghanistan, even if wracked by civil war, had not yet raised this precise set of questions. From 1992 to 1996, the United Nations distributed tens of thousands of tons of food aid and even conducted a national polio immunization campaign that reached 2.4 million children.[135]

[132] Mazower, *Governing the World*, 362.
[133] Ibid., 383.
[134] Samantha Power, *"A Problem from Hell": America and the Age of Genocide* (New York: Basic Books, 2002).
[135] "Afghanistan and the United Nations," available online at: www.un.org/News/dh/latest/afghan/un-afghan-history.shtml.

More strikingly, as data collected by a Peshawar-based umbrella group in the autumn of 1992 showed, international NGOs had invaginated the Afghan state to an extent unimaginable a decade ago. NGOs covered different geographical areas of Afghanistan, had their own external funders, and varied between semi-autarkic fund-raising *and* implementing organizations (like SCA) and groups that tended more often to fund or implement *other* groups' projects. Among the groups administering public health, the Ministry of Public Health was there, but only as one of dozens of "implementor organizations," a colorless term that tossed in the state alongside NGOs.[136] Examined closely, moreover, the Ministry's geographical reach was limited to Kabul and the eastern provinces. Part of the reason for the limited reach of the acronymized "MOPH" was, of course, the fact that many NGOs worked with the sovereign Security Council of the Northern Areas, a quasi-state organization led by Dostum and Massoud.

Left unresolved, however, was the status of these alien NGOs if a strong and xenophobic government ever took control in Kabul. Humanitarian groups owed their presence in Afghanistan, after all, to the weak institutionalization and, later, destruction of the Afghan state. With the Soviet Union freshly collapsed, the spirit of a new world order in the air, and Afghanistan overflowing with wounded, traumatized bodies whose amelioration manifestly exceeded indigenous "state capacity," little suggested a sea change. But Pakistan had not yet completed its quest for "strategic depth." The dream of removing an Afghan state from international society remained incomplete. Distorted by Persianate Kabuli regimes for decades, Pashtun nationalism still smoldered. With Najib languishing in the UN compound, the possibilities for Pakistani transnational projects and Pashtun nationalism to fuse and bring all the old possibilities of territoriality to bear remained untested. If modernization had now been decisively consigned to Afghanistan's past, what was to stop medievalization from constituting its future?

---

[136] ACBAR, "Health Facilities in Afghanistan" (November 17, 1992), Harvard University Map Collection. The data from this report was originally drawn from A.S. Osmani and W. Noori, *Health Facilities in Afghanistan by Location* (Peshawar: November 1992).

Conclusion

The USSR was not a possible object of admiration, but it was an object of solidity. Its defining feature was its permanence. It was an inevitable part of the planet's architecture: obsolete but immovable. Its going suddenly disclosed a set of hidden linkages that pulled various aspects of my familiar, home experience away after it.... This was the biggest intellectual change of my lifetime – the replacement of one order of things, which I had just had time to learn and to regard as permanent, with a wholly different one, in radical discontinuity with it.[1]

As shelling turned Kabul to rubble, Islamabad activated new parts of its regional project. Pakistani Islamic institutions like the World Muslim Congress had begun developing transnational ties with Central Asian, Bashkir, and Tatar Muslim organizations under *perestroĭka*, but as the Soviet Union fragmented, a world of states beckoned.[2] Pakistani diplomats visited and established diplomatic ties with all five Central Asian republics, Azerbaijan, and Russia in November and December 1991.[3] But as the Gulf War, compared to the Battle of Karbala by Pakistani military elites, showed, Islamic unity could not be assumed. Pakistan needed a new regional architecture.[4] The Pakistan Army, noted one newspaper, could not rely on the "gallant but hopelessly inadequate Pakistani fleet" to protect the "jugular vein" of oil shipping lanes in the event of a war with India, but the "new strategic scenario" promised to change everything.[5] Bolstered by thousands of miles of "strategic depth," awash in

---

[1] Francis Spufford, "Response: Part I," *Crooked Timber* Blog, available online at: http://crookedtimber.org/2012/06/11/response-part-i/.
[2] Dietrich Reetz, "Pakistan and the Central Asian Hinterland Option," *Journal of South Asian and Middle Eastern Studies XVII* 1 (Fall 1993), 54.
[3] "Central Asia: Islamic World's New Frontier," *Dawn*, January 15, 1992.
[4] *Dawn*, January 29, 1991.
[5] Naeem Safraz, "The New Strategic Scenario," *Dawn* Supplement, January 15, 1992, 5.

Turkmen, Iranian, and Azeri oil, and in command of a reserve force of Islami-
cized Pashtun bodies, the Pakistani janissary state could become formidable.[6]

And formidable it would have to be, for from Islamabad's point of view,
the end of the Cold War only intensified the merciless competition with India.
In late 1992, US Senator Larry Pressler (author of nuclear proliferation-related
sanctions against Pakistan) traveled to Delhi and argued that Turkey, Iran, Central Asia, Afghanistan, and Pakistan risked becoming "a fundamentalist belt."[7]
To Pakistani policy planners, India was trying to enlist Washington in an anti-
Islamic crusade reaching from Babri to Baghdad.[8] Islamabad had no choice
but to respond. In November 1992, the Ministry of Education ended prefer-
ential quotas for Afghan refugees at Pakistani universities, and a month later,
authorities forced all Afghan political parties operating on Pakistani territory to
close.[9] In mid-January 1993, authorities announced that the 3.3 million Afghan
refugees would have to return home.[10]

As Pakistani-supported parties battled for Kabul, in Qandahar, the situation
that Soviet advisers had once managed spun out of control. "The road from
Qandahar to Quetta, a crucial link for Qandahar's economy, was controlled
by numerous armed bands, each of which demanded from truckers and other
travelers."[11] Tired of supporting Gulbuddin Hekmatyar, but also distrustful
of the local warlords who refused Pakistani truckers transit rights, Pakistani
military élites began negotiating with so-called Taliban, pious militants who
had studied at Pakistani *madrasahs*, to liberate the roads for Pakistani truckers. On October 12, 1994, Taliban militias captured Spinboldak; on November 4, Qandahar. In December 1994, they established a one-toll system along
the Quetta–Qandahar road, opening the route to Pakistani truckers. Benazir
Bhutto's government soon established trade links with Turkmenistan.

Pushing northwards, the Taliban captured Kabul on September 26, 1996.
Najib was now truly doomed: after UN personnel took the last flight out
of town, Taliban forces broke into the UN compound. "The next morning,
Najibullah and his brother were found hanged from a traffic post at the Ariana
traffic circle in central Kabul; Najibullah's corpse was bound by ropes to keep
it from falling apart. Banknotes were stuffed into his mouth and pockets and
cigarettes were shoved into the nostrils of his brother, symbolizing corruption
and betrayal."[12]

The Taliban's public desecration of Najib, not to mention *where* they had
kidnapped the former President from, was telling. Zahir Shah and Daoud had

---

[6] Ahmad Rashid, "Seizing a Historic Opportunity," *Dawn* Supplement, January 15, 1992, 1.
[7] *The Hindustan Times*, January 12, 1992.
[8] Naeem Safraz, "The New Strategic Scenario," *Dawn* Supplement, January 15, 1992, 5.
[9] *Dawn*, December 1, 1992.
[10] *Dawn*, January 7, 1993; Ihtashamul Huque, "Pakistan Unable to Support Afghan Refugees Any
Longer," *Dawn*, January 16, 1993.
[11] Kalinovsky, *A Long Goodbye: The Soviet Withdrawal from Afghanistan*, 210.
[12] Roy Gutman, *How We Missed the Story: Osama Bin Laden, the Taliban, and the Hijacking of
Afghanistan* (Washington: United States Institute of Peace Press, 2008), 76.

represented a Persianate state alienated from Afghanistan's Pashtun population while integrated into the international system; Taraki and Amin, a failed attempt to turn Afghanistan into a Pashtun fascist state that rejected internationalism; and Najib, a reformed attempt for the Kabuli state to speak, act, and be Pashtun while also embedded in nonliberal internationalist institutions. Finally, for a brief window of time, a reformed United Nations and the *mujāhidin* sack of Kabul had given Afghanistan an escape hatch back into the international sphere, as an Islamic State of Afghanistan (the name of the successor state to the Democratic Republic of Afghanistan) entered the organization whose Kabul offices had sheltered Najib. Now, however, in one blow, Najib, the Islamic State, and the UN order that had accommodated both was replaced by a perverse vision of a Pashtun-dominated Afghan state embedded only in select bilateral relationships.

That vision involved a radical break with Afghanistan's traditional relationship to the world. Rather than governing from Kabul, Taliban leader Mohammad Omar resided almost exclusively in Qandahar, former capital of the Durrani Empire and the home of the Shrine of the Cloak of the Prophet Mohammad. Publicly donning the Cloak in 1996, Omar gave himself a new title. Unlike Taraki, Omar did not declare himself to be the "Leader of the Pashtuns." Nor, unlike all leaders of Afghanistan from Dost Muhammad Khan to Amanullah, did he style himself an *Emir*, a sovereign that translated the will of God to the scale of the state. Nor even did he call himself *Shāh*, a Persian term for a king that Amanullah and the Musahibans had used. Instead, Omar called himself by an Arabic term, *Emir al-Mu'minin*, "commander of the faithful," that legitimated his rule not through the state but through a transnational religious community. Rather than speaking Persian, French, or English – hitherto accepted ways for Afghan leaders to engage at the scale of the international – Mullah Omar spoke Pashto and Arabic and scarcely met with outsiders. All the same, Taliban "high medievalism" was not an outright rejection of high modernism but rather a patina of neo-traditional practices affixed to a postmodern state. Rejecting the territorial imaginaries of the nation-state, Taliban rule created a "mobility state" defined by judges administering sharia law, transported on Japanese pickup trucks and protected by Soviet weapons.

Pakistan had defanged Pashtun nationalism. When the Deputy Chief of Mission of the U.S. Embassy in Islamabad visited Taliban-ruled Qandahar, his conclusion was unambiguous: "For Pakistan, a Taliban-based government in Kabul would be as good as it can get in Afghanistan. Even though the Taliban is a Pashtoon movement, they do not seem to covet that part of a 'Pakhtunistan' that would lie on Pakistan's side of the Durand Line. Thus the ethnic factor under a Taliban-based government would be a positive, rather than a negative as in the past."[13] Pashtun statehood had been transformed, realized in a

---

[13] U.S. Embassy (Islamabad) Cable to Assistant Secretary of State for South Asia Robin Raphel, "Scenesetter for Your Visit to Islamabad: Afghan Angle" (January 16, 1997), 7, available online at National Security Archive.

partnership with Punjabis. Islamabad finally found the strategic security it desired. Jallaludin Haqqani explained: "On Pakistan's Eastern border is India – Pakistan's perennial enemy. With the Taliban government in Afghanistan, Pakistan has an unbeatable two-thousand-three-hundred-kilometer strategic depth."[14] By the late 1990s, Taliban commanders had conquered most of the north and the Hazarajat, leaving pogroms of Shi'as behind. Only small patches of northeast Afghanistan, like the Panjshir Valley, remained independent. Writing from his home base there, Ahmad Shah Mas'ud composed an open letter to the American people: "Afghanistan," he wrote, "for the second time in one decade, is once again an occupied country."[15]

Mas'ud was right. The Afghan state's possibilities for international engagement had been dramatically curtailed. Paradoxically, even as UN grain shipments fed Kabul, at the UN General Assembly, the Islamic State (not the Taliban "Emirate") continued to occupy Afghanistan's UN seat. Only Pakistan, Saudi Arabia, and the United Arab Emirates recognized the Emirate. But nor was the regime a mere puppet of its patrons: pressured by Riyadh to hand over former Saudi citizen Osama bin Laden, the Taliban refused even at the cost of losing Saudi aid.[16] Relations with other neighbors were dicey. After ethnic Turkmen fled from Taliban rule into neighboring Turkmenistan, Ashgabat complied with Kabul's demands to return the refugees, who were killed.[17] Türkmenbaşy's regime also conducted several high-level informal talks with the Taliban over possible pipeline projects, but diplomatic recognition remained fleeting. Relations with Shi'a Iran were even worse, for when Taliban armies captured the northern city of Mazar-i Sharif in August 1998, they not only massacred Hazara Shi'a but also stormed the Iranian consulate and murdered Iranian diplomats and journalists.[18] Iran massed 70,000 soldiers on the border, but eventually backed away from intervention to support Mas'ud and Shi'a militias.

All the same, humanitarian aid continued to function. UN agencies delivered hundreds of thousands of tons of food, vaccinated Afghan children against polio, and ran educational programs (including home-schooling programs for girls).[19] NGOs like SCA continued to work in the country, but the Taliban's attitude toward them was inconsistent. "They were hard to love, stupid, and

---

[14] Aslam Khan, "Interview of Jalaluddin Haqqani," *The News*, October 20, 2001.

[15] Ahmad Shah Mas'ud, "A Message to the People of the United States of America," (1998), available online at: www.afghan-web.com/documents/let-masood.html.

[16] Barnett Rubin, "The Political Economy of War and Peace in Afghanistan," in *Afghanistan from the Cold War through the War on Terror* (New York: Oxford University Press, 2013), 59.

[17] Muhammad Tahir, "Peace Talks with the Taliban in Turkmenistan?" *Radio Liberty*, May 27, 2011, available online at: www.rferl.org/content/peace_talks_taliban_turkmenistan/24207460 .html.

[18] Human Rights Watch, *Afghanistan: The Massacre in Mazar-i Sharif*, November 1, 1998, Document C1007, available online at: www.unhcr.org/refworld/docid/45c9a4b52.html.

[19] "Afghanistan & the United Nations," available online at: www.un.org/News/dh/latest/afghan/ un-afghan-history.shtml.

arrogant," recalled Börje Almqvist of his Taliban interlocutors. As an in-house SCA report explained, "the Taliban represents the political power of a state, but the administrative function of a state is largely missing." Some ministers had "a vision of a state, but it remains questionable whether the Taliban leadership's concept of a state goes very much beyond a rigid interpretation of Shariat."[20]

As long Taliban ministers did not have to put their signature to paper – and risk rustication to Qandahar – NGOs enjoyed a degree of freedom. SCA ran schools for more than 20,000 Afghan girls in provinces in northern and eastern Afghanistan.[21] In Kunar Province, a savvy mullah exploited the internal refugee crisis to revamp the school system, replacing incompetent male teachers with overqualified Kabuli professional women who had fled the chaos in the capital.[22] Not only that, the mullah's underlings imposed a ban on employing mullahs from the "crazy crescent" – Ghazni, Wardak, Qandahar, or Helmand Provinces – in public institutions. Neighboring Laghman Province, ruled by a harsher Taliban governor, saw no such liberalizations.[23] Incredibly, even in Qandahar itself, SCA educated 3,000 girls – a huge improvement from the mere hundreds of girls educated under Daoud.[24] SCA's Anders Fänge hired third-party Afghans to investigate whether the figures were bogus. And they were off – but by less than one percent.

Such an arbitrary "system" was, however, obviously vulnerable. International organizations' lack of discretion tested Taliban ministers' patience. When the World Food Programme announced a program to train Kabuli women to work as bakers (to process UN grain shipments), a line of at least 500 women in *burqas* stretched around the block. WFP staff had, however, "foolishly forgot that the entrance to their compound was literally across the street from the Pakistani Embassy." Taliban religious police rushed to shut down the training sessions; WFP counterdemands that "there are no back doors, only front doors" only aggravated Taliban interlocutors.[25] Disastrously, in the summer of 1998, Taliban leaders demanded that Kabul-based NGOs move their operations to the ruins of the Soviet-built Kabul Polytechnic University, part of an effort to monitor foreigners more closely.[26]

[20] "Workplan & Budget 2000–2001," "The Political Situation & the International Assistance," 12; Folder 60 [2000–2004], SCA Institutional Archives.

[21] "Annual Report 1998," "SCA Primary School Statistics"; Folder 56 [1999–1998], SCA Institutional Archives.

[22] "Field Trip Report of a Journey to SCA-Supported Girls Twin School Bibi Ayesha in Kunar Province" (March 24, 1999), Personal Archive of Börje Almqvist.

[23] Author Interview, Börje Almqvist, Stockholm, Sweden, June 22, 2014.

[24] Author Interview, Anders Fänge, conducted via telephone from Berlin, Germany, September 17, 2014.

[25] Author Interview, Börje Almqvist, Stockholm, Sweden, June 22, 2014.

[26] "Annual Report 1998," "The Political Situation & International Assistance 1998," ix, Folder 56 [1999–1998], SCA Institutional Archives.

The aid community protested, but Taliban ministers were firm. "We Muslims believe God the Almighty will feed everybody one way or another," said the Planning Minister. "If the foreign NGOs leave, then it is their decision."[27] Fänge called the Taliban's bluff, ordering all of SCA's office materials moved to Jalalabad; a few days later, police raided SCA's (empty) Kabul offices.[28] Fänge eventually negotiated SCA's return to Kabul – part of "the piecemeal battle for the good" waged by the forty-odd expats present in Kabul from 1998 to 2001. But the Swedes' tenacity constituted the exception to the rule. The Taliban's recklessness encouraged what Fänge dubbed the "big dragons" of aid – the American USAID, the British Department for International Development (DFID), and the European Commission's European Community Humanitarian Office (ECHO) – to close their purses. ECHO, one of the largest donors in the world, cancelled all aid projects in Kabul, where NGOs fed over half of the population.[29] DFID announced "that NGOs sending their international staff to Afghanistan would get their funding from the British Government cancelled."[30] London's politics of life went global at a donors' meeting in Tokyo in the autumn of 1998, when major aid agencies officially encouraged NGOs to withdraw "international staff." Afghan nationals, needless to say, were not so privileged. "The air had gone out of the balloon," recalled Almqvist. Once a developmental hothouse, shattered Afghanistan stood on the margins of the world.

Failed Planets

Afghanistan's Cold War took place in the context of shifts in the relationship between the global projects of socialism, development, and humanitarianism. The "socialist" world was always internally diverse, but even Hungary's János Kádár stressed that "the foundation of Hungary's people's economy is socialist [...] Everything else can be a useful supplement to this, but nothing else."[31] Yet such dogmatism was soon fleeting. In China, Deng Xiaoping scuttled a Soviet-style Ten-Year Development Plan and announced market reforms. Following China's lead, Vietnam shifted to a "socialist-oriented market economy" in 1986. Eastern European economies that had survived by borrowing Western currency to finance export-led growth faced mounting bills and low growth.[32] Lacking the political legitimacy to cut subsidies or fire workers, Eastern Bloc

27 *Agence France-Presse*, "Taliban Reject Warnings of Aid Pull-Out," July 16, 1998.
28 Author Interview, Börje Almqvist, Stockholm, Sweden, June 22, 2014.
29 Ahmad Rashid, *Taliban: Militant Islam, Oil, and Fundamentalism in Central Asia* (New Haven: Yale University Press, 2000), 72.
30 "Annual Report 1998," "The Political Situation & International Assistance 1998," ix, Folder 56 [1999–1998], SCA Institutional Archives.
31 Jason McDonald, "Transition to Utopia: A Reinterpretation of Economics, Ideas, and Politics in Hungary, 1984 to 1990," *East European Politics and Societies* 7(2) (1993), 214.
32 Stephen Kotkin, "The Kiss of Debt: The East Bloc Goes Borrowing," 80–92.

élites plunged into debt and rendered themselves vulnerable to the "political bank runs" that erupted in 1989.[33]

With socialism embodied by Kabul's Pul-i Charkhi Prison, Romanian orphanages, and crumbling apartment blocks, the Left was swimming upstream. When ANC leader Nelson Mandela, whose party had long been allied with the South African Communist Party, was released from prison in 1990, he underlined that "the nationalization of the mines, banks and monopoly industries is the policy of the ANC, and a change or modification of our views in this regard is inconceivable."[34] Two years later, it had become conceivable. Visiting the World Economic Forum in Davos, Mandela "had some very interesting meetings with the leaders of the Communist Parties of China and Vietnam. They told him frankly as follows: 'We are currently striving to privatize state enterprises and invite private enterprise into our economies. We are Communist Party governments, and you are a leader of a national liberation movement. Why are you talking about nationalization?'" With Soviet socialism discredited, both old rivals like China, allies like Vietnam, and Third World friends like the ANC jumped into bed with the sirens of globalization.

Just like that, "structural conflict" turned out to be anything but. Both the Soviet and Third World projects had failed. For many on the Left, this sensation of being betrayed by the future altogether, whether in the form of socialism or the nation-state – "the inability to open freedom onto the unchartered territories of the future" – demanded a shift "from the politics of radicality to the politics of expediency."[35] For those, like MSF's founders, who left the church early, it meant a shift from a politics of class to an antipolitics of humanity. For those who left late, it meant the shift from justice at the scale of the nation-state and the national economy to justice at the scale of Europe, facilitated not in defiance of, but in communion with, financial globalization. Tellingly, it would be over debates like asylum that exposed most painfully the contradictions of a new political imagination of justice. As European countries' immigration officers inspected the scarred bodies and shattered souls of asylum seekers for proof of trauma, the body of power once used against the Soviets had come home.[36]

Not only humanitarians but also superpowers had redefined their relationship with the Third World. As the Soviet threat waned, Washington analysts hyped up the dangers presented by so-called "failed states" that provided limited services or security within their borders.[37] Terrifying future scenarios no

---

[33] Stephen Kotkin and Jan Gross, *Uncivil Society: 1989 and the Implosion of the Communist Establishment* (New York: The Modern Library, 2009).

[34] Andrew Ross Sorkin, "How Mandela Shifted Views on Freedom of Markets," *New York Times* Dealbook Blog, December 9, 2013, available online at: http://dealbook.nytimes.com/2013/12/09/how-mandela-shifted-views-on-freedom-of-markets/.

[35] Achille Mbembe, quoted in Shipley, Comaroff and Mbembe, "Africa in Theory," 675–6.

[36] Fassin, "Truth Ordeal: Attesting Violence for Asylum Seekers," 109–29.

[37] Robert H. Jackson, *Quasi-States: Sovereignty, International Relations and the Third World* (Cambridge: Cambridge University Press, 1990).

longer derived from nuclear standoff. "When the Berlin Wall was falling," wrote journalist Robert Kaplan, "I happened to be in Kosovo, covering a riot between Serbs and Albanians. The future was in Kosovo, I told myself that night, not in Berlin."[38] Without some dexterous mix of immigration control, development aid, and interventionism, the old Third World would overrun the First. In 1993, the CIA began researching the vulnerability of states to collapse and revolution, and the 2002 National Security Strategy placed the former Third World at the center of its foreign policy.[39] "America," it argued, "is now threatened less by conquering states than we are by failing ones."

But the mania of ranking failed states was a troubled enterprise from the start. Enthralled to the territorial state and economy as the only possible unit of analysis, the concept remains a conceptual sleight of hand not particularly helpful for understanding path dependencies that have led polities *away* from imaginaries of the fiscally buoyant, globally integrated nation-state. Empires in the region that today comprise Pakistan and Afghanistan, for example, have never had a centralized system of taxation, a corruption-free bureaucracy, or the ability to subdue tribal rebellions. And many "failed states" fit quite successfully into the global economy. In 2011, some of the top recipients of foreign direct investment outside of the rich world included Angola, Nigeria, Pakistan, and Libya; comparatively stable Tanzania did not crack the top one hundred.[40] Because the "failed state" paradigm assumes a national grid of development as the norm, it fails to articulate the dependent role that countries may articulate in transnational webs of finance, mineral extraction, and even the development industry itself.

More fundamentally, however, perhaps "sovereignty has become a chump's game."[41] Denizens of "failed states" remain shut out of the rest of the international state system: Afghan passport holders, for example, can travel visa-free only to Somalia, Mauritania, and Mali.[42] European countries have classified countries like Serbia, Macedonia, and Bosnia-Herzegovina as a "safe countries" for purposes of asylum policy, making it nigh impossible for refugees to leave unsafe Europe for safe Europe – they are, after all, already in the latter. Ironically, in belittling such migrants as coming for "purely economic reasons,"

---

[38] Robert D. Kaplan, "The Coming Anarchy," *The Atlantic Monthly* (February 1994), available online at: www.theatlantic.com/magazine/archive/1994/02/the-coming-anarchy/304670/?single_page=true.

[39] "PITF Reports and Replicant Data Sets," Center for Global Policy, available online at: http://globalpolicy.gmu.edu/political-instability-task-force-home/pitf-reports-and-replicant-data-sets/.

[40] James Ferguson, *Global Shadows: Africa in the Neoliberal World Order* (Durham: Duke University Press, 2006), 226; *CIA World Factbook*, information for foreign direct investment available online at: www.cia.gov/library/publications/the-world-factbook/rankorder/2198rank.html.

[41] Rosa Brooks, "Failed States, or the State as Failure?" *University of Chicago Law Review* 72, 1193.

[42] "The Wanderers," *The Economist*, August 10, 2011, available online at: www.economist.com/blogs/dailychart/2011/08/visa-free-travel.

nationalist politicians have captured a broader point.[43] Today, in contrast to most of human history, most present differences in income between people in the world can be attributed to one's *country* of origin rather than one's position inside said country."[44] Even equalizing income inequality *within* every country would only reduce global income inequality levels to disparities similar to those inside South Africa today.

Without structural changes to global trade or migration regimes, one might speak less of failed states than a failed planet. What to do? "Failed states," suggests Rosa Brooks, might be persuaded to look into indefinite "nonstate" arrangements: "indefinite international administration by the UN, similarly indefinite administration by a regional body such as the EU or African Union, [or a] long-term 'partnership' or 'affiliation' with one or more 'successful' states."[45] More audaciously, Alden Young wonders if the "brutal realism" embodied by Qatar or the United Arab Emirates – millions of guest workers tolerated as economic migrants but denied the subjectivity of refugees or asylum-seekers – represents an improvement on Fortress Europe.[46] In a world, in short, of manifest hierarchy between nation-states, is it necessary to sacrifice the "thick rights" of the European welfare state if they find geographical expression in Ceuta or Lampedusa? Absent *de facto* equality between states, is there anything worth recovering in the tradition of "sovereign equality" embodied by the UN of the 1970s?[47]

The hesitation we may have in finding answers to these questions accounts for the ironic lens through which one can view Natalia Vasil'evna Ianina and her Komsomol advisers. To us, they represent a fleeting moment when people accepted the legitimacy of the state as a primary actor in development. The difference between their developmental vision then and how we remember it today, on the other hand, highlights how the Soviet collapse transformed the possibilities for development. We may never be, nor should we be, nostalgic for the Soviet Union itself. But without the solidity that the Soviet experiment lent to the global architecture of sovereignty, all that was solid seems to have melted into air; "man is at last compelled to face with sober senses his real conditions of life, and his relations with his kind."[48] For Afghanistan as much as in the rest of the world, the dream of a planet of nation-states has given way

---

[43] The phrase in question (*rein wirtschaftliche Gründe*) comes from a January 2015 report on migration by Germany's Christian Social Union (CSU).

[44] Malcolm Bull, "Help Yourself," *London Review of Books* 35(4) (2013), 15–17.

[45] Brooks, 1191.

[46] Alden Young, "Qatar, Inequality, and the Possibilities for Humanity" (January 21, 2015), available online at: http://redseanotes.com/2015/01/21/qatar-inequality-and-the-possibilities-for-humanity/.

[47] Umut Özsu, "Sovereign Equality Today" (January 19, 2015), available online at: http://blog.oup.com/2015/01/sovereign-equality-today-pil/.

[48] Karl Marx and Friedrich Engels, "Manifesto of the Communist Party," trans. Samuel Moore, available online at: www.marxists.org/archive/marx/works/1848/communist-manifesto/.

to one of human beings. How ironic that a project committed to the withering away of the state came to undergird the nation-state's moment in global history.

The Death and Life of Soviet Development

They travel to the Vostriakovskoe Cemetery. Entering through the gates of this resting place in suburban Moscow, they walk to Plot 24. They bring their wreaths; they lay their flowers at a tombstone along the walk.[49] The small gathering of middle-aged men, some of the eighty-odd living Komsomol advisers, has come to pay their respects one last time. Scattered around the former Soviet Union, these former colleagues and friends struggle to reunite frequently. Yet when they can, they meet to recall their past adventures.[50] Some years, some meet in Moscow to make a pilgrimage to the grave of the woman who changed their lives. Their journeys have diverged, but for one autumn morning, they "remember this spiritual and courageous human being who played a noticeable role in the fates of every one of us." Ianina died over a decade ago – September 27, 1999 – but as long as these men of the last Soviet generation are alive, they return to honor her.

Three decades have passed since Komsomol-1, the first Komsomol team, arrived in Afghanistan. Since the Soviet collapse, many advisers leveraged their connections to forge new lives for themselves. Iusuf Abdullaev, a propaganda adviser for the Central Committee of DOYA from 1980 to 1983, became Uzbekistan's first-ever Ambassador to the Russian Federation and, later, Rector of Samarkand State University, a post he held until he was sacked by the Karimov regime.[51] Today, Abdullaev has retreated to quieter pursuits, running El Merosi, a historical costume theater that recruits Samarkandi youth to entertain the tourist trade and preserve local textile traditions. Alikhan Amirkhanov, an ethnic Ingush born in Kyrgyzstan who worked in Herat, became a representative in the Russian Duma and ran for President of Ingushetia in 2005.[52] Others head their local Afghanistan veterans' organizations; two, Aleksandr Belofastov and Aleksandr Rebrik, run an organization for the Komsomol advisers in Moscow. In Tajikistan, one former Komsomol adviser has reinvented himself as a capital manager; half of the academics at the Oriental Institute are former translators. Others, like Zaidullo Dzhunaïdov, who now works for Germany's international aid agency, pursue the mission of development through new institutions.

---

[49] *Mushavery*, 8.

[50] Author Interview, Vladimir Struchkov, Moscow, Russian Federation, October 23, 2012.

[51] *Mushavery*, 52; Artur Samari, "V Samarkande mitinguiut studenty: vystupleniĭ takovo masshtaba ne nabliudalos' v Uzbekistane uzhe bolee desiati let," February 21, 2005.

[52] *Mushavery*, 61.

Ianina's choice had changed their lives. "I can't find the words to talk about her," said one.[53] Advisers recall how she kicked two would-be advisers out of Chirchiq when they threw away uneaten bread because she could not trust them to live up to Soviet standards when working alongside Afghans; how she spent weeks during the scorching Dushanbe summer visiting wounded soldiers in hospitals; how she wrote letters to military veterans' Komsomol *obkoms* and *gorkoms* to secure them the wheelchairs and three-room apartments to which their "internationalist" service entitled them.[54] Perhaps internationalism had been a lie – a cynical, costly lie that killed Soviet citizens and destroyed states. But people like Ianina found a way to realize the ideals behind the cynicism, to be a model Soviet citizen in the world.

The Soviet collapse had obliterated possible lifeworlds that an earlier generation had embraced. "The whole thing started to unravel," recalled Anna Matveeva of the Soviet area studies establishment. "There was no money, no audience. The Foreign Ministry itself was in crisis. People were trying to make money…you have to have your state machine for this whole thing to make sense. If the state is totally dysfunctional, and you're trying to run some conflict management course…well, it doesn't make any sense, does it?"[55] But Afghanistan had been in the lives of many for so long that it became hard to remember anything else. "June 21, 1979," reflected Vasiliĭ Kravtsov, "… the day I first heard the word 'Pashto.'" Kravtsov's life rotated around that moment.[56] As scholars faced the decline in funding and student numbers at institutes, they were forced to recreate in friendships the intensity of common purpose that scholarship no longer offered. Only in 2000, when Gankovskiĭ retired due to health problems at the age of eighty, could Basov lecture at the Institute and have his works published by the Institute's Press. Gankovskiĭ's students dedicated an edited volume to Basov, with the inscription: "Dear Vladimir Vladimirovich Basov – from the collective of authors with unchanged feelings of friendship."[57] All the same, the legacy of the scholar looms large. In April 2011,Viacheslav Belokrenitskiĭ, the director of the Russian Federation's successor to IV AN SSSR and a Gankovskiĭ student, organized an international conference in honor of the late Gankovskiĭ's ninetieth birthday.[58]

But nor were the friendships or lessons restricted to the "domestic" post-Soviet world. Vladimir Snegirëv, *Komsomol'ksaia Pravda*'s main correspondent to Afghanistan, reflected on his friendship with a young Afghan from Herat. In the spring of 1981, the Komsomol adviser in Herat contacted Snegirëv about "a local sixteen-year-old girl who had recently been killed in the fight with the

[53] Author Interview, Abduzahir Zakhirov, Dushanbe, Tajikistan, July 31, 2012.
[54] Author Interview, Nadmidin Shohinbudov, Dushanbe, Tajikistan, July 28, 2012.
[55] Author Interview, Anna Matveeva, London, United Kingdom, April 18, 2012.
[56] Author Interview, Vasiliĭ Kravtsov, Moscow, Russian Federation, October 23, 2012.
[57] Reprinted in Basov, *Natsional'noe i plemennoe v Afganistane*, 330.
[58] S.N. Kamenev, "Konferentsiia, posviashchennaia 90–letiiu so dnia rozhdeniia Iu. V. Gankovskogo," *Vostok. Afroaziatskie obshchestva, istoriia i sovremennost'*, 5 (2011), 169–73.

dushman. Her name was Fazilya. She became inspired by the ideals of struggle and joined the rows of the young defenders of the Revolution."

Snegirëv sensed a story. "Finally, here we had a real case of heroism and self-sacrifice. We had to write a piece at once." Snegirëv flew to Herat, where he met with Fazilya's brother, Mukhtar, "an officer, a captain by rank who was serving in the 17th Infantry Division. We talked with him for several hours. Mukhtar was about thirty, but his black hair had already greyed. When we started to talk about his sister, he began to cry. Never again did I see a Pashtun crying. As it turned out, he felt guilty for the death of his sister, since it was from him that Fazilya had first heard about the Revolution, the Soviet Union, about the possibility of living without poverty or want."

Soon, recalled Snegirëv, "on April 27, 1981, my piece, 'Fazilya's Last Fight' appeared in the *Komsomol'skaia*. All the major Afghan papers reprinted it. One of the leaders of DOYA, Farid Mazdak, wrote a poem, 'Sister of Victory,' and a little while later they set the lyrics to music, and so there was born a song about Fazilya that they often performed on TV in Kabul. In Herat, they renamed a street after the girl."[59] Upon his return to Moscow, Snegirëv wrote a book on his Afghan experiences, later translated into Dari.[60] Professional security seemed secured.

Yet Snegirëv returned to Afghanistan again and again. He grew to understand Mukhtar and Fazilya as people and as friends. Mukhtar "told me that to this day he held with him the most important desire of his childhood – to feel full after eating, if only once. A handful of boiled corn grains or a dry piece of bread could be considered a luxury in his family." Unlike the thugs who ran the PDPA, Mukhtar "was the first person that I encountered in my journey that you could really consider a conscious revolutionary. [...] I found him imbued with sympathy."

Snegirëv paused. "So what's the point? Why am I remembering all of this now? Am I ashamed of that piece in the newspaper and that book?" Maybe the internationalist myth had been a lie. Perhaps Ianina had represented that lie. Encounters with Afghans like Mukhtar, however, challenged this cynicism. "Times have changed, we all have changed, we have rejected things, denied things...but at the end of it, there's still that girl who took the AK-47 into her hands and went off into battle because she heard stories from her brother about social justice and believed in those bright ideals. She's still there. And there's still her and my own belief in the idea that the world could be built according to the rules of social justice. So that everything would be OK. Of course, it's easier to acknowledge my prior convictions, to wave them away, and strike them out from my memory. But it doesn't work, striking them out and forgetting. That past is a part of every one of us."[61]

[59] "Poslednyiĭ boĭ Fazili," *Komsomol'skaia Pravda*, April 27, 1981, 3.
[60] Vladimir Snegirëv, *Opalennyĭ porokhom rassvet* (Moscow: Molodaia Gvardiia, 1984).
[61] Vladimir Snegirëv, "1981 god. KABUL. GERAT. BAGRAM," in *Mushavery*, 30–31.

One had to redeem that past. Snegirëv did: his article may have exploited Fazilya's death; it had also moved an Azerbaijani reader to name her newborn daughter in the girl's memory. Two and a half decades later, the Azerbaijani Fazilya is married to a Turkish man. Mukhtar, reports Snegirëv, has traveled to Baku to visit the former Soviet family who pays tribute to his murdered sister.[62] Snegirëv joins them on occasion, a reminder that the Soviet project had not only destroyed, but also made, worlds. Sooner or later, however, the trip comes to an end. "I'll remain loyal to my homeland," Mukhtar reminds Snegirëv as he boards the flight to Kabul.

Afghan Pasts, Afghan Futures

More than just the flight approach separates Mukhtar's journey from the one that Viktor Samoïlenko embarked upon from Tashkent thirty years prior. Two days after the Taliban scored a coup through the assassination of Ahmad Shah Mas'ud, Osama bin Laden's al-Qaeda claimed responsibility for the terrorist attacks that killed thousands in New York City, Washington, and rural Pennsylvania on September 11, 2001. Less than a month later, the United States began a campaign to oust the Taliban from power and to capture or kill bin Laden. American forces and their Northern Alliance allies captured Kabul on November 13; Qandahar, a month later. That December, American and Afghan forces came tantalizingly close to capturing bin Laden in the same hills that Nodari Giorgadze had roamed decades prior. But like so many Taliban, bin Laden escaped into Pakistan.

What started as an al-Qaeda hunt transmogrified into the largest developmental intervention in Afghanistan's history – carried out by not only USAID and DFID, but also the biggest dragon of them all, namely the U.S. military. In a significant change from Cold War-era development, the vast majority of aid was routed through militaries, not civilian development agencies, NGOs, or the UN. Once discredited in the rice paddies of Southeast Asia, "counterinsurgency" had a second life – and death – among the opium plantations of Helmand Province. Attempts to bring in nonmilitary expertise were similarly desultory. Since the military and civilian surge of 2009–12, thousands of advisers, along with even more private contractors, bloated the Afghan capital. Few had concrete assignments; fewer still were let out of the Embassy compound. Regional experts drafted into the office of Special Representative Richard Holbrooke were rendered ineffective by White House turf battles.[63] Soon, Holbrooke was dead from a torn aorta; counterinsurgency champion David Petraeus was forced to resign from his position as CIA Director following reports that he had leaked

---

[62] Author Interview, Vladimir Snegirëv, Moscow, Russian Federation, October 22, 2012.
[63] Rajiv Chandrasekaran, *Little America: The War Within the War for Afghanistan* (New York: Knopf, 2012), Chapter 9.

classified documents to a paramour. Petraeus later plead guilty to the leaks, resulting in a sentence of two years' probation plus $100,000 in fines.[64]

Developmentalism appears to be disappearing, replaced by nothing but the brutal scramble for resources and influence. After American geologists discovered old disused Soviet geological surveys in Kabul, the United States Geological Service conducted a comprehensive geological survey, revealing the country's potential to become a major world producer of iron and copper and "the Saudi Arabia of lithium."[65] With China racing to obliterate historical sites situated on top of copper mines, an uncertain regulatory environment hardly bodes well for any fair distribution of the bonanza to the Afghan people, much less for the ecological future of Afghanistan's rivers, soils, and forests.[66] Yet as the United States, Pakistan, India, and China jockey for influence, the only power capable of playing spoiler remains none other than Russia. The Russian Embassy in Kabul has recently announced tens of millions of dollars' worth of aid to revamp old Soviet-era projects: $25 million for the Kabul Housebuilding Factory and $20 million for the old Soviet House of Science and Culture, the latter slated to become a new Russian cultural center.[67] "We want to enlarge our role in the region," says the Embassy's spokesman. "It's not only for Afghanistan, but for our own goals."

Yet these moves also take place within the context of shifts in how Moscow imagines international order itself. If the international community now speaks in terms of R2P, the Kremlin has embraced the concept of *Russkiĭ mir* – "Russian world" – as a transnational ethnic community beyond the state. In Abkhazia, South Ossetia, Transdniester, and Ukraine, Moscow has claimed that citizens of other states are, in effect, disenfranchised Russians.[68] Whereas European states rely on the categories of citizen, refugee, and asylum seeker to keep foreigners *out* of the community of citizens, Moscow has reversed this relationship to *insert* Russians into other states and destabilize them. More concerningly, however, Moscow's relationship with our post-Cold War humanitarian vocabulary is one of appropriation, not just rejection. As part of the ongoing Russian war against Ukraine, Russian President Vladimir Putin has openly compared the March 14, 2014, Crimean referendum with Kosovo's bid for independence, accused Kiev of "genocide" of Russian speakers, and

[64] Michael S. Schmidt and Matt Apuzzo, "David Petraeus is Sentenced to Probation in Leak Investigation," *New York Times*, April 23, 2015.

[65] James Risen, "U.S. Identifies Vast Mineral Riches in Afghanistan," *New York Times*, June 13, 2010, Page A1.

[66] Radio Free Europe/Radio Liberty, "Afghanistan Becomes First Country to Have Minerals Mapped," July 20, 2012, available online at: www.rferl.org/content/afghanistan-minerals-mapped/24651540.html.

[67] Kevin Sieff, "As U.S. War Ends, Russia Returns to Afghanistan With Series of Investment Projects," *Washington Post*, March 21, 2014.

[68] Timothy D. Snyder, Remarks at "Ukraine: Thinking Together" Conference, Kiev, Ukraine, May 16, 2014, available online at: www.youtube.com/watch?v=DUdXGsKuQiQ.

launched "humanitarian convoys" of military aid to rebels, all part of a strategy to obscure the annexation and occupation of Ukrainian territory by the Russian Army.[69]

The meaning of sovereignty; the ideological geography of a region; the possibilities for Russian power in the world: all have been transformed. Afghanistan's Cold War encounters have more to teach us than one might think. Our understanding of development may have changed since the supposed end of a territorial moment in history, but the most recent intervention in Afghanistan has hardly proven more successful at building states and economies than its Soviet predecessor. Once exhausted, Moscow's will to challenge Western internationalism appears recrudescent. The dreams of development, humanitarianism, and Russian power in the world together form an indelible part of Afghanistan's past, but they have become our shared future.

---

[69] "SKR zaiavil o genotside russkikh na Ukraine," BBC Russian, September 29, 2014, available online at: www.bbc.co.uk/russian/rolling_news/2014/09/140929_rn_skr_genocide_charges.

Bibliography

Interviews

Abdulazizov, Abdulwakhov. Worked as a lecturer in Persian language and literature at Tajik State University. Worked as a translator in Kabul from 1980 to 1985 before returning to work as a scholar at Tajik State University. Interview conducted in Dushanbe, Tajikistan, August 21, 2012.

Abdullaev, Rakhmatullo. Born in southern Tajikistan. Graduated from Tajik State University in 1979. Worked as a translator in Qandahar in the late 1980s. Interview conducted in Dushanbe, Tajikistan, July 25, 2012.

Almqvist, Börje. Following engagement in the Swedish anti-Vietnam War movement, worked as a journalist for Swedish newspapers, covering the Soviet occupation of Afghanistan. Worked for the Swedish Committee for Afghanistan throughout the 1980s and 1990s. Interview conducted in Stockholm, Sweden, June 22, 2014.

Begbudiev, Shokhrukh. Born in Samarkand, Uzbekistan, in 1945. Studied mathematics at Tajik State University in the 1960s and worked for the Central Committee of the Tajik SSR's LKSM. Worked as a Komsomol adviser to the Kunduz PC of DOYA from 1980 to 1981, before returning to Tajikistan and, following the dissolution of the Soviet Union, Samarkand. Interview conducted in Samarkand, Uzbekistan, September 20, 2012.

Belofastov, Aleksandr. Born in Moscow in 1952. After completing higher education in economics, worked for Komsomol from 1975 to 1985. Deployed to Afghanistan from 1985 to 1987 as an accounting and financial adviser to the Central Committee of DOYA in Kabul. Interview conducted in Moscow, Russian Federation, October 15, 2012.

Davlatov, Mamadsho. Graduated Tajik State University with a degree in history before working as an instructor at Kabul Polytechnic University from 1976 to 1983. Later studied for a *doktor nauk* title at the Oriental Institute of the Academy of Sciences of the Soviet Union from 1983 to 1985. Interview conducted in Khujand, Tajikistan, September 6, 2012.

Dzhumashev, Askar. Director of the Historical Section of the Karakalpakstan Academy of Sciences. Interview conducted in Nukus, Uzbekistan, September 12, 2012.

Ezhov, Georgiĭ. Studied Persian language and literature at the Oriental Institute of the Academy of Sciences of the USSR, graduating in 1951. Worked as a translator at Russian–Persian Bank in Tehran, Iran, from 1951 to 1958 before working as an adviser in Afghanistan from 1958 to 1961. Later worked as an economic adviser at the Soviet Embassy in Tehran in the mid 1970s. Interview conducted in Moscow, Russian Federation, April 15, 2013.

Fänge, Anders. Following youth engagement in Swedish *FLN-Grupperna*, worked as a journalist covering American politics and the Middle East. Served as field office manager for the Swedish Committee for Afghanistan from 1983 until the early 1990s; later worked for SCA in Taliban-era Afghanistan. Interview conducted by telephone from Berlin, Germany, September 17, 2014.

Forsberg, Anders. Studied in Afghanistan as a university student in Uppsala, Sweden, in the mid 1970s. Later became an organizer for the Swedish Committee for Afghanistan. Interview conducted in Uppsala, Sweden, June 28, 2014.

Häselbarth, Christoph. Worked as lead agricultural adviser for the *Paktia Projekt* for the West German Federal Ministry for Economic Cooperation in Paktia Province in the 1960s and 1970s before moving on to Sumatra, Indonesia. Later, quit career in development work to become a Christian pastor. Interview conducted in Strittmatt, Germany, April 14, 2012.

Hassanov, Hassan. Former military translator for the Soviet Army in Afghanistan; at present, Director of the Association of Veterans of the Afghan War in Samarkand, Uzbekistan. Interview conducted in Samarkand, Uzbekistan, September 20, 2012.

Hultén, Gösta. Following activism in Swedish *FLN-Grupperna*, co-authored *Afghanistan okkuperant* with Jan Stolpe and worked with the Swedish Committee for Afghanistan until 1988. Interview conducted by telephone from Arninge, Sweden, June 27, 2014.

Ivanov, Valeriĭ. Graduated from Oriental Institute of the Academy of Sciences of the USSR in 1965 before working in various capacities in Afghanistan from 1966 to 1974. Worked for GKES in Moscow from 1974 to 1979 before directing GKES' operations in Kabul from 1979 to 1991. Worked as Trade Representative of the Russian Federation to the Islamic State of Afghanistan from 1992 to 1996 and from 2002 to 2005. Interview conducted in Ignatovo, Russian Federation, November 2, 2012.

Karimov, Said. Worked as a translator in Paktia and Paktika Provinces from 1987 to 1989. Now works in the Oriental Institute of Tajik State University. Interview conducted in Dushanbe, Tajikistan, July 24, 2012.

Khaliknazarov, Khudaberdy. Graduated from Tajik State University in the early 1970s before working at the Oriental Institute in Dushanbe. Worked as a translator in Mazar-i Sharif and northern Afghanistan from 1974 to 1976. Worked as a translator for the Soviet Embassy in Tehran from 1978 to 1979. Studied for a *kandidat nauk* diploma at Moscow State University in the mid 1980s, writing a dissertation on reform movements in late nineteenth-century Iran, graduating in 1987. Worked as a translator in Kabul from 1987 to 1989. Interview conducted in Dushanbe, Tajikistan, August 2, 2012.

Kireev, Georgiĭ. Born in Verkhnedneprovsk, Ukraine, in 1956. Graduated from Kryvih Rih Technical Academy in 1975 and the Higher Komsomol School in 1981. Served as an adviser to the Qandahar PC of DOYA from 1985 to 1986. Interview conducted via telephone from Moscow, Russian Federation, November 10, 2012.

Komissarov, Nikolaĭ. Born in Kazan, Russia, in 1953. Graduated from the Kirov Chemical-Technological Institute in 1975 before working for Komsomol in Kazan from 1976 to 1982. Served as the first Komsomol adviser in Faryab, Badakhshan, from 1982 to 1983. Following the Chernobyl disaster, worked near the accident site managing containment teams. Interview conducted by telephone from Moscow, Russian Federation, October 16, 2012.

Korgun, Viktor. Studied Dari and Afghan history in university, taught Dari at Moscow area universities in the late 1960s, and later attended the Oriental Institute of the Academy of Sciences of the USSR from 1971 to 1974. Visited Afghanistan numerous times in the 1970s, serving as an adviser to the Afghan Ministry of Higher Education and translator in 1978–9. While working in *Sektor Afganistan* at IV AN SSSR in the 1980s, traveled to Afghanistan numerous times as an adviser. Interview conducted in Moscow, Russian Federation, October 15, 2012.

Kravtsov, Vasiliĭ. Born in rural southern Belarus in 1951. After serving in the Soviet Army, was invited to take intensive Pashto and Dari courses at the KGB's institutions of higher education in Moscow. Served as a trainer in the languages and cultures of Afghanistan for KGB agents outbound to Afghanistan from 1980 to 1987. Served as an adviser for tribal affairs in the KhAD from 1987 to 1991, coordinating support for Ghilzai tribes in southern Afghanistan. Interviews conducted in Moscow, Russian Federation, October 23, 2012, November 15, 2012, and April 12, 2013.

Kurbanov, Haydar. Worked as a translator for advisers in Qandahar and Kabul from 1987 to 1988. Interview conducted in Dushanbe, Tajikistan, July 26, 2012.

Laber, Jeri. Founder and Executive Director of Human Rights Watch, 1978–95. Interview conducted by telephone from Cambridge, MA, May 7, 2014.

Malik, Hafeez. Born in Lahore, British India, in 1930. Graduated from Government College (Lahore) in 1949 before coming to the United States to pursue his higher education, while also working as a correspondent for Pakistani Urdu-language newspapers. Worked since 1961 as a professor of political science at Villanova University, collaborating frequently with Soviet scholar Iuriĭ Gankovskiĭ. Interview conducted by telephone from Cambridge, MA, September 4, 2013.

Matveeva, Anna. Born in Moscow in the 1960s. Studied under Soviet Afghan specialists at the Oriental Institute of the Academy of Sciences before working for the publishing house Progress, Soviet foreign policy analysis centers, and, after the collapse of the Soviet Union, Western development agencies. Interview conducted in London, United Kingdom, April 18, 2012.

Nekrasov, Vyacheslav. Born in 1954 in Ozhgikha, Sverdlovsk *oblast'*, Russia. After completing higher education in 1977, worked as a turner and technician in Sverdlovsk *oblast'* factories and served in the Soviet Army in the Far East. Worked for Komsomol from 1980 and as Komsomol provincial adviser to Meymana, Faryab Province, in 1982. Has written numerous books on the country, returned to Afghanistan frequently, and held talks with Ahmad Shah Mas'ud, Berhanuddin Rabbani, and former Governor of Herat Province Ismail Khan. Now works as an adviser to the Russian Federal Assembly. Interview conducted in Moscow, Russian Federation, October 17, 2012.

Rachabov, Habibullo. Born in Tajikistan and graduated from Tajik State University, specializing in Oriental Studies with an emphasis on Persian- and Urdu-language cultures. Worked as a translator for Komsomol advisers in Kabul, Farah, Kunduz, Qandahar, and Asadabad from 1982 to 1984. Following return to the USSR, became an academic with research interests in the study of Afghanistan and Pakistan. Interview conducted in Dushanbe, Tajikistan, July 27, 2012.

Sal'nikov, Iuriĭ. Born in Kolomna, Russia. Studied in Leningrad in the 1970s before moving to Volgograd for Party work, eventually becoming the Second Secretary of the Committee of the central *raĭon* of Volgograd. Was tapped to work as a CC CPSU adviser to PDPA officials in Qandahar from 1984 to 1986, before returning to Party work in Volgograd from 1986 to 1991. Interview conducted in Volgograd, Russian Federation, November 4, 2012.

Samodov, Abdulrakim. Born in Kanibadam, Tajikistan. Graduated Tajik State University in 1966. Worked as a translator in northern Afghanistan from 1974 to 1979, and, later, at the Afghan Ministry of Justice, the Procurator General, and the Supreme Court of the DRA. Interview conducted in Dushanbe, Tajikistan, July 19, 2012.

Schori, Pierre. Worked as the international secretary of the Swedish Social Democratic Party and an assistant to Swedish Prime Minister Olof Palme. Later, served as State Secretary for Foreign Affairs of the Swedish Foreign Ministry from 1982 to 1991. Interview conducted in Stockholm, Sweden, June 24, 2014.

Scott, Richard ("Dick"). Worked as a contractor for USAID in Turkey in the late 1960s and early 1970s before working in Helmand Province, Afghanistan, from 1971 to 1978. Helped conceptualize, critique, and implement a drainage improvement program for Nad-i 'Ali and Marja in Helmand, and conducted several surveys on the socioeconomic life of farmers and nomads in Helmand Province. Left Afghanistan in 1978 to continue USAID work in West Africa, but has returned to Helmand both under Taliban rule as well as after 2001 to consult on drainage, irrigation, and agricultural issues in the province. Interview conducted by telephone from Tashkent, Uzbekistan, October 5, 2012.

Sharipov, Shavlat. Graduated from Tajik State University in the 1970s before beginning graduate work at the Oriental Institute of the Tajik SSR. Worked as a translator in the Panjshir Valley from 1984 to 1985, then in Kabul from 1985 to 1986. Interview conducted in Khujand, Tajikistan, September 6, 2012.

Shohinbudov, Nadmidin. Worked as a translator for Soviet military forces in Afghanistan from 1982 to 1983 and as a translator from 1985 to 1986 in Kabul, Khost, Paktia, and Paktika. Interview conducted in Dushanbe, Tajikistan, July 28, 2012.

Snegirëv, Vladimir. Born in Tomsk *oblast'* in 1947 and graduated from Ural State University in 1969 with a specialization in journalism. Worked for *Shakhterskaia Pravda*, a paper in Kemerovo *oblast'*, before accepting a job at *Komsomol'skaia Pravda* in Moscow. Was invited in 1981 to work as an adviser for *Derafsh-i Javānān (Youth Banner)*, the official paper of DOYA based in Kabul for a year, before going on to write war correspondence for *Komsomol'skaia Pravda* from Afghanistan for much of the 1980s. At present, writes for Russian newspapers. Interview conducted in Moscow, Russian Federation, October 22, 2012.

Stolpe, Jan. Born in 1940. Worked as a journalist and the editor of the Swedish newspaper *FiB/Kulturfront*. Later worked as a Stockholm-based organizer for the Swedish Committee for Afghanistan throughout the 1980s, serving as the group's Vice-Chairman and Chairman. Interview conducted in Stockholm, Sweden, June 24, 2014.

Struchkov, Viktor. Born in 1945 in Skopin, Riazanskaia *oblast'*. Worked for Komsomol in the Central Region of the Russian SFSR before becoming the head of the Section for Scholarly Youth of the Central Committee of Komsomol. Served as the lead coordinator for Komsomol advisers in Kabul from 1983 to 1985. Interview conducted in Moscow, Russian Federation, October 24, 2012.

Symington, Leslie. Daughter of Arthur Paul; now lives in Baltimore, MD. Interview conducted by telephone from Oxford, United Kingdom, October 21, 2011.

Tokareva, Galina. Born in the western Soviet Union in the 1930s. After surviving imprisonment in a Nazi concentration camp, went through Soviet orphanages and schools, and later became an *obkom* secretary for Komsomol in several locations, eventually joining the Central Committee of Komsomol. Currently works at the head archivist of the Komsomol archives. Interview conducted in Moscow, Russian Federation, November 19, 2012.

Wahidov, Abduwakhov. Born in Samarkand, Uzbekistan. Studied Persian philology and pedagogy in Samarkand before signing up to work as a translator for economic advisers in Jalalabad from 1987 to 1988. Following his service, returned to Samarkand to work in higher education. Interview conducted in Samarkand, Uzbekistan, September 20, 2012, and July 22, 2013.

Zafar, Chafi. Born in Paktia Province before attending school and university in France in the 1950s and 1960s. Married Anahita Esmatey-Wardak, the daughter of Massouma Esmatey-Wardak, and worked in the Afghan government from 1968 to 1990. Later emigrated to the United States. Interview conducted via telephone from Moscow, Russian Federation, April 30, 2013.

Zakirov, Abzuzaid. Born in Chormogzakonitadzhik, Tajikistan, in 1956. Graduated from Tajik State University in 1977 and the Higher Komsomol School in 1982. Worked as military translator in Bagram and Paktia Province, Afghanistan, from 1977 to 1979. Later, worked as a Komsomol adviser to the Kabul PC of DOYA from 1985 to 1987. Interview conducted in Dushanbe, Tajikistan, July 31, 2012.

Ziar, Modschawer. Born in rural eastern Afghanistan before attending schools in Kabul on a government scholarship. Later received a doctoral scholarship to study linguistics at the University of Bern with Professor Georges Redard, a specialist in Iranian languages and linguistics. Served as a research assistant on a major linguistic atlas of dialects of Afghanistan before returning to Kabul in 1972. Taught at Kabul University from 1972 to 1982 before leaving the country. Interview conducted in Oxford, United Kingdom, July 14, 2011.

Ziar, Sakina. Born in Laghman Province in the 1950s, and attended German-language schools in Kabul in the 1960s. Fled Afghanistan in 1982, working with the United Nations Development Corporation before settling in the United Kingdom to work as an editor for BBC Pashto language services and with international aid organizations in Afghanistan. Interview conducted in Oxford, United Kingdom, July 14, 2011.

Manuscript and Archival Sources

Official Publications

Department of State, Office of the Historian, *Foreign Relations of the United States* (FRUS)

Papers Relating to the Foreign Relations of the United States, 1921 (Volume 1)
Diplomatic Paper 1938 (Volume 2)
Diplomatic Paper 1941 (Volume 2)
1973–6: Volume E-8 (Documents on South Asia)
1973–6: Volume XI (South Asia Crisis)

Archives

Online
Afghan Death Lists. Available online at: www.om.nl/onderwerpen/internationale/
   death-lists/
Dick Scott Helmand Valley Archives. Available online at: http://scottshelmand
   valleyarchives.org/main.html
National Security Archive. Available online at: www2.gwu.edu/~nsarchiv/
RIA Novosti Online Archive. Available online at: www.visualrian.ru/ru/
Wikileaks. Available online at: https://wikileaks.org

Private Collections
Personal Archive of Börje Almqvist (Stockholm, Sweden)
Personal Archive of Anders Forsberg (Uppsala, Sweden)
Personal Archive of Valeriĭ Ivanov (Ignatovo, Russian Federation)
Personal Archive of Leslie Symington (Baltimore, Maryland)

Traditional Archives
   Ann Arbor, Michigan
      Gerald R. Ford Presidential Library
         National Security Advisor's Presidential Correspondence with Foreign Leaders
         Collection
   Ashgabat, Turkmenistan
      Tsentral'nyĭ gosudarstvennyĭ arkhiv Turkmenistana
   Berlin, Germany
      *Bundesarchiv-Lichterfelde, Stiftung Archiv der Parteien und Massenorganisa-
      tionen*
         DY 24 (Freie Deutsche Jugend)
         DY 30 (Abteilung Internationale Beziehungen)
         Bibliothek des Bundesarchivs
      Politisches Archiv des Auswärtigen Amtes
         Ministerium für Auswärtige Angelegenheiten der Deutschen Demokratischen
         Republik
         Auswärtiges Amt
         *Bundesbeauftragte für die Unterlagen des Staatssicherheitsdienstes der ehemali-
         gen Deutschen Demokratischen Republik*
   Bishkek, Kyrgyz Republic
      *Tsentral'nyĭ Gosudarstvennyĭ Arkhiv Politicheskoĭ Dokumentatsii Respubliki
      Kirgizii*
         f. 391 (Institut sotsial'no-politicheskikh issledovaniĭ TsK KP Kyrgyzstana)
   Cambridge, Massachusetts
      Harvard Map Collection

Houghton Library
    The Nation Magazine Collection
Peabody Museum Archives
    Louis Dupree Collection
Schlesinger Library on the History of Women in America
    Collection on Women Peace Corps Volunteers in Afghanistan's Smallpox Eradi-
    cation Program, 1968–71
    Gerda Lerner Papers
Cambridge, United Kingdom
    Churchill Archives Centre, Churchill College
    Vasiliĭ Mitrokhin Papers
College Park, Maryland
    United States National Archives
    Record Group 59, General Records of the Department of State
    Records of the Policy Planning Staff
Dushanbe, Tajikistan
    Bāigāni-yi Markazi-yi Dulati Çumhuriyi Toçikiston
    f. 18 (Sovet narodnykh kommisarov TSSR)
Independence, Missouri
    Harry S. Truman Library and Museum
Ithaca, New York
    Division of Rare and Manuscript Collections, Cornell University Library
    Robert R. Nathan Papers
Koblenz, Germany
    Bundesarchiv-Koblenz
    B 213 (Bundesministerium für wirtschaftliche Entwicklung und Zusammenar-
    beit)
Leipzig, Germany
    Universitätsarchiv Leipzig
Lexington, Kentucky
    Louis B. Nunn Center for Oral History
    Oral History Collections
London, United Kingdom
    National Archives
    Foreign and Commonwealth Office
    Records of the Prime Minister's Office
Moscow, Russian Federation
    Arkhiv Vneshneĭ Politiki Rossiĭskoĭ Federratsii
    f. 71 (Referentury po Afganistanu / Reports on Afghanistan)
    f. 159 (Referentura po Afganistanu / Report on Afghanistan)
    Fond Gorbachëva
    Politburo Records, 1985–91
    Gosudarstvennyĭ Arkhiv Rossiĭskoĭ Federatsii
    f. A-842 (Minzdrav RSFSR)
    f. R-6991 (Komitet po religioznym delam)
    f. R-7928 (Komitet sovetskykh zhenshchin)
    f. R-9606 (Ministerstvo srednego i vyshego obrazovaniia)
    Rossiĭskiĭ Gosudarstvennyĭ Arkhiv Ekonomiki
    f. 365 (Uchrezhdeniia po vneshnoekonomicheskim sviaziam)

Rossiĭskiĭ Gosudarstvennyĭ Arkhiv Literatury i Iskusstva
  f. 2487 (Tsentral'naia studiia dokumental'nykh fil'mov)
Rossiĭskiĭ Gosudarstvennyĭ Arkhiv Noveĭsheĭ Istorii
  f. 5 (Tsentral'nyĭ Komitet KPSS)
Rossiĭskiĭ Gosudarstvennyĭ Arkhiv Sotsial'no-Politicheskoĭ Istorii
  f. 17 (Tsentral'nyĭ Komitet KPSS)
  f. M-3, op. 13 (Sovetniki TsK VLKSM v Afganistane)
New Delhi, India
  Nehru Memorial Museum and Library
    PN Haksar Papers
    NM Kaul Papers
  National Archives of India
    Foreign & Secret Consultations
New Haven, Connecticut
  Sterling Memorial Library, Manuscripts & Archives
    Javier Pérez de Cuéllar Papers
New York, New York
  Human Rights Watch Records, Columbia University
    Jeri Laber Files
  New York Public Library
    Edward Allworth Papers
  United Nations Archives
Omaha, Nebraska
  Arthur Paul Afghanistan Collection, Criss Library, University of Nebraska-Omaha
    Arthur Paul Journals
Paris, France
  Medécins sans Frontières
    Institutional Archives
Stockholm, Sweden
  Riksarkivet
    Collection 730500 (Svenska Afganistankommitén)
  Svenska Afghanistankommitén
    Institutional Archives

Periodicals
  Afghanistan.ru
  Afghanistan-Nytt (Sweden)
  Agence France-Presse
  Agentura.ru
  Amān-i Afghān
  Aziia i Afrika segoniia
  The Atlantic Monthly
  BBC News
  BBC Russian
  Bol'shevik
  Biulleten' pressy Srednego Vostoka
  Bulletin Médecins sans Frontières
  The Christian Science Monitor

The Colgate Scene
Da Afghānistān kālaneh
Dawn
Defence Journal (Pakistan)
DRA Annual
The Economist
Eskilstuna-Kuriren med Strengnäs Tidning
El Universal (Mexico City)
Foreign Affairs
Foreign Policy
Frankfurt Allgemeine Zeitung
Geologiia nefti
God za godom
The Guardian
Hamburger Abend-Blatt
The Hindustan Times
The Hosiery Examiner
Houston Post
IA Regnum
International Committee of the Red Cross Bulletin
IRIN News
Iṣlāh
Journal de St Petersburg
Kabul Times
Karavan (Afghanistan)
Kommuna
Komsomol'skaia Pravda
KM.ru
Krasnaia Zvezda
Le Quotidien du Médecin
Les temps modernes
Los Angeles Times
London Review of Books
Merman (Afghanistan)
Mezhdunarodnye otnosheniia
Mezhdunarodnaia Zhizn'
Millat (Afghanistan)
Mirman (Afghanistan)
Mirovaia ekonomika i mezhdunarodnye otnosheniia
Kommuna
Komsomol'skaia Pravda
Krasnaia Zvezda
Mukomol'no-elevatornaia promyshlennost'
Narody Azii i Afriki
The Nassau Weekly
The Nation
New Left Review
The News (Pakistan)

The New Republic
The New York Review of Books
The New York Times
Novoe Vremia
Ogonëk
Oktiabr'
Open Democracy / Open Security
Parcham
Payām-i Zan
Pravda
Pravda Vostoka
Radio Free Europe / Radio Liberty
Ramparts
RAWA News
Reader's Digest
Reading Eagle
Rossiĭskaia Gazeta
Sālnāmeh-yi majaleh-yi Kābul
Sobesednik
Soobshcheniia turkestanskogo otdela russkogo geograficheskogo obshchestva
Sotsialisticheskaia industriia
Sovetskaia Kirgiziia
Sovetskoe vostokovedenie
Tashkentskaia Pravda
Textile World
Time
Times Higher Education Supplement
Torgovlia Rossii s Vostokom
Upolnomochen zashchishchat'
Veteran Afganistana
The Village Voice
Vokrug sveta
The Wall Street Journal
The Washington Post
Zashchita rasteniĭ ot vrediteleĭ i bolezneĭ

Printed Sources

"1975 World Conference on Women." Available online at: www.5wwc.org/conference_background/1975_WCW.html

Abdelal, Rawi. *Capital Rules: The Construction of Global Finance*. Cambridge, MA: Harvard University Press, 2009.

Abu-Lughod, Janet. "Do Muslim Women Really Need Saving? Anthropological Reflections on Cultural Relativism and Its Others." *American Anthropologist* 104(3) (2002), 783–90.

Adamec, Ludwig W. *Afghanistan's Foreign Affairs to the Mid-twentieth Century: Relations with the USSR, Germany, and Britain*. Tucson: University of Arizona Press, 1974.

"Afghanistan & the United Nations." *UN News Service*. Available online at: www.un .org/News/dh/latest/afghan/un-afghan-history.shtml#Taliban

"International Afghanistan-Hearings," Final Report, March 13–16, 1983. Edited by Bjorn Stordrange. Oslo: Afghanistan Hearings Committee, 1984.

Afghanistan Strategic Intelligence: British Records, 1919–1970. Edited by A.L.P. Burdett. Slough: Archive Editions, 2002.

"Afghanistan/Pakistan–UNGOMAP–Background." Available online at: www.un.org/ en/peacekeeping/missions/past/ungomap/background.html

Afghan Refugees Commissionerate. *Relief Work for Afghan Refugees*. Peshawar: Afghan Refugees Commissionerate, 1982.

"Afghanistan and the United Nations." Available online at: www.un.org/News/dh/ latest/afghan/un-afghan-history.shtml

Afghanistan, Wardak Province: A Socio-economic Profile. Peshawar: UNIDATA, 1991.

Afghānshanāsi-yi shuruvi dar 'arseh-yi chehel sāl. Edited by R.T. Akhramovich. Moscow: Izdatel'stvo Vostochnoĭ Literatury, 1959.

Akhramovich, R.T. "Taqiqāt dar bāreh-yi tārikh-i Afghānistān dar atahād-i shuruvi," in *Afghānshanāsi-yi shuruvi dar 'arseh-yi chehel sāl.* Edited by. R.T. Akhramovich. Moscow: Izdatel'stvo Vostochnoĭ Literatury, 1959.

Alan, Pierre and Dieter Kläy. *Zwischen Bürokratie und Ideologie: Entscheidungsprozesse in Moskaus Afghanistankonflikt.* Bern: Verlag Paul Haupt, 1999.

Alekseenkov, P. *Agrarnyĭ vopros v afganskom Turkestane.* Moscow: Mezhdunarodnyĭ Agrarnyĭ Institut, 1933.

An American Engineer in Afghanistan. Minneapolis: University of Minneapolis Press, 1948.

Andrew, Christopher and Vasiliĭ Mitrokhin. *The World Was Going Our Way: The KGB and the Battle for the Third World.* New York: Basic Books, 2005.

Appadurai, Arjun. *Fear of Small Numbers: An Essay on the Geography of Anger.* Durham: Duke University Press, 2006.

_____. *Modernity at Large: Cultural Dimensions of Globalization.* Minneapolis: University of Minnesota Press, 1996.

Arato, Andrew. "Civil Society Against the State: Poland 1980–81." *Telos* (Spring 1981), 34–6.

Arato, Andrew and Jean Cohen. *Civil Society and Political Theory.* Cambridge, MA: MIT Press, 1992.

Ariana Encyclopedia Society. *Afghanistan.* 1955.

Ariès, Phillipe. *L'enfant et la vie familiale sous l'Ancien Regime.* Paris: Plon, 1960.

Arunova, Marianna. *Gosudarstvo Nadir-Shakha Afshara: Ocherki obshchestvennyk otnoshenīĭ v Irane 30–40 godov XVIII veka.* Moscow: Izdatel'stvo Vostochnoĭ Literatury, 1958.

_____. *Dulat-i Nādir Shāh.* Tehran: Shabgir, 1977.

"Aāsnāmeh-yi sāzmān-i damukrātik-i zanān-i Afghānistān." 1969.

Attwood, William. *The Reds and the Blacks: A Personal Adventure.* New York: Harper & Row, 1967.

The Awakened East: A Report by Soviet Journalists on the Visit of N.S. Khrushchov to India, Burma, Indonesia and Afghanistan. Moscow: Foreign Languages Publishing House, 1960.

Bahro, Rudolf. *Die Alternative: Zur Kritik des Real Existierenden Sozialismus.* Cologne: Europäische Verlagsanstalt, 1977.

Baluch Qaum Ke Tarikh-Ke Chand Parishan Dafter Auraq (A Few Pages from the Official Records of the History of the Baloch Nation). Edited by Malik Allah Bakhsh. Quetta: Islamiyyah Press, 1957.

Banuazizi, Ali and Myron Weiner. *The State, Religion, and Ethnic Politics: Afghanistan, Iran and Pakistan*. Syracuse: Syracuse University Press, 1986.

Barfield, Thomas. "Weak Links on a Rusty Chain: Structural Weaknesses in Afghanistan's Provincial Government," in *Revolutions and Rebellions in Afghanistan: Anthropological Perspectives*. Edited by R. Canfield and M.N. Shahrani. Berkeley: University of California Press, 1984.

———. *Afghanistan: A Cultural and Political History*. Princeton: Princeton University Press, 2010.

Barry, Michael. *Personal Account of Famine Conditions in Northwestern Afghanistan*. Kabul: USAID Afghanistan, 1972.

———. *Massoud: De l'islamisme à la liberté*. Paris: Louis Audibert, 2002.

———. *Kabul's Long Shadows: Historical Perspectives*. Princeton: Liechtenstein Institute on Self-Determination, 2011.

Basov, V.V. *Natsional'noe i plemennoe v Afganistane. K ponimaniiu nevoennykh istokov afganskogo krizisa*. Edited by V.B. Kravtsov. Moscow: NITs FSKN Rossii, 2011.

———. Interview with Russian television. Available online at: www.youtube.com/watch?v=ab6bpIsUg_g&list=WLph1vvPu535MLrryLnpjA_xxiifFGlBog

Basov, V.V. and Genrikh Poliakov. "Afganistan: trudnye sud'by revoliutsii." *U politicheskoĭ karty mira* 8 (1988), 3–64.

———. *Afganistan: Trudnye sud'by Revoliutsii*. Moscow: Znaniie, 1988.

Bass, Gary. *The Blood Telegram: Nixon, Kissinger, and a Forgotten Genocide*. New York: Knopf, 2013.

Bauer, Julia. "Zur Entwicklung einer Frauenbewegung in Afghanistan im Zeitraum von 1946 bis zur Gegenwart." Doctoral Dissertation, Humboldt-Universität zu Berlin, 1985.

Bayly, C.A. *The Birth of the Modern World, 1780–1914*. Malden, MA: Blackwell, 2004.

Beckert, Sven. "Das Reich der Baumwolle: Eine globale Geschichte," in *Das Kaiserreich transnational: Deutschland in der Welt 1870–1914*. Edited by Sebastian Conrad and Jürgen Osterhammel. Göttingen: Vandenhoeck & Ruprecht, 2004.

———. *Empire of Cotton: A Global History*. New York: Knopf, 2014.

Bekmakhanova, N.E. "Kazakhi mladshevo i srednogo zhuzov v krest'ianskoĭ voĭne 1773–1775 pod predvoditel'stvom E.I. Pugachev." Dissertation, Leningrad Section of the Institute of History of the Academy of Sciences of the USSR, 1966.

———. *Legenda o Nevidimke (Uchastie kazakhov v krest'ianskoĭ voĭne pod rukovodstvom Pugacheva v 1773–1775 gg)*. Alma-Ata: Kazakhstan, 1968.

———. *Mnogonatsional'noe naselenie Kazakhstana i Kirgizii v epokhu kapitalizma (60-e gody XIX v.-1917 g)*. Moscow: Nauka, 1986.

Bellers, Jürgen. *Außenwirtschaftpolitik der Bundesrepublik Deutschland 1949–1989*. Münster: 1990.

Bernier, Philippe. *Des médecins sans frontières*. Paris: Albin Michel, 1980.

Benvenisti, Meron. *Conflicts and Contradictions*. New York: Villard Books, 1986.

Bezhan, Faridullah. "The Second World War and Political Dynamics in Afghanistan." *Middle Eastern Studies* 50(2) (2014), 175–91.

Bhutto, Zulfikar Ali. "The Islamic Heritage." In Z.A. Bhutto: *Speeches-Interviews 1948–1966*. 1948. Available online at: http://bhutto.org/Acrobat/Bhutto_Speeches_1948–66.pdf

Bińkowski, Andrzej. *Podróż za rzeke Amu*. Warsaw: Wydawnictwo Ministerstwa Obrony Narodowei, 1960.

―――. *Von Taschkent nach Kabul*. Leipzig: VEB Brockhaus, 1961.

Blackbourn, David. *The Conquest of Nature: Water, Landscape and the Making of Modern Germany*. London: Pimlico, 2007.

Bodemer, Klaus. *Entwicklungshilfepraxis–Politik für wen? Ideologie und Vergabepraxis der deutschen Entwicklungshilfe in der ersten Dekade*. Munich: Weltforum Verlag, 1974.

Bol'shaia sovetskaia entsiklopediia. 2nd Edition. Moscow: Izdatel'stvo Bol'shaia Sovetskaia Entsiklopediia, 1951.

Borowsky, Peter. "Die DDR in den siebziger Jahren. Bundeszentrale für politische Bildung." Available online at: www.bpb.de/izpb/10111/die-ddr-in-den-siebziger-jahren?p=all

Bowles, Chester. *The New Dimensions of Peace*. New York: Harper, 1955.

―――. *American Politics in a Revolutionary World*. Cambridge: Harvard University Press, 1956.

―――. *Africa's Challenge to America*. Berkeley: University of California Press, 1956.

―――. *Ideas, People and Peace*. New York: Harper, 1958.

Braithwaite, Rodric. *Afgantsy: The Russians in Afghanistan, 1979–89*. London: Profile Books, 2011.

Brauman, Rony. *Mémoires*. Paris, Juillard, 1983.

Brechna, Habibo. *Die Geschichte Afghanistans. Historische Ereignisse, Erzählungen und Erinnerungen*. Zürich: Hochschulverlag AG, 2012.

Brenner, M.M. *Ekonomika geologorazvedochnykh rabot na neft' i gaz v SSSR*. Moscow: Nedra, 1979.

Brooks, Rosa. "Failed States, or the State as Failure?" *University of Chicago Law Review* 72 (2005), 1159–96.

Brothers in Arms: The Rise and Fall of the Sino-Soviet Alliance. Edited by Odd Arne Westad. Stanford: Stanford University Press, 1998.

Brutents, Karen. *Tridtsat' let na staroĭ ploshchadi*. Moscow: Mezhdunarodnye otnosheniia, 1998.

Bucherer-Dietschi, Paul. "Bibliotheca Afghanica." *British Society for Middle Eastern Studies* 11(1) (1984), 65–6.

Bullen, Roger. "What Is Diplomatic History?" in *What Is History Today?* Edited by Juliet Gardiner. London: Macmillan Education, 1988.

Butler, Judith. "Contingent Foundations: Feminism and the Question of the 'Postmodern'," in *Feminists Theorize the Political*. Edited by Judith Butler and Joan Scott. New York: Routledge, 1992.

Campbell, Robert W. *Trends in the Soviet Oil and Gas Industry*. Baltimore: Johns Hopkins University Press, 1976.

Carlisle, Donald S. "Geopolitics and Ethnic Problems of Uzbekistan and its Neighbors," in *Muslim Eurasia: Conflicting Legacies*. Edited by Yaacov Ro'i. Newbury Park: Frank Cass, 1995.

Caron, James M. "Cultural Histories of Pashtun Nationalism, Public Participation and Social Inequality in Monarchic Afghanistan, 1905–1960." PhD Dissertation, University of Pennsylvania, 2009.

Caudill, Mildred. *Helmand–Arghandab Valley: Yesterday, Today, Tomorrow*. Lashkar Gah: 1969.

Chandrasekaran, Rajiv. *Little America: The War Within the War for Afghanistan*. New York: Knopf, 2012.

Chavis, Melody Ermachild. *Meena, Heroine of Afghanistan*. New York: St. Martin's Press, 2003.

Cherniaev, Anatoliĭ. "The Afghanistan Problem." *Russian Politics and Law* 42(5) (September–October 2004), 32–3.

Christensen, Asgar and Bernt Glatzer. *Coordinated Rehabilitation in the Khost Region: A Brief Profile of Khost and a Proposal for a Joint Approach*. Peshawar: Danish Committee for Aid to Afghan Refugees/DACAAR, 1991.

CIA World Factbook.

Clinton, Hilary. "Remarks to the U.N. 4th World Conference on Women Plenary Session." September 5, 1995.

Comaroff, Jean. "Beyond Bare Life: AIDS, (Bio)politics, and the Neoliberal Order." *Public Culture* 19(1) (Winter 2007), 197–219.

de Conde, Alexander. "What's Wrong with American Diplomatic History?" *Newsletter* of the Society of Historians of American Foreign Relations 1 (May 1970).

Connelly, Matthew. *A Diplomatic Revolution: Algeria's Fight for Independence and the Origins of the Post-Cold War Era*. Oxford: Oxford University Press, 2002.

———. *Fatal Misconception: The Struggle to Control World Population*. Cambridge, MA: Harvard University Press, 2008.

Cooper, Richard N. *The Economics of Interdependence: Economic Policy in the Atlantic Community*. New York: McGraw-Hill Books, 1968.

Coote, Ann and Beatrix Campbell. *Sweet Freedom: The Struggle for Women's Liberation*. Oxford: Blackwell, 1982.

Corwin, Phillip. *Doomed in Afghanistan: A UN Officer's Memoir of the Fall of Kabul and Najibullah's Failed Escape, 1992*. New Brunswick: Rutgers University Press, 2003.

Couldrey, Marion. "Eastern Paktia: Coordination Status Report." Peshawar: ACBAR, June 24, 1992.

Coutin, Susan Bibler. *Legalizing Mores: Salvadoran Immigrants' Struggle for U.S. Residency*. Ann Arbor: University of Michigan Press, 2000.

———. *Nation of Emigrants: Shifting Boundaries of Citizenship in El Salvador and the United States*. Ithaca: Cornell University Press, 2007.

Crews, Robert. *Afghan Modern: The History of a Global Nation*. Cambridge, MA: Harvard University Press, 2015.

Cronon, William. *Nature's Metropolis: Chicago and the Great West*. New York: W.W. Norton, 1991.

Cullather, Nick. *The Hungry World: America's Cold War Battle Against Poverty in Asia*. Cambridge, MA: Harvard University Press, 2010.

Dale, Stephen. *Indian Merchants and Eurasian Trade, 1600–1750*. Cambridge: Cambridge University Press, 1994.

Dalrymple, William. *Return of a King: The Battle for Afghanistan*. London: Bloomsbury, 2013.

Damm, Ulrich. *Die Bundesrepublik Deutschland und die Entwicklungsländer. Versuch einer Darstellung der politischen Beziehungen der Bundesrepublik Deutschland zu den Entwicklungsländern unter besonderer Berücksichtigung der Entwicklungshilfe.* Coburg: Graphischer Betrieb H. Biehl, 1965.

Davydov, A.D. *Razvitie kapitalisticheskikh otnoshenii v zemledelii Afganistana.* Moscow: Izdatel'stvo vostochnoĭ literatury, 1962.

_____. *O sel'skoĭ obshchine i eë khoziastvennoj znachenii v Afganistane (raĭony s preiumshchestvenno tadzhikskim naseleniem) – voprosy ekonomiki Afganistana.* Moscow: Nauka, 1963.

_____. *Agrarnyĭ stroĭ Afganistana: Osnovnye etapy razvitiia.* Moscow: Nauka, 1967.

_____. *Afganskaia derevniia. Sel'skaia obshchina i rassloeniie krest'ianstva.* Moscow: Nauka, 1969.

_____. *Sotsial'no-ekonomicheskaia struktura derevni Afganistana: Osobennosti evoliutsii.* Moscow: Nauka, 1976.

_____. *Afganistan: voĭny moglo ne byt': Krestianstvo i reformy.* Moscow: Nauka, 1993.

Devji, Faisal. *Muslim Zion: Pakistan as a Political Idea.* London: Hurst, 2013.

Dixit, J.N. *An Afghan Diary: Zahir Shah to Taliban.* New Delhi: Konark Publishers, 2000.

Donert, Celia. "Whose Utopia? Gender, Ideology, and Human Rights at the 1975 World Congress of Women in East Berlin," in *The Breakthrough: Human Rights in the 1970s.* Edited by Samuel Moyn and Jan Eckel. Philadelphia: University of Pennsylvania Press, 2014, 68–87.

Donini, Antonio Eric Dudley, and Ron Ockwell. "Afghanistan Report: Coordination in a Fragmented State." December 1996. Available online at: http://web.cas.suffolk.edu/faculty/druke/UN/UN%20OCHA%20FIELD%20GUIDELINE/documents/145.pdf

Dorronoso, Gilles. *Revolution Unending: Afghanistan, 1979 to the Present.* London: Hurst and Company, 2000.

Dudziak, Mary L. *War-Time: An Idea, Its History, Its Consequences.* Oxford: Oxford University Press, 2012.

Dupree, Louis. *Landlocked Images: Snap Responses to an Informal Questionaire.* American Universities Field Staff Reports Service, South Asia Series, Volume VI(5), June 1962.

_____. *Afghanistan.* Princeton: Princeton University Press, 1973.

_____. *A Note on Afghanistan.* American Universities Fieldstaff Reports, Asia Series, Volume XVIII(8, 12), 1974.

Durdenevskiĭ, V.N. *Konstitutsii Vostoka.* Leningrad: Gosudarstvennoe izdatel'stvo, 1926.

Dvoriankov, N.A. "Amukhtan-i zābānhā-yi *Afghānistān* dar atahād-i shuruvi," in *Afghānshanāsi-yi shuruvi dar 'arseh-yi chehel sāl.* Edited by. R.T. Akhramovich. Moscow, 1959.

_____. *Iazyk pushtu.* Moscow: Izdatel'stvo vostochnoĭ literatury, 1960.

I. Dzhurabekov, L. Vartazar'ian, and E. Zhilin, *Dzhelalabadskĭ irrigatsionnyĭ kompleks v Afganistane.* Tashkent: "Uzbekistan," 1981.

"ECOSOC Resolution 1235 (XLII)." August 1967.

Eighmy, Thomas H. *Afghanistan's Population Inside and Out: Demographic Data for Reconstruction and Planning.* Islamabad, 1990.

Ekbladh, David. *The Great American Mission: Modernization and the Construction of an American World Order.* Princeton: Princeton University Press, 2011.

Eley, Geoff. *Making Democracy Social: A History of the Left in Europe.* Oxford: Oxford University Press, 2002.

Engerman, David. "The Second World's Third World." *Kritika* 12(1) (Winter 2011), 183–211.

Entsiklopediia Pakistana. Edited by Iu. V. Gankovskiĭ. Moscow: Fundamenta Press, 1998.

Ermacora, Felix. "Report on the Situation of Human Rights in Afghanistan, Prepared by the Special Rapporteur, Mr. Felix Ermacora, in Accordance with Commission on Human Rights Resolution 1985/88." United Nations Document E/CN4/1985/21, February 21, 1985.

Ezhov, Georgiĭ. "Razvitiie ekonomiki Afganistana v period pervogo piatiletnego plana (1956/7–1960/61)," *Kandidat nauk* Dissertation, Moscow State University, 1968.

Fassin, Didier. "Subjectivity Without Subjects: Reinventing the Figure of the Witness," in *Humanitarian Reason: A Moral History of the Present.* Translated by Rachel Gomme. Berkeley: University of California Press, 2012.

———. "Humanitarianism as a Politics of Life." *Public Culture* 19(3) (2007), 499–520.

Fassin, Didier and Richard Rechtman, *The Empire of Trauma: An Inquiry into the Condition of Victimhood.* Translated by Rachel Gomme. Princeton: Princeton University Press, 2009.

Ferdinand, Klaus. "Preliminary Notes on Hazara Culture." Copenhagen, 1959.

———. "Nomad Expansion and Commerce in Central Afghanistan." *Folk* 4 (1962), 123–59.

Ferguson, James. *The Anti-politics Machine: 'Development', Depoliticization, and Bureaucratic Power in Lesotho.* Minneapolis: University of Minnesota Press, 1994.

———. *Global Shadows: Africa in the Neoliberal World Order.* Durham: Duke University Press, 2006.

———. "Seeing Like an Oil Company: Space, Security and Global Capital in Neoliberal Africa." *American Anthropologist* 107(3) (September 2005), 377–82.

Ferguson, James and Akhil Gupta. "Spatializing States: Towards an Ethnography of Neoliberal Governmentality."*American Ethnologist* 29(4) (November 2002), 981–1002.

Ferguson, Kathy E. *The Feminist Case Against Bureaucracy.* Philadelphia: Temple University Press, 1984.

Fitzgerald, Paul and Elizabeth Gould. *Invisible History: Afghanistan's Untold Story.* New York: City Lights Publishers, 2009.

Foucault, Michel. *Power/Knowledge: Selected Interviews and Other Writings 1972–1977.* Edited by Colin Gordon. New York: Pantheon Books, 1980.

Fraser-Tytler, William Kerr. "The Expulsion of Axis Nationals from Afghanistan," in *The Middle East in the War.* Edited by George Kirk and Arnold Toynbee. London: Oxford University Press, 1953.

———. *Afghanistan: A Study of Political Developments in Central and Southern Asia.* London: Oxford University Press, 1953.

Friedan, Betty. "Scary Doings in Mexico City," in *"It Changed My Life": Writings on the Women's Movement.* Cambridge, MA: Harvard University Press, 1988.

Friedman, Andrew. *Covert Capital: Landscapes of Denial and the Making of U.S. Empire in the Suburbs of Northern Virginia.* Berkeley: University of California Press, 2014.

———. Interview with *Against the Grain*. July 16, 2014. Available online at: www .againstthegrain.org/program/978/wed-71614-imperial-suburbs

Friedman, Jeremy. "Reviving Revolution: The Sino-Soviet Split, the 'Third World,' and the Fate of the Left." PhD Dissertation, Princeton University, 2011.

Fry, Maxwell J. *The Afghan Economy: Money, Finance, and the Critical Constraints to Economic Development*. Leiden: E.J. Brill, 1974.

Gaddis, John Lewis. *Strategies of Containment: A Critical Appraisal of Postwar American National Security Policy*. New York: Oxford University Press, 1982.

Gankovskiĭ, Iu. V. *Imperiia Durrani: Ocherki administrativnoĭ i voennoĭ sistemy*. Moscow: Izdatel'stvo vostochnoĭ Literatury, 1958.

———. *Natsional'nyĭ vopros i natsional'nye dvizheniia v Pakistane*. Moscow: Nauka, 1967.

———. *Nekotorye mezhdunarodnye aspekty pushtunskoĭ problem*." *Vostok i sovremennost'* 1 (1979), 111–24.

———. "Ibragim-bek Lokaĭ (1889–1932)." *Aziia i Afrika segodnia* 4 (1994): 60–63.

"General Information on Modern Afghanistan." Royal Afghan Embassy (Washington, DC). September 1953.

A Generation of Illiterates? Information from and About the Afghanistan Education Committee. Co-authored by Batinshah Safi, Ingemar Andersson, Anders Fänge. Peshawar: Afghanistan Education Committee, 1985.

Geyer, Michael and Charles Bright. "World History in a Global Age." *The American Historical Review* 100(4) (October 1995), 1034–60.

———. "Where in the World is America? The History of the United States in the Global Age," in *Rethinking American History in a Global Age*. Edited by Thomas Bender. Berkeley: University of California Press, 2002.

"Ghazni Health Facilities Map." UNIDATA, 1989.

Goldman, Marshall L. *The Enigma of Soviet Petroleum: Half-Full or Half-Empty?*. London: George Allen & Unwin, 1980.

Goodrich, Carter. *The Miner's Freedom: A Study of the Working Life in a Changing Industry*. Boston: Marshall Jones & Co., 1925.

Gorbachev, Mikhaïl. "Vystupleniie General'nogo sekretaria TsK KPSS M.S. Gorbacheva na general'noĭ assamblee OON 7 dekabria 1988 goda." Available online at: www.promreview.net/moskva/vystuplenie-generalnogo-sekretarya-tsk-kpss-m-s-gorbacheva-na-generalnoi-assamblee-oon-7-deka?page=0,1

———. "Europe as a Common Home." July 6, 1989.

Michael Gould. *The Struggle for Modern Nigeria: The Biafran War*. London: I.B. Tauris, 2012.

Green, Nile. "Locating Afghan History. Roundtable on The Future of Afghan History." *International Journal of Middle East Studes* 45 (2013), 132–4.

———. "Introduction. Roundtable on The Future of Afghan History." *International Journal of Middle East Studies* 45 (2013), 127–8.

Gregorian, Vartan. *The Emergence of Modern Afghanistan: The Politics of Reform and Modernization, 1880–1946*. Stanford: Stanford University Press, 1969.

Griffith, J.C. *Afghanistan*. London: Pall Mall, 1967.

Gubar, Mir Gulam Muhammad. *Afganistan na puti istorii*. Translated by Mullosho Davliatov. Moscow: Nauka, 1987.

Guibert, Emmanuel. *Le photographe*. Marcinelle: Dupuis, 2010.

Gureev, M.A. *Moia poslednaia afganskaia voĭna.* Moscow: Insan, 1996.

Gurevich, N.M. *Vneshniaia torgovlia Afganistana.* Moscow: Izdatel'stvo Vostochnoĭ Literatury, 1959.

———. *Voprosy ekonomiki Afganistana.* Moscow: Izdatel'stvo Akademii Nauk SSSR, 1963.

———. *Ocherk istorii torgovogo kapitala v Afganistane.* Moscow: Nauka, 1967.

———. *Afganistan: Nekotorye osobennosti sotsial'no-ekonomicheskogo razvitiia, 1919–1977.* Moscow: Nauka, 1983.

Gustafson, Thane. *Crisis Amid Plenty: The Politics of Soviet Energy Under Brezhnev and Gorbachev.* Princeton: Princeton University Press, 1989.

Gutman, Roy. *How We Missed the Story: Osama Bin Laden, the Taliban, and the Hijacking of Afghanistan.* Washington: United States Institute of Peace Press, 2008.

Hall, Catherine. *Civilising Subjects: Metropole and Colony in the English Imagination.* Cambridge: Polity, 2002.

Hanifi, Mohammad J. "Vending Distorted Afghanistan Through Patriotic 'Anthropology.'" *Critique of Anthropology* 31(3) (2011), 256–70.

Hanifi, Shah Mahmoud. *Connecting Histories in Afghanistan: Market Relations and State Formation on a Colonial Frontier.* Stanford: Stanford University Press, 2011.

———. "The Combined History of Pashto Printing and Resistance to Print." Available online at: www.soas.ac.uk/cccac/swat-pathan/file59663.pdf

———. "A History of Linguistic Boundary Crossing Within and Around Pashto," in *Beyond Swat: History, Society and Economy Along the Afghanistan–Pakistan Frontier.* Edited by Magnus Marsden and Ben Hopkins. London: Hurst, 2013, 63–76.

———. "Mapping Afghanistan: Colonial, National, and Post-Colonial Cartographies." Unpublished Paper.

———. "Quandaries of the Afghan Nation," in *Under the Drones: Modern Lives in the Afghanistan–Pakistan Borderlands,* by Robert Crews and Shahzad Bashir. Cambridge, MA: Harvard University Press, 2012, 83–101.

———. "Comparing Camels in Afghanistan and Australia: Industry and Nationalism During the Long Nineteenth Century," in *Camel Cultures: Historical Traditions, Present Threats, and Future Prospects.* Edited by Ed Emery. London: SOAS, 2013.

Harrison, Selig S. *In Afghanistan's Shadow: Baluch Nationalism and Soviet Temptations.* New York: Canegie Endowment for International Peace, 1981.

———. "Making the Russians Bleed," in *Out of Afghanistan: The Inside Story of the Soviet Withdrawal.* Edited by Diego Cordovez and Selig Harrison. New York: Oxford University Press, 1995.

Hashimi, Muhammad Azim, "Osnovnye napravleniia po razvitiiu sistemy *elektrosnabzheniia* Demokraticheskoĭ Respubliki Afganistan." *Kandidat nauk* Dissertation, Moskovskiĭ Energeticheskiĭ Institut, 1984.

Heathershaw, John. "The Global Performance State: A Reconsideration of the Central Asian 'Weak State'," in *Performing Politics in Central Asia: Ethnographies of the State,* Edited by Madeleine Reeves, Johan Rasanayagam, and Judith Beyer. Bloomington: Indiana University Press, 2013, 39–61.

Hein, Bastian. *Die Westdeutschen und die Dritte Welt: Entwicklungspolitik und Entwicklungsdienste zwischen Reform und Revolte, 1959–1974.* Munich: R. Oldenbourg Verlag, 2006.

Hirsch, Francine. *Empire of Nations: Ethnographic Knowledge and the Making of the Soviet Union.* Ithaca: Cornell University Press, 2005.

Hirschman, Albert O. "The Rise and Decline of Development Economics," in *Essays in Trespassing: Economics to Politics and Beyond*. Cambridge: Cambridge University Press, 1981.

Hopgood, Stephen. *The Endtimes of Human Rights*. Ithaca: Cornell University Press, 2014.

Hough, Jerry F. *The Struggle for the Third World: Soviet Debates and American Options*. Washington: Brookings Institution, 1986.

Human Rights Watch. "Afghanistan: The Massacre in Mazar-i Sharif." November 1, 1998, Document C1007. Available online at: www.unhcr.org/refworld/docid/45c9a4b52.html

Iandolo, Alessandro. "The Rise and Fall of the 'Soviet Model of Development' in West Africa, 1957–64." *Cold War History* 12(4) (2012), 683–704.

IMF World Economic Outlook Database. Available online at: www.imf.org/external/pubs/ft/weo/2013/01/weodata/index.aspx

Immerwahr, Daniel. *Thinking Small: The United States and the Lure of Community Development*. Cambridge, MA: Harvard University Press, 2015.

Irwin, Ryan. *Gordian Knot: Apartheid and the Unmaking of the Liberal World Order*. Oxford: Oxford University Press, 2012.

———. "Decolonization and the Cold War," in *The Routledge Handbook of the Cold War*. Edited by Artemy Kalinovsky and Craig Daigle. Abingdon: Routledge, 2014, 91–103.

Iskanderov, Kosimsho. *Molodezhnoe dvizheniie v Afganistane (1945–1990 gg.)*. Dushanbe: 1992.

Jackson, Robert H. *Quasi-states: Sovereignty, International Relations and the Third World*. Cambridge: Cambridge University Press, 1990.

Jansson, Irland. "India, Pakistan, or Pakhtunistan: the Nationalist Movements in the North-West Frontier Province, 1937–47." PhD Dissertation, University of Uppsala, 1981.

Jersild, Austin. *The Sino-Soviet Alliance: An International History*. Chapel Hill: The University of North Carolina Press, 2014.

Jones, Paul S. *Afghanistan Venture: Discovering the Afghan People: The Life, Contacts and Adventures of an American Civil Engineer During His Two Year Sojourn in the Kingdom of Afghanistan*. San Antonio: Naylor Co., 1956.

Judt. Tony. *Postwar: A History of Europe Since 1945*. New York: Penguin, 2006.

Kahn, Jeffrey S. "Islands of Sovereignty: Haitian Migration and the Borders of Empire." PhD Dissertation, University of Chicago, 2013.

Kakar, M. Hassan. *Afghanistan: The Soviet Invasion and the Afghan Response, 1979–1982*. Berkeley: University of California Press, 1995.

Kalinovsky, Artemy. *A Long Goodbye: The Soviet Withdrawal from Afghanistan*. Cambridge, MA: Harvard University Press, 2011.

Kamenev, S.N. "Konferentsiia, posviashchennaia 90-letiiu so dnia rozhdeniia Iu. V. Gankovskogo." *Vostok. Afroaziatskie obshchestva, istoriia i sovremennost'* 5 (2011), 169–73

Kandagar–pobratim Alma-Atinskoĭ oblasti (v pomosch' lektoru–propagandistu po internatsional'nomu vospitaniiu). Alma-Ata: Kabinet komsomol'skoĭ raboty Almatinskogo Obkoma LKSM Kazakhstana, 1988.

Kaplan, Robert. *Soldiers of God: With Islamic Warriors in Afghanistan and Pakistan*. New York: Vintage Departures, 2001.

Kelly, Catriona. *Children's World: Growing up in Russia, 1890–1991.* New Haven: Yale University Press, 2008.

Kassymbekova, Botakoz. "Humans as Territory: Forced Resettlement and the Making of Soviet Tajikistan, 1920–1938." *Central Asian Survey* 30(3–4) (2011), 349–70.

Kishtmand, Sultan 'Ali. *Yāddāshthā-yi siyāsi va ruydādhā-yi tārikhi: khāṭirāt-i shakhṣi bā burah'hā 'i az tārikh-i siyāsi-i mu'āṣir-i Afghānistān.* Tehran: Najib-i Kabir, 2002.

Keohane Robert O. and Joseph S. Nye. "Transnational Relations and World Politics: An Introduction." *International Organization* 25(3) (Summer 1971), 329–49.

Keynes, John Maynard. *The Economic Consequences of the Peace.* New York: Harcourt, Brace, and Howe, 1920.

Khaïtun, Alekseï. *Eskpeditsionno–vakhtovoe stroitel'stvo v Zapadnoĭ Sibiri.* Leningrad: Stroĭizdat, 1982.

Khalili, K. *Yāddāshthā-yi Astād-i Khalili: Maqālāmā Beh Dakhtarash Mary.* Virginia, Herndon: All Prints, 2010.

Khashimbekov, Khadiia. *Uzbeki Severnogo Afganistana.* Moscow: Institut Vostokovedeniia, 1994.

Killen, Andreas. *1973: Nervous Breakdown: Watergate, Warhol, and the Birth of Post 1960s America.* New York: Bloomsbury, 2006.

Kireev, Georgiĭ. "Kandagarskiĭ dnevnik." Available online at: http://kireev.info/

Klass, Rosanne. "Genocide in Afghanistan," in *The Widening Circle of Genocide.* Edited by Isabel W. Charney. New Brunswick: Transaction Publishers, 1988.

Jay Klinghoffer, Arthur. *The Soviet Union & International Oil Politics.* New York: Columbia University Press, 1977.

Kotkin, Stephen. *Magnetic Mountain: Stalinism as a Civilization.* Berkeley: University of California Press, 1995.

———. "Modern Times: The Soviet Union and the Interwar Conjuncture." *Kritika* 2(1) (Winter 2001), 111–64.

———. "Trashcanistan." The New Republic, April 15, 2002.

———. "The Kiss of Debt: The East Bloc Goes Borrowing," in *The Shock of the Global: The 1970s in Perspective.* Edited by Niall Ferguson, Charles S. Maier, Erez Manela, and Daniel J. Sargent. Cambridge, MA: The Belknap Press of Harvard University Press, 2010, 80–93.

Kotkin, Stephen and Jan Gross. *Uncivil Society: 1989 and the Implosion of the Communist Establishment.* New York: The Modern Library, 2009.

Knabe, Erika. *Frauenemanzipation in Afghanistan.* Hain: Meisenheim am Glan, 1977.

Krasner, Stephen. *Structural Conflict: The Third World Against Global Liberalism.* Berkeley: University of California Press, 1985.

Kravtsov, V.B. *Spetsifika afganskogo obshchestva i eë vlianiie na obstanovku v Demokraticheskoĭ Respublike Afganistana.* Moscow, 1987.

———. "Zhizn', otdannaia Afganistanu: K 70-letiiu Vladimira Basova." Informatsionno-analiticheskiĭ zhurnal politicheskoe obrazovaniie. November 2, 2011. Available online at: www.lawinrussia.ru/node/44371#_ftn1

———. Introduction to V.V. Basov, *Natsional'noe i plemennoe v Afganistane. K ponimaniiu nevoennykh istokov afganskogo kriziza.* Edited by V.B. Kravtsov. Moscow: NIF FSKN Rossii, 2011.

Kushkeki, Burhān al-Din Khān. *Kattagan i Badakhshan: dannye po geografii strany, estestvenno-istoricheskim usloviiam, naseleniiu, ekonomike i putiam soobshcheniia.*

Translated by P.P. Vvedenskiĭ, E.V. Levkovskiĭ, and B.I. Dolgopolov. Edited by A.A. Semënov. Tashkent: Obshestvo dlia izucheniia Tadzhikistana i iranskikh narodnosteĭ za ego predelami, 1926.

Kux, Dennis. *The United States and Pakistan, 1947–2000, Disenchanted Allies.* Washington: Woodrow Wilson Center Press and Johns Hopkins University Press, 2001.

Lacey, Jim. *Keep from All Thoughtful Men: How U.S. Economists Won World War II.* Annapolis: Naval Institute Press, 2011.

Langer, V. *The Defence and Foreign Policy of India.* New Delhi: Sterling Publishers, 1998.

Lasch, Christopher. *The True and Only Heaven: Progress and Its Critics.* New York: W.W. Norton, 1991.

Lauterpacht, Hersch. "Freedom of Transit in International Law." *Transactions of the Grotius Society* 44 (1958), 313–56.

Leonov, Nikolaĭ. *Likholet'e.* Moscow: Mezhdunarodnye Otnosheniia, 1995.

Lerner, Gerda. "Women Among the Professors of History: The Story of a Process of Transformation," in *Voices of Women Historians: The Personal, the Political, the Professional.* Edited by Eileen Boris and Nupur Chaudhuri. Bloomington: Indiana University Press, 1999.

Lessar, P.M. *Iugo-Zapadnaia Turkmeniia (zemlia sarykov i salyrov).* St. Petersburg, 1885.

Lewis, Arthur. *Theory of Economic Growth.* London: Allen & Unwin, 1955.

Liakhovskiĭ, Aleksandr. *Tragediia i doblest' Afgana.* Moscow: GPI "Iskon", 1995.

Lieven, Anatol. *Chechnya: Tombstone of Russian Power.* New Haven: Yale University Press, 1998.

Limon, Marc and Hilary Power, *History of the United Nations Special Procedures Mechanism: Origins, Evolution, and Reform.* Washington: Brookings Institution, 2014.

Link, Stefan. "Transnational Fordism: Ford Motor Company, Nazi Germany, and the Soviet Union in the Interwar Years." PhD Dissertation, Harvard University, 2012.

Linton, Ralph. *The Study of Man: An Introduction.* New York: D. Appleton-Century, 1936.

Lodge, David. *Small World: An Academic Romance.* London: Penguin Books, 1984.

Lüthi, Lorenz M. *The Sino-Soviet Split: Cold War in the Communist World.* Princeton: Princeton University Press, 2008.

Lynch, Kevin. *The Image of the City.* Cambridge: MIT Press, 1960.

"Ma'āhadeh-yi fimābin-i Āfghānistān va Rus." February 21, 1921. In *Manāsabāt-i Afghānistān va atahād-i shuruvi dar sālhā-yi 1919–1969.* Kabul: 1969.

Magris, Claudio. "Come i pesci il mare." *Frontiere, Novi Argumenti* 38 (1991), 1–12.

Maier, Charles S. "The Politics of Productivity." *International Organization* 31(4) (1977), 607–33.

———. "Marking Time: Contemporary Historical Writing in the United States," in *The Past Before Us: Contemporary Historical Writing in the United States.* Ithaca: Cornell University Press, 1980.

———. "Consigning the Twentieth Century to History: Alternative Narratives for the Modern Era." *American Historical Review* 105(3) (2000).

———. "An American Empire? Implications for Order, Disorder, and Democracy in World Politics." Unpublished Paper (2004).

_____. *Among Empires: American Ascendency and Its Predecessors.* Cambridge: Harvard University Press, 2007.

_____. "Return to Rome: Half a Century of American Historiography in Light of the 1955 Congress for International Historical Studies," in *La storiografia tra passato e futuro (Il X Congreso Internazionale di Scienze Storiche (Roma 1955) cinquant'anni dopo).* Rome: 2008, 189–211.

_____. *Leviathan 2.0: Inventing Modern Statehood.* Cambridge, MA: The Belknap Press of Harvard University Press, 2012.

Majrooh, Parwin Ali. "Afghan Women Between Marxism and Islamic Fundamentalism." *Central Asian Survey* 8(3) (1989), 95–6.

Makmudov, E.R. *Transport sovremennogo Afghanistana. Nekotorye ekonomicheskie problemy.* Moscow: Nauka, 1983.

Mamadshoev, R., "Vklad Iu. V. Gankovskogo v razvitie vostokovedeniia v Tadzhikistane." Presented Paper. April 6, 2011. Oriental Institute of the Russian Academy of Sciences.

Marx, Karl and Friedrich Engels. "Manifesto of the Communist Party." Translated by Samuel Moore. Available online at: www.marxists.org/archive/marx/works/1848/communist-manifesto/

_____. Letter to Ludwig Kugelmann. December 12, 1868. Available online at: www.marxists.org/archive/marx/works/1868/letters/68_12_12.htm

_____. *Capital,* Available online at: www.marxists.org/archive/marx/works/1885-c2/cho4.htm

Malik, Hafeez. *The Encyclopedia of Pakistan.* Karachi: Oxford University Press, 2006.

_____. "The Soviet Union, Russia: Yuri and I. A Memoir." *Journal of South Asian and Middle Eastern Studies* XXXV(3) (Spring 2012), 56–75.

Manela, Erez. "A Pox on Your Narrative: Writing Disease Control into Cold War History," *Diplomatic History* 34(2) (April 2010), 299–323.

Mann, Gregory. *From Empires to NGOs in the West African Sahel: The Road to Non-governmentality.* Cambridge: Cambridge University Press, 2015.

Markovits, Claude. *Merchants, Traders, Entrepreneurs: Indian Business in the Colonial Era.* Basingstoke: Palgrave Macmillan, 2008.

Martin, Terry D. *The Affirmative Action Empire: Nations and Nationalism in the Soviet Union.* Ithaca: Cornell University Press, 2001.

Mas'ud, Ahmad Shah. "A Message to the People of the United States of America." 1998. Available online at: www.afghan-web.com/documents/let-masood.html

Masov, Sergeï. *A Distant Front in the Cold War: The USSR in West Africa and the Congo.* Washington: Woodrow Wilson Center Press, 2010.

Massey, Doreen. *For Space.* London: Sage, 2005.

Masson, V.M. *Ekonomika i sotsialnyĭ stroĭ drevnikh obshchestvakh.* Leningrad: Nauka, 1976.

Masson, V.M. and V.A. Romodin. *Istoriia Afganistana.* Moscow: Nauka, 1965.

Matn-i asnād-i awalin konferāns-e sartāsari-ye zanān-e Afghānistān. Kabul: 1980.

Mazov, Sergeï. *A Distant Front in the Cold War: The USSR in West Africa and the Congo, 1956–1964.* Washington: Woodrow Wilson Center Press, 2010.

Mazower, Mark. "Governing the World: The Rise and Fall of an Idea." Public Lecture at Columbia University. November 28, 2011. Available online at: www.youtube.com/watch?v=imY8H3TUh88

_____. *Governing the World: The History of an Idea.* New York: The Penguin Press, 2012.

McDonald, Jason. "Transition to Utopia: A Reinterpretation of Economics, Ideas, and Politics in Hungary, 1984 to 1990." *East European Politics and Societies* 7(2) (1993), 203–39.

Medécins sans Frontières. "MSF in Afghanistan." Available online at: www.doctorswithoutborders.org/events/exhibits/thephotographer/msf-afghanistan.cfm

Mead, Lawrence M. "Scholasticism in Political Science." *Perspectives on Politics* 8(2) (June 2010), 453–64.

Miller, Elizabeth. "An Open Letter to the Editors of Ms. Magazine." April 21, 2002. Available online at: www.rawa.org/tours/elizabeth_miller_letter.htm

Miller, L.C., M. Timouri, J. Wijnker, and J.G. Schaller. "Afghan Refugee Children and Mothers." *Archive of Pediatrics and Adolescent Medicine* 148 (7) (July 1944), 704–8.

Ministerstvo Innostrannykh Del SSSR. *Deistvuiushchie dogovory, soglasheniia i konventsii, vstupivshie v silu s 1 ianvaria po 31 dekabria 1985 goda.* Volume XLI. Moscow: Mezhdunarodnye Otnosheniia, 1987.

Missiia v Kabul. 1971. Directed by Leonid Kvinkhidze.

Mitchell, Timothy. *Rule of Experts: Egypt, Techno-Politics, Modernity.* Berkeley: University of California Press, 2002.

_____. "Carbon Democracy." *Economy and Society* 38(3) (2009), 399–432.

_____. *Carbon Democracy: Political Power in the Age of Oil.* New York: Verso, 2011.

Mohmand, Abdul-Qayum. "American Foreign Policy Toward Afghanistan: 1919–2001." PhD Dissertation, University of Utah, 2001.

Molodëzh Afganistana. 1986. Directed by V. Shorokhov. Available online at: http://rutube.ru/video/9cf0c9df01077cfa686506878ac51cad/

Morrison, Alexander. Review of Robert Crews, *For Prophet and Tsar. The Slavonic and East European Review* 86(3) (July 2008), 553–7.

Moscow State Institute for International Relations. "Pushtu." Available online at: www.mgimo.ru/study/languages/list/document6594.pdf

Mouzin, Éric. "Approche de l'Afghanistan à travers six mois de mission humanitaire avec MSF." Doctoral Thesis, Université René-Descartes, 1990.

Moyn, Samuel. *The Last Utopia: Human Rights In History.* Cambridge, MA: Harvard University Press, 2010.

_____. "The Return of the Prodigal: The 1970s as a Turning Point in Human Rights History," in *The Breakthrough: Human Rights in the 1970s.* Edited by Samuel Moyn and Jan Eckel. Philadelphia: University of Pennsylvania Press, 2014, 1–14.

Mushavery. Moscow: Nauka, Tekhnika, Obrazovaniie, 2005.

Munn, Nancy D. *The Fame of Gawa: A Symbolic Study of Value Transformation in a Massim (Papua New Guinea) Society.* Durham: Duke University Press, 1986.

Myrdal, Jan. *Kulturers korsväg; en bok om Afghanistan.* Stockholm: Norstedt, 1960.

Naimark, Norman. *Fires of Hatred: Ethnic Cleansing in Twentieth-Century Europe.* Cambridge, MA: Harvard University Press, 2001.

Nalbandiants, Ruben. *Zapiski vostokoveda.* Moscow: Luch, 2002.

Nathan, Robert R., Oscar Gass, and Daniel Creamer. *Palestine: Problem and Promise. An Economic Study.* Washington: Public Affairs Press of the American Council on Public Affairs, 1946.

Robert R. Nathan Associates. "Economic Advisory Services Provided to the Ministry of Planning, Royal Government of Afghanistan, September 1961 to June 1972, Final

Report. Submitted to the Royal Government of Afghanistan and U.S. Agency for International Development by Robert R. Nathan Associates, Inc., Washington." June 1972.

———. *The Potential Impact of the Delaware Water Gap National Recreation Area on its Surrounding Communities: A Summary of the Report Prepared for the State Planning Board of the Commonwealth of Pennsylvania and the Department of Conservation and Economic Development of the State of New Jersey*. Washington: Robert R. Nathan Associates, 1966.

Nathans, Benjamin and Kevin Platt. "Socialist in Form, Indeterminate in Content: The Ins and Outs of Late Soviet Culture." *Ab Imperio* 2 (2011), 301–24.

National Atlas of the Democratic Republic of Afghanistan. Warsaw: GEOKART, 1985.

Nguyen, Mimi Thi. *The Gift of Freedom: War, Debt, and Other Refugee Passages*. Durham: Duke University Press, 2012.

Nikoforov, V.N. *Sovetskie istoriki o problemakh Kitaia*. Moscow: Nauka, 1970.

Nikulin, Lev. *Chetyrnadtsat' mesiatsev v Afganistane*. Moscow: Izdatel'stvo Krasnaia Nov', 1923.

Noelle-Karimi, Christine. "Maps and Spaces." Roundtable on "The Future of Afghan History." *International Journal of Middle East Studes* 45 (2013), 142–5.

Nye, Joseph S. and Robert O. Keohane. *Power and Interdependence: World Politics in Transition*. Boston: Little, Brown, 1977.

O'Brien, Connor Cruise. *Murderous Angels: A Political Tragedy and Comedy in Black and White*. Boston: Little, Brown, 1968.

Office of the Co-ordinator for United Nations Humanitarian and Economic Assistance Programmes Relatingto Afghanistan. "Operation Salam: First Coordinated Report." February 1989.

Office of the United Nations Co-Ordinator for Humanitarian and Economic Assistance Programmes Relating to Afghanistan. "First Consolidated Report." Geneva, 1988.

Ogle, Vanessa. "Whose Time Is It? The Pluralization of Time and the Global Condition, 1870s–1940s." *The American Historical Review* 188(5) (December 2013), 1376–1402.

———. *The Global Transformation of Time, 1879–1950*. Cambridge, MA: Harvard University Press, 2015.

Okimbekov, Ubaïd Vafobekovich. "Problemy ekonomicheskogo i sotsial'nogo razvitiia Severo–Vostoka Afganistana." *Kandidat nauk* Dissertation, Institut Vostokovedeniia Rossiïskoï Akademii Nauk, 2003.

Olcott, Jocelyn. "Globalizing Sisterhood: International Women's Year and the Politics of Representation," in *The Shock of the Global: The 1970s in Perspective*. Edited by Niall Ferguson, Charles S. Maier, Erez Manela, and Daniel J. Sargent. Cambridge, MA: The Belknap Press of Harvard University Press, 2010.

———. "Transnational Feminism: Event, Temporality, and Performance at the 1975 International Women's Year Conference," in *Cultures in Motion*. Edited by Daniel T. Rodgers, Bhavani Raman, and Helmut Reinitz (Princeton: Princeton University Press, 2013), 231–66.

OMA, Rem Koolhaas, and Bruce Mau. "Field Trip: A Memoir. The Berlin Wall as Architecture," in *S, M, L, XL*. Edited by Rem Koolhaas OMR and Bruce Mau (New York: Monacelli Press, 1995), 212–33.

Once in Afghanistan DVD. Directed by Jody Bergedick and Jill Vickers. 2008; Dirt Road Documentaries, 2008.

Orme, Nicholas. *Medieval Children*. New Haven: Yale University Press, 2001.
Orr, Michael. "The Russian Army and the War in Tajikistan," in *Tajikistan: The Trials of Independence*. Edited by Mohammad-Reza Djalili, Frederic Grare, and Shirin Akiner. Richmond: Curzon Press, 1998, 151–9.
Osman, Wazhmah. "Thinking Outside the Box: Television and the Afghan Culture Wars." PhD Dissertation, New York University, 2012.
Osmani, A.S. and W. Noori. *Health Facilities in Afghanistan by Location*. Peshawar: November 1992.
Osterhammel, Jürgen. *Die Verwandlung der Welt. Eine Geschichte des 19. Jahrhunderts*. Munich: C.H. Beck, 2009.
Oye, Mari Michener. "Government Legitimacy, Local Politics and the 1971–2 Famine in Afghanistan." M.Phil. Thesis, University of Cambridge, 2013.
Özsu, Umut. "Sovereign Equality Today" (January 19, 2015). Available online at: http://blog.oup.com/2015/01/sovereign-equality-today-pil/
Pandolfi, Mariella. "'Moral entrepreneurs,' souverainetés mouvantes et barbelés: le biopolitique dans les Balkans postcommunistes." *Anthropologie et Sociétés* 26(1) (2002), 29–51.
Patterson, Anna R. "Scholars, Advisers, and State-Builders: Soviet Afghan Studies in Light of Present-Day Afghan Development." In *The Heritage of Soviet Oriental Studies*. Edited by Michael Kemper and Stephan Conermann. Abdingdon: Routledge, 2012.
Patterson, David S. "What's Wrong (And Right) with American Diplomatic History?: A Diagnosis and a Prescription." *SHAFR Newsletter* 9 (September 1978), 1–14.
Pérez de Cuéllar, Javier. Nobel Peace Prize Lecture. January 9, 1989. Available online at: www.nobelprize.org/nobel_prizes/peace/laureates/1988/un-lecture.html
del Pero, Mario. "Tra lunghe paci i guerre fredde. La storiografia di John Lewis Gaddis." 2005. Available online at: www.sissco.it/fileadmin/user_upload/Attivita/Convegni/cantieriIII/storiografia_usa/DelPero.pdf
———. *The Eccentric Realist: Henry Kissinger and the Shaping of American Foreign Policy*. Ithaca: Cornell University Press, 2010.
Plastun, Vladimir and Vladimir Andrianov. *Nadzhibulla. Afganistan v tiskakh geopolitiki*. Moscow: Agenstvo "sokrat," 1998.
"Politbiuro TsK RKP(b)–VKP(b) i Komintern. 1919–1943." Dokumenty, Moscow, 2004.
Po obe storone granitsy (Afganistan: 1979–1989). Volume I. Edited by V.I. Gribanov. Moscow: Granitsa, 1999.
Po obe storone granitsy (Afganistan 1979–1989). Volume II. Edited by V.I. Gribanov. Voronezh, 1999.
Poullada, Leon. *Reform and Rebellion in Afghanistan, 1919–1929: King Amanullah's Failure to Modernize a Tribal Society*. Ithaca: Cornell University Press, 1973.
Power, Samantha. *"A Problem from Hell": America and the Age of Genocide*. New York: Basic Books, 2002.
"Preliminary Results of the First Afghan Census." Central Statistics Office, State Planning Committee, Government of the Democratic Republic of Afghanistan. January 1981.
"Province of Paktyka: Tribal Territories." UNIDATA, 1990.

Puar, Jasbir. *Terrorist Assemblages: Homonationalism in Queer Times*. Durham, NC: Duke University Press, 2007.

Qānun-i Asāsi-yi Jumhuri-yi Afghānistān (Constitution of the Republic of Afghanistan). 1990. Available online at: http://afghantranslation.checchiconsulting.com/docu ments/constitution/Constitution_1990-1369_Amdts_OG_0728.pdf

Rakove, Robert. *Kennedy, Johnson, and the Nonaligned World*. Cambridge: Cambridge University Press, 2012.

Rashid, Ahmed. *Taliban: Islam, Oil, and Fundamentalism in Central Asia*. New Haven: Yale University Press, 2000.

"Record of a Conversation of M.S. Gorbachev with President of Afghanistan, General Secretary of the CC PDPA Najibullah, Tashkent, 7 April 1988," Cold War International History Project Bulletin 14/15 (Winter 2003–Spring 2004), 174–81.

Redfield, Peter. *Life in Crisis: The Ethical Journey of Doctors Without Borders*. Berkeley: University of California Press, 2013.

Reetz, Dietrich. "Pakistan and the Central Asian Hinterland Option." *Journal of South Asian and Middle Eastern Studies* XVII 1 (Fall 1993), 28–56.

Reĭsner, Igor. *Razvitie feodalizma i obrazovanie gosudarstva u afgantsev*. Moscow: Izda-tel'stvo Akademii Nauk SSSR, 1954.

Reĭsner, Larisa. *Afganistan*. Moscow: Gosudarstvennoe Izdatel'stvo, 1925.

"Remembering the Past: The Early Years of U.S.–Afghan Relations." *In Small Things Remembered* Online Exhibition. Available online at: www.meridian.org/insmall thingsremembered/about-the-exhibition/remembering-the-past-the-early-years-of-u-s-afghan-relations

"Report of the World Conference to Review and Appraise the Achievements of the United Nations Decade For Women: Equality, Development And Peace," 1986. Avail-able online at: www.5wwc.org/downloads/Report_of_WCW-1985.pdf

Republic of Afghanistan Central Statistical Office. *Economic and Social Indicators March 1979–1984*. Kabul: 1984.

Rethinking American History in a Global Age. Edited by Thomas Bender. Berkeley: University of California Press, 2002.

Rishtiyā, Sayyid Qāsam. *Khāṭarāt-i Siyasi-yi Sayyid Qāsim Rishtiyā, 1311 tā 1371*. Peshawar, Markaz-I Maṭbu'āt-I Afghāni-yi Pishāvar, 1997.

Rich, Adrienne. *Blood, Bread, and Poetry: Selected Prose, 1979–1985*. New York: W.W. Norton and Company, 1986.

Robinson, Paul and Jay Dixon. *Aiding Afghanistan: A History of Soviet Assistance to a Developing Country*. London: Hurst, 2013.

Rodgers, Daniel. *Age of Fracture*. Cambridge, MA: Belknap Press of Harvard University Press, 2013.

Romodin, V.A. "'Siradzh at-tavarikh' (tom III) kak istochnik," in *Pis'mennye pamiat-niki i problemy istorii kul'tury narodov Vostoka*. Edited by Pëtr Griaznevich, Georgiĭ Zograf, Evgeniĭ Kychanov, Iuriĭ Petrosian, and Eduard Temkin. Leningrad: Akademiia Nauk SSSR, Institut Narodov Azii, Leningradskoe Otdelenie, 1968, 42–4.

———. "Poslednye gody domusul'manskoĭ istorii kafirov Gindukusha i politika Abdurrakhman-khana (po 'Siradzh at-tavarikh')," in *Strany i narodov Vostoka*. Vol-ume 10. Moscow: Izdatel'stvo Vostochnoĭ Literatury, 1971.

———. "Eshchë ob avtore 'Siradzh at-tavarikh' i ob izdanii etogo sochineniia," in *Pis'mennye pamiatniki i problemy istorii kul'tury narodov Vostoka*. Volume XVI/1. Moscow, 1979.

————. *Afganistan vo vtoroĭ polovine XIX-nachale XXv. Ofitsial'naia istoriia i istoriografiia.* Moscow: Nauka, 1990.

Roshchin, Michael. "Evgeniĭ M. Primakov: Arabist and KGB Middleman, Director and Statesman," in *The Heritage of Soviet Oriental Studies.* Edited by Michael Kemper and Stephan Conermann. Routledge: Abdingon, 2011.

Rossiia i Afrika. Dokumenty i Materialy, XVIII v.-1960 g., Vol. II: 1918–1960 gg. Edited by Apollon Davidson and Sergey Mazov. Moscow: IVI RAN, 1999.

Rostow, Walt Whitman. *The Process of Economic Growth.* New York: W.W. Norton, 1952.

Roy, Olivier. *Afghanistan, Islam et modernité politique.* Paris: Seuil, 1985.

Rubin, Barnett. *Afghanistan from the Cold War Through the War on Terror.* New York: Oxford University Press, 2013.

————. *The Fragmentation of Afghanistan: State Formation and Collapse in the International System.* New Haven: Yale University Press, 1995.

Rushdie, Salman. *Shame.* New York: Knopf, 1983.

Russo, Ann. "The Feminist Majority Foundation's Campaign to Stop Gender Apartheid: The Intersections of Feminism and Imperialism in the United States." *International Feminist Journal of Politics* 8(4) (December 2006), 557–80.

Rutland, Peter. *The Politics of Economic Stagnation in the Soviet Union: The Role of Local Party Organs in Economic Management.* Cambridge: Cambridge University Press, 1993.

Sadat, Mir Hekmatullah. "The Life of a 102 year-old Afghan Entrepreneur: an Economic Perspective." Available online at: www.afghanmagazine.com/jan99/articles/zabuli.html

Sad rangli sad sol: Točikon dar ḵarni bistum. Edited by Salimi Ajubzod. Prague: Postscriptum Imprimatur, 2002.

Sahadeo, Jeff. Review of Robert Crews, *For Prophet and Tsar. Central Asian Survey* 27(1) (March 2008), 105–6.

Said, Edward. *Orientalism.* New York: Vintage Books, 1978.

Sakharov, Andreĭ. *Memoirs.* Translated by Richard Lourie. London: Hutchinson, 1990.

Sal'nikov, Iuriĭ. *600 dneĭ v Kandagare. Dnevniki 1984–1986.* Volgograd: Izdatel', 2010.

Sánchez-Sibony, Oscar. "Red Globalization: The Political Economy of Soviet Foreign Relations in the 1950s and 60s." PhD Dissertation, The University of Chicago, 2010.

Samari, Artur. "V Samarkande mitinguiut studenty: vystupleniĭ takovo masshtaba ne nabliudalos' v Uzbekistane uzhe bolee desiati let." February 21, 2005.

Samoĭlenko, Viktor. *Kak otkryvaesh' stranu: Afganistan glazami ochevidstev.* Novosibirsk: Knizhnoe Izdatel'stvo, 1986.

Sargent, Daniel J. *A Superpower Transformed: The Remaking of American Foreign Relations in the 1970s.* Oxford: Oxford University Press, 2014.

Schimmelpennick van der Oye, David. *Russian Orientalism: Asia in the Russian Mind from Peter the Great to the Emigration.* New Haven: Yale University Press, 2010.

Schmitt, Carl. "The Großraum Order of International Law with a Ban on Intervention for Spatially Foreign Powers: A Contribution to the Concept of Reich in International Law," in *Writings on War.* Translated and edited by Timothy Nunan. Cambridge: Polity, 2011.

Scott, James C. *Seeing Like a Scott: How Certain Schemes to Improve the Human Condition Have Failed.* New Haven: Yale University Press, 1998.

Scott, Joan W. "Gender: A Useful Category of Social Analysis." *American Historical Review* 91(5) (December 1986), 1053–75.

Seriot, Patrick. *Analyse du discours politique soviétique.* Paris: Institut d'études Slaves, 1985.

Shah, I.A. *Trade with Afghanistan.* Kabul: 1946.

Sharq, Muhammad Hassan. *The Bare-Foot in Coarse Clothes.* Peshawar: Area Study Centre of University of Peshawar, 2000.

Shipley, Jesse Weaver, Jean Comaroff', and Achille Mbembe. "Africa in Theory: A Conversation Between Jean Comaroff and Achille Mbembe." *Anthropological Quarterly* 83(3) (Summer 2010), 653–78.

Shukrullo: Die ohne Leichentuch Begrabenen. Translated by Ingeborg Baldauf. Wiesbaden: Dr. Ludwig Reichert Verlag, 2005.

Siddiqi, Farhan Hanif. *The Politics of Ethnic Difference: The Baloch, Sindhi, and Mohajir Ethnic Movements.* London: Routledge, 2012.

Siegelberg, Mira. *Statelessness: An International History, 1921–1961.* Cambridge, MA: Harvard University Press, forthcoming.

Simoniia, Nodari. "Moĭ marksizm–eto ne marksizm sovetskikh uchebnikov ..." *Mezhdunarodnye protsessy: zhurnal teorii mezhdunarodnykh otnosheniĭ i mirovoĭ politiki* 7. Available online at: www.intertrends.ru/seventh/009.htm

Sinitsyn, Sergeĭ. *Missiia v Efiopii: Efiopiia, Afrikanskiĭ Rog i politika SSSR glazami sovetskogo diplomata 1956–1982 gg.* Moscow: Izdatel'skiĭ dom "XXI vek–soglasie", 2001.

Slaughter, Anne-Marie. *A New World Order.* Princeton: Princeton University Press, 2004.

Slinkin, M. "O politicheskoĭ deiatel'nosti konservativnykh krugov Afganistana v 60–70-x godakh." *Spetsbiulleten' IV AN SSSR.* Volume 2. Moscow: IV AN SSSR, 1980.

Snegirëv, Vladimir. *Opalennyĭ porokhom rassvet.* Moscow: Molodaia Gvardiia, 1984.

Snegirëv, Vladimir and Valeriĭ Samunin. *Virus A: Kak my zaboleli vtorzheniem v Afganistan. Politicheskoe rassledovaniie.* Moscow: Rossiĭskaia Gazeta, 2011.

Snyder, Timothy D. Remarks at Memorial Event to Tony Judt. King's College, Cambridge, United Kingdom. March 23, 2012.

———. Remarks at "Ukraine: Thinking Together" Conference, Kiev, Ukraine, May 16, 2014. Available online at: www.youtube.com/watch?v=DUdXGsKuQiQ

———. "Not Even Past: History, Russia, Ukraine and Europe." Lecture, The Red House Centre for Culture and Debate, Sofia, Bulgaria, June 4, 2014. Available online at: www.youtube.com/watch?v=mgIqL_mxKI8

Sobianin, Sergeĭ. Interview. May 30, 2013. Available online at: www.youtube.com/watch?v=J7Zo6lIg2Jo

Solzhenitsyn, the Voice of Freedom. Two Addresses by Aleksandr I. Solzhenitsyn. Washington: AFL-CIO, 1975.

Spivak, Gayatri. "Can the Subaltern Speak?" in *Marxism and the Interpretation of Culture.* Edited by Cary Nelson and Lawrence Grossberg. Urbana: University of Illinois Press, 1988, 271–316.

Spufford, Francis. "Response: Part I." Crooked Timber Blog, June 11, 2012. Available online at: http://crookedtimber.org/2012/06/11/response-part-i/

Stremlau, John J. *The International Politics of the Nigerian Civil War, 1967–1970.* Princeton: Princeton University Press, 1977.

Suri, Jeremi. *Power and Protest: Global Revolution and the Rise of Detente.* Cambridge, MA: Harvard University Press, 2003.

Tagore, Rabindranath. *Rabindra-Racnabali*. Kolkata: Biśvabhāratī, 1995.

Thompson, E.P. "Outside the Whale," in *The Poverty of Theory & Other Essays*. London: Merlin, 1978.

Tikhonov, Iuriĭ. *Afganskaia voĭna Stalina: Bitva za tsentral'nuiu Aziiu*. Moscow: Eksmo, 2008.

Tolz, Vera. *Russia's Own Orient: The Politics of Identity and Oriental Studies in the Late Imperial and Early Soviet Periods*. Oxford: University of Oxford Press, 2011.

Toynbee, Arnold. *Between Oxus and Jumna*. New York: 1961.

Trachtenberg, Mark. "What's the Problem? A Research Agenda for Diplomatic History." H-Diplo State of the Field Essay. October 10, 2014.

Tribal Analysis Center. "Achakzai Tribe." October 2009. Available online at: www.tribalanalysiscenter.com/PDF-TAC/Achakzai Tribe.pdf

———. "Pashtun Tribal Dynamics." October 2009. Available online at: www.tribalanalysiscenter.com/PDF-TAC/PashtunTribalDynamics.pdf

———. "Afghanistan's Development: An Instability Driver?" August 2010. Available online at: www.tribalanalysiscenter.com/PDF-TAC/Afghanistans%20Development.pdf

Tsuchimoto, Noriaki. *Another Afghanistan: Kabul Diary 1985*. 2011.

Tworek, Heidi. "Magic Connections: German News Agencies and Global News Networks, 1905–45." PhD Dissertation, Harvard University, 2012.

Ukhanov, Ivan. "Ubit po zakazu," in *Victor Polianichko–chelovek i grazhdanin. Ocherki vospominaniĭ*. Moscow: Izdatel'stvo "Kliuch", 1994.

UNOCA. "Afghanistan. Operation Salam Report for 1991." June 1992.

UNOCA. "Operation Salam Programme for 1991. Progress Report January–June 1991. Humanitarian and Economic Assistance Programmes Relating to Afghanistan."

United Nations Office on Drugs and Crime. "UNODC 2010 World Drug Report."

Vallaeys, Anne. *Médecins sans Frontières. La biographie*. Paris: Fayard, 2004.

Vos'moi s"ezd RKP(b): Protokoly. Moscow: Gospolitizdat, 1959.

Wahab Zada, Amina. "Die Notwendigkeit der Gleichberechtigung der Frau unter den Bedingungen der national-demokratischen Revolution in Afghanistan und Aufgaben der Gewerkschaften um Kampf um ihre Verwirklichung." Dissertation, Gewerkschaftshochscule, Fritz Heckert, May–June 1987.

Wakhidi, Zokira. "Strukturnye preobrazovaniia natsional'noĭ ekonomiki Respubliki Afganistan v 80-e gody." Kandidat nauk Dissertation, G.V. Plekhanov Institute for the National Economy, 1990.

Westad, Odd Arne. *The Global Cold War: Third World Interventions and the Making of Our Times*. Cambridge: Cambridge University Press, 2005.

———. Remarks, "A True Alternative? The Nonaligned Movement in the Cold War" Conference, Belgrade, Serbia, May 24–6, 2012.

Wilber, Donald. *Afghanistan: Its People, Its Society, Its Culture*. New Haven: HRAF Press, 1962.

Yate, C.E. *Northern Afghanistan, or Letters from the Afghan Boundary Commission*. Edinburgh and London, 1888.

Yehoshua, A.B. "Facing the Forests," in *Three Days and a Child*. New York: Doubleday & Company, 1970.

Young, Alden. "Qatar, Inequality, and the Possibilities for Humanity" (January 21, 2015). Available online at: http://redseanotes.com/2015/01/21/qatar-inequality-and-the-possibilities-for-humanity/

Yunus, Mohammad. *Bhutto and the Breakup of Pakistan*. Karachi: Oxford University Press, 2011.

Zābali, Abd Almajid. *Yāddāshthā-yi 'Abd Almajid Zābali*. Peshawar, 2001.

Zahra, Tara. *Kidnapped Souls: National Indifference and the Battle for Children in the Bohemian Lands, 1900–1948*. Ithaca: Cornell University Press, 2008.

———. *The Lost Children: Reconstructing Europe's Families After World War II*. Cambridge, MA: Harvard University Press, 2011.

Zaripov, Sh. *Proizvoditel'nye sily sel'skogo khoziaĭstva sovremennogo Afganistana*. 1972.

Index

Page numbers followed by letters *f* and *t* refer to figures and tables, respectively.